X 47948

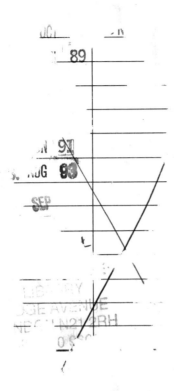

John Maynard Keynes

John Maynard Keynes

A PERSONAL BIOGRAPHY OF THE MAN WHO REVOLUTIONIZED CAPITALISM AND THE WAY WE LIVE

CHARLES H. HESSION

MACMILLAN PUBLISHING COMPANY
New York

COLLIER MACMILLAN PUBLISHERS
London

Macmillan Publishing Company
866 Third Avenue, New York, N.Y. 10002
Collier Macmillan Canada, Inc.

Library of Congress Cataloging in Publication Data

Hession, Charles H. (Charles Henry), 1911–
  John Maynard Keynes: a personal biography of the man
who revolutionized capitalism and the way we live.

  Bibliography: p.
  Includes index.
  1. Keynes, John Maynard, 1883–1946.   2. Economists—
Great Britain—Biography.   I. Title.
HB103.K47H47   1984   330.15′6[B]   83–23888

10   9   8   7   6   5   4   3   2   1

Printed in the United States of America

To our grandchildren—
Elisabeth, John, Meredith
and Michael—
and *their* "economic possibilities"

Contents

CONTENTS

Preface

I BEGAN THIS BIOGRAPHY of the creative life of John Maynard Keynes in 1976 while in Ireland on a Fulbright scholarship. In Cambridge, England, on leave from that assignment, my wife and I came upon a wealth of unpublished material dealing with Keynes's early life at the libraries of King's College and Cambridge University. Both of us were familiar with the previous publications, such as Michael Holroyd's masterly biography of Lytton Strachey and the fascinating *Essays* edited by Keynes's nephew, Dr. Milo Keynes, which had brought to light, along with many other details, the fact of his bisexuality. In his official biography, Sir Roy Harrod had been very discreet, if not reticent, in dealing with his subject's sexual nature. Even today, in one of the finest and most recent books on Keynes's monetary economics, the author, while asserting that another biography must be written with the emphasis on Keynes's complex personality, states that whether "his bisexuality is of much relevance is at present an open question."* This book is addressed to that very question in accordance with the belief expressed some years ago by the late Lionel Trilling: "No curiosity is more legitimate than that which directs itself upon the

*J.C. Gilbert, *Keynes's Impact on Monetary Economics*. London: Butterworth, 1982, pp. 7, 16.

connection between the 'impersonal' creative mind and the 'actual' and 'human' person."

In composing this volume, a close textual analysis of Keynes's various writings has been undertaken in order to determine and to demonstrate what neuroscientists would describe as his "cognitive style." As a consequence of this purpose, there has been considerable quotation of actual texts; it is hoped that this will also enable the reader to gain a better sense of Keynes's literary skill.

In the course of an intensive exploration of the literature on homosexuality and the psychology of human creativity as well as the complexities of Keynes's and Keynesian economics, I have had the assistance of the following people who generously undertook to read part or all of the manuscript: the late Dr. Silvano Arieti, Professor Kenneth E. Boulding, Professor John Kenneth Galbraith, Professor Max Lerner, Professor John E. Mack, Professor Bruce Mazlish, Dr. Albert Rothenberg, and Dr. June Singer. Assistance of one form or another was also given to me by Professors Anthony Alpers, Matthew Besdine, George R. Feiwel, David M. Harrington, Stephen A. Schuker, Lord Kahn, and the late Professor Joan Robinson of Cambridge, England. I benefitted considerably from the suggestions I received from some of the above, but none should be held responsible for the facts or interpretations offered in this work which is altogether my own responsibility.

I am also very pleased to express my indebtedness for the splendid cooperation of the librarians of the following institutions: King's College and Trinity College libraries, Cambridge, England; Cambridge University Library; British Library, Department of Manuscripts; Herbert Hoover Presidential Library; New York Public Library, Henry W. and Albert A. Berg Collection; Princeton University Library; Franklin D. Roosevelt Library; Library of the State University of New York at Stony Brook; and Yale University Library.

My editors at Macmillan, Edward T. Chase and Dominick Anfuso, have been extremely helpful with suggestions for streamlining the manuscript and improving it in other constructive ways. Finally, my wife Marie has been especially kind and understanding and unstinting in her encouragement; she did so much original research, made so many improvements in the writing, and listened to so many of my "inspirations" about this book over the breakfast table that she could well be considered the coauthor.

Acknowledgments

I WISH TO THANK the following for permission to quote from copyright sources:

The Provost and fellows of King's College for permission to quote from the writings of John Maynard Keynes in the college's library;

Cambridge University Press for the material reprinted from *The Collected Writings of John Maynard Keynes,* edited by Sir Austin Robinson and Donald Moggridge, Copyright © Royal Economic Society;

Harcourt Brace Jovanovich, Inc. for excerpts from *The Letters of Virginia Woolf,* edited by Nigel Nicolson and Joanne Trautmann, volumes 2, 3, 5, and 6, © 1976, 1977, 1979, 1980 by Quentin Bell and Angelica Garnett. Reprinted by permission of Harcourt, Brace, and Jovanovich, Inc. and from *The Diary of Virginia Woolf,* edited by Anne Olivier Bell, volumes 1 and 3;

The Strachey Trust, Michael Holroyd, and the Henry W. and Albert A. Berg Collection, the New York Public Library and the Astor, Lenox, and Tilden Foundations for excerpts from the correspondence of Lytton Strachey with Leonard Woolf;

Macmillan (London and Basingstoke) for permission to quote from Sir Roy Harrod's *The Life of John Maynard Keynes;*

Cambridge University Press for permission to quote from *Essays on John Maynard Keynes,* edited by Milo Keynes;

Yale University Library for permission to quote from the Walter Lippmann Papers;

Cambridge University Library for permission to quote from *The Diaries of John Neville Keynes;*

Holt, Rinehart and Winston, Inc., for permission to quote from *Lytton Strachey* by Michael Holroyd (Vols. I and II). Copyright © 1967, 1968 by Michael Holroyd. Reprinted by permission of Holt, Rinehart and Winston, publishers.

King's College Library for permission to quote from the Keynes Papers;

The British Library, Department of Manuscripts, for permission to quote from the Strachey Papers and the Keynes-Duncan Grant correspondence;

Miss Velda Sprott for permission to quote from the letters of W.S.H. Sprott to Lord Keynes in the King's College Library.

Introduction

FROM A SEMANTIC STANDPOINT, the word "Keynes" (in pronunciation, it rhymes with "brains") is one of the most highly charged, emotional surnames in the political discourse of the Western world and, perhaps, even that of the Soviet Union. This is not surprising because its bearer was at the center of some of the most bitterly contested economic controversies of the twentieth century. In 1919, after the conclusion of the Versailles treaty, he was highly praised by some for his stand on that document and reviled by others; in the 1930s, he was regarded as a savior by some, while in other quarters his name was synonymous as a profanity with the New Deal; in 1944, he played a central part in the famous monetary conference at Bretton Woods, again to strong pro and anti feelings about the outcome. Even after his death, in the aftermath of the so-called Keynesian Revolution, popular opinion about the "new economics" associated with his name has been a subject of unremitting dispute. In December 1965, for example, Keynes's picture appeared on the cover of *Time* magazine, and a few weeks later *Business Week* hailed the economic recovery attributed to the Keynesian Kennedy-Johnson tax cut of 1964. A little later, with the institutionalization of Keynesian-like policies in the corporate economy of the United States, President Nixon announced, "We are all

Keynesians now." Then the politico-economic kaleidoscope shifted, with the result that in the seventies with the onset of inflation and the baffling phenomenon of "stagflation," Keynes's prestige and popularity plummeted. In a time of unprecedented deficits and intractable inflation, a critic such as Frederick von Hayek wrote of "exorcising the Keynesian incubus" and compared Keynes himself to the notorious eighteenth-century inflationist, John Law.

In the United Kingdom, too, controversy has swirled just as fiercely about his economics or that of his followers. During this "time of troubles" for that country, one monetary economist found it hard to avoid the conclusion that "Britain has paid a heavy long-run price for the transient glory of the Keynesian Revolution" and wondered whether Keynes was "too expensive a luxury" for it to be able to afford.

So much public and political involvement with Keynes and Keynesian economics would lead one to expect that there would be considerable professional discussion of the man and his work. And so there has been; in fact, in the thirty or more years since Keynes's death in 1946 more books and articles have been written about him than any other economist, with the possible exception of Karl Marx. Most of these works have been primarily concerned with Keynesian economics or with differentiating Keynes's conception of his *General Theory* from that of the so-called Keynesians. While there has always been a keen interest in his protean personality, there has not been a full-fledged examination of his life since Sir Austin Robinson's memorial sketch in 1947 and Sir Roy Harrod's official biography in 1951. Since then, new material published about Keynes's life and personality is enabling us to rediscover the whole man—in particular, the rather surprising portrait of young Keynes in Michael Holroyd's biography of Lytton Strachey and the various aspects of the man and his wide interests as described in his nephew's collections, *Essays on John Maynard Keynes*. In this study of the man, I am especially concerned with relating what is now known about his personality from these later analyses and from my own inquiry into his creativity as an economist, author, and statesman. Such a reevaluation of his life is necessary and timely because, as will be explained subsequently, one cannot fully grasp the implications of his economics for our time without knowing the complete man.

When Harrod's biography appeared in 1951, the reviewers were generally favorable in their appraisals, though some of Keynes's Bloomsbury intimates were not so impressed and complained that the author did not know the "real" Keynes. Kingsley Martin, who was Keynes's close associate for many years, quoted a friend as saying, "This is the biography of Lord Keynes. Someone else must write the life of Maynard." To be more explicit, Harrod touched only lightly on the sexual life of the Apostles and of Bloomsbury. Writing less than five years after Keynes's death, his reticence about that subject was understandable, but as has been pointed out in an Oxford memoir on his life, "Taste and usage in these matters have changed since 1951."

The portraits of Keynes given us by Harrod and Robinson have a tendency to perceive him from the height of his achievements as an economist and a statesman. While these authors have contributed immensely to our knowledge of the public figure of Keynes, they have not been so successful in treating his early, more private life, nor have they related the developments of that phase of his life to his later achievements. The appearance in recent years of Keynes's *Collected Writings,* edited by Sir Austin Robinson and Donald Moggridge, will enable scholars to achieve a deeper understanding of the man and his work.

The biography of a writer and scientist as complex as Keynes is exceedingly challenging because it must concern itself with his subjective, imaginative life as well as his more overt, public behavior, all occurring during a period of profound change in the very structure and culture of the Western world. Henry James has taught us that to comprehend the intimate side of a writer's creation, his work must be related to "the consciousness that gave it birth and to the world in which that consciousness functioned." To understand Maynard Keynes in any significant sense, it is necessary to study his internal, psychological experience in its relation to his personal perception and reaction to the new economic and cultural developments of his age. To examine the one without grasping its relation to the other would be futile and fruitless.

William Butler Yeats once wrote, "There is always a living face behind the mask." The time has come to penetrate the mask of myth and legend that surround the life of Maynard Keynes and to rediscover the whole, authentic man.

CHAPTER 1

Childhood and Early School Years

Oh mystery of man, from what a depth
Proceed thy honors. I am lost, but see
In simple childhood something of the base
On which thy greatness stands; but this I feel
That from thyself it comes, that thou must give,
Else never can receive.

William Wordsworth, *The Prelude*

IN 1983, THE WORLD CELEBRATED the centenary of the birth of two of
the greatest economists of the twentieth century, John Maynard
Keynes and Joseph A. Schumpeter, and recognized also that it marked
the centennial of the death of its most famous Socialist, Karl Marx. The
latter died in London on March 14, 1883, about a month before
Schumpeter drew his first breath in a provincial Austrian town.
Keynes, born in the idyllic city of Cambridge on June 5 of that year,
could truly claim to be a son of that city and its illustrious university
because of his and his family's long association with both. The home in
which he grew up and which still stands at 6 Harvey Road was within
walking distance of the university. His father, John Neville Keynes, at
the time of his first son's birth was a lecturer in logic and political
economy and eventually became the university's registrary, its chief
administrative official, from 1910 to 1925. His mother, Florence Ada,
was an early graduate of Newnham College in Cambridge and a pioneer
in social work in the city. She was Cambridge's first woman councillor
and later its mayor. Prior to 1882, the dons or teaching fellows at
Cambridge had not been permitted to marry. The Keyneses were one
of the first couples to wed after the ban was lifted that year, so when
Maynard was born the following year, he could rightly claim to be the
first son of the marriage of two Cambridge graduates.

[1]

Maynard was their oldest child. A year and a half after his birth, a daughter, Margaret, was born and a second son, Geoffrey, arrived in 1887 to complete the comfortable middle-class family.

Before examining the Keyneses' family life, some account must be taken of its distinguished ancestry. Lord Annan has written that "family connections are part of the poetry of history," and indeed the genealogy of the Keynes family is one of the most colorful and interesting in English annals. When Maynard Keynes was still a student, he drew up a family tree which showed it to be headed by Guillaume de Cahagnes, who previously had been lord of a fief in Normandy. In return for services rendered, William I gave this founder of the family in England a share of land in Northhamptonshire, and the Bishop of Bayeaux also gave him considerable acreage in the village of Barton in Cambridgeshire, only five miles from the present city of Cambridge. The family seat was at Winkley Keynes in North Devon, and there the line continued for fifteen or more generations. The early Keyneses were people of standing in the reigns of the Plantagenets and the Tudors, and their influence can still be seen in local place names in England, such as Horstead-Keynes and Milton-Keynes. During Queen Elizabeth's time they were prominent Roman Catholics, and they showed their intellectual independence by holding to that faith during the years of religious persecution. There was a period when all but one son in the Keynes family became Jesuit priests; the most famous religious figure of that group was Father John Keynes (1625?–1697), who was a professor of logic at Liege and rector of the college there. He established two Jesuit colleges in England and was the author of well-known religious works.

Much later, the family of one Richard Keynes became reconciled to the Anglican church, but then another son, the fifth in succession with the name of Richard, again became nonconformist and served as a Congregationalist minister at Blanford.

The grandfather of John Neville Keynes had grown up in Salisbury, the family home for four generations, where he started a business of manufacturing high-grade brushes and was active in civic affairs. One of his sons, another John, turned from this business and devoted himself to the commercial culture of roses and dahlias, in which he did very successfully. He added to his wealth, Maynard Keynes believed, by judicious investment in land in western Britain at a time when the railroads were being constructed in that region. In 1853, upon the death of his first wife, John married Anna Maynard Neville, and from this union Maynard's father was born.

The maternal side of the family also had a religious background, but it did not have or acquire the social position of the Keyneses. Florence's father, the Reverend John Brown, was of Scottish descent, distantly related to the poet Robert Burns. He had grown up in Bolton-le-Moors, near Manchester, where his father had been a boot- and shoemaker, a trade which had been carried on by the family for two hundred years. Though the family circumstances were such that he had to leave school early, in 1851 he obtained a scholarship to the Lancashire Independent College, and upon graduation he became minister at the Park Chapel in Manchester. Later he accepted the invitation to become assistant pastor of the Bunyan Meeting (or Meeting House) at Bedford where he served faithfully as minister for more than thirty years. During that time he wrote the definitive life of John Bunyan as well as other volumes on Puritanism, and became a celebrated preacher. In 1859, he married Anna Haydon Ford, and they raised a family of three sons and three daughters, Maynard's mother, Florence Ada, being the oldest.

Such was the family history, running back on the Keynes side over the centuries to that magic year 1066 and containing many distinguished names. Maynard himself, reviewing the interesting details of their exploits, often wondered whether his ancestors were as fascinating alive as they were dead.

From this sketch of the Keynes and Brown family histories it is clear that Maynard's parents were of that nonconformist or evangelical group whom Lord Annan has shown provided so many outstanding members of the British intelligentsia. This group consisted of a handful of wealthy, evangelical families, the Clapham sect, to which were joined a number of similar Quaker and Unitarian families. In the nineteenth century they agitated against slavery and later worked for various liberal and philanthropic causes. Prior to 1871, dissenters of this type could not take a university degree, but after that year, this was no longer true. In succeeding years the members of this group entered upon academic careers and, as the Empire expanded in the latter part of the century, those of them who had graduated from Cambridge or Oxford were able to find increased employment opportunities in the professions and in civil service positions overseas. In fact, Lord Annan contends that this academic middle class was central to the stability of British society in that period of its history. Committed as it was to the gradual reform of the accepted institutions, it was able to move between the worlds of intellectual speculation and of government.

What were the social values of this nonconformist group of which Keynes's parents were a part? Basically, though their faith in revealed religion as with most intellectuals of the Victorian period was fading, they were very moral people, and their moral system derived very largely from the Puritan ethic. Bertrand Russell remembered John Neville Keynes as "an earnest nonconformist who put morality first and logic second," though Russell, it must be admitted, was not always an unprejudiced observer. Keynes's mother, in her history of the family, asserts that "a high standard of moral and intellectual effort" was demanded by her parents. The specific values or norms which the Keyneses stressed in raising their own children will become evident in what follows.

John Neville Keynes was the only child of a prosperous Salisbury family. He was educated at Amersham Hall School and University College in London and went on a scholarship in mathematics to Pembroke College (Cambridge) where he became the "Senior Moralist" in 1875. The following year he was made a fellow of the college, and six years later he joined the first golden age of married dons by taking as his bride Florence Brown, who was one of the first graduates of Newnham, a women's college at Cambridge. Shortly after Maynard's birth the following year, Neville Keynes published his *Studies and Exercises in Formal Logic,* which went into several editions and brought him considerable recognition. In 1890, the first edition of his *Scope and Method of Political Economy* appeared; this work was favorably reviewed as a balanced and authoritative treatment of its subject, and in recognition of its worth he was awarded a doctorate of science by the university the following year. From 1884 to 1911, he held the position of lecturer in moral science; during this period he also took on a position as the secretary of the local examinations and lectures syndicate, and this work occupied him until 1911. At the time of receiving his doctorate, he had been elected to the university's council of the senate, and soon he was made its honorary secretary; finally, in 1910, he assumed the office of registrary for the whole university, and he held this post until 1925.

Such is the bare outline of the man's career. But what was he like as a person and a parent? Not surprisingly, though some may feel that it lacks objectivity, one of the most revealing appraisals of his life and personality was made by Maynard himself on the occasion of his father's ninetieth birthday and the diamond anniversary of the Keyneses' wedding. Commenting upon his work first, he said that "for thirty-three years he was one of the best administrators there ever was, and during those years this university was a better place, in my judgement, than it has ever been before or since. Perfect order and accuracy without a shadow of pedantry and red tape, the machine existing for the sake of the university and not the other way round as it sometimes seems to be now." Keynes then observed that his father managed to create a framework for science and learning without interference or restraint, while possessing learning himself at the highest level. He went on to portray him "as he was before I knew him: elegant, mid-Victorian, highbrow, reading Swinburne, Meredith, Ibsen, buying William Morris wallpaper, whiskers, modest and industrious, but rather rich, rather pleasure loving, rather extravagant within carefully set limits, most generous, very sociable, loved entertaining, wine, games, novels, theatre, travel, but the shadow of work gradually growing, as migraine headaches set a readiness to look on the more gloomy or depressing side of any prospect, and then by the withdrawal, gradual, very gradual, to his dear wife and the bosom of his family, but just the same in his firm habits and buttoned shoes. He became a perfect, loveable, dependable parent, generous, reserved, and shy, leaving you always to your will and judgment, but not concealing his own counsel."

This sketch of the man is strikingly substantiated on most points in the pages of John Neville's diary in which he conscientiously recorded the triumphs and tragedies of his dear family over many years. Puritanical in some of his ways, he was a methodical man who scrupulously noted the hours he worked each day and reckoned up carefully his financial standing at the end of each year. (Typically, more than half of his annual income would be from investments, a large part of which were probably inherited.) But he was also a rather anxious, cautious, self-deprecating man who refused to bid for a professorship of political economy at Oxford or to undertake the editorship of the new *Economic Journal,* which his friends, such as Alfred Marshall, insistently urged upon him. He was not nearly as enterprising as his oldest son but preferred his leisure time pursuits of golf, stamps, butterfly collecting, and flower raising when he was not engaged in the complexities of the university administration or the fatiguing routine of marking and setting examinations. Still, he always found time to be a loving parent and to stimulate the growing minds of his children by judicious reading and playing games with them. The possible sources of conflict of his values with theirs will be examined later.

Joined with him in a perfect union of love and temperament was his wife Florence, a gracious Victorian lady who, as *The Times* put it, "refused to become a period piece." She had gone at the age of seventeen as one of the first students to Newnham College, and after graduation and marriage she became one of the busiest social workers in Cambridge. A *Who's Who* published in that city in 1916 said that there was "scarcely a social or public movement in this place with which she is not or has not been associated." As early as 1894, she was the secretary of the Charity Organization Society, which later became known as the Cambridge Welfare Society, and she continued in that work for many years. In the opening years of the century, she was instrumental in the establishment of the Juvenile Employment Registry or Exchange, which was the first in Great Britain. She also pioneered in providing surgical aids for the indigent and in establishing, with others, the Papworth Village Settlement for those suffering from chronic tuberculosis. In 1912, she took part in the formation of the National Union of Women Workers and served as its chairman as well as president of the National Council of Women until 1925. Intensely cooperative, she cheerfully and efficiently accepted new appointments and responsibilities. For example, in 1914 she became the first woman elected to the borough council, and in 1932, her golden wedding anniversary year, she was elected mayor of Cambridge. In addition to being one of the founders of the Folk Museum in that city, she became involved in broadcasting for the BBC and made her last appearance on radio at the age of ninety-two! It is quite possible that Harrod was right in saying: "It may well be that her practical humanity made a deeper impression on Maynard's young mind than the abstract doctrines of the social philosophers, who were sometimes a little remote from the sordid realities. In her activities Maynard could see the reforming spirit of Cambridge taking effect and bringing solace to afflicted persons." How appropriate was William Blake's hymn which was sung at the memorial service for her in King's College Chapel (she had passed away in February 1958 at the age of ninety-six):

> I will not cease from mental fight
> Nor shall my sword sleep in my hand
> Till we have built Jerusalem
> In England's green and pleasant land.

Maynard's parents were not only capable people, but they raised very competent children. Margaret, over a year younger than Maynard, became involved in social work like her mother and married Archibald Vivian Hill, a fellow of Trinity College who later became a famous physiologist and Nobel Prize winner. Geoffrey, four years younger than Maynard, after attending Rugby, went to Pembroke College on a scholarship and became a distinguished surgeon, a surgical specialist major of the Royal Army Medical Corps in World War I and a vice-marshall in the Royal Air Force during World War II, a world-renowned editor of the works of William Blake, and a bibliographer of note. He was knighted and has received many honorary degrees. He married Margaret Darwin, granddaughter of the famous biologist and daughter of Sir George Darwin. The four sons of this marriage have already brought honor to the Keynes-Darwin "connection."

The home at Harvey Road which the Keyneses made for their children and friends was unmistakably Victorian in appearance. Geoffrey Keynes tells us that "the house and small garden were without charm or character, but the place suited our unexacting standards." The walls of the rather dark dining room were covered with a deep blue and crimson Morris paper which was never replaced while they lived there. The furniture was "undistinguished but comfortable," and the pictures were conventional ones of the period. "Our home surroundings afforded no esthetic stimulus of modernity or novelty to our expanding consciousness," but this was offset by the family's contacts with academic society. Their home provided middle-class comfort and security without luxury, but this aspect was less important than its warm, supportive nature.

To historians, the Victorian frame of mind in Great Britain during its formative years, 1830 to 1870, was predominantly middle class in its characteristic modes of feeling and thought. As that class achieved political and financial eminence, its social influence became decisive, so far as the value orientation of the culture was concerned. The early Victorians were prone to regard their age as one of transition and profound crisis; they felt that they lived under the shadow of political revolution, fearing either a revolt of the agricultural and industrial workers, growing out of the distress caused by the vast technological and industrial changes of the time, or the possibility of a social explosion as terrible as that of the French Revolution. These tensions were heightened by the rapid pace of economic and scientific advance which contributed to the widespread feelings of anxiety and religious doubt. The intellectual world, the Christian church, and the social order were all seen to be in great peril, only to be saved by a life of earnest, moral dedication. That earnestness was considerably strengthened by the earlier evangelical movement and the revival of Puritanism with its attendant gospel of work and other prudential virtues.

The principal intellectual ingredient of this early Victorianism was Benthamism with its emphasis on rationality and self-interest, ideas which evolved into the dominant ethics of utilitarianism. Jeremy Bentham denied the validity of feelings and the effectiveness of sympathy in ordering social life, but later Victorians, such as John Stuart Mill, Charles Dickens, and Walter Bagehot, sought to revive sympathetic feelings and benevolent action.

Generally, the middle-class Victorians became worshipers of Progress and, in their individualist culture, of the ideals of individual success and social respectability; they displayed a dogged optimism, a decided dogmatism in moral and intellectual matters, a marked respect for masculine force, and a notable tendency toward hero-worship, thanks mainly to Carlyle and the need for a moral substitute for the waning faith in supernatural religion. Life was earnest and life was hard in this Victorian world, but the family was sheltered from the harsh, competitive struggle for existence; it was regarded as the center of life, served and bolstered as it was by that "angel in the house," the mother, with her numerous children. Of course, the exaltation of woman and family life in that period had its other side in the prudery and repression of sexual need, which was so commonplace in middle-class culture. All this was closely related to the other characteristic which critics felt so strongly about: the hypocrisy of the Victorians, manifested in their conformity, moral pretension, and evasiveness. These shortcomings were to be especially condemned and repudiated by a later generation in rebellion against a repressive ethos.

Though there is not enough information on Maynard's early years as one would like, one can still see some of the elements of his environment which nurtured his developing intelligence and creativity. Fortunately, his father kept a diary for many years in which he faithfully recorded his observations of his growing family. From this and other material it is evident that Maynard was a sickly child from his first year. His parents were delighted with their "little man" from the day of his birth and, as will be seen, when he was able to talk he was very precocious, sweet, and charming. But he was also strong-willed, and two of his nurses accused the parents of "spoiling" him. Even before he was a year and a half, his father wrote, "The little pet tyrant drags us about after him to obey all his behests, and I regret to say that he often cries when he has to retire to the nursery."

The doting parents noted his every accomplishment. When he was one and a half, he cutely began to call himself "Boy" and was quick to throw kisses to onlookers. John Neville quotes the English statesman Richard Cobden as saying that eighteen months was the most disagreeable and annoying of all ages. "At any rate, just now it seems to us the most fascinating and delightful of all ages."

When the Keyneses' second child, Margaret, was born on February

4, 1885, the father recorded that the "little man seemed to realize that he must rise to the occasion, and he was particularly good all day. . . . He would say 'How do' to the baby in a most plaintive way."

Before he was two, Maynard had become very fond of Caldecott's story books, he would run off with them to the nursery and go through the pictures in pantomime. When he was about twenty-one months old, he was repeating the alphabet to his nurse. At this time he was very much in the exploratory state; on walks he would poke into every hole and corner, often running away from his parents and startling the whole neighborhood with his loud laughing.

Busy as they were, the parents devoted much attention to their children, playing with them, for example, in the garden on Sundays. They were taken to parties and even to social occasions at the university. The father noted that when Maynard returned from his first party he was "excited, with a shining face, having much enjoyed himself." Two and a half now, he could repeat "Little Bo Peep" and "Who Killed Cock Robin?" in a pretty way. At Christmas the children were the center of attention at the Manse, their grandfather's house in Bedford. The father remarked about this time that Maynard was showing more and more imagination in his games.

Maynard, though, was not an easy child to raise; apart from his unpredictable health, or perhaps because of it, he could be difficult and even naughty at times. On one such occasion his father slapped his arm: "A mark was raised, lasting some time, and I soon repented of my severity. The rest of the day he was good and sweet." Still again, in November 1885: "Maynard has been rather naughty, and I had to threaten to slap him. 'Please,' he said, and at last the threat was carried out. Then he was pitiful, and Mummy was asked to kiss the spot where Papa hit him. Perhaps this punishment had its desired effect, but I don't feel anxious to repeat the process."

The focus of the trouble with Maynard's behavior at this time was his father's insistence that he stay in the nursery for a large part of the day. Both parents lived busy lives and as good Victorians stressed the importance of regularity and good order in family life. The elder Keynes did not wish to have his son roaming through the house or "tidying up" his office, a matter of which he specifically complained. Often, Maynard would seek maternal support in his resistance to his father's requests, playing one parent against the other; in fact, disagreement developed between his parents over handling the child, as this next incident reveals. When he was nearly three, Mrs. Keynes went on a visit away from home with her mother, and while she was absent

Maynard was suffering from a cold, but apparently was so disobedient that his father felt he had to be disciplined. Later, he copied in his diary a letter from his wife: "I am very sorry my little boy's cold has lasted so long. I am afraid he must have been kept in a great deal, and in that case I don't wonder that he gets restive. I do not think I should have let you whip him, husband, if I had been home. I know he feels as if he can't be good when he is in the nursery all day." John Neville added, "Oh, it is the father who has to maintain discipline, but he does not like it."

Eventually, the parents learned to allow Maynard more freedom of movement and more opportunity to express his growing sense of self. The signs of change became evident soon after their previous disagreement. On Maynard's third birthday, the father wrote, "It is our dear little boy's third birthday. He is quite a little man now, and we can send him to any part of the house by himself on any errand. There is nothing he likes better than being entrusted with an errand."

Now that he was three years old, Maynard was allowed to have breakfast and dinner with his parents. At the table, he continued to fascinate them with "his funny little remarks." He would take note of things said in his hearing and repeat them afterwards. On one occasion, Maynard listened as his father told his wife that the young emperor of Germany had made a very warlike speech and that as a consequence, some shares (securities) had fallen in price on the exchange. "Afterwards, we heard the young man retailing the information to Louisa, a nurse, after his usual fashion. 'And that very evening after the emperor's speech all the chairs upset!'"

On March 25, 1887, the Keyneses' third child, Geoffrey, was born. The father was soon proudly noting in his diary that he was "a most flourishing specimen of babydom" and "such a happy little boy," while Maynard was now being referred to in his journal as "the little shrimp." (John Neville was himself five feet four inches in height.)

While Maynard's conduct from his parents' point of view was improving, there were relapses from good behavior. In September 1887, a diary entry reads: "The little shrimp was naughty this morning and had to be whipped. He preserved his equanimity during the preliminary operations and at the first blow laughed, thinking to have it out. But he soon began to cry bitterly, and then my heart smote me. Florence was nearly crying. He told her afterwards that it stung him so and made him feel so warm down there. I think it did him good. He was good for the rest of the day, although he commenced by being very cranky. He is a dear affectionate little man and kissed his hardhearted father very affectionately after the punishment was over."

Maynard later told his father about his love for his mother, saying that she was "such a clever person." He also remarked, "Mother is so kind. You are kind too, but not so kind as Mother." She was "his greatest friend in the world"; his father came next, but at some distance. When Maynard was eight, he referred to his mother as his "City of Refuge." In his diary, John Neville recorded Maynard's assertion of his love for his mother no fewer than six times in the period up to his seventh year. The most striking expression of his identification with her is found in the diary entry for November 7, 1891; "The one person he would like to be is his mother; at any rate, he would desire to resemble her in everything." Also relevant here perhaps is his remark when he was six that he so loved his parents that "he never wants to leave us—so he doesn't intend to marry, at any rate until we are dead."

Maynard's remark about his mother being "his greatest friend in the world" brings to mind Freud's statement that "people who know that they are preferred or favored by their mothers give evidence in their lives of a peculiar self-reliance and an unshakeable optimism which often seem like heroic attributes and bring actual success to their possessors." Further, some students of creativity believe that mother love may exert unusual influence upon the young son. Writing that "one becomes creative as a by-product of the inspiration of the beloved," J. C. Gowan, a specialist on creativity, adds, "Boys who are affectionately close to their mothers and girls who are unusually close to their fathers during the years from four to seven tend to become more creative than others of similar ability. The child in this period responds to the warm affection of the opposite sexed parent by freely enlarging the bridge between his fantasy life and his real world. The affectionate adult who values the child's ideas stimulates and encourages the child to produce ideas and to show off intellectually. The emotional support encourages the child to draw freely from past experiences and to retrieve half-forgotten ideas from the preconscious. Thus he becomes able to dip further into this area and to produce more creative ideas than another child whose efforts might be inhibited by his parent's disapproval or negative judgments." As will be seen, Maynard's mother and grandmother provided him abundantly with that sort of love and attention. In fact, Mrs. Keynes kept a clipping file of his accomplishments and appearances in the news headlines for practically his entire life and he, in turn, wrote her very frequently throughout his youth and adult life.

In his early years, when he was beginning to read and listen to stories, Maynard seems to have been subjected to many nursery tales about naughty pigs or other animals. Victorian nursery tales were very intent on inculcating obedience in children. His father liked to read Charles Kingsley's *Water Babies* to him, and he would emphasize the moral of the story, especially when his son's behavior was not quite satisfactory. One day Maynard cried out, "I wish that you had not got that book. Do you think that I am a regular Do As You Like?"

As a child, Maynard's tongue was constantly "on the go." His grandmother who lived nearby was very fond of him and loved to repeat his fascinating sayings and doings to her friends. He was unusually bright and witty at the age of four or five. For example, when a friend was leaving their home, she said to him, "I hope that you are not too old to give me a kiss." He replied gallantly, "Oh, I shall never be too old for that."

At about the age of five, Maynard's father began to read *Alice in Wonderland* and Grimm's fairy tales to him before bedtime. He noted that he was "a delightful little man to read to. His attention never wanders for an instant, and he hardly misses a single point." Other favorites at this time were *The Witches of Headcorn* and *Little Remus*.

At five and a half, Maynard began attending kindergarten at the nearby Perse School. While he was "as lively as a cricket," his health was not good. When he was barely past his sixth birthday, he came down with rheumatic fever and complained of pains about his heart. The family physician urged quiet and his recovery was rapid, but this attack may have contributed to his heart trouble in adult life. At another time, according to his father, his eyes were constantly blinking and would sometimes turn up so that the whites would show. A local doctor diagnosed this twitching as "a slight form of chorea [St. Vitus's dance]" and warned that he should not be pressed forward or excited. His parents agreed that he should go late to school and spend more time in the open air. Eventually, he was taken out of kindergarten altogether and given lessons at home by his mother and a hired teacher.

At the age of six, Maynard was beginning to distinguish between right and wrong; he knew that he could be naughty, but it is perhaps significant that he would not let his parents say that Geoffrey was naughty. One can detect a sort of emerging pattern of protection of his sister and little brother in these years; he cried when Margaret was sick and was very emotional and tearful when Geoffrey drank some paint water which he thought contained lead that would make him sick.

As was customary for some middle-class Victorian families, the Keyneses often entertained themselves with games, particularly at Christmas time. They played charades and other games, and John

Neville would compose a play for the family's enjoyment in which all would take part. One such composition, entitled "A Happy Pair," reduced the three children to tears, he says. Certainly, such activities contributed to the growth of imagination in all the children. The family's recreational life, with its picnics, rowing on the Cam, ice-skating in the winter, and longer excursions in the summer, was indeed an ideal one for them.

Maynard's parents fostered their children's spontaneous interests in any way they could. His father helped them in stamp collecting, and when Maynard grew curious about silkworms, his mother assisted him in raising them. The father, who was an avid reader himself, continued to read Maynard such books as Stevenson's *Treasure Island,* Lamb's *Tales from Shakespeare,* and Dickens's *Christmas Carol,* all in addition to the boy's own reading. Still, his behavior at times continued to concern his father. Once, John Neville pointed out to him that he was not behaving as well as he had when a colleague had come to lunch. "That," Maynard responded, "was a great effort. I had prepared for it for days. I cannot always make such a great effort."

Maynard's intellectual development was now becoming more rapid: at seven he was taking great delight in reading poetry aloud, and at eight he was accompanying his parents to the theatre to see scenes from Hamlet. At the annual Christmas party at his grandfather's house at Bedford, he entered into all the games and was quite equal to composing his own poetry.

In Cambridge, the Keyneses lived near Fenner's cricket ground, and as a small boy Maynard spent many hours watching the games and keeping score, though he never became skilled as a player. One sport in which he participated and indeed pioneered in his neighborhood was bicycle riding, often taking long rides with Geoffrey around the city. Then, when he was nine years of age, he had a bicycle collision with a hansom cab on Harvey Road. He was not seriously injured, but his brother remembers him rushing frantically home to have a lacerated finger dressed under an anesthetic by the family doctor. He suffered a slight but permanent deformity in the injured finger. His brother later speculated that this might have accounted for his lifelong interest in people's hands, which he believed were a clue to character.

One personal characteristic that seems to have developed rather early was a certain daring or willingness to take risks. A boyhood friend, Frank Smith, who lived next door to the Keyneses, recalled one instance involving fireworks which he was making. Maynard, it seems, boldly lit one of Smith's homemade sky rockets and it exploded with a deafening roar. Smith was amazed to see him walk calmly out of the enveloping smoke laughing! This old neighbor was of the opinion that Maynard's indifference to personal danger was a contributing factor to his bicycle accident. He further recalled that while Maynard was bored by fishing, he seemed to take immense pleasure from a model theatre which he owned—a most interesting reminiscence because no one else had ever mentioned this possession—and in later life Keynes had a remarkable fascination with the theatrical arts.

In his relationships with his siblings, Maynard was always the superior, partly because of his age and character. Thus, his brother Geoffrey, four years his junior, recalled rather abjectly: "All my young days were lived under the shadow of a much more intellectual and forceful character in the person of my older brother—not that he was ever unkind or even domineering; the division was the natural result of a situation where the elder was leading not so much by virtue of the few years between them, but rather by inborn advantages of mind and body. We were not close friends, and my view of him was rather that of an eminent acquaintance to whom I looked up as a superior and rather distant being."

Margaret, less than two years younger than Maynard, was on a more equal footing with him as a child, but she regarded his privileges "with longing." Geoffrey insisted that he felt no jealousy for his elders and does not recall any family squabbling. "Maynard's supremacy was accepted, and there was no ground for quarrels to disturb our happiness." However, in another place, while saying that "Maynard was treated with admiring respect by us all," he adds, "though sometimes it seemed to us younger ones that he was perhaps given too much consideration when he developed his habit of staying up late at night and refusing to come down to breakfast before the middle of the morning without any protest from *those in nominal authority*."

Maynard's habit of staying late in bed became, in fact, a source of disagreement with his father. Both parents had acquiesced in this when he was small and sickly, but when that inclination persisted into his youth, John Neville would often make critical remarks about his late rising. This difference in attitude between father and son over Maynard's disposition to lie long in bed foreshadowed perhaps the latter's subsequent break with some of the parental values and with much of the Victorian ethos.

He had grown accustomed also to staying in bed reading poetry; at seven he was reading Longfellow's poetry in bed, and this was the beginning of what became a lifelong practice. While he was a very active, even fidgety boy when he was up, he was also cultivating the passive side of his nature—the inner, imaginative side that in Victorian eyes would be thought more appropriate for a female. In short, he was growing in an androgynous direction, down the middle path between the polarities of gender.

Despite the long clerical background of the Keynes and Brown families, the religious education of the children was not strict. When they visited the home of Florence's father, the Reverend Brown, at Bedford, morning prayers were customary and a severe observance of the Sabbath was the rule. On the other hand, at Harvey Road there was a more liberal attitude toward religious ritual and ceremony. In Cambridge, when the children were young, the family attended the services at Emmanuel Chapel every Sunday morning; perhaps it was not typical, but the father's observation that they liked the minister at this Congregational church and "appreciated his short services" tells us something about the parental attitude. Maynard, it is known, often listened to highly intellectual sermons with considerable interest. However, as his brother recalls, while he always showed an intellectual interest in religion, he, like his brother and sister at the age of seventeen or eighteen, "passed painlessly into a natural state of agnosticism." When the children ceased going to Sunday services, the parents followed suit without much discussion or uneasiness. "It is certain that neither Maynard nor his juniors were subjected to any sort of pressure in matters of religion, each taking his or her own course."

John Neville Keynes and his wife were not only eminent Victorians, but earnest ones as well. As close friends of Henry Sidgwick, the noted student of ethics, and of Alfred Marshall, the proponent at the time of what was regarded as a revolutionary approach to economics, they were very active in programs of social reform and improvement. For example, in addition to Mrs. Keynes's social welfare activities already mentioned, they were important members, indeed founders, of the Cambridge Ethical Society which was organized in 1888. This society was part of a larger movement at that time in Great Britain whose purpose was to promote the idea of progress, to arm reformers with "a rational conception of human good," and, above all, to encourage the "development of good character among the citizens." As a result of this and his father's connection with the university, when he was growing up Maynard had the advantage of being able to converse with many of the most capable and famous academicians in Cambridge. These informal talks and associations undoubtedly contributed to his own ethical development, not in a conformist way, but rather along his own intellectual lines.

When he was about eight and a half years old, he began to go as a day student to Saint Faith's preparatory school in Cambridge where Ralph Goodchild was the headmaster. At first he was at the bottom of his class, for he was much younger than the other boys. He gave no evidence of being a mental prodigy; in fact, several of his teachers complained of his carelessness, and sickness again interfered with his work, forcing him to be absent for long periods. In the early years at Saint Faith's he was stammering badly, perhaps because of the competitive pressure. But his teachers were soon remarking about his aptitude for arithmetic and algebra and his large vocabulary. Indeed, by the end of his first term he had gone to the top of his class.

His education went on incessantly, even during vacation. His father, always intent on mental improvement, tells us that on their walks a friend would tell tales of Sherlock Holmes, while he would recount stories from Asgard (in Scandinavian mythology, this was the celestial realm in which the gods dwelled). All this effort paid off handsomely. By the time Maynard was eleven he was first in his class, and in December 1894 he was first again. A mathematics teacher reported that he did "really brilliant work" but added that he "soon tires and has not perseverance in the face of difficulty." At the close of his time at Saint Faith's, the headmaster came to have a very high opinion of his abilities, saying that he was head and shoulders above all the other boys both mentally and physically.

This last remark about his physique will come as a surprise after all that has been said about his chronic illness. But it was a fact that as he approached adolescence, he became more robust; he began to grow very fast, sprouting up three inches in six months. Now he was no longer "the shrimp." Indeed, he was so tall for his age and so forceful that his fellows at the school regarded him with awe. He made one of them his "slave," requiring him to walk behind at a respectful distance, carrying his books from school.

As his stay at this prep school approached its end, the objective of winning a scholarship to Eton College became his and his parents' all-important goal. Solicitous as ever about his progress, they hired special tutors to prepare him for the entrance examination. Maynard rose at 7:00 A.M. to work before breakfast so that he would be accustomed to being examined at that unholy hour, for even then he liked what he called a "long lie" in bed. Despite being ill the day before, he passed the exams which were spread over three days; in fact, he was tenth out of the twenty elected, being bracketed or classified first in mathematics.

Eton at last! He was on his way to being a King's scholar and ultimate admission to the university. His parents were overjoyed; their tireless efforts in behalf of their gifted son had been rewarded. On June 28, 1897, Maynard's father wrote in his diary, "It is a grief to me that the dear boy will not in any case work much longer with me in the study."

In retrospect, one can see that Maynard Keynes had in some respects a very positive relationship with his parents. He was raised and educated in a manner that nurtured both his reason and imagination, his sense and his sensibility, and with further growth and maturation would achieve and fulfill his own distinctive nature of genius. In his case, however, due either to inherited factors or because of his environment or their interaction, he was destined to bear a homosexual orientation into adulthood which would contribute a remarkable character to his life.

The development of a homosexual predisposition is generally thought by modern psychiatrists to occur in the early childhood years. From that standpoint, what factors in the Keyneses' family life could have conduced to Maynard's sexual orientation? The answer to that question is very difficult because there is virtually nothing in Maynard Keynes's medical record upon which to base a tentative explanation. His case does not seem to be that of the "close-binding mother" with an absent or emotionally remote father. On the other hand, in his early years he was a sickly, dependent child, very much attached to his mother, whereas his father was the disciplinarian, and his occasional chastisements of the sensitive boy could have caused his failure to resolve the Oedipus complex and diverted him to the "safer" homosexual object.

Apart from sexuality proper, how did Maynard's parents conceivably affect his sense of maleness? Current studies of masculinity and femininity seem to demonstrate that a substantial number of persons learn or acquire personality traits from both parents, with the result that in terms of gender they can be termed "androgynous."* According to such studies, androgynous parents are most likely to have androgynous children. In Maynard's case, his parents appear to have been somewhat androgynous—the father was a rather modest, retiring sort of man who refused to take opportunities for academic advancement urged on him

---

*See J. T. Spence and R. L. Helmreich, *Masculinity and Femininity, Their Psychological Dimensions, Correlates and Antecedents.* Austin: University of Texas Press, 1978, *passim.*

by his friend, Alfred Marshall; at the same time, he had a considerable interest in reading, the theatre, flower growing, and butterfly collecting, all activities which relate to the expressive side of life and which were associated in the Victorian period with the "feminine." In contrast, Mrs. Keynes was a representative of the new woman of the early twentieth century in Great Britain; an active social worker, she energetically pedaled her bicycle around the city, despite her husband's constant admonitions and a few spills. From descriptions of her it would seem that she combined in her personality an instrumental outlook and characteristics which some of her more sedate neighbors thought of as "masculine." In summary, then, Maynard's parents seemed to have had marked androgynous characteristics, and these may have been acquired by him in the course of his socialization. In his case also, as the oldest son in the sibling set, there were other factors of a birth-order nature which may have lead to "spoiling" him and inducing homosexual tendencies. In succeeding chapters, other influences in his Eton, university, and Bloomsbury milieus will be noted which probably sustained his homosexual nature and reinforced his tendency toward androgyny.

CHAPTER 2

Portrait of the Economist–Artist as a Young Man

In English preparatory and public schools, romance is necessarily homosexual. The opposite sex is despised and treated as something obscene. Many boys will never recover from this perversion. For every born homosexual, at least ten permanent pseudo homosexuals are made by the public school system; nine of these ten as honorably chaste and sentimental as I was.

Robert Graves, *Good-bye to All That*

IN GOING TO ETON, the famous school on the river Thames near Windsor, young Keynes was beginning a phase of life that was to be decisively important in his personal development. He was at this private institution from his fourteenth to his nineteenth years, a period roughly coincident with that of adolescence. In that often troublesome stage of the life cycle, the young are not only confronted with new scholastic tasks but, in the language of Erik Erikson, must relate themselves in loyalty and fidelity to their peers. This period was exceedingly important for Maynard because puberty is a critical transition in sexual maturation. Would the tendencies toward homosexuality which had been influencing his development at home be reinforced or reversed at school? What effect, if any, would it have on his androgynous characteristics?

He did not seem to have as many friends at home as he made at this school; in fact, some of the talented young men he met remained his friends for years to come. And, of course, Eton had a tremendous significance for him intellectually. As David Garnett later wrote, "Eton was important . . . for Keynes because it initiated him into the secret of life. It gave him a view of a larger, freer, wealthier world than that which he had known in the atmosphere of his academic home in

Cambridge. It was a world of high thinking, of learning, and of endeavor noble and admirable, but not unmixed with complacency." He added somewhat wryly, "At Eton, Keynes learned that plain living is by no means essential to high thinking."

It may be useful, especially for the non-British reader, to say something more about Eton at this point. This venerable institution, founded by Henry VI in 1440, has become to some the symbol of the British ruling class. However one may feel about privilege in education, it seems to have had considerable success in educating the sons of the prosperous for a wide range of professions, including the civil service. Indeed, this school has provided the United Kingdom with a disproportionate share of its prime ministers—eighteen out of forty-five since Walpole—as well as preparing some on her famed playing fields to fight the nation's wars.

At Eton, Maynard rubbed shoulders with many who were his superiors in social standing or at least in family wealth. The very style of life and dress at the school was designed to accustom the student to the life of a gentleman, regardless of his social origins. Critics have contended that the public (in Britain, private) schools breed snobs and are often class conscious to an odious extent. In defending his school, one house master at Eton, J. D. R. McConnell, has admitted that "Etonians are surrounded by a kind of patina which often excludes others. Yet it is not a snobbery of breeding or of family. Etonians more than any other schoolboys learn to live with titles. They are not overawed by them and very quickly learn that many a title sits upon a reasonably normal human being. Nor is it a snobbery of wealth. Once again the Etonian has to live with the very wealthy. Eton is one place where money cannot buy success and where the display of wealth does not impress."

The presence of wealth in the home background of its students seems indeed to have shaped its rigorous examination and report practices; a boy who does not measure up, regardless of his parents' social standing or wealth, is eventually eliminated. Weekly trials and exams at the end of every half (or term) require steady study and application by the student. Reports go periodically to subject and house tutors and finally, under a separate cover, to parents.

One of the traditions of Eton with which many are familiar is the dress suit or tails that students wear to class and even in workshops. This "uniform" was adopted in the nineteenth century as a sort of least common denominator of a gentleman's dress in the London of that period. The self-meritocracy, the Eton Society (familiarly known as "Pop"), to which Maynard was elected in his third year, has an even more distinguished style of dress. Its members wear stick-up collars and white bow ties; their tailcoats are braided with black ribbon, and they customarily wear a flower in their buttonhole. Most elaborate of all are their waistcoats, of which most members of Pop possess a half-dozen or so. In his last year at Eton, Maynard wrote home, "I have bought a perfect dove of a waistcoat   lavender with pale pink spots. (*Wycombe papers please copy.*)" [His sister Margaret was attending Wycombe Abbey school at the time.] In this same period the Keyneses provided him with a fresh flower each morning for his boutonniere.

However, Eton had a much greater influence on its young students than merely prescribing their dress. The public schools, as Gathorne-Hardy has argued, have the practical effect of being a total society for their inhabitants in that they meet all their needs while they are cut off from society for an appreciable amount of time. Their activities are performed together, they take place under a rational plan, and they usually have a common set of goals. These boarding schools have an immense socializing effect because their students are under their sole supervision for two-thirds of the year. Furthermore, as single-sex institutions they seal off the male students from interaction with the opposite sex at the very time when their sexual drives are most powerful. It is not surprising, given the difficulty of sublimating this drive, that the public schools are, and were, "the most sexual places in the world." The public school experience, as has been documented in innumerable novels and biographies, is "overwhelmingly one of erotic and romantic passion."

Maynard's going to Eton was a new and challenging experience for him because he had never before been away from home alone for very long. The separation from their firstborn was a matter of anxiety also for his parents. They were most desirous that he should do well; indeed, he was no sooner at the school than Mrs. Keynes wrote to her husband, "Give my love to the dear little boy [*sic*] and tell him he must try to be a K. S. [King's Scholar; that is, obtain a scholarship to King's College upon leaving Eton]." The parents' financial status was a comfortable one but they were not wealthy, and they were therefore very eager to have him win this honor, as will be seen.

Early in the fall of 1897, Keynes's parents prepared him for the opening of the term at Eton by having him measured for new clothing. He was scheduled to enter the school on September 22, but a few days before he fell sick and so arrived three days late. Mrs. Keynes accompanied him to Windsor to see him settled and then left. She wrote her husband, "I am sure you will be glad to hear first of all that the dear boy seemed very much better and when I left him said that he hardly felt more tired than he would under ordinary circumstances. . . . By the way, Miss Mackey says she believes that Maynard is bigger than his fag-master [MacNaghten]! This is a relief to Mother [his grandmother], who seems to be under the impression that fags are beaten and generally ill-treated by their masters." (For those to whom this reference to fags may be obscure, we should explain that they are boys in an English public school who act as servants for other boys in a higher form or class.)

Maynard's being taller than his fag-master turned out to be very much in his favor in getting off to a good start at Eton. Though he was only a few months older than his classmates, his voice had already changed; this characteristic, plus his towering stature, led them to look to him to be their leader and spokesman.

The Keyneses' solicitude for their gifted son showed itself even before he reached Eton. Dr. Keynes had gone to King's College and importuned Samuel Gurney Lubbock, who had just been made a master at Eton, to become his son's tutor. Lubbock was highly recommended, and the choice turned out to be a sound one. He constantly urged the young scholar not to specialize too much in mathematics, but rather to seek a broad, liberal education.

Once settled in, Maynard began the practice of writing weekly or more frequent letters to his parents, a habit which he had begun when he was about seven. These were written in a small, legible hand, usually in very good grammatical style, and demonstrate remarkable maturity for his age. They were invariably signed "your affectionate son." His letters to his father covered a wide range of subjects and were extraordinarily explicit about his scholastic standing, listing grades by subject, and including sample problems; those to his mother contained a great deal about his health, clothes, and other matters. On one occasion he wrote a four-page letter to his father, then an hour later wrote another, "adding three separate and distinct facts to my previous letter." Sometimes he boasted, "The amount of letters that I have written during the last few days staggers the imagination." Or, "How virtuous I feel beginning a second sheet." At another time he despaired, "I am astonished at the amount I find to say in these letters, considering the uneventfulness of my life."

One is impressed with his competitive drive where grades were concerned. He consistently reported the standing of his rivals on different subjects to his father. The intensity with which he worked and the hours he put in would seem shocking to many contemporary students. He would often work ten hours a day, and in one letter he remarked, "If one gives one's mind to it, a good deal can be done in eight minutes." His remarkable ability to shift from subject to subject, and the speed and quality of his writing which elicited much comment in his later years, undoubtedly owed much to the stern discipline and training which he received at Eton. All this effort paid off early in his time at the college. By October of his first half he had already come out on top of his division in the fortnightly order, and at the end of the first half he was first in classics and second in mathematics, despite the fact that early in the half he had been pushed up three divisions. In this first term, too, his verses were "sent up for good." In this traditional practice, superior compositions and mathematical solutions were transcribed on high-quality paper embossed with the pale blue arms of the college and deposited in the library.

At the close of this term he was elected to Chamber Pop, a debating society for those who had acquired rooms of their own. (The freshman at the college slept in large rooms or a chamber, whereas upper classmen were assigned private rooms.) Excellent reports on his work continued to come to his doting parents, Lubbock stating that he had "a real healthy interest in all the doings of the college, athletic and otherwise."

Unfortunately, the next term his progress was interrupted by a bout of measles. Still, he was selected as captain of Chambers and won the junior mathematical prize. "Maynard will be returning to you with honors thick upon him," wrote his admiring tutor to the father.

His parents provided him with relaxation from this tiring regimen of study by taking him and Margaret to theatrical performances in London, especially at the end of term. Thus, father and son met in that city for the Eton-Harrow match, the proud parent describing him as "a resplendent young Etonian with light blue favor, flower, and umbrella tassel." Later, he took him to see *Lord and Lady Algy* at the Comedy Theatre. Constant notice was taken by his parents of his health; the diary reads in the fall of 1898, "Maynard in good spirits but had a slight twitching of the facial muscles."

Apart from the periodic theatregoing, in these years he was also playing golf occasionally with his father or his friends at Royston, Sheringham, or the nearby Gogmagog links. He played with Professor Henry Sidgwick shortly before he died in 1901 and said that he enjoyed his talk as much as the golf. In the summer of 1900, he was off with the family to Tintagel on the Cornish coast for a six-week vacation. Now there was time for that enjoyable reading that he couldn't do during the school year. He read William Lecky's *History of the Eighteenth Century.* History, his father noted, had a great attraction for him.

As the years at Eton swiftly passed, he continued to win additional scholastic awards. In 1899, he was given high marks for his essay on "Responsibilities of Empire," a typical public school topic and a subject of which he was to acquire a very deep personal knowledge later in life. In this same year, he was head of the list for the senior mathematical prize, and in the following year he won it. He had a variety of masters or "beaks," as the students called them; most of them had a very favorable view of him. However, there was one master, a Mr. X (in his letters to his father), whom Maynard thought very dull, and this master in turn had a rather adverse opinion of him. In his July 1900 report to his superiors, he wrote: "Rather a provoking boy in school. Reads notes when he should be attending to the lesson. Apt to talk to his neighbor unless severely repressed. He gives one the idea of regarding himself as a privileged boy with perhaps a little intellectual conceit." While this was definitely a minority opinion, so far as Maynard's teachers were concerned, a bit of narcissism or conceit would be consistent with his homosexual inclination.

In his college work he displayed a striking versatility; he was first of his division in history as well as excelling in classics. In his third year he competed for the Richards Prize Essay in English. The topic was made known to the students in advance—the Stuarts, not a very appealing subject to him—but in three hours in the college library where the examination was held he covered twenty-two pages and captured the prize.

In his next-to-last year at Eton his father became concerned about his prospects in the upcoming examinations. He confided to his diary: "Maynard is working steadily about three hours a day under my direction. I feel quite like a trainer, as if I were training him for a race or a prizefight." A day or two later he wrote, "The boy works in the mornings but is disinclined to put in another hour in the evenings. . . . I am quite convinced that his only chance for the Tomline [the principal mathematical prize at Eton] and afterwards is to grind hard at his book work this vacation." The father believed that Maynard's master at the college, a Mr. Hurst, had not given him sufficient systematic book work, and he was trying to remedy this deficiency. His concern was great; he was much more inclined to worry than Maynard. He talked to the master of another college at Cambridge about his son's instruction at Eton, and Maynard spoke to him also. The father continued to fret: "[Maynard] does not quite rise to the occasion and devote himself to it as I should like to see him do, considering how much is needed in order that he may be properly prepared for his approaching examinations [the Tomline in June, the certificate in July, King's in December]. But perhaps I expect too much." As it turned out, Maynard won the Tomline and the Holiday Task Prize as well.

In addition to the regular courses, the tutors at the college had a practice known as "private business" in which they gave special instructions to a few students. Mr. Lubbock chose for this purpose some translations of the Latin poetry of Saint Bernard of Cluny; the subject interested Maynard so much that he pursued it for the rest of his time at Eton and a year later read a paper on Bernard to the Literary Society. His father was very proud of his interest in medieval Latin poetry, noting it in his diary. Maynard, in fact, had a more personal, emotional interest than he probably knew—Bernard's *De contempu mundi* had a number of verses directed "against intercourse with one sex only" in which he lamented that the "entire universe—alas!—is addicted to this sordid practice." Nevertheless, his tutor was full of praise for his effort in a letter to his father: "I must congratulate you again on your boy's very excellent performances. . . . I am sure that he will go far. He seems to have the power of being interested in everything, and at the same time he seems incapable of doing anything in a dilettante manner. . . .

"I confess I was fairly dazzled by the actual result. It is an extraordinary performance. He certainly does command success to an amazing extent, but then no one deserved it better. His way of accepting it is characteristic—just as quiet, frank, and modest as ever, enhancing all the pleasure his successes give one. I hope that he has not overdone himself and am glad to think of him beginning a complete rest." Fortunately, Maynard got his deserved rest; the family went on an entomological expedition to Switzerland that year.

In his penultimate year at Eton, young Keynes went on to new triumphs. At the end of the second half he won the Chamerlayne Prize, which brought him sixty pounds a year for four years for being in the higher certificate examination, and in addition he stood first in his division in history, mathematics, and the English essay. As the year closed, his greatest Eton honors were conferred on two glorious, red-letter days: he was elected to a college scholarship at King's, Cambridge University, "in mathematics and classics," and almost at the same time he learned of his election to the Eton Society ("Pop"). This society, a self-selected body of boys, had important responsibilities in the governance of the school. "To be elected to Pop," writes a house master, "is a severe test of character, for here there is a danger that a boy may enjoy privileges without having enough responsibility. It is unlikely that he will at any other time in his life enjoy more prestige or wear more glorious apparel."

Many of Maynard's prizes at Eton took the form of books, as this was the custom. He had lengthy discussions with his father about his choices and their bindings. These were the titles that he selected: *Charles I* and *Cromwell,* magnificently bound at six guineas each; Jebb's *Sophocles,* eight volumes in morocco; Robert Browning complete, nine volumes in half morocco; Edmund Burke's *Works,* twelve volumes in published binding; Matthew Arnold's *Essays,* two volumes, speckled calf; Thomas Macaulay's *England,* four volumes, calf; Herbert Spencer, six volumes. In addition to these, he had won other book prizes during previous terms, such as Carlyle's *French Revolution* in two volumes; Tennyson in sixteen volumes, and Wordsworth in eight. The preponderance of poetry and history in this list, both nourishing to the imagination, should not be overlooked. He added these prizes to his library, which he had built up since he was twelve when he had first started buying books from the Cambridge dealer Gustave David, of whom he was very fond. While at Eton he continued buying Aldines and Elsevirs (fine editions of the classics). All in all, by the time he went up to Cambridge in October 1902, he had bought no fewer than 329 volumes!

It does not diminish his scholastic achievements to note that his father was of considerable help to him in his endeavors, sometimes borrowing books from the Cambridge University Library to assist him in his work. When John Neville edited a new edition of Henry Sidgwick's *Principles of Political Economy,* he had Maynard read and correct proof on it. Good training for the future economist.

At the college in his last year he did not rest on his laurels, for he took three extra courses: Lucretius with A. B. Ramsay, history with Henry Marten, and mathematics with his old tutor, Hurst. And then for private business with Lubbock he read the *Choephoroe* of Aeschylus.

Despite the heavy load of course work, he took a very active part in student activities and in the government of the college. As a fag during his first year, in accordance with the hoary Eton tradition, he had to wait on tables and scamper when the fag-master or senior boy uttered that long drawn-out cry, "Boy up." He seems to have taken all this philosophically, entering into the fun of pranks and chamber singing. On one occasion in his first year he rendered the song "Three Blue

Bottles" with such success that it became a favorite. On these happy, gala days he made his first acquaintance with champagne, the taste for which long remained with him, so much so that in later life he was famous for saying that his only regret was that he had not drunk more of it.

In his very detailed letters to his father in these years, he passed discriminating judgment on many aspects of college life and world affairs. Poor sermons at chapel were an especial abomination to him, leading him to write: "The Reverend the Provost preached today. He really ought not to be allowed to." Or stronger still: "This morning I have heard a sermon which, putting my hand on my heart and without hesitation, I can call the worst I have ever had inflicted on me. Sermons may be dull, but you can sleep; sermons may be old, but you can sleep; but this—there is no parliamentary language in which I can express my opinion of it. I sat and writhed for twenty-five minutes."

Sometimes, though, he gave his approval: Benson's youngest brother [Robert H. Benson, a minister] gave the sermon. "I thought that he would preach well as soon as I saw that he had not brushed his hair."

On another occasion, returning from Windsor, he met George Darwin, brother of the famous Charles: "I had a short conversation with Professor Darwin at the end of the journey," he wrote his father. "His hands certainly looked as if he might be descended from an ape." This is another remark reflecting his lifelong obsession with hands of which there is further evidence.

Among the topics of these letters is the Boer War which was fought during part of the period in which he was at Eton (1899–1902). His attitude toward it reveals his budding independence of judgment. As the martial ardor mounted at the college, the Head called for students to join a volunteer military corps. Maynard reported to his father that all the sixth form and the greater part of the college had joined, including most of the people with whom he associated. Many of the "beaks" or schoolmasters had also volunteered. Papa Keynes did not try to influence his decision; he left it wholly to him. Finally, after careful weighing of the pros and cons, Maynard decided against it, saying, "The preliminary drills are a dreadful nuisance. You have to go directly after early school and get no proper breakfast and oh, so cold! We all agree that it is easier to die for your country than to go without breakfast for it. There are about 130 recruits."

When Mafeking, the scene of a critical battle, was relieved, as the tide of the war turned in the British favor, he wrote, "The whole nation has gone in for what we call at Eton an organized rag. The papers call it a fervent thanksgiving from the heart!" His skeptical attitude reflected the fact that he was a pro-Boer. In describing the rejoicing over this victory in the nearby town of Windsor, he revealed his own somewhat snobbish, upper-middle-class view of the crowd: "The men were reeling drunk and the women offensive and gross beyond words." And then somewhat later in the same letter, "The town of Windsor is the fungus on the Royal Oak." That this was not an isolated example of his priggishness where the working class was concerned, consider another letter of June 17, 1900, to his father in which, after recounting a horrible railway accident at Slough, a town close to the college, in which many were mutilated, he added, "Most of the injured are horrible scum who were going to the Windsor races. . . . " The attitude expressed in this letter demonstrates the gulf between the classes in British society at the end of the century and reflects the restricted life which young Keynes lived in the intellectual stratum of Cambridge.

Another of the student activities in which he took an active part at the college was debating; in fact, as a result of his participation he was developing a considerable facility as a public speaker. Once elected to Pop, he made his maiden speech on the proposition that "women are more fitted to rule than men" and later took the affirmative that "old institutions are worthy of our respect as such." At another time he spoke on the Gladstone resolution for a quarter of an hour without notes and added confidently, "I know more of the facts of the case than most people." He remarks about speaking "an unconscionable number of times" and in another place said, "I find that by now I have no modesty when on my legs before a strange audience." Next he was called upon to declaim Burke's Orations [which he knew by no means perfectly] to an audience representative of the college "clad as to my uppers in dress clothes, and as to my lowers in knee breeches and black silk stockings."

By now he was practically a college factotum. We are not surprised to learn that he was elected in his senior year to the Committee of Management of College Stores, composed of students and masters, presumably because of his competence in financial matters. He complained to his father of a tendency with which some are familiar: "I am finding that, like you, when I am appointed to a committee, I am inevitably made to do all the work." In this year he also did yeoman service in reforming the college "Library," a key institution at Eton which consisted of select boys who were responsible for discipline and the general welfare of the students in their various houses (a form of self-government). He amazed his classmates; as one of them put it, "What was so extraordinary was that while he seemed to all of us to be leading such a lovely life, he never refused a dirty job." Still another of his assignments in his last months at the school was his work on the athletic committee in which he was involved in the administration of college sports.

Though he did not have a rugged constitution and was beset with numerous minor ailments in these years, he nevertheless managed and enjoyed a very strenuous round of sports at college. In his first two years he did a lot of rowing. He was not a "drybob," as those who avoided the sport were called; sometimes he rowed every day in the week. In the spring of 1901, however, he began to taper off, taking an oar in one of the first boats on the river which did not have to take part in the "bumping races." (This practice is so named because in a narrow river when a boat catches up to one ahead in a race, the latter is required to pull aside to allow it to pass.) These races were scheduled for May, just before the Tomline examinations for the top math prize which he aimed to win; apparently he was shrewdly rationing his energies. Furthermore, his parents wanted him to cut back on rowing for reasons of health.

As a consequence, he seems to have shifted his interest to the ancient Wall Game, a form of organized mayhem peculiar to Eton, which was perhaps more tiring and ruthlessly rough than rowing. He would come out of one of these contests dripping with sweat, absolutely exhausted, and almost unable to breathe. One time he got on the ball and had three gigantic opponents who collectively weighed 32 stone (448 pounds) struggling to budge him. (At this time he weighed about 140 pounds.) It is no wonder that the *Eton Chronicle* described him as a "scientific wall of great service to his side in spite of his being a lightweight." Possibly because of one of these games, he got boils on his knees, but nevertheless he carried on until he won his college colors. His mother was inclined to think that the strain of this merciless sport contributed to his heart trouble in later years.

In his last year he was back in the boats, but now it was Aquatics, a game of cricket played under aquatic rules. Other sports in which he engaged were Fives, a sort of handball, squash, and occasionally golf. He continued to be an avid and highly involved spectator of cricket matches, some of them leaving him "a mental and physical wreck."

Maynard's social life at Eton was always busy. In contrast to the rough treatment that some homosexually inclined boys received in their public schools, he was never subject to any ragging or bullying by his fellow students. Perhaps his height and active participation in sports were helpful in warding off the unfriendly attention of some of his classmates. In January 1901, when he was seventeen, he was a tenth of an inch short of six feet. Family photographs show him to have been a pretty child, but as a young man at Eton he was not exactly handsome. While he had an interesting face, his lips were thick and sensuous in appearance and he had a somewhat long nose, slightly *retroussé* (which led boys to call him "snout"), but bright and warm blue eyes. His face was especially attractive when he smiled, which was often because he liked fun and gaiety. Strangely enough, according to Holroyd, he "suffered . . . . from an unutterable obsession that he was physically repulsive." In his later years at the school he grew a small mustache which he retained for the rest of his life.

His social life at the college was almost as successful as his scholastic endeavors; he had several good friends and the respect and regard of many others. His closest classmate was Bernard Swithinbank, a very tall and quite handsome young man: his features were well shaped, the nose arched, hair fair and thick, and his voice was rather shrill and boyish. He had an elegant, intellectual look about him. Quiet rather than voluble, when he spoke he enunciated his words precisely and usually expressed his independence of mind and sincerity of character. Joined with his faultless sense of humor, he seemed to Maynard "a veritable king of men."

Robert Hamilton Dundas, called Robin, was another of his great friends. Curiously blended of Scotch puritanism and modern thought, he had "a finely chiseled Roman face" and expressed himself in blunt, terse fashion, revealing a good sense of humor which Maynard always prized. Dundas could be very rude, but Keynes's verbal aggressiveness was always his equal. In his adult years he became a fellow (or student, as they are misleadingly called) at Christ Church, Oxford. Professor A. J. Ayer, the philosopher, who knew him when he was there, states that he was "homosexual in sentiment," though he doubted that he ever practiced. He developed a curious habit of instructing the undergraduates on the facts of life, whether or not they wanted such knowledge. Upon receiving a student's complaint, the authorities compelled him to take a sabbatical leave, apparently in the hope that he would "drop the habit."

Granville Hamilton (later changed to Proby) was another of Maynard's intimates. A young man of aristocratic background, he too had good looks and charm as well as being homosexually inclined, judging from some scraps of evidence. In one of his letters to his parents,

Maynard wrote that "Hamilton's latest freak is female dresses. He stayed out for a day and spent the whole time reading fashion articles."

One of the brightest of Keynes's friends at Eton was Dillwyn Knox, the son of an Evangelical bishop, one of several brilliant brothers, perhaps the most famous of whom was Monsignor Ronald Knox. The former was a capable classical scholar, a field of study which he continued as a fellow of King's and as a colleague of Maynard. His academic honors came so easily that he was able to spend his ample leisure displaying his wit and charm. Later in life he gave long service to the nation in intelligence work in war and peace. Other members of Keynes's circle of friends included W. Hope-Jones who returned to Eton to serve as house master and publisher; and even two who later entered the religious life, R. H. Lightfoot and J. M. Duncan.

Gadding about with some of his aristocratic friends probably gave Maynard some conceit about his noble ancestry. His mother's keen interest in the genealogy of the Keynes family undoubtedly contributed to this. Thus, when he was feeling in high spirits, Maynard would indulge himself in some humorous fantasy of this nature. He would wire home in anticipation of his arrival: "Shall grace platform about [at a certain hour]; please inform District Superintendent order red baize, Albert Edward." Or he would sign a letter JMK, "a descendant of the Royal House of Flanders," indicating that his genealogical investigations had led him to believe that he had an ancestry of nobility.

While at Eton he did not have much association with females; he occasionally had supper with a Miss Ward, an older woman who had been a missionary doctor in East Africa and had retired to the neighborhood of Eton. In her company he met the daughter of the writer Mrs. Humphrey Ward who, he remarked, was "most pleasant and interesting," but nothing came of this introduction. In short, his erotic life at Eton, such as it was, was largely confined to the company of his intimate male friends.

Now that he was in the sixth form, the last class in the college, with most of his scholastic triumphs behind him, he was able to enjoy the company of these friends in almost aristocratic privacy. Harrod says that Maynard was "living in the school rather as in one's own fine country home, cooperating with his classmates in its administration." In December 1901, for example, he arranged a supper for his friends in celebration of his election to Pop and the news of his winning a scholarship to King's. His father had sent him four bottles of claret for the gala occasion, and in addition they had "soup, fish, pilaf, turkeys, partridges, plum puddings, mince pies, *pâtés de foie gras,* dessert, coffee, with claret, Moselle, and champagne." Yet it should not be thought that this feast was typical of the fare at the college; in many letters home he complained of the food and of the cold in the rooms without fires. Life at the school was not all peaches and cream for him, nor was his behavior always exemplary. On one occasion he was, in fact, disciplined in no uncertain terms, as this diary entry reveals: "I was worked over, beaten by Chute for throwing one pellet in hall last Thursday. He said I was going to throw more. He could see it in my eye. It gives him a great deal of pleasure and does not do me much harm." Keynes's imputing a sadistic motive or satisfaction to his Eton master suggests his psychological perceptiveness even at this young age.

One of the extracurricular activities which seems to have flourished in British public schools in this period was homosexuality. In seeking to understand that cultural fact it must be recognized that unconventional forms of sex life had had a long history in European society. In the nineteenth century, to go no further back in the past, homosexuality was found in many of the great capitals of the continent. However, in mid-Victorian Britain, probably because of the central place of the public schools in upper-class culture, it took on the special character of a cult. This variant of homosexuality mainly took the form of pedophilia: the love by men of boys or young men. Most of the men so disposed were not practicing homosexuals; rather, they prided themselves on suppressing or sublimating their desires, and some did not realize that their behavior was at all odd. More often than not, their homosexuality expressed itself in terms which were "sentimental, whimsical, coy, mawkish, extraordinarily naive, and almost unendurably high-minded."

This cult was institutionalized in Great Britain among the upper classes to an extent unknown in any other country. This result came about because of the important part played by the public schools and the ancient universities in the socializing of upper-class youth. These institutions were almost entirely male establishments, and their students lived in them for two-thirds of the year, cut off from any substantial interaction with the female sex. The school holidays provided too little time for these boys to get to know what girls were like, especially in heavily chaperoned Victorian society. Sisters, if they attended school at all, were in separate institutions, and their physical presence in the boys' academies was taboo.

Victorian biographies and memoirs of school years are full of the friendships which these lonely boys formed. The greatest of the public school novels, from *Tom Brown's School Days* to Alec Waugh's *The Loom of Youth,* describe the strong affection between the big and the little boys.

The education which these boys received was based largely on the Christian Bible and the study of classical languages and literature. Indeed, some clever schoolboys knew the classical literature so well that they could quote passages from Greek which justified their romantic attachments. And in this ethos of Hellenic or platonic friendship, the love of man for man was regarded as a higher spiritual one than the carnal love of man for woman. In English literature, the most famous of such friendships was immortalized in Tennyson's *In Memoriam,* his tribute to his platonic friendship for Arthur Hallam. The whole question of the influence of this classical literature on schoolboy morality was never thoroughly debated in mid-nineteenth-century Britain. John Addington Symonds raised the issue in *A Problem in Modern Ethics,* but another authority, the famous Dr. Benjamin Jowett of Oxford, contended that all the references in these works to the love of youths were merely figures of speech, so nothing was done to change the status quo.

Keynes's years at Eton coincided with those of his puberty, and it was therefore very likely that whatever homosexual disposition he had would manifest itself during this period, as did Lytton Strachey's while he was attending public school. Maynard's infatuation with Swithinbank, the young man with whom he was closest, was very likely of a platonic nature. It doesn't seem to have been translated into physical terms, but it is known that Swithinbank later had trouble with the Balliol authorities over his relationship with a fellow student. There is much evidence in Keynes's correspondence with Swithin, as he affectionately addressed him, of terms of endearment and love. This is not surprising or unusual—Freud himself states, in writing of the sexual aims of the invert, that in the latter case "mere effusion of feelings is even more frequent than in heterosexual love."

Keynes's first physical intimacy with another male occurred in his last year at Eton when he and Dillwyn Knox decided to experiment intellectually and sexually with the question of what was necessary to life. Young Knox had had a difficult youth. He had lost his mother when he was eight years old and was raised by a widowed great-aunt who imposed her variety of Protestantism on him. At Eton he broke with the family faith and became a "ferocious agnostic." Keynes told of his "experiment" with Knox six years later in a letter to Duncan Grant. In it he said that he and Swithin had had a long conversation "lasting most of the night" in which the latter told him many details of his past life. "In return I told him about Dil and me long ago at Eton. I've never seen anyone so surprised and so jealous. I thought that he would never get over it, and even the next day he chuckled to himself at intervals. Apparently he had hoped to do likewise himself and had never dared, believing it would be absolutely out of the question; and he very nearly did, not much more than a year ago. But I can't hand on his confidences until we meet."

Incidentally, Knox later married and had two sons, the oldest named Maynard after Keynes who was his godfather. In World War I, Dilly Knox's genius and intuition as a cryptographer enabled the British to break the crucial German flag-code, and in World War II he played a key part in solving the Nazi enciphering system. When he died in 1943, Maynard described his old friend in *The Times* obituary as "skeptical of most things except those that chiefly matter, that is, affection and reason."

Apart from his romantic crushes, Maynard had many other social activities in those happy years at Eton; for example, he participated in the Shakespeare Society, in which he enjoyed the reading and played the parts of the melancholy Dane and Othello. Still, reading between the lines in his letters home, one gets glimpses into his furtive, homosexual existence. As an instance, one notices that when he returned home on leave he made determined efforts to avoid dancing, which would have given him more experience with girls but which he thought extremely distasteful. In a letter to Dundas, he wrote that "with consummate skill he had got off (*all,* mind you) dances. Oh, what fair round lies I have told!" It is also significant that at times he felt he was leading a double life. In writing to his sister he said in part, "One seems to have, in a way, two entirely different lives, one at home and the other at school, and when you are living one of them, the other doesn't seem much more than a dream, a trifle more realistic than usual."

One notices also that despite his hectic pace he was reading a good deal. He enjoyed such books as Mary Cholmondely's *Red Pottage,* George Meredith's *The Ordeal of Richard Feverel,* Thomas DeQuincey's *Confessions of an English Opium-Eater,* and Robert Browning's *The Ring and the Book.* Most interesting was his continued love of poetry combined with his pursuit of mathematics. Modern students of the lateralization of the brain tell us that logic and mathematics involve processes that are carried on predominantly in the left hemisphere, *nonsense* whereas poetry is a creation of or engages more the right side of the brain. In these years Maynard was assiduously cultivating both sides of his. In a letter to his father comparing the length of long poems, we see both aptitudes manifesting themselves side by side. "I made some investigations the other day about the comparative lengths of some long poems. This was among the longest, but I was surprised at the results on the whole.

The longest is W[illiam] Morris's *Earthly Paradise,* which comes to approximately 40,000 lines.

Then Spenser's *Faerie Queen* (35,632), then in order, *The Ring and the Book* (21,116), *Canterbury Tales* (17,386), *The Iliad* (15,692), Dante's *Divine Comedy,* including Paradise, Purgatory, and the Inferno (14,408), *Hudibras* (11,445), *Paradise Lost* (10,665), and the *Aeneid* (9,898). I did not look at the *Odyssey;* I should put it down at eleven or twelve thousand."

But now all these absorbing interests at Eton were drawing to a close. He was in the midst of his final examinations at the school, and as he said to his father in another letter, "I have just reached a very melancholy stage. Last night I received a note of thanks in college Pop, which I think I desired more than anything else that remains to be got here. Eton has been much kinder to me than I deserve."

The vital decision as to which university to attend had already been settled during the previous half. Two of his tutors, Marten and Hurst, had argued for Trinity, the latter contending that mathematics was at a low ebb at King's and would not offer a good atmosphere for one of his chief interests. Lubbock, his general tutor, was inclined toward King's, which was also Maynard's strong preference. The only question was whether his Chamberlayne prize would be tenable with an Eton-King's scholarship. Lubbock heard from King's that it would, and then the momentous news arrived that he had been elected to an Eton scholarship at King's in both mathematics and classics—it was Cambridge for sure, and as for Oxford, he did not want to go there "at any price."

He left Eton a much more mature and developed individual than when he had entered. Given his sexual ambivalence, with the coming of puberty he had to find his gender identity in what was a predominantly heterosexual society. Influencing that adjustment was his continued belief that he was not attractive physically. As late as 1906 he was confessing to Lytton Strachey, "I have always suffered, and I suppose I always will, from an unalterable obsession that I am . . . physically repulsive. . . . The idea is so fixed and constant that I don't think anything—certainly no argument—could ever shake it."

This sense of what the psychotherapist Alfred Adler called "organ inferiority" could have contributed to his homosexual tendency, though other factors in his home environment, previously noted, were probably far more important. At the least, this weakness in his self-image could have predisposed him to compensate for his sense of physical inferiority by developing crushes on the better looking young men. In any case, he made an adjustment to his sexual nature by finding congenial friends who had dispositions and interests similar to his own. At the same time, through his scholastic, athletic, and administrative activities he achieved a meaningful, functional relationship with men and boys who were more masculine than he. Undoubtedly there were compensatory forces at work in his personality whereby he used his superior intelligence and physical stature, for example, to assume leadership roles, which in turn contributed to his growth as an individual. All the while he had the support of sympathetic instructors and loving parents who sustained his sense of self-esteem and general competence.

With its upper-class privileges and perquisites, the power that went with election to the key bodies that ruled the school, such as Pop, and the aesthetic aura of the place, the college was like an "enchanted garden" to some Etonians. The socializing influence was so profound that it cast a spell over them so that they remained "permanent adolescents" long after they left its halls. Brian Howard and Harold Acton, Etonians of a later election than Maynard's (that of 1918), are prime examples of this "dandy" type, of the hermaphroditic *Sonnenkindern* who became conspicuous in the Oxbridge scene of the twenties. In Keynes's time at the school there was more of an intellectual dandyism that prevailed, and so while Eton made a significant contribution to his developing in a homosexual direction, it had some compensating advantages. As an institution it had not succumbed to what has been termed "the Arnoldian blight" so prominent in some other public schools with their excessive emphasis on sports and character formation. At Eton, intellectual achievement was respected and encouraged so that Keynes had to compete with some of the smartest boys in the nation with the aid of some very able and dedicated teachers. Thanks to his earlier upbringing in a Victorian home, he retained and developed his capacity for work and responsibility. In short, he encountered well-defined images and norms of society at the college, and he responded in his own unique fashion; he did not become an "old boy," though he did have a fondness throughout his life for many of his schoolboy friends and for the Eton tradition. He did not cease to grow or lose the capacity for new experience. At Cambridge he was destined to find men and ideas which challenged him toward further self-development.

CHAPTER 3

The King's Scholar at Cambridge

Keynes's intellect was the sharpest and clearest that I have ever known. When I argued with him, I felt that I took my life in my hands, and I seldom emerged without feeling something of a fool. I was sometimes inclined to feel that so much cleverness must be incompatible with depth, but I do not think this feeling was justified.

Bertrand Russell, *Autobiography*

ALTHOUGH MAYNARD'S FAMILY resided in Cambridge, even he must have been thrilled when he first came up as a freshman to that lovely academic town. Of course it was a very different place then from what we know today. Tourists did not jostle one on King's Parade, the road traffic consisted of horses rather than automobiles, and horse trams took visitors from the railroad station to the university. Though the streets were quiet and the students' garb almost dowdy, there was an atmosphere of privileged culture. The ancient structures of the university, set like gems on green plush and towering over the lazy Cam and the surrounding fields, provided an unmatched background for the serious pursuits of the mind and the spirit. Lytton Strachey caught the influence of their ambience well when he wrote: "The real enchantment of Cambridge is of the intimate kind; an enchantment lingering in the nooks and corners, coming upon one gradually down the narrow streets, and ripening year by year. The little river and its lawns and willows, the old trees in the old gardens, the obscure bowling greens, the crooked lanes with their glimpses of cornices and turrets, the low dark opening out onto sunny grass—in these, and things like these, dwells the fascination of Cambridge."

In those years, the secret of Cambridge's success as an educational institution was not to be found wholly in its lectures and laboratories, but in the ample opportunities for open, intimate exchanges of thoughts and feelings among the undergraduates themselves. In the colleges which claim our interest, the student body consisted entirely of men; the women had their separate institutions, for this was before the day of coeducation. In their societies and debating clubs, these men were able to appraise each other candidly and openly, and argue with sincerity and understanding about opposing points of view, in accordance with the old Cambridge ideal of truth and free speaking. As Lord Annan pointed out, it was G. Lowes Dickinson, one of the greatest of Cambridge's dons, who was the leader in establishing a new view of the relations between the generations which was emerging at the close of the Victorian age. Dickinson had come up from his public school, Charterhouse, after a rough time there; he was a sensitive young man not at all sure of what he would make of his life. At Cambridge he was taken up and encouraged by Oscar Browning, the Eton master who had been dismissed from Eton but who was now showing his empathy for the young by making them believe in themselves. Dickinson, with this type of encouragement, went on to receive an M.B. (Bachelor of Medicine) and then later became a fellow of King's. In this latter capacity he began to preach a new ethos, that "boys and young men were no longer to be snubbed and put down by their elders; they were to be taken up, encouraged and befriended." He put his philosophy into practice by encouraging and supporting E. M. Forster and dozens of others to realize their potential. It was this type of faculty-student relationship that Dickinson had in mind when he spoke of Cambridge as "the city of friendship and truth." Forster with his literary genius was even more specific about its magic influence: "Body and spirit, reason and emotion, work and play, architecture and scenery, laughter and seriousness, life and art—these pairs which are elsewhere contrasted were there fused into one. People and books reinforced one another, intelligence joined hands with affection, speculation became a passion, and discussion was made profound by love."

Such an environment was vital to Maynard at this stage in his personality development. While he had acquired a firm basis of knowledge and a certain competency in social affairs and public matters, he had reached perhaps only a tolerable degree of adaptation to life, given his homosexual disposition. He had still to confirm his sexual identity and confront and settle the question of what his life's work would be, and develop an ideology or life philosophy which would serve, in Erik

Erikson's phrase, as a guardian of that identity. Since this process of ego growth is one of "mutual affirmation," he would need the confirmation of significant others for its realization. In a complex way, strangely enough, he acquired an ideology which supported him in his sexual identity, but he was not to attain a satisfactory solution of his occupational identity until after he had left the university.

At Cambridge it was customary at that time to allow lower classmen to have private lodgings, but an exception was made for the King's scholars in their first year. They were brought together in crowded quarters "in the Lane." Nominally, they were in the Royal Foundation, but their rooms were hardly regal. Maynard's was small, but it had the advantage of contiguity with some rather remarkable neighbors. Upstairs there was a hearty and enthusiastic rugger player from Liverpool who was to become a distinguished economic historian, C. R. Fay. He was working for the history tripos (a special examination for a B.A. degree with honors), and since he was interested in social and economic problems, they were soon good friends, involved in absorbing arguments. Across the hall was W. M. Page, a mathematics scholar who was to be elected to a fellowship at King's. Next to Fay upstairs was Robin Furness who became Maynard's best undergraduate friend. A literary man, he was the pleasure-loving sort who enjoyed gossip and anecdote, quite to Maynard's taste. On the ground floor was an old Eton boy, J. W. Capron, an eccentric who was absorbed currently in levitation; he would later become a minister.

Maynard's principal study in his first year was mathematics. The college arranged for him to receive his instruction in that subject from a Mr. E. W. Hobson, a fellow of Christ's College, at 9:00 A.M. on three mornings of the week. Maynard was never one for early rising, but he managed to make his classes on time. Because of his numerous other interests at Cambridge, he did not devote all his time to math, nor did he ever achieve the status of a topflight mathematician. To keep in shape physically, he returned to his old love, rowing, and in his first year he won a cup in the Trial Eights.

What occupied most of Maynard's time were his numerous societies, such as the Walpole Debating Society; the Decemviri, a mixed society of ten men from King's and Trinity; the Apennine Society, the oldest literary society in the university; the Liberal Club for which he spoke often, on and off campus; Lowes Dickinson's Society; the Baskerville Club, in which he could indulge his ardent bibliophilism; and lastly the Union, the University debating society, at which he was a frequent speaker. These club activities sometimes resulted in his attending meetings at breakfast time, and some during the day, and he might even stay up until 3:00 A.M. engaged in some heated or interesting discussion. John Neville disapproved, as usual: "Maynard can go to five debates a week. It is too much. He is still spending his substance at David's [his son's favorite bookstore]. He has just bought a magnificent edition of Virgil in three volumes (which apparently originally belonged to Adam Smith) and a set of about twenty Elzevirs." What his father doesn't mention was that if he went to a lecture, as he often did, he could be stimulated to write a paper; one that he wrote on "Time" was a remarkably erudite work for a freshman.

For relaxation he liked to play bridge, particularly with an old Eton friend, Stephen Gaselee, and others. Gaselee was a great one for "bridge and port and brandy and soda," and Maynard entered into this game, which he enjoyed very much, like a man of the world. While he was not an expert at cards, he played with his usual lightninglike mental speed; he liked, says Harrod, to take risks for the sake of trying out a new idea—striking evidence of his creativity. Another card game which intrigued him was solitaire, partly because he applied the theory of probability to calculate the chance of its coming out twice running.

G. Lowes Dickinson (or "Goldie," as he was fondly called) was one of the most influential younger dons in Maynard's time; he taught history and political subjects. One of his books, *The Greek View of Life*, originally published in 1896, won him wide esteem. In it he expounded the platonic belief that the highest love was homosexual. His fascination with Greece and Plato stemmed, it would seem, from his own ambivalent temperament, the existence of which was not known publicly until after his death. In a posthumous autobiography, Goldie admitted that his life centered upon his sexual difference. Looking back, he wrote, "All the insight I have had in life and the world has been rooted in my friendships. They have struck deep into my intellectual and spiritual life; they have made me what I am. And if anyone values anything that I have done, they should value also the passions that alone have made it possible." His homosexuality, which seemingly accounted for his warm sympathy and perceptiveness, took a curious form—a boot fetishism, in which his friends would give him pleasure by standing and treading upon him.

"In my emotional life," Dickinson wrote, "I have had such experience as I would hesitate to exchange for the normal satisfaction of love and marriage. I am like a man born crippled; will and character may make more of such a life, through the very stimulus of the defect, than many normal men make of theirs. Whatever I feel about my life, it is not shame or humiliation, rather the contrary. It presents itself to me sometimes as tragic, but never base."

In addition to his friends at King's, Maynard had five intimates at Trinity with whom he was especially close: Thoby Stephen, brother of Virginia and Vanessa Stephen; Clive Bell, who was to marry the latter; Saxon Sydney-Turner, called the "quietist" because of his scholarly ways; Leonard Woolf; and Lytton Strachey, one of the thirteen children of Sir Richard and Lady Strachey, a potential claimant to the Scottish throne but known to history later as author of *Eminent Victorians* and other writings.

Strachey had the most influence on Maynard and was closest to him of these men in his Cambridge days. He was older than Maynard by three years, having been born in 1880 when his father was over seventy and Lady Strachey forty-seven. His mother, like Oscar Wilde's, dressed her son in petticoats and left his hair long in his early years because she thought that he looked prettier that way. From his infancy, Lytton was a delicate child and later a somewhat ridiculous boy. He too was passionately devoted to his mother; his chronic illness and insecurity may be partly attributable to the birth of another son, James, who was seven years younger than he.

Lytton's mother was intensely interested in Elizabethan literature and read Shakespeare to him when he was hardly three, and at an early age she introduced him to French letters. As a child he spent most of his time reading, joking, and giggling with his numerous sisters. His father, Sir Richard, was rather remote; he had had a distinguished career as an Indian administrator and in retirement was absorbed in meterology and other scientific interests.

Lytton attended an authoritarian prep school and then went to Leamington College where he was subject to much bullying by his fellow students and had his first platonic "love affairs" with good-looking athletes. Next he went to Liverpool University College for two years in the hope of being admitted to Oxford. Failing admission at Balliol College, he went on to Trinity in Cambridge instead.

It is evident that he was sexually ambivalent, and his nature expressed itself in an emotional dependence on those of his own sex that he admired. He was moody and introspective, and these characteristics, added to his unusual appearance, did not make him a favorite with some men. Physically, at this time he had "long spidery legs and arms, a large nose, mild eyes, a large mustache, and calamitous equine teeth." With his congenital shortsightedness, pale complexion, and rather old-maidish manner, he did not make a very attractive figure. Adding to his afflictions was his voice, which had changed late and tended to go into a high pitch at the termination of a sentence. His intonation made him seem affected and, indeed, he often used this style of utterance to show his displeasure or skepticism of what had been said by another.

Closely examined, Lytton presented to the world two faces. One face, the only one that Harrod sees, was his capacity for personal sympathy, his gentleness and understanding of others as a confidant. He was the very spirit of tolerance, enlightenment, and humanity for those he liked. Yet, says Holroyd in a perceptive psychological assessment of the man, "the humanitarianism for which he stood was erected and maintained against a scathing comtempt for the mass of mankind—the ugly, the boring, the stupid, the ambitious, the powerful, and the ordinary. Toward these classes of persons he sometimes reacted with the unself-conscious brutality of a child, his rude and abrupt behavior being quite as extraordinary as the warmth and kindness he lavished upon those he liked."

While he maintained "a pleasure loving mask," Lytton was deeply insecure, prone to self-doubt and devaluation of himself. Maynard, on the other hand, was an extrovert who was more inclined to celebrate his triumphs than his failures. Lytton wrote fiery, pseudorevolutionary, iconoclastic essays for the Apostles, such as "Christ or Caliban?" and "The Colloquies of Senrab," denouncing Christianity, but as Holroyd points out, these were essentially diatribes against the ironbound Victorian morality which branded his kind as misfits. It must not be overlooked that Maynard and Lytton were aware of Oscar Wilde's trial for homosexuality (1895) and that, under the Labouchere Amendment of 1885, "an act of gross indecency with another male person" could lead to imprisonment for one year with or without hard labor. Further, it is well known that at the time of the Wilde scandal many English homosexuals were so alarmed that they deemed it prudent to leave Britain for a while. Lytton and his friends made little explicit comment about the Wilde case, but "it must have had at least as great an effect on their ideas about sexual behavior as did the Dreyfus case on their ideas about political behavior." These were some of the concerns that Lytton and Maynard shared, plus their interest in the new and handsome men on the campus who might become members of the Society. Harrod, in his biography of Keynes, writes of their having "certain affinities," but his vague musings and rationalizations about the literary and religious reasons for their revolt against Victorian culture altogether ignores this essential element of their homosexual rebellion.

According to Erik Erikson, ideology and the confirmation of one's peers play an important part in the late adolescent's search for identity. This Eriksonian concept becomes very relevant at this point because it seems clear that Maynard, with his complex homosexual nature, was probably as much or more in need of such support as anyone. This role was filled for him at the university by the Cambridge Conversazione Society, better known as "the Apostles" or simply "the Society."

This was an old undergraduate group which had been started at Saint John's College and then moved in the 1820s to Trinity under the leadership of two stalwarts of that day, Frederick D. Maurice and John Sterling. It was a secret society which chose its members with extreme caution; there could be no more than twelve Apostles. They met behind bolted doors on Saturday nights, and after tea and anchovies on toast, would read and discuss papers. Tennyson, Arthur Hallam, James Clerk-Maxwell, and in later years Bertrand Russell and Alfred North Whitehead were members, to mention a few worthies. Through careful choice of its membership, the Society had preserved its character down through the generations. Essentially, it was a secret brotherhood of the elect who sought truth and self-development through absolute candor with each other.

A prime article of the Apostles' faith was unworldliness and the pursuit of truth or the promotion of a good cause, regardless of what ordinary mortals might think. Those who were not members of the Society were called "phenomena"; the Society was the World of Reality; everything else was Appearance. In fact, this society had all the characteristics of religion, with its dogma, its mystique of ritual, and its faith in its credo, humorously summed up in the saying of one of its members: "The world is one great thought, and I am thinking it." Instead of the sacrament, the initiated ate "whales"—sardines, which substituted for the original anchovies. There was a hierarchy of membership, grading up from the "embryos" (those being considered for election) to "angels" (those who had already entered the charmed circle, graduated, or "gone down" from the university).

After being vetted by Lytton Strachey and Leonard Woolf toward the end of his first term, Maynard was elected a member of the Apostles in February 1903. Three months later his astonished father was noting in his diary: "Maynard tells me that in the course of the last term he was elected to an Apostle! This is an almost unprecedented distinction for a freshman. He has only just obtained leave to give us the information." His membership in the Society meant a lot to Maynard too; he retained an ardent loyalty to it all the rest of his life.

In the fall of that year, George Edward Moore, a young Cambridge philosopher—just turned thirty—and a key member of the Society, published his celebrated *Principia Ethica* which was to have a profound influence on Maynard, Lytton, and some of their other classmates. Moore was a moral philosopher, one of the pioneers of the modern analytical or linguistic approach, who insisted that it was important to ask the right question if one hoped to find the correct answer. Rejecting the teachings of either utilitarian or evolutionary ethics, he taught a doctrine that "good" is an attribute the meaning of which is indefinable. As a consequence, what is good depends on direct intuition in each particular case. In his final chapter of the aforementioned work, he states that certain things are intrinsically good: "By far the most valuable things which we can know or imagine are certain states of consciousness which may roughly be described as the pleasures of human intercourse and the enjoyment of beautiful objects. No one, probably, who has asked himself the question has ever doubted that personal affection and the appreciation of what is beautiful in Art or Nature, are good in themselves."

In his memoir, "My Early Beliefs," read to his friends at his estate at Tilton in the fall of 1938, Keynes recalled that his generation of Apostles ignored Moore's chapter on moral obligation. "We accepted Moore's religion, so to speak, and discarded his morals. Indeed, in our opinion, one of the greatest advantages of his religion was that it made morals unnecessary—meaning by 'religion' one's attitude toward oneself and the ultimate and by 'morals' one's attitude toward the outside world and the intermediate. Keynes and his friends were interested mainly in "states of mind," which were associated not with action, achievements, or consequences. They consisted, he says, in "timeless, passionate states of contemplation or communion, largely unattached to 'before' or 'after.'" He called this faith a religion and stated that it had some sort of relation to neo-Platonism. "Thus," he continued, "we were brought up with Plato's absorption in the good in itself, with a scholasticism which outdid Saint Thomas, in Calvinistic withdrawal from the pleasures and successes of Vanity Fair, and oppressed with all the sorrows of Werther. It did not prevent us from laughing most of the time, and we enjoyed supreme self-confidence, superiority, and contempt toward all the rest of the unconverted world."

Infatuated with their new messiah, Lytton and Maynard effused about his significance for the world, their world: The former wrote: "I date from October 1903 the beginning of the Age of Reason." And Maynard exclaimed, "The New Testament is a handbook for politicians compared with the unworldliness of Moore's chapter on 'The Ideal.'" In another place he remarked that the influence of Moore's book was "exciting, exhilarating, the beginning of a renaissance, the opening of a new heaven on earth. We were the forerunners of a new dispensation, we were not afraid of anything." Later in this essay Keynes qualified his enthusiasm, stating, "I see no reason to shift from the fundamental intuitions of *Principia Ethica,* though they are much too few and too narrow to fit actual experience which provides a richer and more varied content." And he added, rather significantly, "One cannot live today secure in the *undisturbed individualism* which was the extraordinary achievement of the early Edwardian days, not for our little lot only, but for everyone else, too."

Keynes and Strachey went on to consider the consequences of their new faith. Having thrown out hedonism, the psychological basis of the utilitarian calculus, they lived entirely in present experience and ignored social action. Keynes wrote, "We were among the first of our generation, perhaps alone amongst our generation, to escape from the Benthamite tradition." But then he noted quickly, "In practice, of course, at least so far as I was concerned, the outside world was not forgotten or foresworn." They felt the Benthamite tradition, more than Christianity which they used to regard as the enemy, was "the worm which has been gnawing at the insides of modern civilization and is responsible for its present moral decay." In truth, he concluded, "it was the Benthamite calculus, based upon an overevaluation of the economic criterion, which was destroying the quality of the popular Ideal"—the general social value system.

For Lytton, Moore's message, apart from its significance for art and esthetics, had a peculiar personal impact. Being insecure, he was inclined to hero worship of older people as intellectual and cultural gods. Moore, as such a figure, seemed to be "the prophet of that divine companionship for which he so urgently yearned." His emphasis on friendship, at a time when there was so little understanding of sexual deviance, meant to him "the glorification of that friendship which, throughout the Victorian Age of Unreason, had dared not speak its name." After Moore, he no longer needed such philosophical crutches to stand up for himself and to go on to claim his place in society and in the world of letters.

And what of Keynes and his homosexual disposition? How was it affected by Moore's new gospel? In the memoir on his early beliefs we find a forthright answer: He stated that as part of their faith they claimed the right to disregard general rules: "We repudiated entirely customary morals, conventions, and traditional wisdom. We were, that is to say, in the strict sense of the term, immoralists." He quipped that this was perhaps "a Russian characteristic ... certainly not an English one" and earned them much suspicion about their motives and behavior. He added somewhat obscurely, "It is, I think, a justifiable suspicion. Yet, so far as I am concerned, it is too late to change. I remain, and will always remain, an immoralist."

Bertrand Russell in his autobiography is more explicit on what Moorism, as interpreted by Strachey and Keynes, meant: "After my time the Society changed in one respect. There was a long drawn-out battle between George Trevelyan and Lytton Strachey, both members, in which Lytton Strachey was on the whole victorious. Since his time, homosexual relations among the members were for a time common, but in my day were unknown."

Strachey was in a strategic position, as a matter of fact, to bring about such a transformation of the Society. He had become its secretary, and in going through its old papers became aware of the fact that one of its traditions was that of the "higher sodomy," a "sort of ideological homosexuality which manifested itself more in words than in deeds." He concluded that many of the past Apostles had been secret but non-practicing homosexuals. This discovery was to have far-reaching consequences because of the close relationship between himself and his young friend Keynes.

By the fall of 1904, Lytton and Maynard were the main figures in the Society, Moore's influence being on the wane. That they were formidable intellectuals was attested fifty years later by J. D. Beazley, who had risen at Oxford to become a renowned professor of archeology. When Harrod was writing his biography of Keynes, he interviewed Beazley who recalled, "When I went over to Cambridge at that time, I thought Keynes and Strachey were the two cleverest men I had ever met; and looking back over the years, I still think they are the two cleverest men I ever met." Harrod asked him whether one was leading or dominating the other. He replied, "No, they seemed to me to be equals, different and complementary."

Maynard had become acquainted with Beazley through Swithinbank who had introduced him on a previous visit to Cambridge. On one such trip, according to Harrod, Beazley caught cold. In such circumstances he was accustomed to taking care of himself, and he was very much surprised, therefore, to find Keynes putting him to bed and offering him different drugs and all sorts of attention. Beazley told Harrod that Keynes had nursed him like a mother, and he repeated, with emphasis, "like a mother." Harrod tells this story straight, commenting that "poor Maynard had much experience of colds, and of worse ailments following on colds, and of his mother's loving care." This ingenuous explanation of the incident completely ignored Keynes's sexual nature and attributed his behavior solely to his mother's treatment under similar circumstances.

Maynard's friendships continued to grow during these years at Cambridge. One of his fondest companions then and for years later when they were both fellows at King's was the classicist Sir John Sheppard. This cherubic product of Dulwich, a public school which produced several geniuses, went on at Cambridge to become an inspiring professor of Greek drama, both on the stage and in the classroom. A striking figure on campus, prematurely gray but amazingly energetic and full of fun, he was a capable speaker at the Union and its president in the year before Maynard. According to Lord Annan, though Sheppard was the "most unbridled of all in his conversation and behavior," his love of other men was "untouched by sensuality."

In his first year at the university, Maynard continued his interest in the classics, doing a paper on Abelard and more on Saint Bernard, while at the same time studying math three times a week with Hobson and Richmond, the latter a fellow at King's. He was an active speaker at the Union, debating the Venezuela dispute, British imperialism, and home rule for Ireland (he opposed it). His mother and grandmother heard him speak in one of these debates; they thought that he did very well. Later, however, his father was more critical: "The *Granta* [a local journal] is severe on Maynard's last speech at the Union. They admit that his arguments were first class, but he spoke in a dreary fashion and displayed 'an utter lack of rhetorical verve.' There is some justification for the criticism, and it might be a good thing for him to take lessons in voice production or in elocution."

However, in Maynard's last year at Cambridge, John Neville proudly quoted the approving *Cambridge Review:* "A speech in the retiring president's best style—cool, logical, and yet full of a regard primarily and above all for the highest and best moral principles of statesmanship. We lose no ordinary speaker in Mr. Keynes, but one who raises the tone of any debate in which he may take part. We look forward to a great career for him in other circles."

After attending lectures by Alfred North Whitehead as the sole student, in the summer term of 1904 Keynes had gone with Leonard Woolf on a walking tour of North Wales. In this period he was working on his mathematics in the morning and on an essay on Edmund Burke in the evening. The following term he was awarded the Member's Prize for this interpretation of the statesman's political thought. It is interesting to note, considering Maynard's love of the traditional in later life, that he found much to admire in the brilliant Irishman's ideas.

His father, more worrisome than Maynard, was anxious about his future. He would make such notes as this: "I am just now feeling very much depressed about Maynard's future. I keep wondering whether we did the right thing in letting him read mathematics. No doubt if he would work regularly six hours a day it would be all right." Maynard was now working with a math tutor from Saint John's. In the summer, probably at his father's suggestion, he worked on the civil service exam in political economy and talked over his answers with John Neville.

While his father, mother, and Margaret went on another vacation to Switzerland, Maynard slaved on at his math, political economy, and history in preparation for the tripos examination, with a good deal of golf thrown in. When his father returned from abroad, he noted that Maynard, in planning for the Michaelmas term, had committed himself to a 9:00 A.M. lecture every day. "I have seen his gyp [a college servant], who at present expresses himself quite confidently and cheerfully as to his ability to get the boy up in good time. I think he hardly knows what is before him."

Believing that he was devoting altogether too much time to his many interests, he had Maynard entered at the Inner Temple as a precaution, but the son never seriously considered the bar as a career. About this time George Trevelyan, in a very friendly letter, urged him as a liberal aristocrat to pursue the law as a prelude to politics for which he seemed to have a remarkable flair. The question of his vocational identity was becoming foremost in his mind, but Maynard was not to make a definitive decision for some time.

Meanwhile, a new heartthrob for Maynard appeared at Trinity in the person of Arthur Hobhouse. "Hobby," with his fine intellect and personal charm, was a perfect "embryo" to both Strachey and Keynes, and he soon became an Apostle. About the same time another personable candidate appeared on the horizon—a freshman named Edgar Duckworth of Clare College, who had studied medicine in Scotland and whom Lytton described as "fair, with frizzy hair, a good complexion, an arched nose, and a very charming expression of countenance." He added, "I'm rather in love with him. . . . He looks pink and delightful as embryos should." When "Dicker" was smashed up in a bicycle accident, Lytton was devastated, expressing his shock and love in verse. But then he discovered that Maynard was "enamored" of him also. An intense rivalry developed between them as to who should sponsor Dicker for election to the Apostles. The victory went to Maynard, and Lytton was left to brood over his "dead, desiccated hope of some companionship, some love." Shortly thereafter he delivered an unprecedented onslaught on Keynes before the Apostles, saying, among other things, "For it is one of his queer characteristics that one often wants, one cannot tell why, to make a malicious attack upon him and that, when the time comes, one refrains, one cannot tell why. His sense of values, and indeed all his feelings, offer the spectacle of a complete paradox. He is a hedonist and a follower of Moore; he is lascivious without lust; he is an Apostle without tears."

Strachey's hatred of Keynes was so deep that he could neither see nor speak to him for several months. But when Dicker drifted apart from his rival, his sympathy for Maynard returned, and he began to realize how much they had in common. By his confidences and transparent honesty about the affair, Keynes had won back Lytton's trust and friendship so much that the two "sometimes wondered whether they might not, just possibly, be in love with each other."

Another insight into Maynard's nature is afforded by his correspondence with Bernard Swithinbank, his old Eton companion who was now at Oxford. In one April 1905 letter, he wrote of "being filled with love for you" and went on to say, "I find my chief comfort more and more in Messrs. Plato and Shakespeare. Why is it so difficult to find a true combination of passion and intellect? My heroes must feel and feel passionately—but they must see too, everything and more than everything. What is there worth anything except passionate perception?"

This youthful expression of belief was to foreshadow or anticipate much of the effort of Keynes's whole life. His wish to combine intellect with emotion reminds one of a similar thought which William Butler Yeats wrote in his diary, "I cannot discover truth by logic unless that logic serve passion." The famous Irish poet believed with Keynes that the energy of a great personality must emanate from the whole man, of "blood, imagination, intellect running together."

At about this time Maynard introduced Swithinbank to Lytton, and these two soon became good friends, writing and visiting each other at their respective colleges. The latter was in dire need of such companionship because he was then experiencing one of his periods of darkest pessimism. He was in the midst of writing his seemingly interminable dissertation on Warren Hastings, the controversial Indian administrator of the late eighteenth century who was related to the Strachey family. Swithinbank was also having his troubles at Balliol where the dons, as Harrod says, "for some reason seemed always a little unfriendly to him." Two years later he was summarily dismissed from that college, apparently on the complaint of a millionaire that he had had improper relations with his son. In deep despair, poor Swithinbank announced his intention to his friends, Lytton and Maynard, to apply for the position of inspector general of brothels in the Fiji Islands! This crisis led these two to frantic letter writing and feverish visiting of officials in an effort to dissuade him from such rashness. After Keynes had written Swithinbank's father, who happened to be a minister, he at last relented and gave up his mad idea. But the next year he was determined to leave for civil service duty in Burma, which he did and eventually wound up having a distinguished career there, and he later served as advisor to the secretary of state in London. The disconsolate Lytton had written Swithinbank before he left, "But go away and be a great man, and rule the blacks, and enjoy yourself among the apes and peacocks."

Time was now running short for Maynard at King's. In June he would have to take the tripos examination in mathematics, and he had a great deal of work still to do. If he failed in that exam, his future would be uncertain. Before his dismissal from Balliol, Swithinbank had written to inform him that he had obtained a degree with honors. He had to put on a spurt; by April he was working six hours a day on the subject and, as he confided to Strachey, "actively loathing almost the whole time I was at it."

On the eve of the examination his mother wrote, expressing her love and confidence in him: "I must send a line of greeting. For half my life you have occupied a large place in my thoughts and affections, and it is natural that I should think of you and hope for you today. I hope for—and expect—success this time as so often before, but whatever the result may be next week, I shall be proud of your university career and satisfied that you have spent your time well."

The tripos examination was long drawn out—there were four days, then an interval of two weeks, followed by another four days. At last it was over and the list was read out in the august Senate House. As he had expected, Maynard was bracketed or classified with another examinee as twelfth wrangler—that is, in twelfth position in this highest class of honors; the redoubtable Page, who went on to be a mathematics fellow at King's, was only bracketed eighth.

Maynard's father was very relieved and wrote, "On the whole we are satisfied. Most people congratulate—some few console. At King's they appear to be very well pleased, as far as Maynard is concerned. They were evidently fearing that he might do badly." In other words, while he had won high honors, Keynes had not excelled all others in the field. Mathematics was to be one of his main interests, but it was not to be his life's work. The clarification of that aspect of his emerging identity was still before him.

CHAPTER 4

Keynes's Quest for Identity

Man can be defined as the animal that can say "I," that can be aware of himself as a separate identity. The animal, being within nature and not transcending it, has no awareness of himself, has no need for a sense of identity.

Erich Fromm

IN HIS WRITINGS on the subject of human identity, Erich Fromm explained that because man has broken the "primary bonds" which tie him to mother and nature, he has an urgent need to find his sense of identity, for without it he may fall victim to role diffusion or even insanity. He pointed to the possible development of human destructiveness as a response to "unlived life," and Erikson, too, in his work states that in the face of threatened identity loss, rage can accumulate because of "unfilled potentials." Despite or because of their talented, complex natures, Maynard Keynes and Lytton Strachey did not find it altogether easy to establish their place in the cultural world of their day. They were both brilliant young men, but Keynes achieved a sense of his occupational identity more readily than his emotionally insecure friend. It is possible to follow Keynes's wavering steps toward his ultimate profession of economics.

Before the close of the 1904 academic year, Maynard had been studying Alfred Marshall's *Principles of Economics* assiduously, according to his father, and about the same time he discovered the "curiously exciting style of writing" of another master economist, W. Stanley Jevons, whose life and letters led him to conclude that he was "probably apostolic." It is evident that he was sampling economics to see whether it appealed to him. He discussed with his father whether he should take a second tripos in moral science or economics, but decided to do neither, returning to an earlier decision to study for the civil service examination.

With the coming of the autumn term, he returned to the university and attended Marshall's lectures. He was doing a lot of work for the famous economist who thought that some of his answers were brilliant. He wrote Dr. Keynes, "Your son is doing excellent work in economics. I have told him that I would be greatly delighted if he should decide on the career of a professional economist. But of course I must not press him." In addition to this work, another university economist, Professor Alfred C. Pigou, tutored him in the subject once a week at breakfast. He continued to buy books and did much reading as well in psychology, particularly in the writings of the "superb Hume."

In the fall of the following year, 1905, Lytton finally "went down" after six years at the university, though Maynard and he continued their almost daily correspondence about the state of the Society, the most likely embryos, and who was boosting whom for membership. The sophistication and interest of these letters illustrates in a way Strachey's dictum: "Perhaps the really essential element in a letter writer's makeup is a certain strain of femininity."

Maynard continued to read papers on such subjects as "Beauty" and "Egoism" at the university, and he also led a discussion at the Jowett Society at Oxford based upon a paper on "Time and the Absolute." Moore's essay on "The Nature and Reality of Objects of Perception," read about this period to the Aristotelian Society, fascinated him. Then at Christmas he indulged his old interest, genealogy, by reading aloud a history of the Keynes family at his home.

His interests continued to be broad, though there is a significant letter to Strachey in 1905 in which he declared, "I find economics increasingly satisfactory, and I think that I am rather good at it. I want to manage a railway or organize a trust. . . . It is so easy and fascinating to master the principles of these things."

A week or so later he again wrote Lytton, saying that "Marshall is continually pestering me to turn professional economist and writes flattering remarks on my papers to help on the good cause. Do you think that there is anything in it? I doubt it. I could probably get employment here if I wanted to. But prolonging my existence in this place [Cambridge] would be, I feel sure, death. The only question is whether a government office in London is not death equally. I suppose that I shall drift."

In his letters to the absent Strachey, Maynard continued to enthuse over Moore, the philosopher. In one he wrote, "Oh! I have undergone a conversion. I am with Moore absolutely and on all things—even secondary qualities. . . . Something gave in my brain, and I saw everything clearly in a flash. But the whole thing depends on intuiting the universe in a particular way—I see that now. There is no hope of converting the world except by Conversion, and this is pretty hopeless. It is not a question of argument; all depends upon a particular twist in the mind."

In the midst of his very active social life, Keynes was studying ethics for the civil service examination, while poor Strachey in London, lonely as ever, envied his friend's erotic opportunities and dreamed of the future: "I suppose it really doesn't matter whether you get into the C.S. [civil service] or not, does it? If you didn't, wouldn't you get a fellowship and take rooms in the Temple? That you might in any case—very charming. Oh, dear me! When will my heaven be realized—my castle in Spain? Rooms, you know, for you, Duncan, and Swithin, as fixtures—Woolf, of course too, if we can lure him from Ceylon; and several suites for guests. Can you conceive of anything more supreme! I should write tragedies; you would revolutionize political economy; Swithin would compose French poetry; Duncan would paint our portraits in every conceivable combination and permutation; and Woolf would criticize us and our works without remorse." Sweet dreams of youth—but how many of them were to be realized!

Lytton was more than a little envious not only of Maynard's romantic affairs, but of his other achievements as well. When the latter was first elected to the Apostles, Lytton was already a major figure in the Society, but at Cambridge Keynes went on to become president of the Union and of the University Liberal Club. He won a first, whereas Lytton had obtained only second class honors. The more ambitious Keynes was later made a fellow at King's, but Lytton never attained that status at Trinity, nor was he accepted at the education board despite the efforts of his mother in his behalf, while Maynard was to pass the civil service examination with relative ease. Their old friendship was strained by the disparity in their material and sexual success, and it was only when Keynes suffered periodic reverses that their former intimacy was restored.

Early in 1906, Henry Sidgwick's *Memoir* appeared, and almost immediately it became a subject of discussion in Cambridge intellectual circles. Sidgwick had been professor of ethics and of political economy at Cambridge in the years before Moore; he had been an Apostle and was a good friend of the Keyneses. Maynard's reaction to the book was quickly expressed. He wrote Swithinbank that it was

very interesting and depressing and, the first part particularly, very important as an historical document dealing with the mind of the Victorian period. Really—but you must read it yourself. He never did anything but wonder whether Christianity was true and prove that it wasn't and hope that it was. . . .

I wonder what he would have thought of us; and I wonder what we think of him. And then his conscience—incredible. There is no doubt about his moral goodness. And yet it is all so dreadfully depressing—no intimacy, no clear-cut boldness. Oh, I suppose he was intimate, but he didn't seem to have anything to be intimate about except his religious doubts. And he really ought to have gotten over that a little sooner because he knew that the thing wasn't true perfectly well from the beginning. The last part is all about ghosts and Mr. Balfour. I have never found so dull a book so absorbing.

Lytton summed up his reactions to the volume in more explicit language: "What an appalling time to have lived! It was the Glass Case Age. Themselves as well as their ornaments were left under glass cases. Their refusal to face any fundamental question fairly—either about people or God—looks at first sight like cowardice; but I believe that it was simply the result of an innate incapacity for penetration—for getting either out of themselves or into anything or anybody else. They were enclosed in glass. How intolerable! Have you noticed, too, that they nearly all were physically impotent? Sidgwick himself, Matthew Arnold, [Benjamin] Jowett, [Frederick] Leighton, [John] Ruskin, [George Frederick] Watts. It's damned difficult to copulate through a glass case."

The Keynes-Strachey revulsion against Sidgwick's Victorian ethic shows, of course, that they had revolted against the older way of life and its values long before Lytton composed *Eminent Victorians*. Theirs was truly a generational revolt—a reevaluation of the values of the father by the sons. Robert Wohl, in his authoritative study, *The Generation of 1914,* demonstrates beyond a doubt that there was a widespread rebellion of European youth before World War I against the ideas and values of the previous generation. Writing of that phenomenon in England, he remarks that "these privileged young intellectuals at Cambridge were rebelling with the understatement and good manners typical of the English ruling classes, against the nineteenth century and Victorianism. They got their ethics from G. E. Moore, their politics from the Webbs, their attitude toward relations between the sexes from Ibsen and George Bernard Shaw, their vision of the future from H. G.

Wells, and their ideas of what art and literature should be from Roger
Fry and E. M. Forster. They wanted to be modern." Moore's influence
on Keynes has already been described, and there will also be ample
evidence of the appeal which the powerful ideas of Ibsen, Shaw, and
Wells had for him.

Perhaps Keynes's decision at this time not to take a second tripos but
to prepare instead for the civil service examination reflected this same
discontent with the ethos of the Sidgwick era. Despite Marshall's
importuning, he was determined to sample London life instead. Although he regarded his mentor as a very great man in the field of
economics, he thought him "a rather silly one in his private character."
On the other hand, he felt that Mrs. Marshall was "charming." While
he later wrote an admiring biographical essay on the Cambridge
professor as an economist, he told Harrod in private conversation that
"he [Marshall] was an utterly absurd person." The older man's moraliz-
ing was apparently too much for the young Keynes.

At about this time Keynes had been invited by Alys Smith, Bertrand
Russell's first wife, to join her sister, Mary Berenson, on a reading party
and motor tour of Tuscany. A thoroughgoing Oxford esthete, an
undergraduate of New College by the name of Geoffrey Scott, was to be
in the party. He was just twenty-two, a year younger than Maynard,
and a very dashing figure indeed. He was the youngest son of a family of
seven children, his father being a prosperous flooring manufacturer,
and his mother was said to come from "a large family of exceptionally
strong and original characters." Young Scott was very original and very
unconventional; in appearance he was tall, slim, and nearsighted; his
hair was usually uncombed so that he gave the impression of a charming
intellectual unable to take care of himself. He was a delightful conver-
sationalist, a real raconteur who could hold people late into the night
with his stories and repartee. Maynard could not resist a holiday with
such a jolly companion, and soon they were at their hostess's home
where Scott's audience included Ray and Karin Costelloe (daughters of
Mrs. Berenson by her first husband), Mary Berenson herself, and
Bernard Berenson, the internationally known art critic. The setting
was "I Tatti," their fabulous villa overlooking Florence which at that
time was just being rented but was later to be converted into a
strikingly beautiful home. Maynard wrote Lytton describing the spot
and their way of life there: "The comfort is incredible; the cypresses and
sun and moon and the amazing gardens and villas in which we picnic
every day high above Florence have reduced me to a lump of Italian
idleness. We go to bed later and later and gradually find methods of
working five meals into the day."

Mary Berenson, the mother of the family, "full of Italian and money," as Keynes described her, footed the whole bill for their automobile tour, even paying the entrance fees to the art galleries. And so they motored over the lovely Tuscan countryside, laughing almost the whole time. In the past Keynes had been very critical of the new motor vehicles, perhaps because he associated them with Americans, but now he exulted over the pleasure of motoring in that uncongested day: "But I must confess rather a conversion to the engine. The mere pleasure of the motion is exquisite, and you visit so many places and so many different hotels in a week that it really seems weeks and months since we started. One symptom which overcame all of us (except Mrs. B.) was motor slackness—an intense disinclination to get out of the car to look at wayside frescoes and a mere desire to go on forever in a kind of trance.

The countryside of Italy (Do you know it?) is incredibly beautiful, and it is really that which has been the *pièce de résistance*. I don't think I have ever spent a more pleasant week."

Keynes wrote to Lytton that he seemingly had fallen in love with Ray Costelloe "a little bit," but Scott, while he was amusing, "makes me angry by plotting at the greatest inconvenience to himself never to leave me and Ray alone. Everybody tried to bring it about occasionally, but no, he forbids."

Mary Berenson, a very liberated woman, was somewhat disappointed with her marriage and looking for a romantic diversion. In a later letter to Maynard, Scott told of his assignations with her on what she called "Morpeth nights." She said that she wanted to meet him again at Dover, but "this is too much. She is a good sort all the same, and I look a dream in my blue silk pajamas. (The Bond Street tailor is amused by her simultaneously ordering some of B. B.'s lesser dimensions.) What a jolly Aristophanic world this is! But you would have played my part differently. I am not worthy of the situation. Embraces."

While Maynard stayed a week in this lap of Italian luxury, Scott remained a month; indeed, the wily Mary managed to keep her lover at her side for many years. Later he returned to the Berenson villa in the role of secretary-librarian, and when it was renovated he was hired as architect. Truly, he was a man of many parts, witness that he went on to write a famous book, *The Architecture of Humanism,* which Bernard Berenson claimed borrowed heavily and unfairly from his own writings.

As for Maynard's original visit to I Tatti, one should note that while it was a delightful holiday for him and Scott, it had its disturbing moments. Some time later the latter wrote Keynes to say that Mrs. Berenson had received a letter warning her of him who she hears has been invited to be "the companion of her innocent (*sic*) children in Venice. This young man," Scott continued, quoting the letter, "is known in Oxford as a disciple of the deplorable practices (*sic*) of Oscar Wilde. He and some of his friends *whom I could name* under the pretense of 'Greek friendships' (*sic, sic*) cloak the most unnatural and shocking forms of vice, etc. Funny thing, what? You and I will pick oakum yet. If you get off, I look to you to raise a fuss in the press and to petition the Home Secretary. . . . It is very stimulating to find oneself a notorious character. But I am just a little exercised as to what she may 'feel it her duty' to do next. I wonder if other people are getting these warnings—the police, for example."

On his way home from this Italian holiday Maynard planned to stop over in Germany to visit his brother Geoffrey who was on a mountain-climbing trip there. The latter replied and said that he would be delighted to see him, but then expressed surprise and suspicion at his going on a motor trip at all: "But what do you, the antimotorist motorphobe, the giber of all forms of motoring, mean by thus suddenly hurling all your principles to the wind and arranging to go for a week's tour in one of the despised, accursed, and work-of-the-devil vehicles? Perhaps it is a 'dream of Fair Woman' (Who is this Mrs. Berenson? I have never heard of her) that is the attraction, but this is improbable, and I prefer to think that it is an unconditional surrender on your part to the charms of The Pastime." From this letter one can conclude that Geoffrey, who was nineteen at the time, knew of his brother's sexual inclination and shrewdly deduced what was behind the Italian tour.

On his return to England, Maynard had to buckle down to the study of history and political science for the civil service examination. When the date of the civil service examination arrived, Mrs. Keynes, always concerned about her son's health, took a flat in London for the duration of the ordeal which extended unmercifully from August 3 to 25. Maynard slogged his way through the endless papers, confident now of being in the first ten of the examinees, most of whom he despised as "a talentless crew." "I trembled for our Indian empire when I saw the bulk of them," he wrote to James Strachey, and he told Lytton that "perpetual examinations of various kinds by day and night have reduced me to a state of excessive weakness and dependence on brandy. Good God! Here I am in a brief lull between two three-hour papers on English history, and I only got one-half hour's sleep last night. Pray for me."

While he was awaiting the results of the examinations, Keynes went off with the two Stracheys and Harry Norton to visit Scotland for a rest and for work on a subject which he found most intriguing—the theory of probability. He apparently had decided to submit a dissertation on this topic as a candidate for a fellowship at King's. Each year the college offered a small number of prize fellowships. If he won one of these, he would not have to resign from the civil service; though the fellowship would pay only a very small stipend, winning it would be an honor and would provide him with a hedge, supposing that he should decide to return to Cambridge life. His father noted that he was pleased with his initial work on probability and claimed that his method was quite new.

The civil service authorities did not publish the list of vacancies until after the examinations; the only two that interested Keynes were the Treasury and the India office. When the results appeared late in September 1906, he was shown to be second out of the field of 104 candidates. His father commented that it was "a wonderful achievement," considering how little he had prepared. Otto Niemeyer was first and he chose the Treasury, and thus Keynes had no recourse but to take the India office. He was enraged by his marks on the exams. He was eighth or ninth on the economics paper, and he scored higher marks for English history than for mathematics. He was first in political science, logic, psychology, and essay. His characteristic comment was, "I evidently knew more about economics than my examiners."

At the time Lytton wrote an amusing poem which wonderfully portrays Maynard's attitude toward the results:

In Memoriam J. M. K. Ob., September 1906

Here lies the last remains of one
Who always did what should be done.
Who never misbehaved at table
And loved as much as he was able.
Who couldn't fail to make a joke,
And, though he stammered, always
        spoke;
Both penetrating and polite,
A liberal and a sodomite,
An atheist and a statistician,
A man of sense, without ambition.
A man of business, without bustle,
A follower of Moore and Russell,
One who, in fact, in every way,
Combined the features of the day.
By curses blest, by blessings cursed,
He didn't merely get a first.

A first he got; on that he reckoned;
But then he also got a second.
He got the first with modest pride;
He got the second, and he died.

There are other glimpses into Keynes's inner life in this period which one gets in his letters, but only two significant ones will be noted. In one to Lytton Strachey on June 20, 1906, Maynard returned to the question of publishing their unconventional views and asked whether their opinions on various subjects were too violent to publish. He said that to think so was absurd, they must crusade, but he urged that they should employ moderate or gradual means to that end. He felt strongly about the matter and used an expletive to express his feelings about conventional public attitudes; this letter is important because it shows the depth of his emotions over these questions and may help to explain his later interest in social reform. The second letter, containing a more poignant note, was written by Maynard to his father about three years later, telling him of some mail that had arrived at home: "An interesting report from Cambridge from the medical officer of health has arrived for mother. . . . It states also that one-third of the boys in the higher grade school are deformed! (I wonder if, on their standards, I am?)"

In the fall of 1906, Keynes began his work at the India office where he remained for almost two years, to the summer of 1908, employed as a junior clerk at the same time that he was busy with his study of probability. He was initially assigned to the military department where the business was very slow—sometimes he averaged an hour's official work a day—so he had ample time to work on his dissertation. His first official responsibility was to arrange the shipment of ten Ayrshire bulls to Bombay; having accomplished this and other duties to their satisfaction, his superiors offered him a resident clerkship, but he declined it because he wanted the evenings for his own work.

At the beginning of March 1907, he was transferred to the revenue statistics and commerce department where he had much more to do. He read everything that came into the department—commercial negotiations with Germany, conflicts with the Russians in the Persian Gulf, regulation of opium in India—and prepared a very realistic memorandum on the jute trade in India. Attending his first meeting of the committee of council, he was plainly contemptuous: "The thing is simply government by dotardy; at least half of those present showed manifest signs of senile decay, and the rest didn't speak."

In time, he came to like the work in this new department much better, though he was restless and critical of bureaucracy, as an autonomous person would likely be. Still, he grew very dissatisfied with his India office position and by September 1907 was informing Strachey that he was "thoroughly sick of this place and would like to resign. Now the novelty has worn off I am bored nine-tenths of the time and rather unreasonably irritated the other tenth, whenever I can't have my own way. It's maddening to have thirty people who can reduce you to impotence when you are quite certain that you are right."

During this period Maynard had a service flat at Saint James Court in London. From there he went on excursions with Lytton and others, helped in the "Mud March" for women's suffrage, and even went to Paris to visit Duncan Grant. Since the latter was to play a large role in the lives of Maynard, Lytton, and others in the Bloomsbury circle, his background needs to be known. Duncan had come into contact with Keynes through his relationship to the Stracheys. He was the only son of Major Bartle Grant, Lady Strachey's youngest brother. In January 1885, nearly two years after Maynard's birth, Duncan was born in Rothiemurchus, the site of the Grants' ancestral home. Father and mother had returned home from India so that their child could be born there, but most of Duncan's early life was spent in the subcontinent, the color and excitement of which left a lasting impression on him.

When he was old enough to attend preparatory school, he was shipped back to England to attend Hillsboro Prep School at Rugby, where his cousin James Strachey and Rupert Brooke were fellow students. He spent his holidays with the Stracheys at that preposterous and dowdy structure, 69 Lancaster Gate, which Lytton described so humorously in a famous essay. In the spring of 1899, after two terms of boarding school, he went to Saint Paul's as a day student, living with the Stracheys or with his parents when they were on leave in England. Years later Duncan described himself as "the dumped grass-orphan of an Anglo-Indian major."

At Saint Paul's, Duncan was placed in the army class—his father thought that he should follow him in the military—but he had no aptitude whatever for mathematics, and that ruled out an army career. An art master noticed his talent for drawing and painting, and Lady Strachey finally persuaded his parents to let him study at the Westminster School of Art, where he was from 1902 to 1905. Duncan was also influenced in those years by a French artist, Simon Bussy, who had married Dorothy Strachey; the latter gave the neophyte much good advice, particularly to copy the old masters. In 1904, young Grant and his mother went to Florence for the winter so that he had plenty of opportunity to do that in the Uffizi and other Italian galleries.

Though Duncan was relatively uneducated compared to Lytton,

Maynard, and their university friends, he had other compensating assets. He was good-looking and had a winning personality and a very good intellect. In later years David Garnett said that he was "the most entertaining companion" he had ever known. "He had a liveliness of mind which never struck upon the obvious; he was intensely observant and amused and interested in everything he saw; and the things he saw were those to which the majority of people are blind. One had only to walk down the street with him to find this out. . . . All the little dramas which were going on were instantly perceived." Garnett does not mention that Duncan was musical, taking after his father, and could dance Scottish reels and sword dances with great style. Often in wild spirits, he loved to mimic and tease and be a prankster. One can see his appeal to Maynard and Lytton, both of whom loved gaiety.

Lytton had liked his cousin when he was still a young boy, but now that he was older his friendship took on more the character of love. He described Duncan in a letter to Leonard Woolf: "His face is outspoken, bold, and just not rough. It's the full aquiline type, with frank, blue eyes and incomparably lascivious lips." Lytton's insecurity was such, according to Holroyd, that he would abandon his own personality and substitute that of the person he loved. His confusion about his own identity and what he was to do in the world after he left Cambridge led him to want to submerge himself in another's identity. "Perhaps," he wrote, "the truth is that I'm not an artist. But what the devil am I?"

In this sort of mood, Lytton came to regard Duncan as a genius who, as an artist, worked in one of the most creative media known to man. Thus, writing of his cousin to Keynes, he said, "He sees everything, you know, and he's probably better than us. I have a sort of adoration. When I hear people talking about him, I'm filled with a secret pride." His love for Duncan reached its peak in the winter of 1905–06 when he penned Clive Bell, "I have fallen in love hopelessly and ultimately. I have experienced too much ecstasy, I want to thank God, and to weep, and to go to sleep."

But this sense of euphoria was usually followed by one of despondency, as Lytton wondered whether Duncan returned his love. While on holiday with the young artist at Ledbury in Herefordshire, he was "blissfully happy" until something that Duncan said made him realize that he didn't really care for him, and he wanted to escape. He now became wretched and even thought of death.

Despite his misgivings, in the spring the two cousins went off together to France; Duncan was to paint in Paris, and Lytton would go on to Menton to stay with his aunt, Lady Colville. While he was there, amidst old dowagers and paralyzed majors, with nary a decent-looking boy in sight, he received a letter from Duncan informing him that Duckworth was with him and that he had "fallen in love with him and he with me." (This was the same Duckworth, or "Dicker," whom Keynes had taken away from Strachey before.) Lytton now began to wonder at the complications of this "new style" of homosexual love; all the possible permutations and combinations, without limit or logic, could leave one not knowing who was in love with whom.

Numbed and shocked by the disastrous turn of events, Lytton shook off the dust of Menton as fast as he could. "This place is so vilely relaxing that I believe that it's undermining my health," he wrote to Duncan, and headed for Paris. On the way there he developed a severe fever so that he was compelled to remain in bed for several days under a doctor's care, wretched and depressed. He broke the news in a letter to Keynes and later, after further weeks of doctoring and despair at Lancaster Gate, he wrote again to his Brother Confessor, as he was accustomed to calling Maynard: "That that little devil should despise me, and with justice, is my lowest infamy. That he should register my tears and dishonor my abandonments, my failures, the miserable embraces I can't withhold—I want to shake the universe to dust and ashes! Hell! Hell! Hell!"

If this development had shaken Lytton, far worse was still to come. He had introduced Duncan to Keynes but apparently did not realize their attraction for each other. Actually, Maynard had spent his Easter vacation with Duncan in Paris and then in the fall of 1907 took a flat with him in Belgrave Road. When Lytton heard of this, he was devastated. All the while that he was writing to both of them, calling Keynes's attention to Duncan's elusiveness and lack of responsibility and making fun of Maynard's lack of passion to Duncan; they had been deeply in love with one another. Concluding that his best reaction was to be overtly altruistic toward his "treacherous friends," he wrote to Keynes (whom Holroyd says "he detested now more than at any moment of his life"): "Dear Maynard, I only know that we've been friends far too long to stop being friends now. There are some things that I shall try not to think of, and you must do your best to help me in that; and you must believe that I do sympathize and don't hate you, and that if you were here now I should probably kiss you, except that Duncan would be jealous, which would never do!"

Maynard's reply was lacrimose but brief: "Your letter made me cry, but I am very glad to get it." He asked to come to visit him, but being refused, inquired whether he would like to go with him to see Isadora Duncan dance. In his reply Lytton ignored the pun and the invitation, and informed Keynes instead that he had sent him a present of some books for his rooms at King's. Maynard wrote back, thanking him for the books and saying, "Oh, Lytton, it is too good of you to behave like this." The same tactics worked with Duncan. Lytton offered to pay for some art lessons which the impecunious artist wanted to take in London. "You're too kind," he wrote Lytton. "You made me burst into tears; I cannot bear your being so completely good and generous. I think it is cruel of you to plunge me into such contradictory emotions." Duncan obviously saw through his cousin's hypocritical generosity.

In one of his woeful letters to Duncan, Lytton wrote, "The world is damned queer, it really is," and then wailed, "O Lord, Lord, why do we live in such a distorted, coagulated world? I feel all topsy-turvy and out of place, as if I were a pocket handkerchief that somebody had dropped on top of Mount Blanc." He was hoping that Maynard's affair with Duncan might be just "a flash in the pan," but when the summer came he soon realized that was not so. At that time Duncan was in the Orkney Islands, off the north coast of Scotland, and he wrote Maynard that he had found a perfect place for a holiday: "Rackawick is a largish fishing village about ten miles up the coast, with no road to it and right on the sheer Atlantic near the highest rocks in this part of the world. The people are superstitious and frequently mad from too frequent incest. One of them is a Red Indian, and the others are the remains of the Spanish Armada mingled with the heroes of the Iceland saga. There is no priest, no church, *and* no policeman. Don't you think that we'd better go there at once? I shall make inquiries today."

Maynard quickly joined his lover in these remote islands where they remained for two months on what Lytton called their "honeymoon." It was not altogether a romantic interlude, for while Maynard thought and wrote on probability, frequently putting in five hours a day on the subject, Duncan sketched the landscape and did a striking portrait of his friend which now hangs at King's College.

Still desolate over his loss of Duncan, Lytton poured out his soul in long letters to Leonard Woolf, his old Cambridge friend who was in the civil service in faraway Ceylon, writing, "I've heard nothing from them [Duncan and Maynard] for more than a week. I expect they've quarreled or begun to find each other out. I shouldn't be surprised if they were to ask me to join them, and I were to do so. [*sic*] Dieu! It's a mad mixture; are you shocked? We do rather permutate and combine. I've never been in love with Maynard and I've never copulated with Hobbes [Hobhouse], but at the moment I can't think of any more exceptions."

Less than two weeks later he dolefully admitted that it was all wishful thinking: "Keynes's love affair isn't in the least wearing out. Idyllic letters come from the Orkneys—blue seas, blue skies, and most convenient bedrooms—one's mouth waters. Ah! Ah! Imagination now all that's left to me on my heights and hearths. I walk out, contented or half-contented, and brood over conceivables; I linger in the theatres among glimpses of exquisite young men; I come home to my bed-sitting room to remember, to relapse, and to write to you."

All that fall and winter Lytton went on feeling unloved, forsaken and rejected over Duncan's affair with Keynes, toward whom he felt increasingly bitter. He would break out in his letters to Woolf, "Can you imagine the torture of imagining, of knowing for a *fact* that someone for whom you would be disemboweled is prostituted to Keynes?" Finally, he poured out the full depth of his resentment in a long denunciation of his friend:

As for poor old Keynes, he's absolutely sunk—it's really remarkable, the unveiled collapse. If ever a human soul was doomed, it's he. And by God he deserves his fate. Looking back I see him, hideous and meaningless, at every turn and every crisis, a malignant goblin jibbering over destinies that are not his own. . . . What's curious is that he, at this moment, must be imagining—if he imagines anything—that he's reached the apex of human happiness. Cambridge, statistics, triumphant love, and inexhaustible copulation—what more could anyone desire? His existence is the thinnest shell, and he believes it's solid and will go on believing so, until one day it shivers into smithereens, and even then he'll believe that it can be patched. He'll end a spiritual nixon, with a whole internal economy of metal makeshifts for lungs and lights and heart and genitory organs; but he'll never know; he'll never hear the clank.

Despite Lytton's constant wishful thinking that *le affaire* Duncan would be short, Keynes and his artist friend's intimacy persisted and continued until 1914. After their short stay at Belgrave Road in London, they moved late in 1909 to the Bloomsbury area, 21 Fitzroy Square, where Duncan had a studio and Maynard a bedroom which he could use when he came to the city. Maynard had left the India office and returned to the university in the fall of 1908 as a lecturer in economics, while Duncan remained in London. Their physical separation created problems, as well as the fact that the artist was not a very diligent letter writer. Keynes would write in exasperation after a long lapse in hearing from him, "Why aren't you a Cambridge undergraduate, damn you, instead of a wretched Londoner? Come, and I will make King's Chapel into a studio for you." In their relationship it is clear that Maynard was the dependent one, always anxious for some sign of Duncan's love and frequently depressed when it wasn't forthcoming or he didn't write for long periods. Independence, on the other hand, was a strong feature of Duncan's character. He was totally committed to his work as an artist; other obligations were secondary. In these very years, 1908–1911, he was very productive and his talents were being recognized; by the latter year he was considered a leading contributor to the English Postimpressionist movement.

Contrary to what one may have expected, Keynes's love for Grant under these circumstances of frequent separation interfered with rather than inspired his work on probability. Certainly he said as much in his numerous letters to his absent lover. Thus, on August 2, 1908, he wrote, "I seem to be getting very little work done, which is a pity, as I tend to spend almost the whole day being in love with you. Probability, I find, will not drive you out of my mind and does not occupy it jointly very well." Frequently he would moon about the whole day, thinking of what Duncan was doing in London. In November of that year he was back home at Harvey Road, ill with influenza and writing Grant about himself, while "you've been whirling about London as if you were an American."

Fortunately, by the end of the year he was in better health, doing a good deal of work, writing an article on Indian affairs. He was engaged, he stated, "chiefly on statistics of verification, the production of which takes me into a tremendous state of excitement—like the scientist who watches the results of his experiments. Here are my theories—will the statistics bear them out? Nothing except copulation is so enthralling, and the figures are coming out so much better than one could possibly have expected that everybody will believe that I've cooked them."

Nevertheless, despite his emotional involvement in this work, as the year closed he was again depressed, for he had received only one letter from Grant in ten days. He burst out, "Really you are wicked about letter writing. . . . If I wasn't in such rude health, I should be in tears." He added that notwithstanding his disappointment, he had done a lot of work and sent off his Indian article to the publisher.

In one of these 1908 letters to Duncan, Keynes expressed the opinion that in his two years' absence from Cambridge in the India office, pederasty or homosexuality in some form had "grown by leaps and bounds" and "practically everybody in Cambridge, except me, is an open and avowed sodomite." A few months later he remarked, "The outstanding and terrifying fact is that James Strachey? or . . . some-body or other has fertilized inversion in the place. The thing is absolutely universal; nothing else is talked about, and everybody considers himself one. . . . There are at least half a dozen embryos spoken of—wits, beauties, and intelligences—but I've seen none of them." How much of this is romantic imagination or exaggeration for Grant's benefit or projection on Keynes's part, it is difficult to say; he was probably intent on impressing Duncan with his own love and faithfulness. Generally, one thinks of the cult of dandyism and homosexuality as becoming more general in Cambridge and Oxford in the twenties than in the prewar years.

There is surprisingly little mention in Keynes's correspondence of the celebrated case of Oscar Wilde. The brilliant playwright had been convicted in 1895 on a charge of homosexuality and sentenced to imprisonment. His life and death (he died impoverished in Paris in 1900) was still a subject of intense interest in Cambridge eight years later, as witness this bit of family conversation which Keynes reported to Duncan about this time:

Margaret, Keynes's sister, was going to a fancy dress dance during the 1908 Christmas festivities. Maynard and his brother Geoffrey had been invited but had refused to go. In the course of the morning at Harvey Road when Maynard was at home, Margaret said, "I think you had better go as Oscar Wilde!"

Maynard, thinking that she was speaking to him, said that he turned with a dreadful start, only to find that she was addressing Geoffrey. He heard his mother say, "Oh, that would be a horrid thing to do!" "But the females," wrote Keynes, "can't keep off the subject."

About this same time, late December 1908, the Keynes family had tea with the Darwins. Maynard noted in this connection that Geoffrey "seems to me almost a little bit in love" with Margaret Darwin, whom he said he liked very much. (She and Geoffrey were subsequently married.)

Maynard said that he heard the following dialogue at this tea:

Margaret Darwin (aged 17 or 18): "Was Oscar Wilde imprisoned for stealing?"

Margaret Keynes, slightly confused: "Oh, I don't know. For that and other things."

Keynes concluded, "Perhaps she may have known what she was saying in the morning." He added that from a letter he had seen, written by Margaret Darwin to Margaret Keynes, Geoffrey was known as "the curate" and he as "the sailor brother from China." Less than two years later the matter of the "sailor brother's" sexual inclination came up again in family discussion, and Keynes wrote to Duncan, "I had a dreadful conversation on Sunday with my mother and Margaret about marriage, and had practically to admit to them what I was! How much they grasped I don't know." In his reply, Duncan remarked among other things, "What an appalling avowal you have made to your parents!"

In the spring of 1908, Keynes had submitted his work on probability as a dissertation in a bid for a fellowship at King's College. As it happened, the two assessors assigned to review his work were not unknown to him: W. E. Johnson, a mathematician and a logician, was an old family acquaintance, and the philosopher Alfred North Whitehead, whom Maynard had studied under. However, after voting fifteen times, the electors chose two other candidates rather than Maynard. His parents were especially depressed at this result because, from prior conversations with other Cambridge faculty members, they had become quite confident about the outcome. They both wrote their son very supportive letters, the father, two the same day. In her letter Mrs. Keynes said, "We cannot help feeling that they have chosen very badly. . . . Still there is another chance. We do not think that an official career is to be despised. We would love to have you in Cambridge, and what we want most of all is that you should have occupations and surroundings that are congenial and a career that will give you the opportunity of using your life in the best and most satisfactory way— meanwhile, let us possess our souls in patience. Ever your loving mother."

In his letter Keynes's father stressed his hope that if Maynard had to settle down to official life, he would keep up his interest in it and make "a big success"; he expressed his belief that he had "administrative powers of a high order" and would have a chance to manifest them either in the India office or in the Treasury. Maynard thanked his parents for their very sympathetic letters, but he was not easily reconciled to his setback, saying that he was very disappointed because "the decision affects not honor or reward, as these things usually do, but one's whole manner of life." Evidently after his stint in government bureaucracy the academic life was becoming more attractive.

His self-confidence where his work on probability was concerned may be seen in the remarks he made in a letter to Strachey concerning Whitehead's criticisms. He said flatly that the latter's report was not "competent." Whitehead had written that the two most important chapters of Keynes's dissertation were novel and "are really excellent discussions and expositions, but—as I suspect—contain little that is new to a fairly well-instructed philosopher." The sharpness and cogency of Keynes's thinking can be seen in his comment that "Whitehead ought not to have said that it was old, unless he himself knew of some passages where it had been said before. It is no good 'suspecting' that it must have been said before because it seems reasonable." Nevertheless, he was mollified by the kind things that had been said about his thesis and by the news that the electors preferred a revision of his manuscript rather than a new one. He was sustained, too, by having a long talk with Professor Johnson, who he thought was the one person who really understood probability theory; the latter lent him some very valuable notes on the subject, and so he was determined to persevere in his investigations.

Toward the end of this rather disappointing month (March 1908) he had a touch of fever, and in the following May he began to worry about approaching baldness. He wrote his mother that "baldness was reaching such portentous dimensions that I feared to have no hairs at the end of the week. Under the influence of panic I have purchased a drug—the Celebrated Mrs. Parker's Quin Julep (applied to the late Prince Consort by Her Majesty), and hope to have a fine new growth by next Saturday."

Despite his annoyance with the slow-moving bureaucracy of the India office, he had spent almost all of 1908 in the department, compiling the annual report on "The Moral and Material Progress of India" and handling much administrative work and even being in charge of the revenue department for the greater part of his last two days there. Most of those he talked to in the office thought that he was probably right to leave, and thus, he said, he did so with "no regrets." A former colleague in the office later informed him that "Kisch, who migrated from the post office to succeed me, is doing well. So they will miss me as little as I miss them!"

In the spring of 1908 he had received a rather mysterious letter from Professor Marshall in which he stated that he had heard that he might be willing to return to Cambridge and that his chances for election to a fellowship at the college during the next year were good. In rather cryptic phraseology, Marshall informed him that a proposal would be made to the board in June that he be asked to teach general economics as a lecturer and that one hundred pounds would be paid to him by some source or by himself. (At the time lecturers were not paid by the university but received a fee of a certain amount per capita from the colleges of the students who attended their lectures. The one hundred pounds that Marshall offered was entirely unofficial.) The latter had been tentative in his offer because he was scheduled to step down from the professorship shortly, and he did not wish to commit the incoming board.

Maynard consulted with his father on this obscure proposition. John

Neville cautioned him against making too quick an acceptance, saying that if he had to prepare a course of lectures he would not have any more time, or even as much, for his dissertation than if he remained in the India office.

When the economics board met in June, it was faced with a shortage of lecturers for the next academic year. Marshall himself was retiring from lecturing in order to give Alfred C. Pigou the chance to become established as the principal lecturer. H. S. Foxwell, a senior lecturer who was piqued at the election of Pigou, a younger man, to the chairmanship, indicated that he did not intend to continue lecturing. To make matters worse, D. H. MacGregor, another senior man who taught the economics tripos, had just been appointed to a chair at the University of Leeds. There was an urgent need for additional staff, and it was in these circumstances that Pigou, following Marshall's precedent, offered to pay two hundred pounds from his own funds for two lecturers. The board offered one of these lectureships to Walter Layton and the other to young Keynes.

The latter accepted the assignment and shortly thereafter received a letter from Marshall stating that he was "delighted indeed that you are to join our economic staff. I think that it is a brilliant, compact group of earnest men, full of the highest promise for the future." Marshall was certainly right about this distinguished group of men; they included, beside Pigou, Walter Layton (later Lord Layton), W. E. Johnson, G. Lowes Dickinson, J. H. Clapham, C. R. Fay, H. O. Meredith, and L. Alston.

Two days after his appointment at King's, Keynes resigned from the India office, and in a letter to his former superior, Sir Thomas Holderness, he said that "for many reasons I am sorry to do this, and I have only made up my mind after a great deal of doubt and hesitation. But the desire for scientific and theoretical work and for a life here [at Cambridge] is so great that I think I am probably right in giving way to it.

"Please do not think that I have disliked my work in the revenue department or have been discontented. I have liked it very much and have learnt a great deal from it and from you. But the choice has been between two quite opposed ways of life, and on the whole, now at any rate, the way here is better." His mother had aided him in preparing this tactful letter of resignation, and he himself did not wish to seem ungrateful to his superior at the India office who had been, in fact, very kind to him.

In accepting the lectureship at King's he would have only the certainty of approximately £200 a year as income—£100 from his father as an allowance and £100 from Pigou. In addition, he might pick up additional fees from lecturing and tutoring, though the rates at that time were extraordinarily low. Also, if he were elected to the King's fellowship the following year, he would receive an additional stipend of £120 a year. It was a gamble, but it was his nature to take risks. His father, who doubted the wisdom of leaving the India office even if he had the fellowship, wrote in his diary: "He will be throwing up a certainty and taking risks. That fits in with his scheme of life, not with mine." Here again there is evidence of a character trait which is often associated with creativity. In Keynes's case, he had the personal ability to turn this risky opportunity into the making of a master economist.

In considering how he reached his tentative occupational identity at the age of twenty-five, whereas his crony, Strachey, was still struggling as an impecunious journalist, one should not overlook the fact that he had a role model of an economist in the person of his father. At various times he discussed stock transactions with the older man. Furthermore, the two years that he had spent at the India office served somewhat as a moratorium in which he could experience London and the appeal of a civil service career, while he was still working on his treatise on probability. Despite his joking that all he had achieved during his time at the India office was to get one pedigreed bull shipped to Bombay, it was a very valuable experience for the budding economist. He learned how a government department worked; he gained an interest in Indian affairs, especially in the currency issue; and, most important for his future, he made the acquaintance of government officials who became aware of his unusual abilities. The occupational identity that he ultimately developed was an open, creative one in which he moved brilliantly and in accordance with his own personal inclination and involvement. In a word, his identity as an economist was his own unique creation.

CHAPTER 5

Don, Editor, and Royal Commissioner of Finance

The work of a don is the hardest work in the world.

J. M. Keynes

UPON LEAVING the India office, Keynes immediately returned to the university where he had the pleasure of meeting two new men who were to make their mark in economics—Gerald Shove and Hugh Dalton. The former studied under Keynes for two years and ultimately became a fellow of King's College and an intimate of the Keynes-Strachey circle, so much so that in one of his letters to Maynard he asked about his "disease" and discussed buggery. Dalton did not move so much in Keynes's company, but he did go on to become an important member of the Labor party and chancellor of the exchequer in the years 1945–47.

Later in 1908, Keynes also got to know Francis "Frankie" Birrell, a son of Augustine Birrell, the Liberal minister and man of letters, and the two remained intimate for the rest of their lives. Another new friend at this time was George Mallory, who became especially close to Duncan Grant and Geoffrey Keynes; an ardent mountaineer, he was lost mysteriously in 1924 while climbing Mount Everest.

After recovering from an attack of influenza in the fall, Maynard resumed his work on his treatise and then submitted it for reconsideration. Professors Johnson and Whitehead were favorably impressed with the changes he had made in his manuscript, and it was accepted the following March when he was elected a fellow of King's, a position which he held to the end of his life. The master of Trinity Hall, E. A. Beck, wrote his father on this happy occasion: "It gives me joy to see your son has got his fellowship at King's. . . . A feather in the cap of his father, who up to now has had, for the labors of a life, not much emolument, but may well console himself with the regard of all who know him." In later life, when someone addressed the son as professor, he was fond of remarking that he would not suffer the indignity without the emolument.

The economics tripos at the time Maynard began lecturing was under the chairmanship of Alfred C. Pigou, a brilliant disciple of Marshall. The number of candidates at first was small, six in 1906, but it rose to twenty-five by 1910. The teaching staff was equally small, but capable. J. H. Clapham lectured on the economic history of France and Germany; C. R. Fay on British economic history and general economics; H. O. Meredith lectured in place of Pigou; G. Lowes Dickinson held forth on political science; and W. E. Johnson taught advanced economic theory. In addition to these, Walter Layton taught what we now call industrial organization and labor problems. Keynes's specialty was money, credit, and prices, a topic on which he could expound the oral tradition of Marshallian economic doctrine. In the years before World War I he also typically taught a course on principles twice a week and gave lectures once a week on company finance, the stock exchange, the money market, and the foreign exchanges. In 1911, he gave a weekly lecture on Indian currency and finance. As Harrod rightly claimed, "In this prewar period he certainly went through the mill of hard university teaching." On January 19, 1909, Maynard made his debut in the academic role, later describing it drolly to Grant: "I delivered my lecture this morning before an enormous and cosmopolitan audience—there must have been at least fifteen, I think, but a good many of them really had no business there, I am afraid, and I shall have to tell them that the lectures are not suitable for their needs."

During this period he was occupied with writing as well as teaching. In the previous year he had published a statistical analysis of the social and economic conditions in the West Ham area of London and two notes criticizing index numbers used by the Board of Trade. During December of that year he also composed a paper on "Recent Economic Events in India" for the *Economic Journal,* for which he was able to draw upon his recently acquired expertise. This was his first major article to appear in print, and it dealt with the foreign exchange fluctuations of the rupee and, interestingly enough, took a stand in favor of currency management rather than relying on automatic forces. In the spring of the following year he again returned to Indian economic matters, contending in *The Economist* in a series of letters that estimates of British investment in that country were exaggerated.

While engaged in all this teaching and writing, his friends and he continued a discussion group which was held by John Sheppard on Sundays. In addition, the Apostles were holding some stormy sessions in which, among other matters, they condemned Rupert Brooke for admiring H. G. Wells's thinking and disagreed over the election of Gerald Shove. There was plenty of intellectual stimulus and diversion for Keynes in these gatherings, as he told Duncan: "The excitement of this place combined with a good deal of work is enough to unhinge anyone, and I really do not know how any of us last through the eight weeks of it." In actual fact, judging by his other letters to his artist friend, he was often depressed and miserable, mainly because of the dearth of letters from the latter.

Teaching was trying for him at times, so much so that he decided to give up instructing females: "I seem to hate every movement of their minds. The minds of men, even when they are ugly and stupid, never appear to me so repellent." It would be a mistake, however, to take this remark as expressing his more mature attitude toward women. Later, in 1921, he strongly protested the discrimination against women by the university, writing in *The Cambridge Review* that they should not be debarred from degrees or teaching positions on the sole ground of their sex. He also held that it was a grievance for men to be denied the intellectual contributions that women could make.

During the Easter vacation he spent another two weeks with Duncan at Versailles. While abroad he wrote an essay on index numbers and submitted it for the Adam Smith Prize at the university, which he duly won—he was back at his old specialty of winning academic prizes. In commenting upon the criticism of this essay by Professor F. Y. Edgeworth of Oxford, he also displayed his characteristic cockiness. Though he later came to have a different view of him, in a letter to Duncan he wrote that though Edgeworth was "supposed to be the leading authority on the subject of this essay, he seems to me hopeless. I feel convinced that I'm right on almost every point he attacks, and that where my argument is novel he simply has not attended to it. His criticisms show a closed mind, and I feel that I could never convince him since he wouldn't ever properly attend to what I was saying." This, as will be seen, was a complaint that he often made of critics' reactions to his innovations, and with some justification.

Toward the end of the spring term the academic routine was lightened for him by the appearance at Cambridge of a distinguished visitor. Geoffrey Keynes and some friends had the idea at New Year's to address greetings to some of the world figures whom they most admired. Most of those so greeted did not reply, thinking very likely that it was just an undergraduate lark. But to the amazement of all concerned, when Geoffrey saluted Henry James, the expatriate novelist, and invited him to come to Cambridge for a visit, the invitation was accepted! Maynard himself, encouraged by this, invited James to breakfast, and he replied that he would be "enchanted" to come.

Harry Norton, James Strachey, Duncan Grant, and Gerald Shove were all on hand to entertain this distinguished guest at that breakfast, but it fizzled badly. The trouble was that Maynard's friends all spoke endlessly on their own individual esoteric interests, and James could hardly get a word in and understood little of their conversation. The situation was only partially saved when Desmond MacCarthy, a late arrival, engaged James in talk about the photogenic poet Rupert Brooke. From all accounts MacCarthy gave less than a glowing appraisal of Brooke's talents as a poet, whereupon James is reported to have said, "Thank goodness. If he looked like that and was a good poet too, I do not know what I should do."

In July, Keynes went off on vacation with his family to the Pyrenees for some mountain climbing and for what he called "a moderate amount of work." He didn't get much done in the way of writing, explaining to Duncan that he couldn't think or feel in his family's company. He told him also that there were few beauties at his resort and that he was far from the barest possibility of an adventure and was very homesick. Depressed, he withdrew even from the family, working on probability and almost hoping for cloudy weather so that he would have an excuse for not going on a day's excursion with them. Pining for his absent lover, he could still appreciate Biarritz which they visited and where, he said, he fell in love with his barber!

In one of these letters to Grant from the Pyrenees, Maynard remarked, "Geoffrey [his brother] is quite hopeless." Years later, after Maynard's death, Geoffrey came across this sentence in these old letters and in his autobiography, written at the end of a long, distinguished life, he wrote, "This seemed a harsh judgment, though the context of the remark showed that it was justified." Maynard, he explains, in his companionship with Duncan was cultivating an esthetic appreciation of the arts to which he could not contribute, especially because Geoffrey's own mind was completely centered on entomology and could not provide anything of interest to Maynard's. "He had been mistaken to come on this family holiday and he never made the same mistake again." He adds, however, that after Maynard's marriage, his attitude changed immediately; whereas before he had taken very little notice of his younger brother, "from that time onwards he became a kind and affectionate brother."

Later that summer Maynard rented a house at Burford in Oxfordshire so that he could work without distraction on probability. So many of his friends as well as his mother and sister came to stay that he had to have them in relays, but Duncan came last and stayed longest.

In the fall he complained to Grant about his uneventful life as "a pastor among pupils." He was in excellent health except for a cold, but was beginning to feel overworked, probably because he had undertaken to tutor private pupils, of which he had eighteen who added sixty pounds to his income. It was at this time that he informed Duncan, "The work of a don is the hardest in the world. . . . I'm becoming little more than a machine for selling economics by the hour. It is impossible to exaggerate the degrading effect of such work."

About this time he agreed to serve as examiner at the Mercers' Grammar School in Holborn at the rate of fifteen pounds for five days' work, and soon other new opportunities for additional income arose. In 1909, he was appointed director of studies for economics students at Trinity, and in the following year the University Council awarded him an annual lectureship in the subject with a stipend of fifty pounds. "For this," he wrote his father, "I am to lecture to members of the college free of charge and do any supervision if it is required. I think the terms are very generous." As a result of these supplements to his income, he was earning seven hundred pounds a year by the end of 1909, including the one hundred pounds that his father gave him. In terms of our inflated price level and the changed standard of living, the sum seems small, but he had to work exceedingly hard to earn it.

One of the most important academic innovations that he was responsible for at Cambridge in these years was the formation of the Political Economy Club for undergraduates, which developed in the course of time into his famous Monday Evenings. In agreement with the directors of economic studies in the various colleges, he would select the most promising graduates. One or more of the other dons would usually attend, a paper would be read by one of the undergraduates, and then the other students, chosen by lot, would comment on it before the fireplace. Keynes himself usually would sum up, in Austin Robinson's words, "in friendly but utterly devastating manner."

These Monday evenings continued each term, with the exception of the World War I period, from their inauguration in 1909 until 1937. In this fashion Keynes came to know the best of each generation of Cambridge economists down to his illness in the latter year. And, as Robinson stated, he "exercised a more personal influence upon them than anyone else." He asserted further that these sessions were "a wonderful training, because in Keynes's presence there were certain forms of nonsense that one did not enjoy perpetuating once, and remembered for life not to perpetrate a second time." Lest this image of Keynes appear to make him seem harsh and censorious toward undergraduates, it is necessary to add the impression that Harrod offered of these discussion sessions. He pictured Keynes "very cosily arranged in the corner of the sofa beside the fireplace, his legs outstretched, his hands tucked into his cuffs, on his face an expression of kindly interest. One might know that ruthless criticism would come in due course; for the time being, one had the impression that he was eager to hear what one had concocted and that he was esssentially one's friend, covering one with his support and protection." This additional touch to the Robinsonian portrait seems both appropriate and authentic because it accords with what we know of Keynes's androgynous nature, especially his sympathetic receptiveness toward the underdog, coupled with his ability and willingness to disparage and insult, if need be, the top dogs of this world. Thus, as an outsider, a homosexual in a predominantly heterosexual society, he seemed to look at his fellows in both a kindly and a critical fashion, depending upon their place in the human pecking order. Others, in his later life, noted this curious characteristic about him.

In the winter of 1909–10, Great Britain went through a general election as a result of Lloyd George's budget being rejected by the House of Lords. At this time Keynes returned to his old interest in liberal politics, first, by writing a long letter to the *Cambridge Daily News* in support of the liberal cause, then in January rushing off to speak in support of an old Etonian and Cambridge friend, Edward H. Young, who was standing for election as a Liberal in East Worcester, near Birmingham. Writing home to his mother and bragging a bit for her benefit, he told her that "J. M. Keynes, fellow of King's College, Cambridge, is billed to speak somewhere every night" and added, "I am going to enjoy myself very much, I think."

In the two general elections of 1910, he battled the tariff reformers as a free-trading Liberal and as secretary of the Cambridge University Free Trade Association, and as a Liberal he spoke to the Indian undergraduates on India and protection. In an article entitled "India During 1907–08," he, in effect, defended British rule in that country, stating "The apologist of our Indian administration still asks in vain for the simple statistical data which would upset the statistical fiction of an India declining under British rule." Obviously, politics was more than a fair substitute for bridge at this time, and at least it was a change from the burdens of teaching, for he loved variety in life very much.

After this short stint of politics, at the Easter vacation he was off again with Duncan to Greece and Constantinople. Sharing a steamer cabin, Maynard stayed in bed late to avoid seasickness on the Ionian Sea and later read nearly half of Adam Smith's *Wealth of Nations,* concluding that it was "a wonderful book." In Greece he and Duncan had a room overlooking the Parthenon and the Temple of Theseus, and he helped his artist friend by photographing the nude sculptures they saw in that country. It was an exciting holiday, what with their dragoman cooking for them, Maynard's wallet being stolen, and the dancing dervishes they witnessed in Turkey. Later Keynes wrote to Duncan, "I wonder if you realize how immensely happier I was than if you had not been with me."

Back home, during the early summer after a visit to the luxurious home of the Berensons, he resumed examining at Hammersmith in order to earn fifteen pounds. Toward the end of the vacation period he returned to the little house he had rented at Burford for some more work on probability. At times the completion of that treatise seemed in sight, but he later confided to his father that while the first draft on induction was finished, "first drafts never do." To relieve the strain he went bicycling over the Berkshire Downs and Salisbury Plain, later telling James Strachey, "I had a very happy four days on the North Downs, full of flirtations with shepherds and young farmers. They are a charming people on the uplands—not cold and sulky as they are here."

In the autumn, back at King's, he was asked to take on some administrative work in addition to his teaching; he was elected secretary of the special board for economics and politics, and about the same time his father was appointed chairman. Apropos of these developments, Harrod stated that the Keyneses toward the end of 1910 might be said to have had Cambridge economics "in their pocket," yet the impression one gets from Maynard's letters to Grant in these months is that of a rather depressed, overworked, and dissatisfied young man. The fall term had barely begun when he was writing Duncan that he found "Cambridge society rather stale, and I don't seem at present to be much amused by it. I expect it's because there's no one here with whom I feel the least bit in love." Seemingly, he was distressed because of the fluctuations in his affair with Duncan and his uncertainty as to whether the artist reciprocated his love. This same letter stated very directly, "I must try, if I can, to fall in love with someone else besides you." In London, Duncan had been going out with other young men, with Adrian Stephen in particular, and this had not made Keynes at all happy.

His need for emotional interest was so strong that it even led him to make friends with some of the freshmen. A week after the previous letter, he wrote Grant: "Hardly enough time has passed yet for the freshmen to have made their debut in my circle, or for me to tell one from another. I've seen one or two, however, including this afternoon, a rather lascivious one with whom I made friends—long hair, velvet coat, brick-red face, fat legs, but very young and with rather beautiful, excessively well-kept hands and highly aesthetical. Do you think that you would like him?" Was he telling Duncan about these sexual opportunities in order to make him jealous? It is a possible motive, but one cannot be certain. His state of mind at this period is revealed also by the long talks he had with "Goldie" Dickinson about his homosexual affairs; the older man told him that everybody he had been in love with in the course of his life had turned out to be a womanizer. (The latter term, as used by Cambridge homosexuals, seems to have been a derogatory one referring to those males who made love to women instead of men.)

In a previous letter to Duncan, Keynes remarked, "The sooner we all become womanizers the better, I am sure." Did this sentiment, so casually expressed, presage a change in his own sexual inclinations? At any rate, he was still strongly drawn to other men; his next amour, in fact, was Justin Brooke (no relation to Rupert) with whom he and others had recently gone camping in Devon. In June, he wrote that he "fell, once more, deeply in love" with Brooke, who had reminded him on that trip of a fawn of the woods in the frolicsome dance he led.

About this time he also formed a more dangerous attachment to an Indian student by the name of Rimala Sarkar, whom he had recommended for admittance to Clare College and who had been accepted, against the advice of others. The Indian had complained to Keynes that in walking through the streets of Cambridge the residents would make derogatory remarks about him, such as "that black man" and "that Indian." Maynard must have felt real sympathy for him, but as it turned out, it was more than that; he told Duncan that to him the Indian was "a strange and charming creature. . . . I have had all today the most violent sexual feelings towards him; and he on his part has paid me four or five visits on one pretext or another, finally saying that he was so miserable when he was anywhere else. When he is away he writes me long letters to the effect that I am the only person on earth to whom he can open his thoughts freely and that he must come to King's for the sake of my blissful company! And yet I don't feel at all certain what feelings there are in his old Indian head. What will happen tomorrow if he again wants to spend the day here? I did in the end stroll out on Tuesday night and bring a boy back."

That boy told him that there were fewer of his kind about because the police the previous week had been active and locked ten up. Maynard then described for Duncan the speeches made at Marble Arch in which the park orators deplored "the hundreds of painted boys fighting the women for a living!" He added a thought which is puzzling to those of more conventional sexuality: "What a sublime scene. And what a superb place London now is. But I'm afraid it must have reached or about reached the zenith of its accomplishment."

During these difficult emotional months he was simultaneously engaged in increasingly complex academic questions. In 1910, he participated in a controversy with the well-known statistician Karl Pearson, growing out of his review in the *Journal of the Royal Statistical Society* in which he attacked the methods of a study by Pearson and Miss E. M. Elderton denying that children of alcoholic parents were adversely affected by their parents' drinking. The dispute was part of a larger controversy between the conservative disciples of the eugenicist Francis Galton and the more liberal social scientists, such as Marshall, Pigou, and Keynes, who claimed that environmental change could promote social progress. The latter, well versed in statistical inference, criticized Pearson's article in sharp, witty, and confident fashion. At twenty-seven years of age he was ready to challenge the most authoritative figures in academia.

He was publishing and lecturing in economics as well. Early in 1911, he gave a series of six lectures on Indian finance at the London School of Economics, a task for which he had been preparing since the previous May; it is clear from their content that he was very up-to-date and expert on the subject. The lectures in turn provided material for a paper he read to the Royal Economic Society in May, which Harrod regarded as "the first manifestation of his pathbreaking capacity as an economist." In these talks he presented himself as the champion of the gold exchange standard which, he asserted, the government of India had been the first to adopt on a large scale. He boldly predicted that it would become, in effect, before very long the monetary standard of half the world. "And out of it, in my belief, will evolve the ideal currency of the future." Thus, he very definitely made his debut as a monetary reformer in a field which was to command his attention for virtually the rest of his life.

In assuming this role he was aided considerably by officials of the India office, especially Lionel Abrahams, the financial secretary of that body, who was practically his mentor. He submitted everything he wrote to Abrahams for his criticism, and the latter in turn took advantage of the young economist's growing expertise. Again, one notes the Keynesian capacity for receptivity and for converting the suggestions and criticisms of others into his own conceptual framework and idiom of expression.

In the fall of 1909 he had brought a group of officials from the India office to Cambridge to discuss Indian monetary matters with Alfred Marshall. Previously, his former colleagues in that agency had generously supplied him with information and their views on the subject. Just prior to the publication of his essay, Abrahams had written him, "I am sure that we have much to learn from you. . . . Your knowledge of both the practical official's and the economist's standpoint will enable you to say much more helpful things." The India office official agreed with Keynes on most points, so much so that he had copies of the essay prepared and circulated in his office and in the government of India. Over the next two years the latter developed into Keynes's first full-length book, *Indian Currency and Finance.*

His stature now as an economist was growing, as his father and others could see. About this time John Neville was elected to an honorary fellowship of his alma mater, Pembroke College, and in writing to congratulate him, Alfred Marshall said, "Among your many honors there is none perhaps greater than that of being father of J. M. Keynes." Maynard's self-esteem, never anemic, was also pretty high at this time. Somewhat earlier, his brother Geoffrey had done well in some examinations, and Maynard wrote to congratulate him via the father: "We're really a wonderful family, take us all around, at examinations. Probably the finest in the kingdom, I expect. If only the examination system lasts another two or three hundred years, we shall end, I'm sure, by becoming the Royal Family."

During the Easter vacation of 1911, after his strenuous intellectual and emotional involvements of recent months, he was off again on an ambitious holiday to Tunis and Sicily. While on these holidays he maintained almost a daily correspondence with his family and they with him. His mother, always apprehensive about his health, expressed her concern about him in this fashion: "When you are so far away and I do not know what you are doing, I can't help being a little fussy, so you must make allowances for me as well as for the weather. Don't forget my anxiety about you and your promise not to make your father uneasy. Ever your loving Mother." While her reference to the father's uneasiness is ambiguous, from the previous passages quoted it may be surmised that Maynard's father was concerned about appearances and possible scandal resulting from his son's unconventional sexual behavior.

Indeed, one may speculate further that Keynes's tendency to take his holidays with Duncan in places remote from home may have been designed to allay any such criticism or suspicion. But that is mere speculation; what is incontestable is that while Keynes, as Harrod contended, found Duncan "an ideal companion," their love affair at this time was not going at all well. Keynes had gone ahead to Sicily before his companion whom he missed very much, but they had agreed to meet at Naples. When they did they had quite a scene, with Keynes sending Duncan away one night because, after all his high expectations, his lover seemed sad and unable to show much open affection for him. Later they were reconciled and went to visit the Berensons at their villa, I Tatti.

Back home in July, while his father was winning numerous prizes at the horticultural show in Cambridge, Maynard was at Covent Garden watching the Russian ballet dancers—indeed, he went twice a week. This was an interest that was to grow with the years and one that, incidentally, appealed deeply to him even before the appearance of Lydia Lopokova in London.

His uncertain health in these years did not make him the perfect outdoorsman, but he didn't allow it to hamper him too much. In the latter part of September, he took off on a strenuous tour of Ireland with Gerald Shove in a venture that was sponsored by the Eighty Club, a Liberal party organization. The Liberals at this time were split over the issue of home rule for Ireland, and Maynard too was apparently "on the fence" on that question. In several letters to his mother and others, he gave glimpses of the troubled isle, larded with his characteristic, caustic comments on all and sundry. He told his mother that he left the group to tour more leisurely. "I don't like crowd life and couldn't support any longer the perpetual chatter of fifty pomposities at close quarters or bear to hear a single additional speech. However, it's been interesting and I enjoyed it." In Killaloe, County Clare, he told her, "We were magnificently received here—with illuminations, bonfires, and a band playing 'Rule Britannia' and 'God Save Ireland.'" He informed Duncan, on the other hand, that he was having "a good deal of depression and wishing very much that I could see or hear from you. . . . You have not, I suppose, ever mixed with politicians at close quarters. They are *awful.* I think some of these must have been dregs anyhow, but I have discovered what previously I didn't believe possible—that politicians behave in private life and say exactly the same things as they do in public. Their stupidity is inhuman."

He found the Irish landscape very charming, especially in the evening, but he concluded that he preferred England: "A great part of Ireland seems to me unexpectedly to lack mystery and not to make up for this by peacefulness." He added, however, that Galway, the Aran Islands, and perhaps Connemara were romantic and reminded him of Greece and the Orkneys. Furthermore, he met some politicians, priests, and others in Ireland whom he liked. "I'm a very much more convinced home ruler than I was before I started, but it is perfectly plain that the people are now on the whole prosperous, and that the conditions and feelings of twenty years ago have gone away altogether. But my impressions are much too full and complicated for a letter."

In October 1911, he was appointed editor of the *Economic Journal,* the official organ of the Royal Economic Society, a signal honor for a man not yet thirty who himself had relatively few publications to his credit. As Harrod surmised, quite correctly, "Marshall's support was no doubt critical." An editorial committee was appointed, but it had little need to interfere, so Keynes had sole control of the publication— the only exception being in 1919 when F. Y. Edgeworth was made joint editor while Keynes was busy in the Treasury.

The month before his appointment he had published a significant review of Professor Irving Fisher's important book, *The Purchasing Power of Money,* in the British journal. He praised the American economist's volume, stating that it was "marked by extreme lucidity and brilliance of statement" and that it supplied "a better exposition of monetary theory than is available elsewhere." He criticized Fisher for thinking that an increase of gold in a monetary system automatically raised prices and found fault with his determination of certain magnitudes in the equation of exchange. On the whole, however, he endorsed the American's ideas for monetary reform, asserting that the main outlines of the latter's proposal of combining a tabular standard and a gold exchange standard "seem to deserve careful consideration, and if he can revive general interest in such proposals, he will have done a great service to the progress of monetary reform."

His first editorial act had involved the rejection of an article by the

doughty Archdeacon W. J. Cunningham. Edgeworth, who had preceded him in the editorial post, had trouble making up his mind and
had vacillated about approving the archdeacon's piece. But Maynard
had no compunctions, writing his father that "it had to be—for it
couldn't possibly be printed; it was the most complete wash and
nothing whatever to do with economics." On the whole, he ran the
journal simply and economically, saying upon his retirement that "his
only apparatus was one drawer in his desk for his papers and some
porcupine clips to hold them in bundles." He invested much time and
effort in reviewing manuscripts, suggesting improvements, especially
to younger authors. Despite his growing responsibilities in other areas,
he continued this practice and regarded his editorship as a most
important honor and duty. In later years, he was especially keen on
writing biographical sketches of colleagues and of others who had
passed on, an art in which he was unexcelled because of his sharp eye for
salient trifles. In all, he retained the editorship of the *Economic Journal*
for thirty-three years—solid testimony to his scholarly stature in the
controversial field of economics.

As his emotional condition improved, he became even more involved
in the finances of King's College. At the opening of 1912, he wrote
Duncan that his state of mind had become "much more peaceable, and I
am horribly engulfed in Cambridge." He went on to say that "as for the
young men here, I lose more interest in them every day; and indeed
seldom speak to them. There are one or two who row on the river and
whom Gerald Shove and I go to look at. But a duller collection, on the
whole, I have seldom seen. Or is it that I no longer care? Anyhow,
Cambridge presents itself to me more and more as a sort of machine. . . . Still there is always *just* a chance [of amorous adventure?].
Meanwhile, I improve the machine. . . . " He was probably referring
mainly to his work on the college's finances. The year before he had
been appointed a member of the estates committee and an elector to
fellowships, and by the fall of 1912 he had introduced three revolutionary motions challenging the maintenance of large cash balances,
investigating the contracts of the kitchen, buttery, and combination
room departments and the employment conditions of the staff and, most
disturbing of all, proposing an increase in the Fellowship dividends
from £120 to £130 a year. This last resolution was, in effect, a vote of no
confidence in the incumbent bursar and, though it was defeated,
Keynes was elected to the council which governed the college and later
made a member of the committee to discuss the bursar's resignation.
Actually, with the war intervening, he did not assume the post of
second bursar of the college until November 1919.

During the Easter vacation he was on the Riviera again with Gerald Shove, with whom he was quite intimate. Still later he went horseback riding with Archie Rose, an old government "hand" with whom he corresponded over many years. On their jaunt they stopped at the Crown Hotel in Everleigh, and Maynard so liked the place that he arranged to take over the whole establishment for his friends in July. To this delightful spot they came—Duncan, Grant, Gerald Shove, Jack Sheppard, Frankie Birrell, Dilly Knox, Rupert Brooke, the Olivier sisters and Katherine Cox, Archie Rose, Chester Purves, Justin Brooke, Ferenc Bekassy, G. H. Luce, and Geoffrey Keynes. Many of them were Apostles who had come into the Society since Maynard's day. Only recently he had come to know Luce, the poet, and young Bekassy, an undergraduate at the college. He was particularly fond of the latter and later visited him at his baronial home near Budapest.

Keynes told Grant that the landlady of the Crown Inn was shocked by the behavior of some of his guests and charged him, as a consequence, forty pounds "blood money" beyond what he had contracted for. It certainly must have been a memorable occasion, for in future years those who were at Everleigh looked back on that holiday as symbolizing the peace and culture of the prewar period. In the same letter mentioning this detail he made another remark which reveals his state of mind about relations with the opposite sex. Through a window at the Crown Inn he had seen Rupert Brooke making love to a female, leading him to exclaim, "Oh, these womanizers. How on earth and what for can he do it. . . ."

In the fall of that year another figure who was to have a peculiar fascination for him made his appearance on the Cambridge scene—Ludwig Wittgenstein, a handsome young man destined to become the renowned philosopher. He had been born into a rich, cultured Viennese family in 1889, six years after Maynard's birth, of a Jewish father and a mother of the Roman Catholic faith, and he had been baptized in the latter religion. Now grown, he had gone to Manchester to study engineering and then, attracted by Bertrand Russell's lectures on mathematical logic, had enrolled at Cambridge University. Possessed of a brilliant mind and a charismatic personality, young Wittgenstein was soon elected to the Apostles. Both he and Bekassy, by the way, were homosexuals. Maynard was attracted to Wittgenstein in a platonic way. He wrote Duncan, "Wittgenstein is a most wonderful character— what I said about him when I saw you last is quite untrue—and extraordinarily nice. I like enormously to be with him." In the near future he was to help him mightily as a friend.

During most of 1912, apart from his work on probability, Keynes was absorbed in writing *Indian Currency and Finance* which had grown out of the lectures he had given on this general subject in the two preceding years. Behind the sober, technical analysis of that book there is a strong polemical argument for the gold exchange standard. Rather than being backward in monetary affairs, he argued, India was "in the forefront of monetary progress." Under this standard India kept her exchange rate pegged to sterling, but did not redeem the local currency, the rupee, in gold. In this respect, he maintained, it contained one essential element in "the ideal currency of the future."

This first book by Keynes was definitely policy-oriented and contained few of the sharp "put-downs" of the establishment that one finds in some of his other works, though there are precursors of the latter even in it. In discussing the views of certain leading financiers who had opposed the gold exchange standard, he wrote, "Financiers of this type will not admit the feasibility of anything new until it has been demonstrated to them by practical experience. It follows, therefore, that they will seldom give their support to what is new." On the other hand, he took a strong stand for what was new and different—combining thought and feeling ("passionate perception") in its behalf in this and in his other major work.

However, it should not be thought that he approved everything in the prevailing monetary system of India. He believed that the lack of a central bank in that country was a grave defect because there was no institution to act as the government's fiscal agency; the government of India, in effect, was maintaining an independent treasury system such as existed at that time in the United States and of which proponents of the proposed Federal Reserve System were highly critical. Internally, as a result of not having a central bank, he stated, the Indian currency was "absolutely inelastic." India, he held, ought to have a state bank "associated in a greater or less degree with the government."

He strenuously contended that a gold standard did not require the domestic circulation of gold coins, stating that "a preference for a tangible currency is no longer more than a relic of a time when governments were less trustworthy in these matters than they are now" and when it was the fashion to imitate uncritically the English system of the second quarter of the nineteenth century. In India's case, in fact, he held that her love of the precious metals had been ruinous to economic development. "The government ought not to encourage in the slightest degree this ingrained fondness for handling hard gold"; rather, it should seek to counteract "an uncivilized and wasteful habit." These, as will be seen, were to become familiar phrases in his later works; so too is the note of prophecy which he injected into his analysis when he stated that "the time may not be far distant when Europe, having perfected her mechanism of exchange on the basis of a gold standard, will find it possible to regulate her standard of value on a more rational and stable basis. It is not likely that we shall leave permanently the most intimate adjustments of our economic organism at the mercy of a lucky prospector, a new chemical process, or a change of ideas in Asia." Clearly these sentences foreshadowed his later advocacy of managed currency.

Early in 1913, Keynes learned that his sister Margaret was publicly engaged to be married to Archibald Vivian Hill, a fellow of Trinity College and a physiologist who later was to win a Nobel Prize. He was very happy for her, even though he confided to Duncan that he thought her fiancé was "frightfully puritanical."

During the Easter vacation he was off alone on a long trip to Egypt to visit his old friend Robin Furness who was stationed there. He told Grant that he had traveled out in a deluxe train with the ballet dancer Nijinsky, and then added casually that in Cairo he had "had a woman." This disclosure, coming so incidentally and so soon after his denunciation of "womanizers," strikes one like a bombshell and alerts one to a transformation in his personality toward bisexuality.

While in Egypt he received a confidential letter from Sir Thomas Holderness, his former superior at the India office, in which he was offered the secretaryship of a proposed Royal Commission on the Indian Currency. The need for such a body and the inquiry which it was to undertake had grown out of rumors of scandal surrounding the secret purchase by the Council of India of large amounts of silver by the bullion broker, Messrs. Samuel Montagu and Co. Secrecy in these purchases had been followed in order to prevent speculation, and the transaction had been executed in accordance with the standard practices of the Indian office. Nevertheless, critics in Parliament alleged that the firm's partners were in that legislative body and connected with the under secretary of state for India in such a way as to profit from their position.

At the same time an anonymous correspondent of *The Times* of London published a series of five long articles on a similar controversial subject, basing his criticisms of the handling of the Indian currency system on an earlier government inquiry. The gist of this complaint was that the government of India had established a gold standard without encouraging the circulation of gold and that it kept part of its monetary reserves in London earning interest. The author of the series argued that increasing the proportion of the gold in circulation would correspondingly improve the stability of the system.

As a consequence of these articles, a host of questions was raised in the House of Commons. At this point Keynes wrote Lionel Abrahams in the India office, inquiring who was behind *The Times* articles. The latter replied that he didn't know for certain, complimented him on his forthcoming book, and asked, "But can't you send a letter to *The Times* as well in a day or two? There is so little said. I should be most grateful."

Keynes lost no time in obliging, sending off a letter to the editor that very day. It was, as usual, a lucid, succinct brief for the government's policy of centralizing reserves rather than encouraging the circulation of gold from hand to hand. In effect, he was defending the Establishment practice—the gold exchange standard—and he argued that a number of countries, including France, Russia, Austria-Hungary, Holland, and Japan, had substantially similar systems. William Robinson of the India office was enthusiastic about his refutation of the contrary view, writing him to say that it was "the best statement on our side that has appeared, and my only regret was *The Times* did not print it in letters of gold and silver and issue it as a special supplement." Many other letters were written to *The Times* criticizing its correspondent, but it persisted in its editorial campaign for a parliamentary inquiry and was ultimately successful.

In cabling a reply to Holderness about the secretaryship of the proposed commission, Keynes was concerned that his acceptance of such a post would compromise his freedom to publish *Indian Currency and Finance* which was already in proof. He therefore sent the proofs to the chairman of the new commission, Austen Chamberlain; without examining them, Chamberlain informed him that he was free to publish forthwith. Indeed, Keynes was now offered a seat on the commission rather than the secretaryship. Upon hearing this news, his father proudly noted "a great honor" in his diary, and Keynes's faithful mentor at the university quickly penned his congratulations: "My dear Keynes, I am delighted to know the youngest member of the youngest commission, and I think the youngest of any. You are the right man for the place. But you will need to husband your strength. Yours happily, Alfred Marshall."

Later, after the commission had held meetings but before it recessed for the summer, Chamberlain, who was the financial authority of the Conservative party, got around to reading Keynes's book from cover to cover. He wrote him a private letter, saying in part, "It is, if I may say so, admirably lucid, but I scarcely know whether to congratulate you on it or to condole with myself! You will certainly be considered the author of the commission's report whenever that document sees the light. I am amazed to see how largely the views of the commission as disclosed by our informal discussions are a mere repetition of the arguments and conclusions to which your study had previously led you."

Keynes's work won the acclaim of professional economists as well as that of Chamberlain. H. S. Foxwell, a respected economist at Cambridge, in a long and enthusiastic review, said that it was "a timely achievement ... of the highest practical importance" and that it was "likely long to remain the standard on its subject." Foxwell, perhaps erroneously, compared Keynes to Bagehot and Jevons, even though the latter's lasting contribution to economics was neither in monetary theory nor monetary policy.

In retrospect, it appears that Keynes's creativity was shown not only by his authoritative book on Indian money matters but also by the "creative role" he played while on the royal commission. Though he had just turned thirty, he was not at all daunted or overshadowed by the older and more experienced civil servants and bankers who participated in its proceedings. Some of his colleagues were formerly his superiors at the India office, and one, Sir Robert Chalmers, was later to be over him at the Treasury. Still, he took a most conspicuous part in the hearings from the start, as shown by the fact that although he was only one of the ten members of the commission, he asked nearly one-sixth of the questions directed at witnesses and was throughout a tough, incisive interrogator.

After hearing witnesses, the commission could not ignore two proposals for reform: the establishment of a gold mint in India and the organization of a central or state bank. Lionel Abrahams had prepared a memorandum on this latter subject, but he was not optimistic about its reception by the other members of the commission. "You are my chief hope," he had written Maynard.

When the commission recessed in August, Keynes and Sir Ernest Cable, a big jute manufacturer in India, were designated to draw up a state bank proposal for the commission's consideration. The latter wrote a skeleton memorandum, dealing with the bank's capitalization, but Keynes wrote a fifty-page document with three appendices, covering all aspects of a proposal for a state bank in India. "It was a scheme," he later wrote, "which ought to make any banker's mouth water." Ultimately, though it was not adopted, it was published as an annex to the royal commission report.

One of the commissioners, R. W. Gillian who was finance secretary to the government of India, appreciated Keynes's work very much. He wrote of this document, "It clears up things immensely. In the past one had not a single proposition but a number of phantom shapes melting into one another and had really to meet criticism directed against all or any of them. You have brought out in the most definite way how irrelevant much of this criticism is, and at any rate we now have a straight issue."

In getting this proposal considered by the other commissioners, Keynes had to be very tactful because many of them were not enthusiastic about the establishment of a central bank in India. One of these was Sir Shapurji Braacha, who objected strongly to the idea as a solution to India's financial problems. As a result of his protests, a compromise was finally achieved in the commission's report to the effect that continuance of existing banking practice would be assumed and no recommendation on a central banking system would be made in the main body of the report; Keynes made his point in the third and final revision of section five of the report by drafting it in a manner which prominently called attention to that supplementary material.

In this part of the report he had written, "A state bank of the kind proposed might really get the best of both worlds. It is difficult to predict how a new institution will work out in practice. But the advantages of a state and of a private institution may be, partly at any rate, combined."

In general, in his memorandum, he displayed a masterful grasp of central banking as it applied to India. He called attention to the fact that that country and the United States were alone in having no rediscount market, no elasticity in their note issue, no bank rate policy, and operated with independent treasury systems instead of a government bank. In America, he pointed out, steps were currently being taken to remedy these defects; the Federal Reserve system was at the time in the very process of establishment by Congress. In a manner which reminds one of his old debating style, he carefully analyzed the advantages and disadvantages, or criticisms, of a state bank.

The commission held further hearings in the fall, and the chairman, desirous of winding things up, drew up a draft report which he hoped his colleagues would accept without substantial change. A few of the commissioners, including Keynes, were critical of the chairman's draft, but most were hesitant to dissect the whole work. Not so he; he wrote Chamberlain outlining his specific points of disagreement, and the latter accepted his redrafting of the gold currency section at once. He was, indeed, "gracious and accommodating" in his reply, while Keynes, judging from the comment of a commissioner who had been in communication with him, was not so kindhearted toward the chairman. In a letter that has been lost, this individual stated, "Your description of the chairman's brain makes me shriek with laughter." This characteristic trait of intellectual arrogance is also evident in a letter he wrote to his mother late in the month. The commission had met for three grueling days before Christmas to discuss the draft report. He described the strain of those meetings:

The commission is very nearly finished now, and most of the report is in its final form. The last three days have been the most exacting to character and intellect that I have been through, and I feel rather a wreck—wishing very much that I was off to the south of France for an immediate holiday. We sat for seven hours a day, and one had to be drafting amendments at top speed and perpetually deciding within thirty seconds whether other people's amendments were verbal and innocent or substantial and to be rejected. I must say that Austen Chamberlain came out of the ordeal very well, and I believe that he may yet be prime minister—I don't suppose on the purely intellectual score that he is any stupider than Campbell-Bannerman [Liberal prime minister, 1905–1908].

When the commission adjourned for the Christmas vacation, Keynes immediately left on his badly needed holiday with Duncan Grant to stay at Roquiebrunne on the Riviera. While there he suffered a most untimely setback—he fell ill with what was first diagnosed as tonsillitis, then "quinsy," and lastly, something far worse, diphtheria. He was nursed first by Mrs. Bussy's sister and then moved to a nursing home in Mentone. His mother flew to his side as always.

In the middle of January the commission reconvened for the last two sessions on the final report, but still being under a doctor's care in France, Keynes was not on hand. His absence, one commissioner declared, was "little short of a calamity." The other members had accepted his redrafted section of the report on "Gold in Internal Circulation" pretty much as he had worded it, but then got into a desperate muddle over the complications of the gold standard and the paper currency reserves. On the latter, which interested him most, the other commissioners changed his proposal in such a way as to make it practically unworkable so far as contributing to an elastic currency was concerned. The chairman wrote to him, arguing that his proposal regarding the paper currency reserve could not be carried out without the establishment of a state bank, and expressed the hope that he would sign the report and not add an addendum to it.

From his sickbed Keynes indicated in forthright fashion that while he would sign the report, he reserved the right to append a note on the paper currency proposals. He rejected the chairman's suggestion that the worse the paper money scheme they proposed, the more likely there would be an acceptance of the state bank proposal as "too jesuitical," and insisted that the whole tenor of the report was not "shut your eyes and blindly accumulate gold." In another place he wrote, "I do not like a facile make-believe at reform, which when analyzed comes to nothing."

Some of the commissioners friendly to his point of view sought to reconcile him to what had happened in his absence, but when he returned to England he wrote still another memorandum on the paper currency proposals, making two small simple changes in the wording which convinced Chamberlain and carried the day. It was an amazing demonstration of his persistence, verbal brilliance, and political sense— "a smashing document," an admiring colleague called it. He even got an addendum into the final report in favor of an amalgamation of the gold standard and paper currency reserves, which just reversed the previous version as well as covering other emendations which he had urged.

The report of the Royal Commission on Indian Currency and Finance was finally published on March 2, 1914. However, the outbreak of the War the following August prevented the government from implementing any of its recommendations, and in any case the financial situation in India had undergone a radical change in the interim. The consequence was that a central bank was not established for that vast country until 1935, after two other subsequent committees and one White Paper on constitutional reform had laid the groundwork.

When Alfred Marshall received a copy of the Indian Currency Commission's report, he wrote Keynes that he was busy with other matters: "But I dipped in here and there, and then read the conclusions; and finally turned negligently to the annex. But that held me. I had no idea you had written it. Much of it, as the report itself, deals with matters beyond my knowledge and judgment. But there is quite enough of it within my understanding for me to have been entranced by it as a prodigy of constructive work. Verily we old men will have to hang ourselves if young people can cut their way so straight and with such apparent ease through such great difficulties."

In retrospect, it is evident that Keynes accomplished much in the years after he left the India office. Behind his achievements one can now perceive and understand somewhat better his inner life, mainly because of his revealing correspondence with Duncan Grant in the years 1908–

12 which has only recently become available. That exchange of letters makes it clear that in those years he was often unusually depressed, mainly, it seems, because of emotional conflict and anxiety over his relationship to the young artist. Then in 1912, in the letter quoted above, he remarked that his "state of mind had become much more peaceable," adding, "I am horribly engulfed in Cambridge." The change from depression to one of greater equanimity was probably due to his burying himself in work and in part projecting his conflict to the external world. It may be that defense mechanisms of this nature became a relatively persistent mode for him in his coping with life. Bertrand Russell, who knew him well at Cambridge and elsewhere, commented on his hyperactivity, and Michael Holroyd, who studied his life closely for his biography of Lytton Strachey, perceptively observed, "The constant overwork which pressed in on Keynes all his life did not create itself accidentally from without, but was attracted by some urgent, personal necessity. He went through life as if he had to fill an eternal vacuum within himself, and appeared scarcely capable of relaxing." Holroyd did not endeavor to explain the nature of the personal necessity which drove Keynes, but psychologists know that work is often used as an escape from pressing emotional problems.

At several notable crises of twentieth-century history—during World War I, the Great Depression of the thirties, and in the financing and economic management of World War II and its aftermath—the British relied heavily on Keynes to diagnose and deal with enormously complex financial and economic problems. The drive and intensity of effort which he brought to those challenges, the last of which ultimately contributed to his death, are incomprehensible without taking account of the peculiar psychodynamics of his personality. However, before recounting his role in those historic events, the influence on his creativity of that much discussed and much misunderstood circle known as "Bloomsbury" must be examined.

CHAPTER 6

Bloomsbury and Its Influence on Keynes's Creativity

Would it be fair to say that originality was one of the fixations of the Bloomsbury
Group, and that this partly accounts for Keynes's emphasis on originality?

B. A. Corry in *Keynes and the Bloomsbury Group*

A S A SOCIAL GROUP, Bloomsbury had its origins in Cambridge at
the turn of the century in the meetings of such Cantabrigians as
Leonard Woolf, Lytton Strachey, Thoby Stephen, and Clive Bell at the
Midnight Society. When Keynes arrived at the university in 1902, he
came to know these young men through being made a member of their
elite circle. A couple of years later, Strachey reluctantly left his beloved
Cambridge and returned to London, to what he despairingly called "a
limbo of unintimacy." This was not the castle in Spain of which he had
dreamed, and he was wretched and dispirited. But about three years
after his departure from the cloistered halls, he found a substitute, a sort
of commune in the very heart of the city which served as a reasonable
facsimile for a Spanish castle.

It came about quite accidentally. While at the university he had
occasionally been invited by Thoby Stephen to visit 22 Hyde Park Gate
where his two sisters cared for their invalid father, the well-known
scholar Leslie Stephen. The old man was deaf and suffering from cancer
from which he died early in 1904. Later that year, the Stephen
children, Virginia, Vanessa, Thoby, and Adrian, moved from their
fashionable Kensington home to a less respectable address in Bloomsbury—46 Gordon Square. Virginia Stephen's relatives were shocked

by such unconventional behavior, this move to a relatively unfashionable area of the city, but to her the Bloomsbury squares seemed "the most beautiful, the most exciting, the most romantic place in the world."

Strachey's visits to the Stephens now became more frequent. With characteristic exaggeration he said that he found Virginia "rather wonderful, quite witty, full of things to say, and absolutely out of rapport with reality. The poor Vanessa has to keep her three mad brothers in control. She looks wan and sad."

Unfortunately, death reduced the number of the Stephen household in 1906 when the handsome Thoby suddenly died, and in the following year Vanessa married Clive Bell, a jovial, sport-loving art critic. Virginia and her brother, Adrian, then moved to 29 Fitzroy Square, which was nearby, in order to enable the newly married couple to live undisturbed at the old address. It was in Adrian's ground-floor study at Fitzroy Square that their friends met on Thursday evenings, continuing the gatherings which had begun at Gordon Square. This, according to Duncan Grant, was the beginning of Bloomsbury.

The rather amorphous group consisted of Vanessa and Virginia Stephen; their brothers, Thoby and Adrian; Clive Bell; Leonard Woolf; Maynard Keynes; Duncan Grant; Roger Fry; Desmond and Mollie MacCarthy; Lytton, Oliver, Marjorie, and James Strachey; Saxon Sydney-Turner; Harry Norton; E. M. Forster; and Gerald Shove. On the other hand, Leonard Woolf insisted that Bloomsbury came into existence in the three years from 1912 to 1914, after he had returned from Ceylon, and in his version there were only thirteen members in the group. He excluded Gerald Shove, Harry Norton, and Lytton's brothers and sisters. Of the ten men he included, he stated that six had been "permanently inoculated with Moore and Moorism."

It is obvious that Bloomsbury differed quite significantly from the Cambridge Conversazione Society by its inclusion of women, in particular the remarkable Stephen sisters whose background needs description. They had grown up in an upper-middle-class home with a tradition of talent and beauty in that their father was a respected Cambridge intellectual who had resigned his position as a don because of religious doubt to become the editor in London of *The Cornhill Magazine* and later the prestigious editor of *The Dictionary of National Biography*. He was the friend of famous British and American men of letters, one of whom, James Russell Lowell, the author and United States ambassador to the Court of St. James's, was Virginia's godfather. The mother of the family, a strikingly attractive woman, was a granddaughter of one of the Pattle sisters who were renowned for their beauty.

When Virginia and Vanessa were growing up, the Stephen household was crowded because each of the parents had been married before and then widowed. Virginia, born the year before Maynard Keynes, was the third child of the Stephens, junior to Thoby and Vanessa, and a year older than another brother, Adrian. Unfortunately, the mother of the family died in 1895 when Virginia was just thirteen, and it was then that she suffered her first mental breakdown in the course of which she tried to commit suicide.

The family life at the Stephen household then came to depend upon Stella Duckworth, Virginia's half-sister, but she married soon after assuming that responsibility and then tragically passed away within the year. As a consequence, the care of the aging father became the burden of the two young daughters. This was difficult enough, but to make matters worse, upon his wife's death Leslie Stephen became increasingly inconsolable and imposed a regime of sorrow, solemnity, and hypocritical emotion upon their home. For instance, to the great disappointment of the girls, he gave up the summer home at Saint Ives in Cornwall, where as children they had passed many happy vacations—it reminded him too much of his departed spouse.

To his daughters his self-pity seemed to be emotional blackmail, and his ranting over the family household accounts was a further cause of friction. Virginia spoke scathingly of "the angels of the house" who had to perform the innumerable services of a subordinate female; later she wrote too of "the arid scimitar of the male, which smote mercilessly, again and again demanding sympathy." It is plain that the father's emotional conduct at the time of his bereavement made his daughters ripe rebels against the Victorian moral code and its manners.

Yet, when they were free of this tyrannical way of life, the sisters, paradoxically, could be most sympathetic to those who were ill or could not find acceptance in the rough, heterosexual outer world. Virginia, for example, was generally indulgent toward the hypochondriacal Strachey, and Vanessa seemed to have had "a special relationship with homosexuals who felt safe with her and confided in her." The psychology of these two young women, it is evident, was such that they could afford a sort of asylum to Cambridge Apostles in London, several of whom were sexually ambivalent. Maynard was one of these, and he became a part of the Bloomsbury circle rather early through his close friendship with Duncan Grant and Lytton Strachey. Toward the end of 1910, as previously mentioned, he and Duncan had moved to 21

Fitzroy Square in Bloomsbury, and the following year they transferred to 38 Brunswick Square where they shared a house with Adrian and Virginia Stephen, Gerald Shove, and Leonard Woolf. So Keynes was close physically and intellectually to the Bloomsbury group from its very beginning.

In the course of its long, colorful life Bloomsbury was seen by outsiders in many different lights. To its enemies it was pictured as "an intellectual Mafia" intent on praising the work of its members, but being unfairly and highly critical of others. This image of the group would seem to be seriously flawed because, as Quentin Bell has convincingly shown, it was never monolithic. In fact, its members were so critical of each other that Virginia Woolf in one of her letters described Bloomsbury as a lion's house: "Gordon Square is like nothing so much as the lion's house at the zoo. One goes from cage to cage. All the animals are dangerous, rather suspicious of one another, and full of fascination and mystery. I'm sometimes too timid to go in at 46 Gordon Square and trail along the pavement, looking in at the windows." It is a striking metaphor, this leonine conception of Bloomsbury, and it raises the question whether it was in fact a group. To constitute a social group the members must have something more in common than "roaring" at each other. What was it? What did they discuss at their numerous meetings?

To young Virginia Stephen the answer to this question lay in the difference between a party in fashionable Belgravia and one in the more bohemian Bloomsbury. The tacit purpose of the former, she candidly said, was marriage, while at Gordon Square the real purpose of a get-together was to exchange ideas. The latter kind of human interaction was more interesting to her at that time because she was glad to be free of the marriage mart. In her recollection of early Bloomsbury, she wrote of it as forever "talking, talking as if everything could be talked—the soul itself slipped through the lips in thin silver discs which dissolve in young men's minds like silver, like moonlight. Oh, far away they'd remember it, and deep in dullness gaze back upon it, and come to refresh themselves again."

Bloomsbury talk was unusually frank and uninhibited for those days. "We did not hesitate," Vanessa Bell said, "to talk of anything. This was literally true. You could say what you liked about art, sex, or religion; you could also talk freely and very likely dully about the ordinary doings of daily life. There was very little self-consciousness I think in those early gatherings. . . . But life was exciting, terrible, and amusing, and one had to explore thankful that he could do so freely." As an illustration of the freedom of conversation in that faraway Edwardian age, consider the following report by Virginia Woolf (the Virginia Stephen of the preceding pages had married Leonard Woolf, "the penniless Jew from Putney," in August 1912) of what happened at 46 Gordon Square in 1908:

It was a spring evening. Vanessa and I were sitting in the drawing room. The drawing room had greatly changed its character since 1904. The Sargent-Furse age was over. The age of Augustus John was dawning. Suddenly the door opened, and the long sinister figure of Mr. Lytton Strachey stood on the threshold. He pointed his finger at a stain on Vanessa's white dress.

"Semen?" he said.

Can one really say it? I thought, and we burst out laughing. With that word all the barriers of reticence and reserve went down. A flood of sacred fluid seemed to overwhelm us. Sex permeated our conversation. The word bugger was never far from our lips. We discussed copulation with the same excitement and openness that we had discussed the nature of the good. It is strange to think how reticent, how reserved we had been and for how long.

If Bloomsbury had become licentious in its speech in 1908, two years later it had become very liberal in its conduct as well, as compared with the conventional mores of Victorian times. Virginia Woolf once said that human nature changed on or about December 1910, and historians have noted that the pace of social change was accelerating in the prewar years. Still, when the young men assembled at Fitzroy Square, Virginia often found that they could be dull. Describing a typical evening, she wrote that "they sat around mostly silent, and I wished for any woman—and you [i.e., her sister, to whom she was writing] would have been a miracle. I talked to Frankie Birrell and Keynes most of the time. But it was desperate work." She was beginning to prefer the magic gatherings of writers at the home of her aristocratic friend Ottoline Morrell to the society of the buggers.

One standard subject of conversation among the Bloomsberries—when they did talk—was the visual arts. To one such as Virginia Woolf, these arts were of the highest importance because she held that truth might be found by intuition and sensibility as well as by reason. The interest in the arts had been stimulated significantly in those years by the work of Roger Fry in arranging the Postimpressionist exhibitions in London in 1910 and 1912. Breaking with tradition, this Cambridge Apostle rocked the British art world by his championship of the art of Paul Cezanne and other unconventional French painters. As Sir Kenneth Clark was later to write, " . . . Insofar as taste can be changed by one man, it was changed by Roger Fry." In various ways one can see that the Bloomsbury group was very partial to things Gallic; while they looked back to ancient Greece for part of their philosophy, they turned toward the Continent for other necessary values because they sought to establish on French lines a society fit for the discerning minority.

That times were changing very fast was shown when the second Postimpressionist exhibition closed and a ball was given to celebrate the event. The Bloomsbury ladies, with some help from the Slade Art School contingent, appeared dressed in Tahitian sarongs (Gauguin had been one of the painters whose work had been exhibited). Some of the more respectable dowagers of Victorian background whose skirts more than reached the floor fled from the room, and even Roger Fry was said to have made a slight protest.

Of one fact we can be certain: in those prewar years and after, Bloomsbury provided Keynes with "a home away from home." Because of his split way of life—he was accustomed to spending part of the week in Cambridge and part in London—he needed a congenial abode in the capital. However, as Harrod rightly says, Bloomsbury provided more than that; his talkative friends gave him as well "the specific image of what is meant by the good life," and in another place he wrote that Bloomsbury sought to achieve "a way of life." Bloomsbury felt, he said, that it was "on the eve of a great awakening" and that its leaders would head "a new movement for emancipation" in line with its guiding ethos, "a return to the Greek city-state," but he didn't elaborate on the implications of that statement.

These, then, were the shared values of this "group of friends"—the stress placed on personal affection, esthetic enjoyment, candor in expressing one's feelings and thought, clarity in reasoning, and a sense of being different from others. But these characteristics do not enable us to "understand" Bloomsbury until we put it into historical and sociological context. From the standpoint of some historical distance, the more than half a century that has elapsed since Bloomsbury ceased to be, it is now possible to appreciate its significance as a social and cultural group. In a closely reasoned, astute analysis, Professor Raymond Williams has explained that it was "a true fraction of the existing English upper class." Its members were "at once against its dominant ideas and values and still willingly, in all immediate ways, part of it." Composed as it was of the second and third generations of the new professional and highly educated sector of this class, this intellectual aristocracy turned a critical eye on the "vast system of cant and hypocrisy" in contemporary English institutional life—the "monarchy, aristocracy, upper classes, suburban bourgeoisie, the Church, the army, the stock exchange." Conscious that they were carrying on what had been started by the social critics of the previous generation, Shaw, Ibsen, and the Fabians, the Bloomsberries were acutely conscious of the deprivations and exclusion of women from the established institutions. Moving from the "comprehensive irreverence for established ideas and institutions" that was most prominent before 1914, after the war they engaged in political action directed at systematic reform at a ruling-class level, relating to the lower classes as a matter of conscience. Leonard Woolf had expressed the strong feelings of his original Cambridge friends: "We were convinced that everyone over twenty-five, with perhaps one or two remarkable exceptions, was "hopeless," having lost the elan of youth, the capacity to feel, and the ability to distinguish truth from falsehood. . . . We found ourselves living in the springtime of a conscious revolt against the social, political, religious, moral, intellectual and artistic institutions, beliefs, and standards of our fathers and grandfathers. . . . We were out to construct something new; we were in the van of the builders of a new society which should be free, rational, civilized, pursuing truth and beauty." At this specific moment in the development of liberal thought, these friends did not offer any alternative idea of a whole society or any general system of theory which might degenerate into a dogma, but appealed rather to "the supreme value of the civilized individual, whose pluralization, as more and more civilized individuals, was itself the only acceptable social form." In other words, the social conscience's ultimate purpose was to protect the private consciousness.

To understand fully this protest group and particularly certain aspects of Keynes's economic thought, one has to go back to its roots in what John Stuart Mill called the "Germano-Coleridgean" school. Mill and the early Apostles regarded the Sage of Highgate with reverence, and the former thought him to be the most influential teacher of youth in the period 1820–40. In the latter year Mill declared that "every Englishman of the present day is by implication either a Benthamite or a Coleridgean." This division in the way of conceptualizing man's nature and society was the result of the political, technological, and economic changes which had accompanied the French and later the industrial revolution. To some it was a contrast between a mechanical and an organic view of life, between analysis and synthesis. Bentham had sought to discover social laws as immutable and as abstract as Newton's laws of physics, while Coleridge, a romantic idealist, chose to formulate a view of man and society compatible with the highest human aspirations. "It is the difference between rationalism and romanticism, utilitarianism and anti-utilitarianism, and these are perhaps the best tags for the opposing sides. But the antagonism was less often labelled than felt and acted upon intuitively."

Coleridge lived and wrote in an increasingly Benthamite society. He saw and deplored the social devastation and environmental disruption that the new industry was bringing. He feared its effects not only on man's labor and society, but on the human imagination. To the rationalists or Benthamites, on the other hand, the material progress of the industrial revolution was an unalloyed good; to the romantics it seemed that "progress" brought with it a denial of something basic and eternal in human experience, a denial of what Carlyle called "unconsciousness."

The two groups, Benthamites and Coleridgeans, differed fundamentally in their attitude toward religion. The more radical Benthamites were either atheist or anticlerical and thought of religion as an opiate. The early Apostles, ardent Coleridgeans for the most part, though they were discourteous to clergymen, respected what they felt to be true religion. They followed the philosophic idealism of Goethe, Kant, and Hegel, and read the English Romantics who sought divinity in man and nature, quite apart from revelation. They discovered, as Thomas Huxley did later, that "a deep sense of religion was compatible with the entire absence of theology."

Though Coleridgean thought was very helpful to John Stuart Mill in his "mental crisis," the Romantics, on the whole, were not successful in persuading most Victorians to accept their philosophy of life; the latter rejected the proposed change in their attitudes and held fast to the rational faith of utilitarianism and their conventional sexual code. However, the rationalism and the repressions of the Victorian era in Great Britain and on the Continent were challenged again by bold new thinkers in the last decades of the nineteenth century as the old cultural epoch drew to its close. Friedrich Nietzsche, Henri Bergson, Sigmund Freud, Emile Durkheim, and Max Weber were the principal intellectual giants who transformed the way Western man thought of his nature and of society. The year 1895 was particularly significant in that respect because it was then that Freud and Josef Breuer published their work on hysteria which, in effect, inaugurated the era of psychoanalysis, and Paul Cezanne had the first one-man show of modern paintings in Paris. These intellectual and artistic developments represented a fundamental reappraisal of the rationalism that had been questioned by the "Germano-Coleridgean" school years before.

Basically, what the thinkers and scientists of that crucial decade did
was to restore and honor the values of imagination and intuition that
their immediate predecessors had scorned and neglected. In a fundamental sense they were rebelling not only against rationalism but also
against positivism, that is, the tendency to discuss and analyze human
behavior in terms of analogies drawn from the natural sciences. As a
consequence there was a recovery and recognition of the unconscious
and the irrational, and a new appreciation of the profound part they play
in human life. This perspective led to a deeper understanding of the role
of the subjective and of human values in the functioning of society.

At Cambridge, the philosopher G. E. Moore was an important figure
in this revolution of thought. Prior to the publication of the *Principia
Ethica* in 1903, John McTaggart, a Hegelian idealist, and Lowes
Dickinson, a sort of mystic humanist, were the favorites of the undergraduates. Moore demolished their philosophical positions and popularity with his more cogent analysis of ethical questions, contending
that the "good" was indefinable and that the attempt to define it in
terms of naturalistic qualities was an illustration of what he called "the
naturalistic fallacy." He then suggested that the highest goods, those
"good in themselves," were "certain states of consciousness which may
roughly be described as the pleasures of human intercourse and the
enjoyment of beautiful objects." Keynes later referred to these "fundamental intuitions of *Principia Ethica*" and said that they were too few
and too narrow to fit actual experience and that "one cannot live today
secure in the undisturbed individualism which was the extraordinary
achievement of the early Edwardian days."

Strachey and Keynes had interpreted Moore's thought to give
sanction to their homosexual inclinations, but in addition other elements of Moore's thinking were now blended with Apostolic principles
to form the Bloomsbury outlook. These intellectual aristocrats felt that
they had discovered new conceptions of morality, justifying them in
rejecting Victorian earnestness and sexual respectability. As a consequence, Bloomsbury tended to be gay and "remorselessly frivolous."
For example, according to one account, in the twenties some of its
members, like the recent "counterculture" of this generation, showed
their contempt for bourgeois culture and morals by joining what Isaiah
Berlin called "the Homintern." In other words, they made a cult of
homosexuality. Mentioning this sociological aspect of Bloomsbury is
not intended to minimize or ignore the psychological factors which
contributed to the sexual inversion of some of its individual members.

In summary, it can be seen that Bloomsbury as a protest group was a complex sociological phenomenon, tracing some of its heritage back to Coleridge's day, yet reflecting the current discontents and emerging ideas of the Edwardian years. Its liberalism was mainly one of ideas, though Keynes, Leonard and Virginia Woolf, and the militant pacifists of the group sought to put some of those ideas into practice more than some others. While ideas are potentially subversive of institutions, there is always the problem of their translation, no matter how desirable, into the realities of political power. Bloomsbury became a prime carrier of general ideas with revolutionary possibilities, but it always exalted the individual as the touchstone and criterion of state action, and in so doing showed its deeply conservative nature.

In several recent analyses of Virginia Woolf's work, especially those of a feminist orientation, there has been a tendency to see androgyny as a key element in the Bloomsbury ethos. In one of these studies, Professor Carolyn Heilbrun asks,

"What made the Bloomsbury group unique? Two things: First, it produced more works of importance than any similar group of friends, and second, it was androgynous. For the first time a group existed in which masculinity and femininity were marvelously blended in its members. Is it any wonder that they should have brought upon themselves so great an avalanche of hatred? In addition to their androgynous qualities, which should not be confused with the homosexuality of many of its members, these friends were the first to lead their lives as though reason and passion might be equal ideas; hitherto (so far, hereafter) reason always demanded the moderation of the passions, as sexuality and outspokenness took for granted the denigration of reason. Harrod has suggested that within the Bloomsbury group was discovered a "return to the Greek city-state," and indeed, reason and passion have elsewhere rarely been allowed equal sway; more usually, reason has been imitated and passion distorted.

In her feminist tract, *A Room of One's Own,* written in 1928, Virginia Woolf speculated about the possible relationship between androgyny and creativity. She told how the sight of two people getting into a taxi made her

ask whether there are two sexes in the mind corresponding to the sexes in the body, and whether they also require to be united to get complete satisfaction and happiness? And I went on amateurishly to sketch a plan of the soul so that in each of us two powers preside, one male, the other female; and in the man's brain the man predominates over the woman, and in the woman's brain the woman predominates over the man. The normal and comfortable state of being is when the two live in harmony together, spiritually cooperating. If one is a man, still the woman part of his brain must have effect; and a woman must also have intercourse with the man in her. Coleridge perhaps meant this whan he said that a great mind is androgynous. It is when this fusion takes place that the mind is fully fertilized and uses all its faculties. Perhaps a mind that is purely masculine cannot create, any more than a mind that is purely feminine, I thought.

The resemblance of Woolf's thought in this vivid passage to Carl Jung's concepts of the *animus* and the *anima* in the two sexes is obvious, though it is not known whether she was familiar with the work of the Swiss psychiatrist at the time she wrote.

To comprehend how Virginia Woolf and her fellow members of Bloomsbury, such as Keynes, thought about androgyny and its possible relation to creativity, one needs to examine the psychological image of the homosexual in Edwardian times. In exploring this matter, the broad historical context of the period must be kept in mind. The Edwardian years were witnessing a marked acceleration of social change, the patriarchial value system of the Victorians was under attack, but the pace and success of social reform was very uneven. Whereas women had made some gains in politics and there were advances in labor relations and social welfare, homosexuals as a minority group still lived under a regime of repression and fear of persecution. The position of homosexuals in Great Britain and other countries at that time was made even more difficult because of the backward state of psychiatry and psychology and the many erroneous conceptions about human sexuality in the public mind. Homosexuality was generally regarded as a form of moral degeneracy. However, toward the end of the nineteenth century, medical authorities such as Richard Krafft-Ebing, Karl Heinrich Ulrichs, and later Havelock Ellis advanced theories that explained homosexuality in terms of hereditary or congenital factors, and their works were read and discussed in the Bloomsbury circle as early as 1918. In 1920, Freud noted that what was called "the trapped soul theory" was the one "commonly depicted in popular expositions." According to this view, the homosexual embryo's emotional and nervous regions develop along a masculine line, while the outer body follows a feminine one, or *vice versa*. Lowes Dickinson expressed the belief that this was his situation when he said, "It's a curious thing to have a woman's soul shut up in a man's body, but that seems to be my case."

Another major view of homosexuality held that all human beings are innately bisexual and therefore capable of both heterosexual and homosexual love. While he subscribed to this view, Freud believed that the adult who remained homosexual had been arrested at an immature stage of sexuality. So while the hereditary theories removed the stigma of sin from the homosexuals, the Freudian approach led to a classification of them as neurotic. In 1908, Freud stated that some homosexuals often possessed unusual intelligence, spiritual insight, or artistic gifts, and that homosexuals of both sexes often have such strong constitutions that they are able to sublimate frustrated sexuality into artistic expression.

Encouraged emotionally and morally by these new theories of homosexuality, its defenders in Bloomsbury and elsewhere searched the records of the past to find evidence of sexual variance among the great. Joyfully they discovered many homosexuals in the annals of art, drama, music, literature, and even science, yet they probably asked themselves whether the world was ready to learn, for example, that Michelangelo or Leonardo da Vinci had been "buggers." They found many sexual inverts in the Renaissance and even came to regard Shakespeare as a homosexual. Lowes Dickinson called Plato and Shakespeare "the only two people who have given expression to the homosexual experiences which to me are intimate and profound." Virginia Woolf also set the beginnings of her ambivalent figure Orlando in the Renaissance and in one of her books used Shakespeare as an example of the androgyne.

In retrospect, it now appears that Bloomsbury itself was a most creative group, though some of its members perhaps (such as Desmond MacCarthy) have become eminent by association. Let us consider the record: G. E. Moore, although not a member, was close to the group and contributed importantly to ethics and linguistic analysis in philosophy; Lytton Strachey introduced a new type of biography; Keynes gave us the "new economics"; Virginia Woolf pioneered in innovative forms of the novel; Roger Fry and Duncan Grant blazed new paths in art criticism and painting; and easily forgotten, Leonard Woolf contributed substantially to the new idea of a League of Nations at the end of World War I. What accounts for this rather extraordinary record of creativity by this small group at that particular time and place? It is an intriguing but complex question, and it will only be possible here to indicate the broad outlines of an answer; to do so, it will be useful to review briefly some psychological aspects of the creative process, as it is understood by contemporary students of the matter.

In modern analyses of creativity there is a pronounced tendency to conceive it as a rhythmic process involving an interplay between opposite aspects of the mind. Silvano Arieti, for example, in his lucid exposition of the subject, describes "the dichotomy of the creative process" and conceives the creative mind as integrating primitive or primary process thinking with secondary (logical) processes in a magic synthesis that produces something new and original. Similarly, Dr. Albert Rothenberg of the Austen Riggs Center contends that creativity involves what he calls "Janusian thinking," which includes conflict and the functional, simultaneous coexistence of opposites. In an earlier work, Arthur Koestler analyzes the bisociative process by which two different frames of reference are brought together to produce wit and creative thought. Also, more recently, students of the lateral functioning of the brain have stressed that it is the polarity and integration of the two hemispheres, the complementary workings of the intellect and of intuition, which underlie creative achievement.

Bisexuality or cross-sexual identification in the creative personality was emphasized by Freud and in recent years by several other psychoanalysts. For example, Professor Matthew Besdine claims that the life-history pattern of a weak or an absent father and an over-protective, solicitous mother who extends her first-year symbiosis with the child as far as adolescence occurs at above-chance levels in the biographies of a number of famous artists. Such "Jocasta mothering," he holds, leads the son toward a distinctly feminine orientation to the world. Geniuses, he further believes, have a typical family constellation; though it tends to vary somewhat, the one constant factor in their lives is Jocasta mothering. "Its salient features are an unresolved Oedipus complex, fear of love, an underlying sense of guilt, strong masochistic tendencies, a significant homosexual component, paranoid trends, extraordinary egocentricity, exorbitant striving for recognition, and overall narcissism." In short, in his view, Jocasta mothering plays a significant part in the germination of genius. He cites Michelangelo, Leonardo da Vinci, Oscar Wilde, Marcel Proust, Isadora Duncan, and George Sand, among others, as examples of this type of mothering. In several respects, one can see the effects of such "mothering" in Keynes's life also, as has been previously noted.

Incidentally, Besdine emphasizes that while Jocasta mothering appears to be a necessary ingredient and condition of genius, it is not a sufficient one; other factors, both hereditary and environmental, must be favorable for a creative mind to develop. He insists that his analysis does not warrant the conclusion that all geniuses are homosexual or that all homosexuals are geniuses. With this view the present author is in total agreement; in stressing the importance of Keynes's mothering and of his homosexuality and androgyny as factors in his creative personality, it is by no means suggested that other influences did not have a significant part in shaping the man.

In the light of this relatively recent research and writing on the creative process, it is a striking fact that various members of Bloomsbury sensed and expressed the idea years before that creativity depended upon the "double nature" of the intellectual process. Virginia Woolf speculated upon the double nature (masculine and feminine combined) of the creative person. It has been said that in her particular kind of feminism there were in a sense two kinds of truth—the masculine truth of reason and the feminine truth of imagination—and together these truths made up what she called reality. In her view, the artist Roger Fry had a double side to his nature—a remarkable capacity for receptivity, for fresh experience, combined with an ability for independent thought and action—so that he arrived at a balance in his psyche, "a balance between the emotions and the intellect, between Vision and Design." Likewise, as will be presently seen, Keynes attributed the creativity of several economists to their double nature.

Of course, the creativity of individual members of Bloomsbury who have been mentioned did not occur or function in a vacuum; they received input from the external world, and their creative efforts were greatly facilitated or enhanced by their mutual interaction with others. Dr. Arieti, in discussing the differences among societies in their effects on creativity, notes that there has been a clustering of innovations in certain historical periods or cultural eras, and he suggests several social factors that may have contributed to this phenomenon. A consideration of Bloomsbury as a subculture discloses that many of these factors were at work during the period of its emergence and development. It had the availability of cultural means, and its members were open to varied cultural stimuli from the outside world. It stressed becoming (or self-development) rather than being (or duty), and it had the financial means to pursue its ideals. Insofar as it was homosexual, the liberalization of social norms about sexuality during the Edwardian period and later (as opposed to the prudery and hypocrisy of the Victorian era) gave its members a sense of release. It had a high tolerance for and interest in divergent views, witness its absorption in French impressionism, Russian ballet, unconventional economics, and new ways of writing novels.

In recent years Virginia Woolf's work has been the subject of intense analysis from the standpoint of androgyny and its possible relation to her creativity. One of her biographers, Phyllis Rose, has described the interplay of the conscious and unconscious in her writing in a most graphic way. Regrettably, Keynes did not leave us so explicit a description of his manner of working, though it is possible to deduce something about his intellectual processes from his various publications. In his biographical essays on W. Stanley Jevons and Alfred Marshall, one can indirectly gain some interesting insights into his conception of the creative process. When he was twenty-two and reading economics in an exploratory way, he came across Jevons's *Investigations into Currency and Finance* as well as his letters and journals. In an essay which he wrote in 1936 as a centenary memoir of the man, he said that he had been known to him "from my early years, as, in my father's mind, the pattern of what an economist and logician should be." From his remarks one can readily see that he regarded Jevons, particularly when the latter was young, as "a genius." Earlier during his years at Cambridge, Moore had had an unusual fascination for him because of his remarkable intuition and saintly personality, but Jevons was an economist who, he thought, was "probably apostolic."

What were Jevons's characteristics as an economist which made him so admirable, so creative? First, according to Keynes, there was his manysidedness, which he felt was necessary in an economist. In addition, as an empiricist he was adept in "the black arts of inductive economics," and "he was the first theoretical economist to survey his material with the prying eyes and fertile, controlled imagination of the natural scientist." Second, as a logician he was equally skilled in logic and deductive analysis, and in this work he had "genius and divine intuition." A very introverted person, "he worked best alone, with flashes of inner light." Third, he had an unusually strong historical and antiquarian interest. His *Journal,* wrote Keynes, "records depression but also the delight of a creative mind in moments of illumination." He had "a passionate sense of devotion" and, in matters of morals and sentiment, was and remained "an impassioned individualist." From this panegyric, exceeding in some respects Keynes's eulogy of Marshall, one can perceive that Jevons was probably a magnificent inspiration and even a model when he was seeking his own sense of identity. Inspired by Jevons's life, Keynes concluded that economics was a most agreeable branch of the moral sciences, in which "theory and fact, intuitive imagination and practical judgment, are blended in a manner comfortable to the human intellect." Jevons largely failed in his attack on the dominant Ricardo-Mill school of economics in the late nineteenth century, but Keynes, from his own nonconformist background—religious, moral, and sexual—was to be more successful in his rebellion against the citadel of orthodoxy.

Closely considered, one can discern analogies in the nature and careers of the two men. As has been seen, Keynes had experienced periods of depression in the years prior to World War I and had an experience similar to Jevons's youthful period of isolation in Australia, namely, those critical years of his adolescence at Eton and later when he was struck by the difference in his life at home and at school. In this connection, an acute student of the visionary imagination states that a new, synthetic vision "often requires in its carrier a special experience, one which makes him especially fertile ground for a recombination of old and new elements. He is often the man who has gone away, who is of his culture but has also served an apprenticeship in an alien world." Deeply touched by the alien, such a person responds to conflicting world views to a heightened degree. It seems very probable that Keynes's furtive homosexual experience in the years before World War I constituted such an "apprenticeship" and contributed substantially to the development of his imagination and appreciation of alternative visions of society's future.

The only analysis of the requisites for creativity in economics which compares with this piece on Jevons is Keynes's famous description of the master economist in his essay on Alfred Marshall. In it he asked the question: "What explains the paradox that though, intellectually considered, economics is a relatively easy subject, compared to the higher branches of philosophy or of pure science, good and even competent economists are 'the rarest of birds'? An easy subject at which few excel!" He continued, "The paradox finds its explanation, perhaps, in that the master economist must possess a rare *combination* of gifts. . . . He must be a mathematician, historian, statesman, philosopher, in some degree. He must understand symbols and speak in words. He must contemplate the particular in terms of the general, and touch abstract and concrete in the same flight of thought. He must study the present in the light of the past for the purposes of the future." Marshall, said Keynes, possessed much but not all of these qualities, but he had his limitations as well: He had a poor memory; he lacked the power of continuous concentration and was consequently unable to complete any major work "at white heat"; he also lacked "the continuous artistic sensibility to the whole," which is necessary for the successful production of a treatise.

In these perceptive, eloquent remarks on Jevons and Marshall, one notices that in many ways Keynes was stressing the need for that double nature which Edward Carpenter and others had contended was the peculiar endowment of some gifted homosexuals. Creativity, he seems to have been saying, requires the combining of thought and feeling, the union of opposites, the harmonizing of what were commonly regarded in Victorian times as masculine and feminine traits. In his biography of Keynes, Harrod had emphasized his subject's "curious conjunction of contrasting qualities," which he saw as the explanation of his creativity, but he did not trace the duality of Keynes's nature back to his most paradoxical peculiarity—his homosexuality.

Where had Keynes himself gotten this insight that creativity required a double nature? It is known that he owned a copy of Coleridge's *Table Talk*—it had been given to him by his sister—and the present author discovered that in it he made a marginal notation opposite the poet's observation that "talent, lying in the understanding, is often inherited; genius, being the action of reason and imagination, rarely or never."

Did he also know of Coleridge's definition of "the character and privilege of genius"? "To contemplate the ANCIENT of days and all his works with feelings as fresh, as if all had then sprung forth at the first creative fiat. . . . To carry the feelings of childhood into the power of manhood; to combine the child's sense of wonder and novelty with the appearances, which every day for perhaps forty years had rendered familiar. . . . This is the character and privilege of genius." He probably did, but one does not know for sure. It is known that he often made the remark in talking to Roy Harrod and Richard Kahn that "every morning I wake up as innocent as a newborn babe."

Keynes was an implicit Coleridgean and an ardent anti-Benthamite until his last days, but it is unclear to what extent he was indebted to Coleridge for his understanding of the creative process. It seems more probable that his emphasis on the double nature of the creative person derived from his own self-knowledge or from the psychological literature cited above which gave so much comfort to the homosexuals, especially the writings of Edward Carpenter (1844–1929). The latter, a Cambridge graduate, was very friendly with Lowes Dickinson and corresponded with Walter John ("Sebastian") Sprott. Keynes does not seem to have had any of Carpenter's many books on homosexuality in his private library, but in view of their wide circulation it is unlikely that he was unfamiliar with them—Carpenter, after all, was "the leading exponent of Whitmanism in England" during these years. It seems clear, however, that he was acquainted with them because in 1907, while he was still at the India office, he and J. L. Hammond, the historian, signed an appeal circulated by Carpenter which urged the establishment of a British academy to promote a simpler way of life. This interesting and important fact has only recently come to light in a new biography of Edward Carpenter; otherwise, a check of the latter's extensive correspondence reveals no letters to or from Keynes.

In his volume, *The Intermediate Sex,* Carpenter had emphasized the "double nature" of the healthier homosexuals, which he asserted gave them "command of life in all its phases" and claimed that with their intuition and artist-nature they had the artist's sensibility and perception. From his other writings one can see that he had an understanding of the dual nature of the self, of its conscious and unconscious aspects, and believed that from this hidden, unconscious self came "the wonderful flashes of intuition, the complex combinations of ideas, which at times leap fully formed and with a certain authority into the field of men's waking consciousness. These flashes and inspirations 'obviously proceed from a deep intelligence of some kind, lying below, and are the product of an immensely extended and rapid survey of things, brought to a sudden focus.' They do *not* proceed from the conscious brain, but are felt by the latter to 'come from beyond it." These are crude formulations of the functioning of the creative process, to be sure, but they are the kind of psychological literature that would be known to the educated homosexuals of Keynes's day. From this and other passages in Carpenter's writings one can see that if Keynes had been acquainted with them he could come to believe that the double nature of some homosexuals equipped them admirably, if not exclusively, for creative tasks.

In this connection it should be noted that in several modern empirical studies of creativity the male subjects often show high scores on scales measuring "femininity." D. W. Mackinnon, frequently quoted in literature on this subject, states, "In the realm of sexual identification and interests, our creative subjects appear to give more expression to the feminine side of their nature than do less creative persons." Recent empirical research on homosexuality also indicates that homosexual males, rather than being more feminine than heterosexual males, actually might be more androgynous. Such androgynous individuals have been shown in other studies to be more flexible in their behavior than sex-typed persons in a wide variety of situations. Studies such as these may explain why some homosexuals are able to combine thought and feeling in the manner contemplated by Professor Heilbrun above, and such behavior may be considered conducive to creativity.

Whatever may be the intellectual capacity of androgynes in general, it does seem significant that both Lytton Strachey and Keynes have been described by close students of their lives and personalities as being androgynous. Professor Leon Edel writes of the former as "a busy, ardent, oversexed homosexual with an androgynous mind," and he recalls that Leonard Woolf told him privately that Keynes was "a mental hermaphrodite," which is not an inaccurate way of defining an androgyne. Several others who knew Keynes personally, including his colleague Sir Austin Robinson, his niece Polly Hill, and Lord Balogh, commented upon the "feminine" quality of his mind.

Some androgynes seem to have an unusual capacity to passively absorb the stimuli and impressions which they receive from their environment and to transform them imaginatively into intuitions or, in the case of writers, into the stuff of their stories and novels. Henry James, Jr., often stressed the necessity to "convert, convert" in this sense, and in discussing Keynes's *Indian Currency and Finance,* his capacity for such receptivity has been noted. Other instances of this ability to take others' ideas and to convert them into an idiom and conceptualization of his own making will subsequently be pointed out. When he said that he awoke each morning "as innocent as a newborn babe," he was referring, of course, to the freshness and innocence of his imagination. This capacity for passivity as well as for active involvement in his environment may be related, too, to a peculiarity of his that has never been adequately explained. Several of his intimates, as well as his father, commented upon his penchant for lying in bed until late in the morning and doing most of his "office work" in that manner. Milo Keynes, his nephew, has stated that "characteristically, when writing and reading, Maynard would be on a bed or a chaise longue." Harrod explained rather apologetically that his late rising was to conserve his energies, but it may have served other purposes of which even Keynes was not conscious. Students of creativity have noted that a passive state, such as lying in bed or meditation, or sleep itself, may be favorable to the bisociative or creative process. A well-known physicist in Great Britain is reported to have said, "We often talk about the three B's, the bus, the bath and the bed. That is where the great discoveries are made in our science." So far as is known, Keynes did not spend an inordinate amount of time on buses or in the bath, but like Descartes he did like his bed—and with what extraordinary results! Of course, as will be seen more fully later, if he did experience useful intuitions in the prone position, he later had to note, verbalize, or describe and present his insights in an "intellectually negotiable" form so that they could be validated by others—and this required intense logical analysis and expository effort on his part.

Reference has been made earlier to the "Germano-Coleridgean" challenge to the dominant rationalist outlook in early nineteenth-century Britain. Despite that protest, the patriarchal culture in that country remained strongly committed to the rational, analytic mode of knowing; the more holistic, intuitive way of perceiving was practically associated with feminine nature. This dominant world view was dealt a number of staggering blows in the latter part of the century and the opening years of the twentieth. Darwin's ideas on the evolution of the species tended to undermine the metaphysical support given to patriar chal culture by orthodox Christianity. Later, Freud challenged the rationalist world view by showing the enormous influence of the irrational and unconscious on human behavior. Bergson about this same time emphasized the importance of intuition in perception with his important work, *Creative Evolution* (1907), and G. E. Moore a few years earlier laid the basis for an intuitionist ethics with his *Principia Ethica*. Virginia Woolf had begun, with others, the process of revolutionizing the novel by introducing the stream of consciousness technique. Then, World War I further eroded and undermined the old Victorian way of life, with the result that Britain's consciousness became more receptive to some of Bloomsbury's insights and values. During that protracted, bloody struggle, as Quentin Bell has pointed out, in seeking to live a life of more humane and pacific freedom, Bloomsbury was prepared to sacrifice the heroic, masculine virtues in order to avoid its associated vices, chief among the latter being violence. Needless to say, this was in accordance with its cherished ideal of androgyny.

Toward the close of that war this small group of British intellectuals indeed became prolific. Lytton Strachey published his *Eminent Victorians* in 1918; Keynes, *The Economic Consequences of the Peace* the following year; Roger Fry brought out his *Vision and Design* in 1920, and Virginia Woolf began a period of remarkable productivity with *Night and Day* in 1919. The fruits of the Bloomsbury ethos were finally blooming profusely.

In employing his intuition as well as his reason in his theoretical work, Keynes, too, was in a sense transcending the dichotomy between masculinity and femininity which Victorian culture had fostered and maintained. He was extending the challenge to the rational world view to another field of thought, economics. In the past, the dominant sexist culture had severely repressed and punished the unconventional behavior of the sexual minority, hampering and frustrating its creativity as well. Just as the attainment of freedom or even retention of a moderate degree of racial discrimination, after severe oppression or exclusion, produced a burst of creativity among the Jewish people (as Dr. Silvano Arieti demonstrated so persuasively), so the more liberal outlook of twentieth-century Britain fostered novel creative achievements by this formerly despised sexual minority. In breaking through a confining value system and demolishing its rigid categories and dichotomies of thought to reach a fuller actualization of their potential, the androgynous pathfinders of Bloomsbury opened up a new world of arts and letters and ultimately of economics for all human beings.

In appraising the influence of the Bloomsbury milieu on Keynes's creativity, it seems indisputable that its liberalism and especially its latitudinarian sexual ethic sustained and confirmed his own inclination in that direction. As an "immoralist," as he characterized himself in *"My Early Beliefs,"* it provided him with a sense of community and an indispensable opportunity for play and recreation. The Bloomsberries were his reference group, his sounding board; and even a genius or a potentially creative person needs cultural feedback if he is to realize his full capacity. It is clear that Keynes had such a need; in fact, he needed and desired praise, even after he was a world-famous figure, and the critical, discriminating endorsement of his Bloomsbury peers meant more to him than the plaudits of the larger, outside world. Indeed, subsequent chapters will demonstrate that its criticism played a significant part in prodding or motivating him to write *The Economic Consequences of the Peace.*

In his biography of Keynes, Sir Roy Harrod expressed the view that "although Keynes's intellect reached its full development when he was very young, his creative impulse came to maturity slowly." Though it is possible to misunderstand Harrod's conception of creativity or to be confused by his restricting evidence of it to economic theory, his related contention that Keynes was not really creative until after his marriage in 1925 seems very questionable. This especially is the case when one notes that Keynes himself believed that "the powers of originality are at their highest" in the early twenties of life. On the contrary, it is contended here that the elements of Keynes's creativity manifested themselves earlier in his life than Sir Roy realized, and Bloomsbury played a more important part in the enfolding of his genius than the Oxford economist appreciated.

CHAPTER 7

World War I and the Preparations for Peace

[Keynes] is a very clever man and has the talent of the good learner. ... His opinions are in a perpetual state of progress, and therefore of apparent flux.

Sir Eyre Crowe

FOR MOST PEOPLE in Great Britain the weekend on which World War I broke out was very ordinary. It was a bank holiday and seemed like any other summer weekend. The well-to-do had house parties at country estates, the regatta was held at Cowes, there was racing at Goodwood, flying displays at the Hendon airport, and cricket at Canterbury. For the more plebeian, there was a new exhibit at Madame Tussaud's, ironically described as "the European crisis." There was a rally against the war in Trafalgar Square, staged by the Labor and Socialist leaders, but the crowd was so militant that it shouted down the speakers.

Among the writers who recorded their feelings at the war's outbreak, only Henry James immediately saw its meaning. He wrote to a friend that very day: "The plunge of civilization into this abyss of blood and darkness by the wanton feat of these two infamous aristocrats is a thing that gives away the whole long age during which we have supposed the world to be, with whatever abatement, gradually bettering; that to have to take it all now for what the treacherous years were all the while making for and *meaning* is too tragic for any words." James saw that the war, by breaking out almost accidentally, destroyed and contradicted "the benevolent assumptions of the Edwardian age, denied liberalism and progress and the goodness of the human heart, and left men with no cause but war itself." That age had seemed like a long "golden afternoon" or "a garden party"—but now the party was over.

On the day that Great Britain declared war, August 4, Keynes was not in government service, but the man who had taken his place as secretary of the Indian Currency Commission, Basil Blackett, was in the Treasury struggling with the complex financial issues of the impending conflict. On August 1 he had written Maynard: "I tried to get hold of you yesterday and today, but found that you were out of town. I wanted to pick your brains for your country's benefit and thought you might enjoy the process. If by chance you could spare time to see me on Monday, I should be grateful, but I fear the decisions will all have been taken by then. The joint stock banks have made absolute fools of themselves and behaved very badly."

When this message was received by Keynes on Sunday, he discovered that he could not get a train in time, so he persuaded his brother-in-law, A. V. Hill, who owned a motorcycle and sidecar, to drive him to London. They arrived at Whitehall late in the afternoon, so Keynes alighted at the end of the street because he did not think it proper to approach the majestic Treasury in so incongruous a fashion. He was a man in a hurry; he did not wish to miss an opportunity to serve his country at so critical a time.

The financial situation at the outbreak of the war in 1914 was serious because of the possibility of panic. The joint stock banks had been arguing that in view of the domestic and foreign deposits their gold reserves were inadequate, and they thought that the government should assume more responsibility for them. In the last week of July 1914, indeed, as the international situation deteriorated, there had been a run on gold, not by the depositors but by the banks themselves; they withdrew extraordinarily large amounts from the Bank of England, but paid out only notes to their customers—this was the conduct to which Basil Blackett objected. As a Treasury official, he had hired Keynes as a monetary expert, hoping that he would be able to counter the plans of the private bankers whom he opposed.

These banks had just proposed a plan whereby they would pay in gold to the Bank of England, which, in turn, would issue special Bank of England notes, and gold payments would be suspended outside the country. Lloyd George, who was then chancellor of the exchequer, was said to favor this idea, but it was vehemently opposed by the Treasury and the Bank of England. In short, Britain was on the verge of abandoning the gold standard, and Keynes was urged by Blackett to prepare a memorandum condemning the folly of such precipitous action. He did this the very next day, arguing cogently that "the *future* position of the City of London as a free gold market will be seriously injured if at the first sign of emergency specie payment is suspended." The heavy drain of gold from the Bank of England was due, he stated, to "a fit of hoarding" by the joint stock banks, and when they regained their equilibrium, the gold would again be available; furthermore, no large foreign drain was immediately probable.

When Lloyd George was given this memorandum the next day, he asked, "Who is this Keynes?" He was told that he was a friend of Blackett's, an expert in currency, at which George replied that it was monstrous that Treasury officials could call in outsiders on their own responsibility, but he read the memorandum. The next day, in meetings with the bankers, he came out strongly against suspension of specie payments. A compromise was reached: the banks' reserves were placed in the Bank of England, and an emergency currency, issued by the Treasury, was brought out so that it was not necessary to suspend the Bank Act. Blackett noted in his diary that the chancellor had "clearly imbibed much of Keynes's memorandum. . . . We are in high spirits at the prospect of victory for Treasury views." Lloyd George's conversion to support of the gold standard at this juncture was really a signal triumph for Keynes; Great Britain and the United States were the only countries which did not go off gold at this time. He wrote to his father, "Specie payment by the Bank of England has now been saved— by the skin of its teeth. . . . I've just heard that they consider I played an important part in preventing the suspension of specie payments, as it was my memorandum that converted Lloyd George."

He was now truly "on the inside" at the Treasury during these momentous times, and he found the work "very exciting." He wrote another memorandum for the Treasury on the acceptance houses, which were also in trouble as a result of the sudden outbreak of the war. Apparently hoping that he might receive a Treasury appointment at this time, he supplied the permanent secretary with the names of several Cambridge men who were eligible for war work, but that body was not inclined to expand its staff. Instead, he returned to his study of probability and thought of bringing out a small book, a financial history of the early days of the war.

This didn't come off, but somewhat later he wrote a short article on "Currency Measures Abroad" for the *Morning Post* and engaged in a controversy in the columns of *The Economist* on the amount of gold held by the joint stock banks. In the latter he showed a marked antipathy toward the bankers, accusing them of a failure of courage and public spirit in the recent financial crisis. Their leadership, he stated in a letter to Alfred Marshall, was lacking because they were staffed with "second-division men" and had directors who had been appointed on hereditary considerations or because they could bring a certain class of business to the banks.

In his September 1914 article, "War and the Financial System," he was even more caustically critical of the financiers. One of them, Felix Schuster, who was chairman of the London Clearing Banks, was so annoyed by this article that he arranged an interview and succeeded in convincing Keynes that he had been unfair to these institutions. In a subsequent article in the same journal, Keynes admitted that imperfect knowledge had caused him to describe the Clearing Banks, as distinguished from some others, with less than fairness. "My disappointment," he wrote, "was that of an admirer, my complaints those of a true lover of the banking system."

In a letter to his father dated September 3, 1914, Keynes said that he had "seldom written so industriously." In the next few months he expounded on German financial expedients, "The Cost of the War to Germany," a "Note on Government Loans," and "Notes on French Finance." The latter essay was a considerable piece of work compiled in part while he was on a visit to his brother Geoffrey, who was serving as a medical officer at a Versailles hospital. About this time he also composed an article on "The City of London and the Bank of England" for the November 1914 issue of an American periodical, the *Quarterly Journal of Economics*. He was obviously seeking to be noticed during these months, and early in 1915 his efforts bore fruit. In another letter to his father he wrote, "I've been offered a position in the Treasury alongside of Paish for the period of the war. No time for details, as I have a very heavy piece of work to do for them by Friday when L. G. [Lloyd George] (private) sails for France. . . . The governor of the Bank of England has been reading my works and has asked me to come and visit him at the bank."

Sir George Paish, a well-known monetary expert, was a special advisor to the chancellor of the exchequer; Lloyd George liked to have a "brain trust" (or, as the British termed it, a "garden suburb") to check on the regular officials of the bureaucracy. Keynes was temporarily appointed as his assistant at an annual salary of six hundred pounds, with the understanding that he would be allowed to do what he pleased on one day of the week, excepting a public emergency, and that he could continue his editorship of the *Economic Journal*. He was soon very busy serving as a secretary of a secret cabinet committee which was inquiring into the rising cost of food. With his usual extraordinary sense of involvement, he dashed off a paper on wheat prices for the use of the Cabinet.

By the end of January 1915, he was off to Paris with a most select party, including Lloyd George, Montagu Norman, the governor of the Bank of England, and a private secretary. He wrote, "We are to be guests of the French government. There was another meeting of my Cabinet committee today. The amount of things I've got to think about in the next few days, in order to be able to advise at a moment's notice, appalls me. I wish I hadn't a cold coming on." At this meeting in Paris, the first financial conference of the allies, England and France agreed that they would share equally in support of Russia in the war.

The range of questions on which Keynes had to be expert now widened even more amazingly: the financing of Russian wheat exports to the allies, proposals for a joint loan by the major allies, the wheat position of India and of the United Kingdom, and matters of Treasury finance. He supplied the prime minister, Herbert Asquith, with notes for his speech in the House of Commons on the cost of living on February 11 and also argument by way of rebuttal to the opposition. His experience on all matters of finance at this time was remarkable, and his ability to state a case with succinctness and clarity was unmatched.

At the end of May 1915, his position at the Treasury became even more important. At this time Asquith formed a coalition government with Lloyd George as minister of munitions and Reginald McKenna replacing him as chancellor of the exchequer. As a result of this governmental reorganization, Keynes became a member of the Treasury's number one division whose domain was finance. McKenna immediately tapped him to accompany him on a trip to Nice to meet the finance minister of Italy. Maynard wrote hurriedly to his father, "I am overwhelmed with work (and naturally much excited). As usual they have given me just twenty-four hours to get up and write memoranda on a more or less new subject."

This was an arduous mission for him, for in addition to laboring for thirteen of the twenty-three hours spent at Nice, he then immediately returned across the Channel in a destroyer at a speed of thirty-five miles per hour. The passage and possibly overeating, as one wit had it, at the government's expense took its toll; upon disembarking he suffered an acute case of appendicitis and had to undergo an emergency operation, and after that ordeal he came down with pneumonia. He convalesced until the beginning of August, and each of his parents served as his secretary until his return to work.

Restored to health by August 20, he was off again to Boulogne to participate with other British and French representatives in a discussion about raising a joint loan in the United States. He had prepared "A Summary of the Gold Position" for this consultation, in which he minimized the significance of the gold reserve in countries which had suspended specie payments. At Boulogne the banks of England and France agreed that they would hold $200 million in gold for export to the United States and would urge Russia to do the same. The British were to negotiate the loan, and each country would share in the proceeds in proportion to the amount of gold provided.

As the war entered its second year, the economic pinch really began to grow serious. General Kitchener was pressing for seventy divisions, but the supply of recruits was falling off. At the same time, Great Britain had heavy commitments to subsidize its allies. In a memorandum to the chancellor of the exchequer, Keynes maintained that a considerably increased army and a continuance of subsidies to the allies were alternative options, unless a drastic reduction of consumption was achieved. He calculated the cost of the subsidies in real, manpower terms, a technique of analysis which clearly brought out the "guns-versus-butter" dilemma that the British were facing; this approach, of course, foreshadowed the similar analysis of manpower budgeting in World War II. McKenna presented Keynes's memorandum to the Cabinet committee on war policy, but it found his arguments "ingenious but unconvincing." In short, the decision was made to continue the effort to maintain an army of seventy divisions by voluntary means or by conscription, if necessary. To these officials, conscription of men for war was evidently easier to accept than conscription of wealth.

The cost of the war was escalating frightfully in human terms as well. Late in November 1914, Keynes wrote Lytton Strachey of his grief at its toll: "For myself I am absolutely and completely desolated. It is utterly unbearable to see day by day the youths going away, first to boredom and discomfort, and then to slaughter. Five of this college, who are undergraduates or who have just gone down, are already killed, including, to my great grief, Freddie Hardman." Maynard had written to Hardman before his death and sent him some pamphlets. The young man had asked him his opinion about the length of the war, and he replied that he thought it would be short because of economic considerations. Upon hearing the sad news of his friend's death, he sent his condolences to his mother, and she thanked him for his sympathy.

In April 1915, more shocking news from the battlefront reached Cambridge. Keynes wrote Duncan Grant at this time, "This has been a horrible weekend, and I feel again, although I should not, as I did after Freddie's death. Yesterday came the news that two of our under-graduates were killed, both of whom I knew, though not very well, and was fond of. And today, Rupert's death. It is too horrible, a nightmare to be stopped anyhow. May no other generation live under the cloud we live under."

The reference in this letter is, of course, to Rupert Brooke, the handsome poet who had been very friendly with Maynard's brother. To understand this letter and Maynard's reaction to the news of his death, it is helpful to recall the life and personality of this famous figure. Before the war, Brooke had been part of a group of young people whom Maynard called the "neo-pagans"; it included Justin Brooke, Catherine ("Ka") Cox, the Olivier sisters, Geoffrey Keynes, Virginia Stephen, and Rupert himself. Maynard had joined them once on a camping party in Devon, but he really was not one of them. As one can see, the social background of the neo-pagans was not unlike that of Bloomsbury, and, indeed, there was some overlapping of membership, but the real neo-pagans were less unconventional in their sexual behavior and given to sports and camping out. They reacted against the esthetes and those they regarded as decadents; they looked in general to the opposite sex for love, and marriage was their ideal.

As these young people grew older, some married, but the Shelleylike Brooke had not found his mate and seemed envious of those who had. Emotionally he was torn between Noel Olivier and Ka Cox. After a disastrous love affair with the latter, he suffered a nervous breakdown, in the course of which in his depression he accused Lytton Strachey of playing the role of Pandarus, namely, of involving him in homosexual intrigues with others. He felt that he was ruined and contemplated suicide. Upon his recovery, he continued to express his hatred and repulsion not only for Strachey, but for the whole atmosphere of Bloomsbury. In his estrangement from his old friends, he turned from a rational to an intuitive approach to life. His intuition now told him that the world was only to be saved by virility. The mixture of the sexes was all wrong, "male was male and female was female, and any intermingling of the two was calamitous." Manliness in man was "the one hope of the world."

When the Great War came, Brooke was among the first to volunteer.

He served in the Royal Navy as a lieutenant, but died of septicemia while at sea on April 22, 1915. He was buried on Skyros in the Aegean, the island of Achilles, under a cairn with a Greek epitaph, a fit resting place for a classical scholar and a fellow of King's. His sonnet that begins with the famous lines made him immortal for many:

> If I should die, think only this of me:
> That there's some corner of a foreign field
> That is forever England. . . .

As the war progressed in 1915, it came closer even in a physical way to the civilians of Britain. In September of that year Keynes was in London at 3 Gower Street. It was about 11:00 P.M. as he sat writing to his mother:

"As I write, Zeppelin bombs are dropping all around, about one every minute and a half I should say, and the flashes and explosions are terrifying. I am much more frightened than I thought I should be. Miss Chapman [a secretary] is sitting with me in the dining room, which we have decided is safest—I don't know why. She doesn't seem in the least nervous and spends her time soothing Rex [a dog]. I daresay we shall find in the morning that the bombs have not been within a mile of us; but it does seem very near. I am extremely busy at the Treasury, but am enjoying the work. Today I have been commissioned by the chancellor to write an important memorandum, and as usual have only a day to do it in."

Early in September 1915, Keynes had taken over Basil Blackett's work at the Treasury while he was on a financial mission to the United States. In that capacity, in an important memorandum entitled "The Financial Prospects of This Financial Year," he assessed the probable deficit for the next six months at £120 million a month on top of the existing deficiency of £700 million. He asked how far it would be possible to meet this deficiency from "real resources" rather than by "inflationist borrowing." He contrasted Germany's fiscal policy of currency depreciation (which had resulted in an increase of food prices of sixty-four percent since the beginning of the war, with wages frozen) with the more liberal approach in Britain (which was resulting in higher income and consumption by the working classes). The moral was clear: Expenditure in excess of real resources would be financed by "inflationism" brought about by increasing the money supply. Additional resources for the war could be made available if consumption was curtailed. The alternatives were increased taxation or inflation, and Keynes argued strongly for the former.

Lloyd George, suspicious that the Treasury was campaigning against his massive munitions program, attacked Keynes for his dismal analysis and prognostication. "Mr. McKenna's nerve was shaken by these vaticinations of his chief advisor, Mr. J. M. Keynes," he fulminated. Calling Keynes "a volatile soothsayer" who "dashed at conclusions with acrobatic ease," he added, "Mr. Keynes was for the first time lifted by the chancellor of the exchequer into the rocking chair of a pundit, and it was thought that his very signature appended to a financial document would carry weight."

Though this was somewhat of a left-handed compliment, it was very true that Keynes needed the skills of a mental acrobat at this time, for while he was grappling with these complex domestic problems, he was delegated simultaneously to negotiate with the Russians on their finances. In preparation, he wrote a long note on the subject in which he analyzed monetary and price developments within that country and the influence that these might exert on her external finances and foreign exchange position. Subsequently, an agreement was reached providing for the shipment of Russian gold to support the American loan and imposing limitations on the purposes for which the credit was spent.

Keynes had a remarkable talent for detailed, administrative work, and his quick mind enabled him to dash off complex papers on all sorts of subjects. Like a true androgyne, his ability to shift attention and alternate between different types of tasks conserved his energy and at the same time often contributed to synergistic results. The rare combination of an acute, logical mind with a highly feminine capacity for sensitiveness and empathy was commented upon by Harrod. In one passage, in particular, he caught this latter aspect of the man: "But when he was in a position of responsibility himself, he had a superb capacity for picking the brains of others. When in the presence of one who knew his subject, he was completely modest. He sat watching with his steady, searching eyes; tentacles seemed to go out in search of any weak spot, any falsity in his interlocutor, any axe he had to grind. He absorbed all good information readily, welcoming it from the humblest source, and knew how to reject the shoddy. . . . There was none of the self-importance, of the reluctance to discard a view that has become associated with one's ego, of the terror of renouncing what one has committed oneself to in public, which are the besetting sins of great persons."

On the other hand, Keynes could become very impatient with theorists whose logic he could appraise for himself, and with the pompous, the self-opinionated, and the long-winded whom he "snapped off . . . with a sudden rudeness." Perhaps the most amusing example of such aggressiveness was the incident when he was accompanying Lloyd George, who was then chancellor of the exchequer, on an early mission to France. In the railway carriage, George gave his opinion of the state of affairs in that country and then asked for comment. When Keynes gave his reaction, and it must be remembered that he was a relatively new man in the Treasury at that time, he replied, "With the utmost respect I must, if asked for my opinion, tell you that I regard your account as rubbish."

During these years Keynes's position in the Treasury was more that of the "brains" and chief of staff than the administrator. His quick, fertile mind provided innumerable officials and members of the Cabinet with memoranda and advice on all matters of finance. In addition, he was instrumental in establishing the procedure whereby Treasury approval was necessary for Allied purchases financed by British credits. This technique enabled a comprehensive system of control to be maintained which prevented competitive bidding for scarce supplies by the allies and contributed to the stability of foreign exchange rates. Further, despite the increasing pressure on the British pound as the war dragged on, he was adamant against suspension of specie payments. From May 1916 on, the exchange situation deteriorated still more, forcing large sales of United States securities and of gold. By October of that year, he reported, "Of the five million pounds which the Treasury had to find daily for the prosecution of the war, about two million has to be found in North America."

Early in 1916, the British Treasury, acting through J. P. Morgan and Company, pegged sterling at $4.76, thereby stabilizing the exchanges of the allies in New York and other financial centers. Henceforth, and to the conclusion of the conflict, the support of this rate became one of his major responsibilities. Truly, as he said in a talk in March 1916, he acted as "paymaster to the allies."

During these years his life brought him into association with the highest officials in the government and some of the most prominent figures in social life. He spent many weekends at the McKennas' and the Asquiths' as well as at Garsington Manor, the residence of Lady Ottoline Morrell. In all these relationships he made himself very welcome; his multidimensional personality made him a favorite in high society as well as in the deliberations of the conference room.

Inevitably, however, as the war transformed society, the pattern of his most intimate relations changed. In October 1914, Adrian Stephen married Karin Costelloe, and this brought an end to the community arrangement that he had enjoyed at Brunswick Square. He moved to rooms at 10 Great Ormond Street, while Duncan took a room at the Bells' house at 46 Gordon Square. Later he established another community in his own house at 3 Gower Street, where he shared the ground floor with John Sheppard, his classical colleague at King's who was serving in Intelligence for the duration, and Gerald Shove, his economist friend. (The latter didn't stay with him very long; in 1915, he married poet Fredegond Maitland, the daughter of F. W. Maitland, and moved away.) On the second floor of this Gower Street house were Dorothy Brett, the daughter of Lord Esher, and Dora Carrington, both students at the Slade Art School; and at the top were John Middleton Murray and Katherine Mansfield, who later married and became famous as critic and writer, respectively.

Keynes himself became friendly with a number of young ladies at this time, principally Faith Bagenal, an ex-student at Newnham College who later married Hubert Henderson, the economist; Dora Carrington; Dorothy Brett; Alix Sargant-Florence, who married James Strachey; and Barbara Hiles. These young women were called the "Bloomsbury Bunnies" or "Cropheads" (they wore their hair bobbed) by the younger members of the group. Barbara Hiles, who had studied painting at the Slade School, was Maynard's favorite, according to Harrod. She is said to have been "very pretty, lively, and good natured" and was appreciated by several of the men in the Bloomsbury group. Years later when Maynard and Lydia were dining with the Woolfs and reminiscing about the past, Keynes told "how he met Barbara Hiles and did more than meet her fifty years ago." As it turned out, Barbara, after dallying with the retiring Saxon Sydney-Turner, married Nicholas Bagenal in 1918. Maynard very obviously had a warm spot in his heart for her—years later he offered her advice on the sale of a house and financial assistance to put her boys through college, writing in one letter: "When you have one or both boys at King's, will any financial difficulties arise? If so, I am sure something can be arranged. Will you let me know if, say, two hundred pounds a year during the period of the residence of one or both would be a comfort?"

There were a number of factors which may have contributed to this transformation in Keynes's sexual behavior at this time. With the conscription of men and the heavy losses on the battlefront, there certainly was a shortage of eligible bachelors, and with the improvement in his financial and social status, he was extremely attractive to women. Furthermore, his friends were growing older, marrying, or forming new romantic relationships. Duncan Grant was growing closer to Vanessa Bell, the painter, as she, after a love affair with Roger Fry, was becoming estranged from her husband. Duncan and she traveled abroad in 1914, and in the following year he and David Garnett lived with the Bells in West Wittering in Sussex. For the remainder of the war, Grant was engaged in farm work at Wisset Lodge, Suffolk, as well as at Charleston. Shortly after the armistice, on Christmas Day 1918, Vanessa gave birth to a daughter, Angelica. Duncan was the father. From that time and even before, Duncan and Vanessa worked and lived together, and while both of them remained on very friendly terms with Maynard, the latter's relationship to Duncan was not as close as it had been in the prewar period. Late in 1916, Keynes took over the lease of Clive Bell's house at 46 Gordon Square, with the understanding that Clive would have a room there. He brought Sheppard and Harry Norton to share his new lodgings with him; this was to be his London residence for the rest of his life.

Faced with the mounting need for more men on the battlefront, in January 1916 the Asquith government introduced a conscription bill in Parliament. Almost immediately Bloomsbury was reunited in its opposition to the measure. Clive Bell made a forthright attack on the war itself in a pamphlet entitled *Peace At Once,* and soon Bertrand Russell (not part of Bloomsbury but friendly with many of its members) was defying the authorities as a pacificist. Many of Maynard's most intimate friends were conscientious objectors, though few if any of them could claim exemption on the basis of a religious affiliation which forbade the taking of life. Lytton Strachey was exempt from military sevice because of a physical disability, as was Leonard Woolf; James Strachey was allowed noncombatant service. Duncan Grant and David Garnett discharged their obligation under the National Service Act by doing agricultural labor, as did Clive Bell and Gerald Shove. Bloomsbury's skepticism about the war manifested itself in Lytton Strachey's famous answer before a tribunal to the cliché put to the "conchies," as they were called by the local citizenry: "What would you do if you saw a German officer attempting to rape your sister?" Lytton's not very subtle homosexual reply was, "I should try to interpose my own body."

Keynes himself was strongly against the government's resort to conscription. His father recorded in his diary, "Maynard talks of resigning his post at the Treasury, and we are very much worried about him." Just then he was sending a letter to the *Daily Chronicle,* under the pseudonym Politicus, in which he argued that expediency and practical good sense made it unwise to recruit more men at the expense of properly supplying the troops already in uniform, both British and allied; he cited the strain in shipping resources and made the prediction that if Germany did not win the war within the year, she would never win. All the while he intrigued with the Cabinet to persuade some of its members to favor the cause of conscientious objection. His father thought that he took an extreme view about conscription, and even his mother wondered in one of her letters whether some of his friends weren't being "coddled."

Maynard appreciated the objections of his friends to serving in the war, appeared several times before local tribunals in their behalf, and even gave little dinner parties after these ordeals to restore their shattered nerves. He was himself exempt initially for six months because he was engaged in work of national importance. In February 1916, he made a special application to be completely exempted on the specific grounds of conscientious objection to "surrendering my liberty of judgment on so vital a question as undertaking military service. . . . I am not prepared," he wrote, "on such an issue as this to surrender my right of decision, as to what is or is not my duty, to any other person, and I should think it morally wrong to do so." Eventually he was formally exempted by the authorities.

As the war progressed, his pacifist friends needled him about his participation through his service to the Treasury. On one occasion, in February 1916, Lytton Strachey put under his dinner plate a news report of a formerly liberal journalist who had changed his views and enlisted. He wrote on an attached sheet of paper, "Dear Maynard— Why are you still in the Treasury? Yours, Lytton." The latter said that Maynard was really put out when he read the extract and argued "that part of his reason for staying at the Treasury was the pleasure he got from being able to do the work so well. He also seemed to think that he was doing a great service to the country by saving some millions per week. . . . He at last admitted that there was a point at which he would think it necessary to leave, but what that point might be he couldn't say."

Keynes seems to have held the view that the war, having been started, had to be finished. Strachey and some of the others remembered that he had once said that he would resign if universal conscription was introduced. The reverberations of this split in Bloomsbury opinion over conscription are evident in Virginia Woolf's letters. In one to her sister, Vanessa, she asked, "Did you hear of Maynard's terrible outburst at Easter, when he said that Asquith is more intelligent than Lytton? Lytton thinks this a very serious symptom." The strain that Maynard was under is shown by another incident at Gordon Square.

He came home late after a strenuous day at the Treasury, and in conversation with some of his friends declared that he did not think anyone could have a genuine conscientious objection. When Vanessa Bell and Harry Norton objected to this, he snapped, "Go to bed, go to bed." Jack Sheppard remonstrated with him over this, saying, "Maynard, you will find it a mistake to despise your old friends."

The pressure on Maynard from his friends who were opposed to the war and to his part in it was pretty steady and unrelenting. This badgering of Keynes and his possible sense of guilt over his position on the war undoubtedly played a considerable part in motivating him to write his passionate polemic against the Paris peace treaty, of which more will be said in the next chapter.

An interesting light on his attitude to the war is revealed in a short essay which he probably wrote for the pacificist monthly *War and Peace,* an organ edited by his friend Gerald Shove. Once again using the pseudonym Politicus, Keynes carefully assessed the arguments for "peace now," namely that the military outcome of the war would be a deadlock and that there was a deep-seated hatred of war in all the belligerent countries, but that the only obstruction standing in the way was "the pride of governments."

Meanwhile, at the Treasury, his responsibilities and recognition were growing apace. In February 1917, he was promoted to be chief of the new "A" Division in that department whose jurisdiction included all external finance. Under Lloyd George's new War Cabinet, Bonar Law had replaced McKenna as chancellor of the exchequer, so Keynes reported directly to him and to Robert Chalmers, the joint permanent secretary of the Treasury. By the end of the war he had a staff of seventeen under him, including the redoubtable and reliable Dudley Ward and Oswald T. Falk, both of whom relieved him of onerous detail work.

At about this time Keynes's name was submitted in the final list to get a C. B. (Commander of the Bath), but when Lloyd George, who was then prime minister, saw it, he struck him off the list—an unprecedented act and done purely out of revenge, in Maynard's view, because of a memorandum which he had written. Four months later, however, he was awarded the honor, thanks to the earnest intercession of Sir Robert Chalmers. Alfred Marshall wrote in congratulation:

My dear Keynes, I do indeed hope that you will not abandon science for administration. But you have a better chance than any economist has ever had in this country of rendering high services to the State on critical occasions: for you will know more of economics than any professional statesman has ever done; and you will know of Whitehall difficulties—whether founded in the nature of things or in the Whitehall bureaucracy—than any other professional economist has ever done. So when you are K. C. B. [Knight Commander of the Bath] and are yet thinking out your best thoughts to their foundations, and from your foundations, you are to suppose that my shade is hovering over you and dropping an ethereal wreath from Elysian fields on your head. Yours till then and after.

The United States declared war on Germany on Good Friday, April 6, 1917. Financially, whatever one may believe about the political wisdom or military significance of America's entry into the war, this development came none too soon. Britain's American resources, drawn down at the rate of $75 million a day to support her own and the allies' purchases, were approaching a dangerous low point. On February 22, 1917, Keynes had reported to his superiors that the available funds would not last "for more than four weeks from today."

The American entry into the war therefore seemed to the British Treasury its salvation. Even Keynes wrote his mother on May 6 that the financial negotiations with the American officials were going extremely well. "If all happens as we wish, the Yanks ought to relieve me of some of the most troublesome of my work for the future." His expectations were partially confirmed soon after when Congress quite promptly authorized a loan of $3 billion for the support of the allies. But misunderstandings between the United States and the latter came to another climax in the financial crisis of June and July 1917. The American credits were available for purchases only within the United States, but Britain was financing Allied expenditure throughout the world. This external burden contributed heavily to the further deterioration in the British exchange position. By July 17, 1917, a message to the British ambassador in Washington, Sir Cecil Spring-Rice, which Keynes partially drafted, stated that "in short, available funds for payments in America are exhausted. Unless the United States government can meet in full our expenses in America, including exchange, the whole financial fabric of our alliance will collapse. This conclusion will not be a matter of months but of days."

It was apparent that without American assistance the British could not maintain the pegged rate of exchange. Difficult as the economics of the situation were, politics muddied the waters because some congressmen were suspicious about the uses to which the American funds were being put. In a Democratic Congress, Britain's reliance on the House of Morgan did not help matters, but once the American Treasury understood the situation, the financial picture cleared and the funds were provided for the support of the exchange.

In September 1917, Keynes made his first visit to the United States, accompanying Lord Reading, the chief justice, on a financial mission. Frankly, he did not make a very favorable impression on Americans on first contact. To those in London he appeared "rude, dogmatic, and disobliging," and even Blackett, in writing confidentially from Washington, stated that "he made a terrible reputation for rudeness out here." Later, however, one of these official correspondents thought that the Americans might have modified their view of him. Keynes himself remained critical of the former colony and its officials, writing Grant on the liner which carried him home, "The only really sympathetic and original thing in America is the niggers, who are charming."

As part of the effort to avoid such misunderstandings as that of July 1917, the Americans at this juncture insisted that an inter-Allied council for war purchases and finance be established. Keynes was designated as the British representative on this body, which he contemptuously called "this monkey house." He wrote his mother, "I should imagine the only possible analogy to government by the inter-Allied council is government by the Bolsheviks, though judging by results the latter are more efficient. I can't believe these things happen at Potsdam."

As the year approached its end, he grew more pessimistic as "the watchdog of the Treasury." In another missive to his mother, dated December 24, 1917, he gave vent to his misgivings: "My Christmas thoughts are that a further prolongation of the war, with the turn things have now taken, probably means disappearance of the social order that we have known hitherto. With some regrets I think I am on the whole not sorry. The abolition of the rich will be rather a comfort and serve them right anyhow. What frightens me more is the prospect of a general impoverishment. In another year's time we shall have forfeited the claim we have staked out in the New World, and in exchange this country will be mortgaged to America.

Well, the only course open to me is to be buoyantly Bolshevik; and as I lie in bed in the morning I reflect with a good deal of satisfaction that, because our rulers are as incompetent as they are mad and wicked, our particular kind of civilization is very nearly over."

Keynes was, of course, depressed at the dwindling supply of American dollars and securities held by Britain and what it portended for her financial future. As one way of relieving this situation somewhat, he suggested to the chancellor of the exchequer that the French balance of payments to Britain might be aided by purchasing some French art. Duncan Grant had noticed that there was to be an auction in Paris of Degas's private collection. Bonar Law was won over to the idea, and Keynes was given twenty thousand pounds to use on one of his Treasury trips to France. Vanessa Bell wrote him, urging that he consult Roger Fry before he left. Duncan told him to buy "Ingres's *Portrait of Self,* Cezanne, Corot, even at cost of losing others." Keynes was accompanied on this unusual mission by Sir Charles Holmes, the director of the National Gallery. At the time of the Degas sale, Paris was under fire from "Big Bertha," and this is said to have depressed prices, yet the unimaginative Holmes refused to buy any Cezannes, passed up an El Greco which he might have had, and came back with five thousand pounds unspent. Maynard bought for himself a still life, *Pommes* by Cezanne, for nine thousand francs, an Ingres drawing, and two works by Delacroix. This was the beginning of his own art collection; he was able to finance these early purchases from gains in shrewd wartime speculation. Vanessa Bell and Duncan were furious over Holmes's idiotic behavior, but they were proud of Maynard and wrote him, "You have been given complete absolution, and future crimes are also forgiven."

Keynes was involved in plans for peace as early as January 1916, when he prepared a "Memorandum on the Effect of an Indemnity" with Professor W. J. Ashley for the Board of Trade. The two authors pointed out that the indemnity paid by France to Germany after the Franco-Prussian War had damaged the victor as well as the loser because it had thrown Germany's foreign payments out of balance and contributed to the inflation which preceded the financial crisis of 1883. German reparations after the current war to make good the damage done in France and Belgium, it was contended, would very likely increase employment and prosperity at the expense of the allies. It was evident from this study that reparations could be an extremely complicated business.

Nevertheless, some politicians in Britain were whipping up public opinion in terms of vengeance and just compensation from Germany, as the general election of December 1918 approached, altogether oblivious of the so-called "transfer problem." In October 1918, Keynes made a preliminary estimate of Germany's capacity to pay reparations and concluded that only about £1,000 million could be obtained, even if spread over thirty years, "without crushing Germany."

His "A" Division examined the whole matter in a detailed memorandum later that year, finding that the cost of the war to the allies, including military pensions, came to £25,000 million, a sum far in excess of Germany's capacity to pay in reparations. Two policy options were open to the British, the report maintained: (1) to obtain all the property which could be transferred immediately over a period of years, and (2) to nurse Germany back into a state of high productivity by supplying her with raw materials and developing her export trade so that she could be exploited over a long period of years. The report starkly argued that "if Germany was to be 'milked,' she must not at first of all be ruined." It preferred the first of these alternatives because the latter would be injurious to Britain's own export trade and would pose serious political problems. Total reparations could not exceed £3,000 million, and having regard to Britain's own selfish interests, the limit might be as low as £2,000 million.

The political difficulties that the British faced on this problem can be appreciated when one realizes that a Cabinet committee under the chairmanship of William Hughes, the Australian prime minister, recommended in December 1918 that Germany should pay the allies' total war costs of £24,000 million. Harrod noted that this report was written "in total ignorance of the most elementary points, especially the whole question of transfer payments from Germany to the allies." He added, "In this utter nescience Hughes may not have been different from many other politicians of the time, who conceived the indemnity simply in terms of writing a cheque for that amount and levying it upon the citizens. The transfer problem was not envisaged. Keynes told them about it, but they turned a deaf ear."

In the sequel, the Cabinet was not able to resolve the differences between the policy that Keynes had recommended and that urged by the Hughes committee, and so this matter continued to divide the British delegation at the Paris peace conference. While he had worked on this memorandum, Keynes also proposed that at the opening of this conference Great Britain should advocate the complete cancellation of the inter-Allied war debt. Britain should forego her share of reparations and make it available as aid to the newly created states. Although Britain was a net creditor, he believed that she would gain from cancellation. She owed £800 million to the United States and was owed £1,450 million by her allies. She would be renouncing paper claims against her allies, but be relieved of real debts to the United States. His forward-looking proposal was considered at the peace conference as he continued to declare that "a settlement of inter-ally indebtedness is, therefore, an indispensable preliminary to the people of the Allied countries facing with other than a maddened and exasperated heart the inevitable truth about the prospects of an indemnity from the enemy."

At Versailles and later, the Americans were not inclined to accept a total cancellation of the war debts. Never daunted by rejection, Keynes within two weeks produced an alternative scheme for the joint guaran tee of reparations bonds as part of a plan for the economic reconstruc tion of Europe, but this too failed to gain acceptance. The war debts and reparations were left to plague the postwar generation, confirming his belief that "the existence of the great war debts is a menace to financial stability everywhere."

By 1918, by reason of his important service to the Treasury and the nation, Keynes's financial and social status had been transformed from that of the relatively impecunious don of the prewar period. The difference did not escape the sharp eye of Virginia Woolf, who observed in her diary for October 12 of that year: "Maynard, who has the generosity and manner now of an oriental prince, had hired a brougham for Nessa—an infinitely small, slow, antiquated carriage drawn by a very livery stables-looking quadruped. Roger, Duncan, Maynard, Nessa, and I crammed in and padded slowly across London to Chelsea." The reason for Maynard's princely consideration was that Vanessa Bell was pregnant. They were all going to the Sitwells' party in Carlyle Square.

Just about a month later, on Armistice Day when all London went wild with joy at the end of the "great War for Civilization," as it was officially called, many of the artists and intellectuals who had opposed the war spirit assembled at Monty Shearman's rooms. Maynard came with Lydia Lopokova, the star of the Russian ballet, and even D. H. Lawrence and his wife Frieda showed up, the former looking "ill and unhappy." "Bunny" Garnett, who was a great favorite of the novelist, and others gathered around him to hear what he thought was the lesson of the struggle: "I suppose you think the war is over and that we shall go back to the kind of world you lived in before it. But the war isn't over. The hate and evil is greater now than ever. Very soon war will break out again and overwhelm you. It makes me sick to see you rejoicing like a butterfly in the last rays of the sun before the winter. The crowd outside thinks that Germany is crushed forever. But the Germans will soon rise again. Europe is done for; England most of all countries. The war isn't over. Even if the fighting should stop, the evil will be worse because the hate will be dammed up in men's hearts and will show itself in all sorts of ways which will be worse than war. Whatever happens, there can be no Peace on Earth." Lawrence's fierce prophecy of evil was to be remembered by many at that party.

At the end of the war, Keynes was only thirty-five years old, yet he had won an estimable position for himself in the Treasury. He had served under a succession of chancellors of the exchequer and under Robert Chalmers and John Bradbury; he had brilliantly handled the external finance of the war, including the delicate financial relations with the United States; he had shown unusual perception in the defense of Britain's economic interest in all this, and had brought to his advice and consultation a humane and broad view of economic affairs. Since he and his Division had done most of the preliminary work on reparations and war debts, it was only proper and fitting that he should be the Treasury's chief representative at the peace conference.

CHAPTER 8

The Paris Conference and *The Economic Consequences of the Peace*

The Economic Consequences of the Peace "was the child of much emotion."
J. M. Keynes

IT HAS RECENTLY BEEN REMARKED that the statesmen of World War I—Lloyd George, Woodrow Wilson, and Georges Clemenceau—are not remembered with the same reverence that we hold for Franklin Roosevelt and Winston Churchill. Perhaps one of the reasons for the difference is that the latter two were spared the task of preparing a treaty of peace. Whatever one's view of this, we know that from the time of its signing almost to the present day, the terms of the Treaty of Versailles have been an object of severe criticism and even ridicule. One of the persons responsible for this negative image of the Paris peace conference was Maynard Keynes. His brilliant indictment of the chief peacemakers and of the controversial treaty which they fathered and endorsed contributed, it is generally agreed, to its rejection by the United States.

To understand this much debated matter it is essential to be clear about Keynes's exact status at that conference. He attended it as the senior representative of the British Treasury, with the power to speak, if required, for the chancellor of the exchequer and also as deputy for the chancellor on the Supreme Economic Council. Members of his "A" Division went with him—Dudley Ward, Oswald Falk, and Geoffrey Fry. Yet it is important, as Harrod pointed out, not to overestimate

Keynes's role at the conference; he was relatively young and comparatively unknown outside the Treasury. Lloyd George did not nominate him to the critical reparations commission, installing instead William Hughes, the Australian prime minister; Lord Cunliffe, a former governor of the Bank of England; and a high judge, Lord Sumner. None of these men had an adequate knowledge of finance, and earlier, it will be remembered, both Lloyd George and Bonar Law had regarded the conclusions of the Hughes committee as "a wild and fantastic chimera." The Treasury and the British Board of Trade were also excluded from representation on that key commission. As a consequence, Keynes had to spread his views by unofficial means, except when he was consulted by the prime minister himself.

The political situation in the treaty-making democracies must be kept in mind in seeking to understand the outcome of the conference. In Great Britain, Lloyd George's coalition government had just been reelected with a massive majority on a platform of "Hang the Kaiser" and "Make Germany Pay." These electioneering slogans were reflected in the famous promise of Sir Eric Geddes "to squeeze the lemon until you can hear the pips squeak." Lloyd George himself, deftly equivocating on the issue of reparations, promised in one speech that "as far as justice is concerned, we have an absolute right to demand the whole cost of the war from Germany. . . . We propose to demand the whole cost of the war," but then he went on to say that "we must exact it in such a way that it does not do more harm in the country that receives it than the country which is paying," thus implying that full compensation might be impossible. Many members of Parliament thought that the government's mandate was to make a Carthaginian peace, and Lord Northcliffe's newspapers propagandized incessantly for a severe treaty.

In France, Clemenceau, whose policy was moderate by French standards, was sniped at by President Raymond Poincaré and the Chamber of Deputies, while the old, grizzled military commander, Marshal Foch, made direct appeals to the French people over his head.

Perhaps least affected by the pressures of democracy was President Wilson. He was insulated from such influence by his own arrogance; it is notable that he took few congressmen and no Republicans to the conference. In addition, his political position was not secure because his party had been defeated at the midterm elections the preceding November.

While the treaty-making process cannot be examined in much detail in this chapter, it is important to keep in mind also that the freedom of maneuver of the conferees was limited by the secret treaties, such as those with Italy and Japan, which had been made to secure allies during the war. In general, as a result of factors such as these, the atmosphere at Paris almost from the beginning of the conference was not auspicious. Keynes was no sooner present at the conclave when, as he wrote later, "the feverish, persistent, and boring gossip of that hellish place had already developed in full measure the peculiar flavor of smallness, cynicism, self-importance, and bored excitement that it never was to lose."

Having comfortably ensconced himself in the Hotel Majestic, he had almost immediately sought out Norman Davis, the chief representative of the United States Treasury, to discuss a pressing financial issue. At the end of the war, American credits were to cease because foreign loans were only constitutional for war purposes, but the British had already received a loan of $250 million to tide them over the transition to peace; they were now seeking an additional $500 million. This request had earlier been refused by Albert Rathbone of the American Treasury, who annoyed Keynes by "his habit of writing what can only be described as solicitors' letters and the threatening and lawyerlike language that he seems sometimes to use." The then secretary of the Treasury, Carter Glass, had also turned down the matter, but finally, thanks to Keynes's conversations with Davis, the latter persuaded Glass to allow the additional credit.

However, there was soon a much more urgent problem demanding Keynes's attention, and that was the feeding of the defeated Germans. Under the terms of the armistice, there was specific provision for the continuance of the blockade against Germany; the British regarded it as their one instrument for imposing the peace terms on that country. The armistice also stated that "the allies contemplated the provisioning of Germany to the extent that shall be deemed necessary." Further, a supplementary armistice of December 1918, negotiated by France and Belgium without the knowledge of the United States, prohibited Germany from disposing abroad any gold, foreign securities, or other liquid assets, since they were under lien for the purposes of reparation. Some way had to be found to feed the Germans to avoid starvation and the ultimate disaster of collapse and possible Bolshevikism. The trouble was that the French wished to block the use of any of Germany's liquid resources for such purposes.

At that time, Herbert Hoover was director-general of the Inter-Allied Supreme Council for Relief and Supply. His huge task was somewhat lightened by the fortunate fact that his wartime campaign in the United States to expand food production under the slogan "Food

Will Win the War" had resulted in bumper crops of corn, and in turn this had produced a vast supply of hogs. Under these circumstances the Americans were very willing to sell their surplus of pig products; President Wilson spoke eloquently at the Supreme War Council on how Bolshevikism could thus be defeated and a new era begun. Keynes, with his firm economic grasp of the international commodity situation, readily saw what was involved. In a report to the chancellor of the exchequer, he wrote, "But really the underlying motive of the whole thing is Mr. Hoover's abundant stocks of low-grade pig products at high prices which must at all costs be unloaded on someone, enemies failing allies. When Mr. Hoover sleeps at night, visions of pigs float across his bedclothes, and he frankly admits that at all hazards the nightmare must be dissipated."

The memoir, "Dr. Melchior: A Defeated Enemy," is Keynes's autobiographical account of the negotiations with the German financiers over the question of compensation for food for the defeated nation. According to David Garnett, it was read to the Memoir Club probably in the summer of 1931 but not published until 1949, after Keynes's death. Garnett subsequently stated that this essay was "the finest of Maynard's writings: It combines deep personal feeling, a passion for humanity and justice, the unraveling of all the tangled threads in the negotiations, wit, and an almost uncanny observation of tiny but very significant detail. It is so real and so profoundly moving that I would compare it not to any other piece of historical writing that I know, but to a chapter from some great work of the imagination—by Tolstoy, perhaps. It is a work of art." The value of the piece, apart from its literary appeal, lies in the frankness and outspokenness with which Keynes wrote, though the psychological implications or significance of crucial passages obviously require close interpretation.

Keynes described the first meeting with the German financial representatives which took place in a railway carriage pulled up at the Treves station. He reminded his listeners that this town was in Germany and that it was "an extraordinary adventure in January 1919 to step on German soil." He and his conferees wondered what the economic situation would be like in the defeated country, or more specifically, in his vivid imagery, "whether children's ribs would be sticking through their clothes." He tells of their shame as "alien conquerors" at being shown German apartments for their possible occupancy, and describes his feeling about this imposition that "we were really committing an atrocity, and that was what was so enjoyable." His cynical description of some of the major military figures at the meeting was likely to find approval from some of his listeners who, we remember, were inclined to be pacifists and conscientious objectors during the war. Admiral Browning of the British Admiralty, he wrote, was "a most surly and ignorant seadog with a real and large hook instead of a hand, in the highest nautical tradition, with no idea in his head but the extirpation and further humiliation of a despised and defeated enemy." Marshal Foch's mind and character likewise are described as being of "an almost medieval simplicity." His "narrow and impervious intellect" had simply been added to "a strong and simple character"; though he was Jesuit trained, he was incompetent as a chairman and feeble in the art of oral expression; he was, in short, "a peasant." His spokesman, General Maxime Weygand, was described as "his attendant sprite."

Norman Davis, the American representative of the Treasury, presided over that first meeting, and the German spokesman was Dr. Carl Joseph Melchior of the firm of Messrs. Warburg of Hamburg. He was, wrote Keynes, "a small man, exquisitely clean, very well and neatly dressed, with a high stiff collar, his round head covered with a grizzled hair shaved so close as to be like in substance to the pile of a close-made carpet, the line where his hair ended bounding his face and forehead in a very sharply defined and rather noble curve, his eyes gleaming steadily at us, with extraordinary sorrow in them, yet like an honest animal at bay. This was he with whom in the ensuing months I was to have one of the most curious intimacies in the world, and some very strange passages of experience."

In his official report on these financial conversations, Keynes observed that "the general demeanor of the German representatives was strikingly conciliatory and even submissive. They made no complaints, refused no information for which they were asked, were perfectly clear and businesslike, seemed to indicate their willingness to do whatever was told them, and only allowed themselves by way of reply to make what were in effect veiled pleas for mercy. Dr. Melchior himself showed great ability in the conduct of the proceedings."

Keynes also described the two other German representatives, the elderly Dr. Kaufmann, president of the Reichsbank, and a representative of the Foreign Office, but it is evident that he was most intrigued by Melchior, who always spoke deliberately and in a way which gave one "an extraordinary impression that he was truthful. . . . This Jew, for such, though not by appearance, I afterwards learned him to be, and he only upheld the dignity of defeat."

This first conference accomplished little. The French futilely tried to get the Reichsbank gold transferred to occupied territory; the Germans equally vainly pleaded for a loan, but a provisional agreement was reached by which they turned over £5 million in gold and foreign currencies for an immediate supply of fats and condensed milk. In the afternoon, another conference of which Keynes was not a part arranged for the exchange of the German mercantile marine for the badly needed food.

On his return to Paris, Keynes found that there was still no provision for the finance of the German food imports, nor had steps been taken for the surrender of the German ships. Another conference was called for, and again at this meeting the Germans dallied on the transfer of the ships, asked for a loan, and when this was refused, stated flatly that they would not deliver the ships. They foresaw the collapse of their economy and the flooding of Bolshevikism over the whole of Europe.

Meanwhile, as time passed and Germany's food organization approached breakdown, a third conference was arranged for Spa, a fashionable watering place on the frontier of Belgium, formerly the grand headquarters of the German army. In a setting that reminded Keynes of nothing so much as third-rate Wagnerian opera, the conferees again reached a stalemate. General Haking, the British representative on the armistice commission who had the best information on economic conditions in Germany, was issuing dark and convincing reports on the imminent collapse of organization in that country unless the physical privation ended. Two months had passed since Treves—it was now the middle of March—and a rupture between the negotiators seemed to be in sight. Keynes was in a state of despair, as he looked across the table at Melchior who reminded him again of "an honorable animal in pain." As they drifted despondently out toward the cloakroom, he whispered to Rear Admiral Hope who was the presiding officer, "May I speak to Melchior privately? It seems the only possible chance of getting on." "Do what you like," Hope answered.

Quivering with excitement, Keynes managed to get Melchior to a private room where he insisted that the Germans must make up their minds to handing over the ships and urged him to secure from Weimar some discretion to act, and that the British, in turn, would find a formula to allow the food supplies to move and thus evade the obstruction of the French. "I allowed that our recent actions had not been such as to lead them to trust our sincerity, but I begged him to believe that I, at least, at that moment was sincere and truthful. He was as much moved as I was, and I think he believed me. We both stood all through the interview. In a sort of way I was in love with him."

This last sentence has both fascinated and puzzled many readers in the past. What did it mean? What did those who were present at the reading at the Memoir Club back in 1931 take it to mean? The only one of the Bloomsberries to record her impression was Virginia Woolf; in her diary she quoted Keynes as saying, "I was rather in love with him," and then added, "I think he meant it seriously, though we laughed."

Woolf's comment may be said to represent the homosexual interpretation of Keynes's behavior; he was having a flirtation with Melchior similar to those which he had had with other males in the past. The difference here was that he was being amorous toward a representative of a government with whom Britain and her allies were only recently at war. In all probability, this "escapade" with Melchior, as Keynes refers to it in this essay, was platonic in nature, although some have speculated that his "love" for the banker may have influenced him in espousing the German cause then and later.

An alternative explanation would emphasize not the homosexual element so much as Keynes's humanitarian concern for the underdog. In this view he represented the outlook of those Britons who were critical of the war or were conscientious objectors. Now that it was over they would reject the balance of power concept, which in their minds led to the conflict, and stand up in a moralistic way for the defeated. In terms of his psychic makeup, Keynes was peculiarly suited for this role because of his dual consciousness which led him to feel keenly for the weak. In his conscious mind he could appreciate Melchior's overt attributes—his truthfulness, his neatness, his integrity—but added to these were his other characteristics: "the honest animal at bay," the "honorable animal in pain," the Jew, the outsider which registered unconsciously and reinforced the other impressions. Indeed, his sympathetic evocation of the figure of Melchior was so powerful that it has been seen as the classic description of "the good German."

In any case, Keynes's friendship for Melchior paid off, but not immediately. The German authorities at Weimar to whom the latter appealed still vacillated, so Keynes urged that a dramatic step be taken to break off the conference and in that way bring the food crisis to the attention of the "Great Ones" in Paris (Lloyd George, Wilson, Clemenceau, and the others who were conferring on other features of the treaty in that city). In line with this strategy, the British and the Americans, to the consternation of the French, abruptly left Spa in the early hours of the morning of March 5 for Paris.

In the capital, Keynes persuaded Lloyd George to oppose the French strenuously on their refusal to allow Reichsbank gold to be used for the food supplies. Clemenceau argued that the Germans should work for their food, and Keynes archly noted that "this demand, the old atheist oddly added, would be found to be in agreement with the teachings of Christianity." Next, it was M. L. L. Klotz, the French finance minister, who most obstinately insisted that the German gold should be saved for the payment of reparations. Keynes gave a characteristic, thumbnail sketch of the man: "a short, plump, heavy-mustached Jew, well groomed, well kept, but with an unsteady, roving eye, and his shoulders a little bent in an instructive deprecation."

Lloyd George, he wrote, "had always hated and despised him; and now he saw in a twinkling that he could kill him. Women and children were starving, he cried, and here was M. Klotz prating and prating of his 'goold.' He leaned forward and with a gesture of his hands indicated to everyone the image of a hideous Jew clutching a money bag. His eyes flashed, and the words came out with a contempt so violent that he seemed to be spitting at him. The anti-Semitism, not far below the surface in such an assemblage as that one, was in the heart of everyone. Everyone looked at Klotz with a momentary contempt and hatred; the poor man was bent over his seat, visibly cowering. We hardly knew what Lloyd George was saying, but the words 'goold' and Klotz were repeated, and each time with exaggerated contempt. Then turning, he called on Clemenceau to put a stop to these obstructive tactics; otherwise, he cried, M. Klotz, would rank with Lenin and Trotsky among those who had spread Bolshevikism in Europe. The prime minister ceased. All around the room you could see each one grinning and whispering to his neighbor, 'Klotzky.'"

Lloyd George's speech ended the matter, for the Americans agreed with him, as did the Italians; the gold was to be used after all. But the French later demanded that the Germans make an unqualified statement about the surrender of the ships before the food would move. Keynes again saw Melchior privately and got his assurance in advance that the Germans would comply; and so the problem was settled, and the food trains started to roll.

Keynes saw Melchior several times more before he left Paris. The last occasion on which he was with him alone, he said, was in October 1919, when he was invited to visit Amsterdam. He then realized for the first time that for Melchior the war had been against Russia; the Jewish banker was obsessed with the "dark forces" that might issue from the East. Keynes said he understood now what a precisian he was, "a strict and upright moralist, a worshiper of the Tablets of the Law, a Rabbi." What shocked him was the decay of honorable behavior on the part of the Germans and the insincere acceptance by the allies of "impossible conditions which it was not intended to carry out; it was these offenses against the Word which so much wounded him."

The economic disruption caused by the war and the blockade of the Central Powers had caused widespread want and starvation, with the consequence that at the close of hostilities food had to be found for Austria as well as Germany. Keynes had taken the initiative on this matter in the Supreme Economic Council in arranging a joint loan for famine relief early in 1919. Sir William Goode, the British director of relief, stated in a report at the time that "without his [Keynes's] resourceful vision of an England humane although victorious, it would have been almost impossible to carry out the finances in connection with British relief."

In his preparatory work for the peace conference, Keynes had proposed an all-around cancellation of inter-allied debt. In March 1919, he revived his memorandum on that subject, adding a credit rehabilitation scheme, and submitted it to the new chancellor of the exchequer, Austen Chamberlain. In this document he expressed skepticism that intercountry debts were really sound, even though bankers in analogy to private debts believed them to be "a necessary part of the permanent order of society." In contrast, he predicted that none of "these tributes will continue to be paid, at the best, for more than a very few years. They do not square with human nature or march with the spirit of the age."

The Americans in Paris did not think much of the idea of canceling the inter-ally debts, so Keynes quickly formulated a new, imaginative plan, the joint guarantee of reparation bonds, or as he termed it in a letter to his mother, *a grand scheme for the rehabilitation of Europe.* Chamberlain enthusiastically commended the idea in a letter to Lloyd George, saying that it was "marked by all of Mr. Keynes's characteristic ability and facility of resource." In an explanatory memorandum which was submitted to the American, French, and Italian heads of state, written by Keynes, he contended that the economic mechanism of Europe was "jammed" and that the problem of restoring the continent economically was too great for private enterprise alone—the risks were too heavy, the amounts of credit required too big, and the terms too long. Under this farsighted scheme, which was akin to the Marshall Plan, the Central European governments would issue bonds, mostly German securities, to the value of £1,000 million. These bonds would be backed by reparations, and they would be guaranteed by the Allied powers in stipulated proportions, Britain and the United States each guaranteeing twenty percent of the bond issue.

Lloyd George sent the proposal to President Wilson, but the latter rejected it, contending that the authority was lacking under the Constitution to guarantee bonds of European origin; furthermore, he inquired, why should the United States be expected to turn over new working capital to Germany to replace that which the European nations had taken from her? The stands of Hughes, Cunliffe, and Sumner on the reparations commission had alienated the Americans so much that they now refused to aid in the reconstruction of Europe.

Keynes was horrified by the president's rejection of his plan. In a letter to Philip Kerr, Lloyd George's secretary, while conceding that there was substantial truth in the American point of view, he averred that the president's reply "indicates a spirit far too harsh for the human situation facing us. In particular, it is surely impossible for the Americans to disclaim responsibility for the peace treaty to which, wisely or not, they have put their names equally with other governments."

During April, the financial clauses of the treaty were being approved by the Supreme Economic Council in Lloyd George's flat and at President Wilson's house in Paris; Keynes was frequently present at these meetings, but he could not do anything to modify their nature. When the draft treaty of peace became available, he expressed the view that the reparation chapter showed "a high degree of unwisdom in almost every direction." The members of the American delegation, he believed, after fighting the preposterous demands for reparations by Britain and France week after week, were so frustrated that their sympathies were now much more with Germany than with any of the allies. He concluded that the conference "has led us into a bog which it will take more statesmanship to lead us out of than it has taken adroitness to lead us in." His letter to his mother showed his state of desperation: "It must be weeks since I've written a letter to anyone— but I've been utterly worn out, partly by work, partly by depression at the evil around me. I've never been so miserable as for the last two or three weeks; the peace is outrageous and impossible and can bring nothing but misfortune behind it. Personally I do not believe that the Germans will sign, though the general view is to the contrary (i.e., that after a few moans and complaints they will sign anything). ... Certainly if I was in the Germans' place, I'd rather die than sign such a peace."

Two weeks later, in a letter to Austen Chamberlain concerning his possible resignation, he said that if he could be of any real use, he was willing to stay another two or three weeks, but his disgust with the whole prospect was very evident: "The prime minister is leading us all into a morass of destruction. The settlement which he is proposing for Europe disrupts it economically and must depopulate it by millions of persons. The new states we are setting up cannot survive in such surroundings. How can you expect me to assist at this tragic farce any longer, seeking to lay the foundations, as a Frenchman put it, *'d'une guerre juste* and *durable'*?"

One of the most respected participants at the peace conference was Field Marshal Jan Christiaan Smuts, the prime minister of the Union of South Africa. He had served on the Austrian reparation commission, but when the draft reparation treaty for that country became public, he resigned from the body and stated that the imposition of reparations on "a broken, bankrupt, economically impossible state like Austria, or a new friendly allied state like Czechoslovakia ... seems to me a hopeless policy, which could only lead to the most mischievous results."

Keynes's similar reaction to the Austrian reparation provisions was expressed in a letter to Sir Maurice Hankey, secretary of the War Cabinet. His exasperation manifested itself in his characterization of the whole proceeding as "pure humbug"; he felt that the entire document was purely an academic effort which ignored the actual appalling condition of Austria, where many people were without food, clothes, coal, or employment. He alleged that "one-third of the children of Vienna now remain constantly indoors as they are naked." In the light of such conditions, the draft reparation chapter appeared to him to be "a frivolous and unreal document."

By the end of May, Keynes was alerting his superior, Sir John Bradbury, to his imminent separation from the delegation, saying, "At any rate I am so sick at what goes on that I am near the breaking point, and you must be prepared for my resignation by telegram at any moment."

Indeed, on the very day that he wrote this letter he became completely exhausted and retired to bed. But within a few days he rallied and rose to write a new memorandum for Lloyd George; it was to be his "last try." This proposal gave Germany the whole task of physically restoring France and Belgium, and would set a sum in the treaty for all other forms of damage; he estimated that the aggregate claim against Germany might be £6 300 million. The further details of the idea are of no consequence. The prime minister had asked Cunliffe and Sumner, whom Norman Davis had dubbed "the heavenly twins," for a memorandum also, and then adopted neither. The "jig" was up. Three days later, Keynes wrote Lloyd George: "I ought to let you know that on Saturday I am slipping away from this scene of nightmare. I can do no more good here. . . . The battle is lost. I leave the twins to gloat over the devastation of Europe and to assess to taste what remains for the British taxpayer."

Keynes's disappointment and exhaustion were very deep and real. He wrote his mother, explaining his condition as follows: "Partly out of my misery for all that's happening, and partly from prolonged over-work, I gave way last Friday and took to my bed, suffering from sheer nervous exhaustion. There I've remained ever since, rising only for really important interviews and for a daily stroll in the Bois, with the result that I'm already much better." In another letter two days later, he told her that he was living alone in a flat and that he was so much better that his extreme prudence kept him secluded at all. "But I distinctly looked over the edge last week and, not liking the prospect at all, took to my bed instantly." It is generally believed that Keynes on that occasion was on the edge of a nervous breakdown. In that same letter he went on, "The P. M. [prime minister], poor man, would like now at the eleventh hour to alter the damned treaty, for which no one has a word of defense, but it's too late in my belief, and for all his wrigglings Fate must now march on to its conclusion."

In another letter to Norman Davis, his "opposite number" from the United States Treasury, a few days later, he said, "I can do no more good here. You Americans are broken reeds, and I have no anticipation of any real improvement in the state of affairs." While Keynes soon thereafter left Paris, he was not yet finished with that "damned treaty."

In his participation at the conference he had brought intense feeling as well as his finely honed intellect to bear on the numerous, complex issues with which he dealt. He was able to imagine and feel what the legalistic phraseology of the treaty would mean for the people of the world more so than some of the heterosexual politicians and officials. He could be very objective intellectually, but at the same time highly involved emotionally. It is indicative of his attitude that at one point in his Dr. Melchior memoir, when he was describing the debate over food for the Germans (this was years after the event, of course), he complained that "there was no passion in the proceedings—debating points, technical objections, the whole issue was niggled away." Harrod, too, in deploring the fact that Keynes was not on the reparations commission, remarks, "He would have been at the top of his bent, keyed up by his *passionate intellectual* contempt for the trash of Hughes and Cunliffe, and from far away, from some remote recesses of his being, would have come the distant but distinct voices of Duncan and the others—'Go on ... go on ,,, remember your pledge, remember all that we hold dear and all that you hold dear is at stake, and that decent livings for many generations will depend on how you state this case.'"

Though he was not a member of the most important commissions at the peace conference, Keynes had several substantial accomplishments to his credit, apart from the advice and memoranda that he gave to the various officials. First, he had been influential in securing agreement on reasonable terms for feeding Germany. Second, when the conference became bogged down on the amount of reparations to be demanded of the defeated nation, it was his suggestion that the exact sum be left undetermined. The amount could be fixed by an inter-Allied commission and take account of what Germany should pay over thirty years; this solution was the one ultimately adopted in the final version of the treaty. He had several setbacks, also; he was deeply chagrined over President Wilson's rejection of his scheme for the economic reconstruction of Europe. He expressed his feelings on this matter quite explicitly to Duncan Grant: "One most bitter disappointment was the collapse of my scheme for putting everyone on their legs. After getting it successfully through the chancellor of the exchequer, and the prime minister and seeing it handed to Wilson and Clemenceau, the American Treasury (from whom no more was asked than any one else) turns it down formally as a most immoral proposal which might cost them something and which senators from Illinois would not look at. They had a chance of taking a large, or at least a humane, view of the world, but unhesitatingly refused it. Wilson, of whom I have seen a good deal more lately, is the greatest fraud on earth." In this letter and in the one previously quoted to Phillip Kerr, one can see some of the elements and feelings which influenced Keynes's portrait of the president in *The Economic Consequences of the Peace*.

Upon his resignation from his position as representative of the British Treasury at the peace conference on June 7, 1919, Keynes had returned immediately to London. From there he wrote General Smuts, with whom he had been closely associated in the latter months of the negotiations, and expressed the hope that he "would feel one ought to do something about what was happening at Paris—revelation, protestation." In his answer, Smuts advised him to write "a clear connected account of what the financial and economic clauses of the treaty are and mean, and what their probable results will be." It should not, the general added, be too long or technical, "as we may want to appeal to the plain man more than to the well-informed or the specialist."

Keynes was not alone among the experts and officials at Paris who were dismayed at the terms of the treaty. The late President Hoover was convinced that peace could not be built on its foundations. He was so disturbed that he arose early on the morning of May 7, 1919, upon receiving a copy of the treaty at 4:00 A. M., and went for a walk in the deserted streets of Paris.

Within a few blocks I met General Smuts and John Maynard Keynes of the British delegation. We seemed to have come together by some sort of telepathy. It flashed into all our minds why each was walking about at that time of morning. Each was greatly disturbed. We agreed that the consequences of many parts of the proposed treaty would ultimately bring destruction. We also agreed that we would do what we could among our own nationals to point out the dangers.

General Smuts had full knowledge of Old War diplomacy, an independent mind and real statesmanship. Keynes was the economist for the British delegation. Lloyd George apparently did not like him and referred to him as the "Puck of Economics." He had a brilliant mind, powerful in analysis, and the gift of expression. Like most intellectuals, he was usually groping for new shapes and forms for the world, rather than for wisdom in what to do next. That sort of mind has a high place in the world, although it sometimes gets on the nerves of the fellow who must keep the machinery of civilization operating in the meantime. However, Keynes and I agreed fully on the economic consequences of the treaty.

Apparently Keynes began writing a book such as he had discussed with Smuts in the latter part of June, but he did not get down to serious work on it until August. In the meanwhile, he enjoyed the end of the social season in London, attending "a rather amusing party" at the Asquiths at which he won handsomely at bridge; played host to a large dinner party of his own at Gordon Square; attended the ballet; "kept various business appointments; gave evidence before the Indian currency committee; addressed the Fight the Famine Council; opened a discussion on the peace terms at a city dining club; and lunched and dined out every day"—after which he was quite ready for the country. He remarked, "It's amusing to pass from Cambridge, where I'm a nonentity, to London, where I'm a celebrity."

He settled down to a regular routine at Charleston, the new home of Vanessa Bell, where after breakfast at eight he would devote the morning to writing. In two months he composed a classic denunciation of the treaty, creating, as Harrod said, "a great masterpiece" in "a white heat of passion." Though he had most of the facts of the subject at his fingertips, he did not seek to write a definitive history of the peace conference; it was designed rather as a polemic—as Harrod rightly said, "one of the finest pieces of polemic in the English language." If before he had been a celebrity in London, after its publication he became world-famous. "Perhaps," as his most able critic was later to remark, "only Edmund Burke's *Reflections on the Revolution in France* may be said to have wielded over the destinies of Europe such a widespread and immediate influence."

Harrod, in writing of Keynes's book, comments that it has an "artistic unity," but he does not identify the elements of that quality. From a psychological standpoint, it truly possesses that characteristic because it combines reason and imagination, logic and sympathy, and thus reflects the dual nature of its author. One of the most relevant commentaries on the motivation behind the volume was made by Keynes's close friend, David Garnett, in his autobiography. He recounted Maynard's differences with his Bloomsbury intimates over the war and stated his opinion that the latter's skeptical attitude toward him at that time was "a factor of critical importance" in his career. "It was because his friends kept him aware of the danger that he might, for the sake of a brilliant official career, be a party to bringing about terrible evils, that he finally took the course he did in resigning his post rather than accept the reparation clauses of the treaty. That resignation led to the writing of *The Economic Consequences of the Peace,* which was the foundation of his subsequent fame.

"The habit of going beneath surface appearances, of analyzing and detecting far-reaching consequences, was native to his mind. But the criticism of his most intimate friends encouraged him to criticize and justify the work that he was doing during the war and made his ultimate resignation necessary for his own peace of mind."

The book itself, with its numerous classical allusions, gives the reader a sense of an appraisal of the tangled political scene from a great height of authority and judiciousness. In its introduction, Keynes stated that at Paris he had become "a European in his cares and outlook"; he was concerned with the organic unity of the European economy, and persuasively and graphically demonstrated the delicate and fragile nature of its economic organization. He singled out for emphasis several factors of instability—"the instability of an excessive population dependent for its livelihood on a complicated and artificial organization, the psychological instability of the laboring and capitalist classes, and the instability of Europe's claim, coupled with the completeness of her dependence, on the food supplies of the New World." This sketch of the economic peculiarities of Europe on the eve of the Great War was clearly and masterfully done. Its emphasis on the fragility of the European economy reflected a view which his master, Alfred Marshall, had frequently expressed about British society.

Keynes's assessment of the psychology of European society is particularly interesting because it foreshadowed his later ideas. He described a Europe that was organized socially and economically as to secure the maximum accumulation of capital. Nineteenth-century society, he contended, was framed "to throw a great part of the increased income into the control of the class least likely to consume it. . . . Thus, this remarkable system depended for its growth on a double bluff or deception. On the one hand, the laboring classes accepted from ignorance or powerlessness, or were compelled, persuaded, or cajoled by custom, convention, authority and the well-established order of society into accepting, a situation in which they could call their own very little of the cake that they and nature and the capitalists were cooperating to produce. And on the other hand, the capitalist classes were allowed to call the best part of the cake theirs and were theoretically free to consume it, on the tacit underlying condition that they consumed very little of it in practice. The duty of saving became nine-tenths of virtue and the growth of the cake the object of true religion." Keynes asserted that in this description he was not necessarily disparaging the practices of that generation. "In the unconscious recesses of its being, society knew what it was about." He remarked further that "the principle of accumulation based on inequality was a vital part of the prewar order of society and of progress as we understood it" and then emphasized that this principle depended upon unstable psychological conditions, "which it may be impossible to re-create." This whole passage contains a vision of the economic process that later was to emerge in his writing as the fallacy of oversaving.

Professor Hans Jensen has acutely pointed out that Keynes's image or "vision" of European society was considerably influenced by Alfred Marshall's conceptualized version of social reality. In the latter's *Principles of Economics,* which Keynes had thoroughly mastered, the national income was pictured as being produced by four factors of production: land, labor, capital, and entrepreneurship. In *The Economic Consequences of the Peace,* the social structure is composed of three recognizable counterparts of Marshall's world: a rentier class of investors who own, but do not manage; an active class of business entrepreneurs who manage but do not own much enterprise; and a class of wage earners. Anticipating the theme of his magnum opus, *The General Theory,* Keynes bluntly voiced the value judgment in this polemic that "it was not natural for a population, of whom so few enjoyed the comforts of life, to accumulate so hugely." Then he closed his tract by stating ominously that "the war has disclosed the possibilities of consumption to all and the vanity of abstinence to many. Thus, the bluff is discovered, the laboring classes may no longer be willing to forego so largely, and the capitalist classes, no longer confident of the future, may seek to enjoy more fully their liberties of consumption so long as they last, and thus precipitate the hour of their confiscation."

From his presentation of the postwar situation it is clear that in Keynes's mind the task of the peace conference was not only to honor the terms of the armistice and to do justice, but also to reestablish the economic life and to heal the wounds of Europe. His largely unexamined premise, as Harrod shrewdly pointed out, was that "these tasks were dictated as much by prudence as by magnanimity which the wisdom of antiquity approved in victors." Whether that criterion, based as it was on precedents from ancient history, was the proper one will require further examination.

In another chapter of the work, Keynes also described the personalities of the Council of Four, justifying such an assessment by stating that the world needed light, "even if it is partial and uncertain," on the complex struggle of human will and purpose, which was concentrated in these four individuals almost as "the microcosm of mankind."

The remarkable portraits, etched in acid, of the chief peacemakers revealed his penetration as a psychologist as well as his skill as a biographer. His eye for every significant detail, his wit, and his mastery of the art of writing made some of his sketches superior even to those of Lytton Strachey, in the opinion of the writer David Garnett. His focusing on the consciousness of the Big Three, on how they perceived the world, have given us almost indelible impressions of these men. (He omitted the Italian prime minister, Vittorio Emanuele Orlando, presumably because of his lesser role in the negotiations.)

He insisted at the outset that "insofar as the main economic lines of the treaty represent an intellectual idea, it is the idea of France and of Clemenceau." He said of the latter that one could not despise or dislike him, but "only take a different view as to the nature of civilized man, or indulge, at least, a different hope." While this sentence conveys to the reader a sense of Keynes's fairness and impartiality, it embodied his own perception of the European realities and certainly doesn't do justice to Clemenceau's. Then he painted an unforgettable picture of the French statesman by saying that "he wore a square-tailed coat of a very good, thick black broadcloth, and on his hands, which were never uncovered, gray suede gloves; his boots were of thick black leather, very good but of a country style, and sometimes fastened in the front, curiously, by a buckle instead of laces." He sat on "a square, brocaded chair in the middle of the semicircle facing the fireplace, and the prime minister opposite on the other side of the fireplace on his right." As Garnett rightly says, this sketch of the physical Clemenceau has "the solidity of a portrait by Ingres."

Next, he presented a critical vignette of the man and his policy: "He felt about France what Pericles felt about Athens—unique value in her, nothing else mattering" (the Greek leader was famous for his determination to make Athens supreme among the Greek cities); "but his theory of politics was Bismarck's." In other words, Clemenceau, like the Iron Chancellor, was a believer in power politics and nationalistic strength. But, continued Keynes, "he had one illusion—France; and one disillusion—mankind, including Frenchmen, and his colleagues not the least." France's demand for a Carthaginian peace, Keynes wrote, "is the policy of an old man, whose most vivid impressions and most lively imagination are of the past and not of the future. He sees the issue in terms of France and Germany, not of humanity and of European civilization struggling forwards to a new order. The war has bitten into his consciousness somewhat differently from ours, and he neither expects nor hopes that we are at the threshold of a new age." This passage is an amazing revelation of the gulf in the perception of the two men, between the cold realism of the older man and the idealism of the younger one who was envisaging, rather prematurely, a European economic community in 1919!

Keynes's portrait of President Wilson was equally sharp and provocative and no less controversial. He said of him that "the great distinction of language which marked his famous Notes seemed to indicate a man of lofty and powerful imagination. His head and features were finely cut and exactly like his photographs, and the muscles of his neck and the carriage of his head were distinguished. But, like Odysseus, the President looked wiser when he was seated; and his hands, though capable and fairly strong, were wanting in sensitiveness and finesse." Garnett states that Lytton Strachey persuaded Keynes to keep this reference to the President's hands. The latter went on to assert that

Wilson did not have "much even of that culture of the world which marks M. Clemenceau and Mr. Balfour as exquisitely cultivated gentlemen of their class and generation." The President seemed to Keynes to be insensitive to his environment and therefore to be like "a blind and deaf Don Quixote" in his encounters with the telepathic instincts and skills of Lloyd George. In temperament, the President seemed to him most like "a nonconformist minister, perhaps a Presbyterian. His thought and his temperament were essentially theological, not intellectual, with all the strength and weakness of that manner of thought, feeling, and expression." His mind, it seemed to the younger man, was slow and unadaptable, and he was liable, therefore, to be outwitted by "the mere swiftness, apprehension, and agility of a Lloyd George."

Keynes's comment that the President seemed like a Presbyterian minister was close to the mark. He was, in fact, the son of one, and he had almost as many clergymen in his family background as Keynes; Wilson once remarked himself that he was frequently taken for a man of the cloth. On the other hand, the disparagement of the President's culture seems to reflect Keynes's anti-American bias because Wilson, it is generally agreed, was a man of considerable learning. Further, at least one reputable scholar holds that the image which Keynes presented of the President as a visionary Don Quixote was one which served in a way as scapegoat for those English liberals and radicals who had placed such hope in his coming to Europe and now, faced with their own frustrations and failures at the conference, found their hero was a figure of clay.

At the suggestion of friends, Keynes had also drawn a portrait of the British prime minister, but he was not satisfied with it, and because of his closeness to him during some phases of the negotiations, he did not include it in his book out of "certain compunction." It was published fourteen years later in his *Essays in Biography*. It was fortunate that he showed some sense of discretion in this matter—one can almost visualize Wales seceding from Great Britain over the Keynesian insults to her favored son, if he had brought it out in the postwar period of inflamed emotions. Though some Americans were very annoyed by Keynes's delineation of the President's character, they would have been mollified by his rendering of the prime minister.

In mock modesty, Keynes wrote that he did not aspire to this task, for "who shall paint the chameleon, who can tether a broomstick?" He summed up the peace conference by saying, "The President, the tiger, and the Welsh witch were shut up in a room together for six months, and the treaty was what came out. Yes, the Welsh *witch*—for the British prime minister contributed the female element to this triangular intrigue. I have called Mr. Wilson a nonconformist clergyman. Let the reader figure Mr. Lloyd George as a *femme fatale*. An old man of the world, a *femme fatale,* and a nonconformist clergyman—these are the characters of our drama. Even though the lady was very religious at times, the Fourteen Commandments could hardly expect to emerge perfectly intact." (The allusion was, of course, to President Wilson's famous Fourteen Points.) The outrageous satire and sexual innuendo of this passage describing a "triangular intrigue"—the latter was a term used in reference to homosexual affairs—could only be written by one intent on shocking or titillating heterosexual sensibilities.

In Keynes's view, Lloyd George's good qualities, such as his industry, were offset by his lack of "a policy grounded in permanent principle, tenacity, fierce indignation, honesty, loyal leadership." With the British jingoes and the Northcliffe papers at his heels, the Welshman took the political course of a middle path, the path of compromise. So it became his role "to explain the president to Clemenceau and Clemenceau to the president and to seduce everybody all around. . . . The president's very masculine characteristics fell a complete victim to the feminine enticements, sharpness, quickness, sympathy of the prime minister."

Keynes knew that Lloyd George was very different from his political contemporaries. He had become known as "the Welsh Wizard" because he was thought to have almost supernatural political gifts—the ability to read the minds of those with whom he was conversing or to hold an audience spellbound by his oratory. The epithet, we are told, was probably first admiring, but in time became derogatory. "His quickness, flexibility, and resourcefulness were taken for dishonesty, insincerity, and lack of principle. His self-confidence, his reputation for amorous adventure, and his lack of personal inhibitions made him appear to more conventional contemporaries to be not just immoral but beyond morality. Agility and sexuality combined with his shaggy white hair to lend him the derisive nickname, 'the Goat.'"

Keynes took this image of Lloyd George to its extreme in his essay: "How can I convey to the reader who does not know him any just expression of this extraordinary figure of our time, this siren, this goat-footed bard, this half-human visitor to our age from the hag-ridden magic and enchanted woods of Celtic antiquity? One catches in his company that flavor of final purposelessness, inner irresponsibility, existence outside or away from our Saxon good and evil, mixed with cunning, remorselessness, love of power, that lend fascination, enthralment, and terror to the fair-seeming magicians of North American folklore. . . .

"Lloyd George is rooted in nothing: He is void and without content; he lives and feeds on his immediate surroundings; he is an instrument and a player at the same time, which plays on the company and is played on by them too; he is a prism, as I have heard him described, which collects light and distorts it and is most brilliant if the light comes from many quarters at once; a vampire and a medium in one."

This extravagant profile of the British statesman was written by Keynes when he was the personal friend and follower of the Asquiths, who could not abide Lloyd George. It is instructive, too, to read Keynes's sketch of the personality of Lord Oxford (Herbert Asquith) which portrays him as a cultured gentleman and scholar, "a wise and tolerant umpire," supremely gifted for the positions which he held and for which "there has been no man in this century by any means his equal." Despite this lavish encomium, Keynes was to be reconciled with the more creative Lloyd George in the late twenties in his effort at industrial reconstruction (the Liberal Industrial Inquiry) and break politically with Asquith. When asked in 1929 whether his opinion of Lloyd George's character had changed since he wrote *The Economic Consequences of the Peace,* Keynes replied, "The difference between me and some other people is that I oppose Mr. Lloyd George when he is wrong and support him when he is right." However, when the *Essays in Biography* appeared in 1933 with its harsh portrait of Lloyd George, the latter strongly attacked Keynes in the second volume of his *War Memoirs,* which was published in the fall of that year.

But, to return to more substantive issues at stake in the treaty, what were the causes of the failure at Paris? In Keynes's opinion the explanation was to be found in the fact that President Wilson was undone when there "began the weaving of that web of sophistry and jesuitical exegesis that was finally to clothe with insincerity the language and substance of the whole treaty." Jesuitical sophistry was a favorite Keynesian *bête noir.* Hypocrisy, too, was anathema to his nonconformist morality and particularly rankling perhaps to a homosexual in a heterosexual society. What was most intolerable to him was that "the honest and intelligible purpose of French policy, to limit the population of Germany and weaken her economic system," was "clothed, for the President's sake, in the august language of freedom and international equality." He then went on to argue that once the President had been entangled in such inconsistent sophistry, his self-image was at stake. "In the language of medical psychology, to suggest to the President that the treaty was an abandonment of his professions was to touch on the raw a Freudian complex. It was a subject intolerable to discuss, and every subconscious instinct plotted to defeat its further exploration."

Keynes, as we see here and elsewhere in his writing, was not reluctant to engage in psychological analysis, and he showed familiarity with Freudian terminology, as one would expect given his Bloomsbury background and his friendships with the Stracheys. (James and Alix Strachey, after World War I, went to Vienna and were psychoanalyzed by Freud himself; they became the translators and editors of his collected works in English.) But he could revert to the colloquialisms of everyday conversation just as quickly, as he does in this instance. He writes that Lloyd George, desiring at the last moment to moderate the terms of the treaty, "discovered that he could not in five days persuade the President of error in what it had taken five months to prove to him to be just and right. After all, it was harder to debamboozle this old Presbyterian than it had been to bamboozle him, for the former involved his belief in and respect for himself."

He closed his Lloyd George sketch with this summation of the personalities of Paris: "Clemenceau, aesthetically the noblest; the President, morally the most admirable; Lloyd George, intellectually the subtlest. Out of their disparities and weaknesses, the treaty was born, child of the least worthy attributes of each of its parents, without nobility, without morality, without intellect."

In retrospect, when one considers closely what happened in the preparation of Keynes's tract on the peace treaty, it seems that the omission of the Lloyd George profile in the original had the effect of shifting the onus of blame for the weaknesses of the document to President Wilson. Yet it is clear from the Lloyd George sketch which Keynes wrote later that to him the *femme fatale,* the Welsh witch, was much more to blame for its unsatisfactory nature. It is in this light that there is some support for the interpretation that the President was made a scapegoat, or so it appeared to many readers of *The Economic Consequences of the Peace,* whatever Keynes's intention.

Keynes argued three main theses in his famous book: "the economic unity of Europe; bad faith on our part (i.e., the allies) in the reparation clauses; and demands which were economically and financially impossible." His contentions under these heads will be briefly outlined here, but the reader must refer to the book itself for the full details of the argument.

On the first point he insisted that Germany was "the central support" of the European economic system, and the prosperity of the rest of the continent mainly depended on its prosperity and enterprise. He cited numerous statistics showing the continent's economic interdependence to uphold this key supposition of his analysis.

The allies' bad faith consisted of securing an armistice with Germany on the basis of President Wilson's Fourteen Points and four of his subsequent addresses, and then ignoring the commitments made. With the German acceptance of the President's Note of November 5, 1918, these constituted to Keynes a contract which was plain and unequivocal. In short, the allies were committed to a peace based upon the Fourteen Points and upon the principle that "there shall be no annexations, no contributions, no punitive damages." At the time of the armistice, he stated, no responsible authority among the allies expected any indemnity from Germany beyond reparation for direct material damage resulting from invasion or from the submarine campaign.

But when the allies discovered how hopeless the German position was, the atmosphere changed. In the interim, Lloyd George had participated in the general election of 1918, in which out of political exigency he gradually came out for full indemnity from Germany, even suggesting that she should pay the full cost of the war. Keynes made much of the bad faith and insincerity of the allies in that a war ostensibly waged in defense of the sanctity of international agreements was now being ended by a definite breach in one of the most sacred possible of such engagements.

In general, he deplored the fact that Lloyd George and President Wilson did not apprehend that their most serious problems in peacemaking were not political or territorial, but financial and economic; the perils of the future lay not in frontiers or sovereignties, but in food, coal, and transport. None of them, he stated, paid adequate attention to these problems at any stage of the conference. Their main excursion into that field was reparations, and here the amount demanded of Germany was impractical and uncollectible. He particularly denounced the inclusion in reparations of all the military pensions and separation allowances, which the allies had paid or were to pay, arising out of the war. He estimated these as totalling $25 billion which, when added to his maximum estimate of $15 billion for direct damage, resulted in a total claim against Germany of about $40 billion.

The treaty did not fix a final amount that the defeated nation was to pay, but left its determination to a reparations commission. Keynes argued that the terms of the German liability were altogether beyond her capacity to pay, considering the almost total loss of her colonies, her overseas possessions, her mercantile marine, and her foreign properties. In addition, she had ceded ten percent of her territory and population, about one-third of her coal, and three-quarters of her iron ore; she suffered two million casualties in the war, and her civilians had been subject to practical starvation. Germany could not export sufficient goods, which was the only practical way in which indemnities could be paid; the coal clauses (the treaty provided for reparation to be paid partly in kind instead of cash), providing for about forty million tons annually to be shipped to the Allied countries, were impossible in the light of her loss of Alsace-Lorraine, the Saar Basin, and Upper Silesia. He considered all these and other subjects with as much statistical documentation as possible and concluded on a high moral note that "nations are not authorized, by religion or natural morals, to visit on the children of their enemies the misdoings of parents and rulers."

In the following chapter he painted a pessimistic picture of postwar Europe, stressing the disorganization and decay of its economy, the absolute decline in its internal productivity, the breakdown of its transport and exchange systems, and its inability to purchase supplies from abroad. He graphically described the inflationism of the currency systems of Europe, quoting Lenin to the effect that "the best way to destroy the capitalist system was to debauch the currency." In short, he contended that "an inefficient, unemployed, disorganized Europe faces us, torn by internal strife, fighting, starving, pillaging, and lying." Under such conditions, and he referred here to "the flames of Russian Bolshevism which seem for the moment, at least, to have burnt themselves out," he asked how much is endurable, or in what direction will men "seek at last to escape from their misfortunes."

In his chapter on remedies, he boldly surveyed the European political scene and asserted that escape from the atmosphere and methods of Paris could only be achieved by "replacement of the existing governments of Europe." Analyzing the proposed League of Nations, he correctly surmised that the assembly might become "an unwieldy polyglot debating society," but agreed that the initial efforts to revise the treaty must be made through the league rather than in any other way. His main reliance and hope was that the new governments would show a more profound wisdom and greater magnanimity than their predecessors. He suggested new, more practicable terms of reparation and proposed a free trade union of the European countries, including Great Britain. In vague foreboding, anticipating the Nazi horror, he stated that "if we aim deliberately at the impoverishment of central Europe, vengeance, I dare predict, will not limp. Nothing can delay for very long that final civil war between the forces of reaction and the despairing convulsions of revolution, before which the horrors of the late German war will fade into nothing, and which will destroy whoever is the victor, the civilization and progress of our generation."

More positively, to restore the European economy to a functioning state, he outlined a possible settlement of the inter-Allied indebtedness. Britain should waive her claim for cash payment from Germany in favor of Belgium, Serbia, and France so that priority would be given to repairing the material damage suffered by the countries actually invaded. Then the entire inter-Allied indebtedness, totalling some £4,000 million incurred for the purpose of the war, should be canceled. These "paper shackles," he forcefully insisted, were a menace to financial stability everywhere, and he predicted that "any of these tributes will continue to be paid, at the best, for no more than a very few years."

Next, he proposed an international loan, provided by the neutrals, the United Kingdom, and for a very large part, the United States, perhaps to the amount of £200 million, to furnish foreign credit for all the belligerent countries of Europe, Allied and enemy alike. Thus, they would be able to supply themselves with the minimum food and materials necessary for European reconstruction. In addition, a guarantee fund of £200 million should be established by the members of the League of Nations to permit a general reorganization of European currencies.

In line with his policy of reintegrating Germany into the European economy, he urged that the country should be encouraged and assisted to take her place as a creator and organizer of wealth for her eastern and southern neighbors. He even envisioned that German agents and organizers would be able to "set in train in every Russian village the impulses of ordinary economic motive." At the time no one could anticipate how stable the new Soviet regime would be. Though he conceded that there was little moral solidarity among the races of Europe, there was an economic solidarity, at least potentially, which could not be disregarded. Here he argued quite patently in terms of Britain's own economic interest, stating that "if we do not allow Germany to exchange products with Russia and so feed herself, she must inevitably compete with us for the produce of the New World."

Moving to his peroration, Keynes, in effect, reassured his readers that there was still time "to view the world with new eyes." While for the immediate future the destiny of Europe was at the mercy of hidden currents, which no man could control, the latter could be influenced by "setting in motion those forces of instruction and imagination which change opinion. The assertion of truth, the unveiling of illusion, the dissipation of hate, the enlargement of men's hearts and minds must be the means." With stirring eloquence he closed his book with the sad observation that "never in the lifetime of men now living has the universal element in the soul of man burnt so dimly."

As an essay, Keynes's tract is so brilliant in its dramatic rendering of the principals at the Versailles conference that it is easy to overlook the nature of its composition or forget the background factors which probably contributed to its controversial success. To take the latter first, one needs to go back and follow somewhat the career of his old friend Strachey after he had left Cambridge. Lytton for many years lived a dependent, hypochondriacal life as a sort of hack journalist, without much sign of the recognition which Keynes was achieving in those years. Shortly before the beginning of the Great War he had gotten the idea of writing a series of silhouettes of the Great Victorians, and with encouragement from Virginia Woolf he kept at it. As he composed his famous psychological portraits of Cardinal Manning, Florence Nightingale, Dr. Arnold, and General Gordon, he tried them out on his Bloomsbury friends, and they were generally enthusiastic also. Then, in 1915, he met a young Slade School girl by the name of Dora Carrington, with bright blue eyes and bobbed hair, who so despised herself as a woman that she simply called herself "Carrington," as if she were a man. But Lytton liked her, and she adored him in her strange, neurotic way. Their "love affair" was helped along when Carrington found the Mill house at Tidmarsh near Reading, which Keynes and some of Strachey's other friends helped to acquire with the understanding that they could stay there from time to time.

In May 1918, Strachey with some help from Clive Bell finally published his *Eminent Victorians,* which was such an instant success that it went into seven printings within the year. Almost immediately he was a celebrity, with money, the attention of duchesses, the press, and an adoring mistress. Though there were critics who did not think well of Strachey's new, mocking style of biography, Leon Edel points out that in a sense he was "the first practitioner of 'psychohistory'" in which he used elements of the psychoanalytical method, which even the

Viennese master himself approved, especially in his later books, *Elizabeth and Essex* and *Queen Victoria*.

Strachey's technique in deflating the evangelic humanitarians who he felt were indirectly responsible for World War I involved much irony, skillful use of diaries, and a reduction of masses of dull historical fact into a scintillating paragraph or sentence. He dared to interpret his facts, to spell out their meaning, and soon there were numerous imitators who sought to "debunk" the famous or knock them off their pedestals. David Garnett, who personally knew both Keynes and Strachey, believes that the former's description of Lloyd George definitely shows the influence of his friend's literary style, and it has been noted earlier that Strachey urged Keynes to keep his reference to President Wilson's hands.

The newly available correspondence of Keynes with Duncan Grant suggests that he was not able to dash off his book "in white heat," as Harrod said. In one letter in July 1919 from King's College he said that he was enjoying himself enormously and found his room, books, and solitude very agreeable. "I see the young men very little and have no desire for company whatever. I wonder how long this will last. . . . But writing is very difficult, and I feel more and more admiration for those who can bring it off successfully. I've finished today a sketch of the appearance and character of Clemenceau and am starting tomorrow on Wilson. I think that it is worthwhile to try, but it's really beyond my powers."

Keynes's vignettes of the Big Three, though they have a certain resemblance in tone and treatment to Strachey's longer sketches of his eminent Victorians, were the product of his own peculiar genius. Imagination, as many thinkers such as Schopenhauer and Coleridge recognized, is an essential element of genius, and it is a curious fact, noted by writers from Greek times to today, that some homosexuals or bisexuals have had a high degree of imagination and insight, amounting at times even to the power of prophecy.

What explains this possible relationship between the bisexuality of some men and women and their heightened imaginative powers? The answer may lie in the fact that homosexuals (bisexuals) are "outsiders" or marginals in a predominantly heterosexual society, and some develop a peculiar sensibility and imagination, a sort of bifocal sense of perception, because they are constantly forced to imagine what it is like to be in the shoes of the "normal."

Whatever view one takes of this matter, there can be little doubt of the richness and fertility of Keynes's imagination as it manifested itself, almost excessively, in the form of multiple images of the statesmen at Versailles. President Wilson was described as "a blind and deaf Don Quixote" and as "a nonconformist clergyman"; Lloyd George was portrayed at one and the same time as a chameleon, a broomstick, a Welsh witch, and a *femme fatale*. In another place he appeared as "an instrument and player, a prism, a vampire, and a medium in one." Dr. Rothenberg has stated that this curious use of multiple metaphors may be presumptive evidence that Keynes engaged in "homospatial thinking," which he regards as indicative of creativity.

Keynes's indictment of the statesmen of the Paris conference, with its emphasis on the need for magnanimity on the part of the victors, was not argued at length, yet it is implicit throughout the work. It was obviously a product of his whole upbringing and environment, so much so that any other view was unthinkable. Harrod writes that he was merely reminding his British readers of what was "bred in their bones, and scorned to develop the case further. . . . High-minded Cambridge of the great Victorian era, 'the Society,' the sage thinkers of refined feeling who were his immediate seniors, Whitehead, Trevelyan, Goldie Dickinson, all this world would accept the precept of magnanimity without question. . . . The question is not simply, Was Keynes wrong? but, Were the presuppositions of British civilization, as established during the Victorian period, impracticable in 1919? What was peculiar about Keynes was that he kept his head in the maelstrom and voiced the sentiments of the civilization to which he belonged."

There have been others since, however, who expressed the view that there were serious defects in this moral outlook as applied to international affairs. Etienne Mantoux, that arch-Keynesian critic, challenged it forthrightly in his *The Carthaginian Peace* and more recently, Corelli Barnett has presented a much more powerful critique. He holds that British evangelicism and nonconformity contributed to a romantic idealism and evangelical morality which was then "exported" into international relations. The British "forgot that no other nation—except perhaps America—had shared their own transforming religious experience, and that therefore no other nation now shared their world outlook. And so, in applying the qualities of gentleness, trustfulness, altruism, and strict regard for moral conduct to a sphere of human activity where cunning, cynicism, opportunism, trickery, and force, all in the service of national self-interest still held sway, the twentieth-century British stood disarmed and blinded by their own virtues." Further, he alleges that in "the very shortcomings of Keynes's book—its sentimentality, its moral indignation, its sense of guilt, its lack of strategic comprehension" lay "its particular appeal and guaranteed its immense, far-reaching, and catastrophic success."

How valid are these sweeping charges? It is true that Keynes's tract, though it was entitled *The Economic Consequences of the Peace* and insisted that food, coal, and transport were more important than the frontiers and sovereignties to which the statesmen were devoting so much of their attention, had little analysis of the French concern about military security. Keynes dealt only obliquely with that issue by asserting that France's demand for a Carthaginian peace was the policy of an old man, concerned with the past rather than the future. Yet Winston Churchill was to write later that French security was "the root problem of the peace conference" and that while Keynes's "qualifications to speak on the economic aspect were indisputable ... on the other and vastly more important side of the problem he could judge no better than many others." Like President Wilson and other idealists, Keynes rejected the idea of the balance of power and looked to the League of Nations to provide collective security. He was very vulnerable to criticism on this matter; even Harrod admits that he did not do justice to the problem of French security, adding that his failure to apply his mind to this key problem was "a fault."

Keynes's controversial work appeared in magazine form in the United States even before it was published as a book. He had met Walter Lippmann, the brilliant young staff writer of the *New Republic,* in Paris, and the American later urged him to let his journal publish parts of the volume in serial form. Keynes agreed to do this, though in a letter to Felix Frankfurter he made it clear that he did not wish his manuscript to be used as part of a campaign against the League of Nations. "I am as much in favor of this [the League] even in its present, vicious form as I am against the rest of the treaty. . . . But I should not like my ms. to be used as part of a campaign against the League. If the N. R. [*New Republic*] is taking this line, I should prefer not to publish with them anticipatory installments." The objection overcome, that periodical published the first of three installments of *The Economic Consequences of the Peace* at Christmas 1919, and it had an extraordinary impact on public opinion. Soon Keynes's malicious characterizations of the peacemakers were being quoted widely, even in the United States Senate.

As to the book itself, Keynes had arranged for its publication by Macmillan. He was so sure that it would sell and so anxious to secure a wide circulation that after a discussion with the officers of the firm it was agreed that he would take the risk of publication himself and pay all the costs, giving Macmillan a royalty of ten percent. Again, being creative, he reversed the usual publishing agreement and assumed the risk himself. In assuming it, he undoubtedly expected that he would improve his chances of much higher profits, but as it turned out, he was disappointed in this. The book was printed by an Edinburgh firm, and in coming from that city to London by sea, it encountered misfortune. The ship carrying it was wrecked, and two thousand copies were jettisoned. Amazingly enough, however, the book's sheets were not damaged so much by the water; when they finally reached land on the coast of Denmark, they were sold at public auction in that country.

Professor Frankfurter of the Harvard Law School had become acquainted with Keynes at the peace conference, and he arranged for the book's American publication by Harcourt, Brace, and Howe. (Lippmann, in fact, had first suggested the firm to Keynes and he, in turn, urged Lytton Strachey to use it; through the latter, Harcourt, Brace secured most of the Bloomsbury authors, the novels of Virginia Woolf being the most lucrative sellers.) After the first reviews in Great Britain and the United States, the sales of the volume made publishing history. In these two countries alone, more than 60,000 copies were sold in the first two months, more than two-thirds of these being in the United States. In the United Kingdom, the Labor party sponsored a special cheap edition of 10,000 copies for members of the trade unions and the cooperative societies. Translations were quickly made into German, French, Dutch, Flemish, Danish, Swedish, Italian, Spanish, Rumanian, Russian, Japanese, and Chinese. In short, Keynes's classic essay was literally read all over the world; by 1924, by one estimate, its sales totalled some 140,000 copies. The book ws debated, mentioned in popular sermons and in public legislatures, and its themes discussed by international organizations of all sorts. Keynes received numerous congratulatory messages from famous persons as well as equally enthusiastic ones from persons in every walk of life.

Upon its publication he had sent many presentation copies of the book to officials, friends, and members of his family. His friends were delighted with its brilliance and savored the personality sketches particularly. On the other hand, opinion among high officials who had been in Paris or who were "in the know" generally was mixed. While Austen Chamberlain, then a member of Parliament, enjoyed the lampooning of the President, he regretted that Keynes felt the need to criticize his country's part in the peace negotiations and felt that the imputation of bad faith to the Allied negotiators over the Fourteen

Points was unnecessary; further, he would have omitted the moral denunciations. Lord Reading was also in despair about the possible harm the book would do in America, but Sir Robert Chalmers and Reginald McKenna had no such fears. A copy was shown to Lloyd George, and while parts of it "made him wild," on the whole he liked it because "it showed he was a cleverer man than Wilson." General Smuts termed it "a most terrible indictment," and Melchior, in a serious letter, said that reading the book gave him a feeling of "a lugubrious, bewildering, and lofty drama of which—fortunately or unfortunately— only the first acts may be over." He expressed the wish that Keynes's volume might be "a landmark for a new development in the postwar history" and opined that his practical remedies could make possible European reconstruction, "provided the peoples concerned and their governments are already ripe for such wise action."

A typical British reaction appeared in some verses which were published in the January 14, 1920, issue of *Punch* (with no thanks to Gilbert and Sullivan):

The Candour of Keynes

(Suggested by the perusal of *The Economic Consequences of the Peace*)

There was a superior young person named Keynes
Who possessed an extensive equipment of brains
And, being elected a fellow of King's,
He taught economics and similar things.

On the outbreak of war he at once made his mark
As a "tempy," but principal, Treasury clerk
And the permanent staff and the CHANCELLOR too
Pronounce him a flyer and well worth his screw.

So he went to the conference, not as a mute,
To act as the chancellor's chief substitute,
And in this extremely responsible post
He mingled with those who were ruling the roost.

The Big and redoubtable Three, 'tis confessed,
By his talent and zeal were immensely impressed;
But, conversely, the fact, which is painful, remains
That they failed to impress the redoubtable Keynes.

So, after five months of progressive disgust,
He shook from his feet the Parisian dust,

Determined to give the chief delegates beans
And let the plain person behind the Peace scenes.

Though his title is stodgy, yet all must admit
That his pages are seasoned with plenty of wit;
He's alert as a catfish; he can't be ignored;
And throughout his recital we never are bored.

For he's not a slinger of partisan ink,
But a thinker who gives us profoundly to think;
And his arguments cannot be lightly dismissed
With cries of "Pro-Hun" or of "Pacificist."

And yet there are faults to be found just the same;
For example, I doubt if it's playing the game
For one who is hardly unmuzzled to guy
Representative statesmen who cannot reply.

And while we're amused by his caustic dispraise
Of President WILSON's Chadbandian ways
Of the cynical TIGER, laconic and grim,
And our versatile PREMIER, so supple and slim—

Still we feel, as he zealously damns the allies
For grudging the Germans the means to arise,
That possibly some of the Ultimate Things,
May even be hidden from fellows of King's.

Wickham Steed, the editor of *The Times,* had set the tone of the British reaction in the January 5, 1920, issue when he damned the book as "clever" and expressed wonder at Keynes's political inexperience and his special concern for Germany. He acknowledged that it did have value as a constructive criticism of the economic clauses of the treaty. Many of Keynes's critics in Britain and in Europe simply lashed out at what they regarded as pro-German propaganda.

In Keynes's own opinion, the "first serious and responsible criticism" of his book came from John Foster Dulles, who had served as the legal advisor to the American financial delegation at Paris. In a letter to *The Times,* February 16, 1920, Dulles contended that the evils of the treaty which Keynes criticized were offset by the provisions which made possible correction of these shortcomings. President Wilson's alleged capitulation to the demand that pensions and separation allowances be considered as claims upon the enemy was not due to "a masterpiece of subtlety," to which Keynes referred, but came about rather as the result of a memorandum prepared by General Smuts, one of the leaders of liberal thought at the conference. Dulles defended the treaty for its practicality in establishing the reparations commission to consider and pass upon claims in a manner akin to that of a receiver, a procedure which he said was "consecrated by the jurisprudence of the world." If the reparations commission exercised its powers with the true interests of the nations represented in mind, it could be regarded as a statesman-like accomplishment.

In a long and respectful reply, Keynes defended his indemnity figures and insisted that while two months has passed since his book had been published, during which he had been criticized on various grounds, personal and otherwise, "no one has made a serious attempt to traverse my main conclusions." He argued for a formal revision of the treaty rather than relying upon the process of adjustment by the reparations commission, and he blamed the statesmen at Paris for "not guiding, enlightening, and elevating the minds of the people rather than succumbing to the passions of the hour."

Later, in a revealing letter to Norman Davis dated April 18, 1920, he dealt, among other matters, with what he had written about President Wilson. He stated that what he "deemed to be the President's psychology was necessary for the purpose of my book" to explain how a perfidious peace was enacted, in spite of the President's sincerity. At this time he was inclined to attribute Wilson's weakness to the shadow of his impending illness. Woodrow Wilson, for him, was "a fallen hero," and in another letter to Professor Allyn Young of Harvard University he admitted that "in spite of everything I say about him, and of all my disappointments, I still believe that essentially the President played a nobler part at Paris than any of his colleagues."

There was much more American criticism and commentary on his book in this first year after its publication. One of the few serious analyses, in Keynes's mind, was written by Dr. Alonzo E. Taylor, an economist who was in Paris with the American Food Administration. He and Paul Cravath, an American lawyer who was also at the conference, thought that Keynes should have recommended the return by Britain of some of the German merchant ships or some other economic concessions. Cravath did, however, write a review of Keynes's volume for the *New York Times* which was very complimentary and approving.

One of the most surprising sequels to all this was a review by Keynes himself of a book by Bernard Baruch, who had played a prominent role at the peace conference. He agreed with the latter that the American delegation had defended honorable and sensible courses at the conclave and even conceded that "the President, being what he was, and the Allied leaders, being what they were, then in the situation that Mr. Baruch describes the result could not have been otherwise." Still, he differed with Baruch in thinking that words, such as those in the Fourteen Points, should be taken seriously and in holding that the reparations commission would not be a reliable agency in reforming the terms of the treaty.

In October 1919, before his book had been published, Keynes was in Amsterdam with Melchior, as we have observed earlier. He later recounted how he went for a stroll through the city with him and Paul Warburg, the brother of Melchior's Hamburg partner. After lunch he took both of them to his hotel room, where he read the chapter on the President from his manuscript, noting, as he said, "its effects on the two Jews." Warburg, who for personal reasons hated the President, laughed and giggled and thought that it was "an awful good hit." But Melchior, as he listened, became ever more solemn until he was almost in tears. "This, then, was the other side of the curtain; neither profound causes, nor inevitable fate, nor magnificent wickedness. The Tablets of the Law, it was Melchior's thought at that moment, had perished meanly."

Whether Keynes's portrait of the President was "a good hit" is certainly debatable, but there can be no disputing the fact that when the book was published on December 12, 1919, it almost immediately became a publishing sensation. What accounted for its astonishing success?

Apart from its literary merit or its deflation of the images of eminent statesmen, it would seem that it satisfied some deep, widespread need for a clarification of the confused economic and political situation at that critical juncture of world history. In socio-psychological terms, Keynes perceived that situation differently from the conventional statesmen of the time. Even General Smuts, though he had talked earlier of doing something at home about the treaty, had grown fatalistic. In a letter to Keynes, he had written, "After giving the matter my closest consideration, I have seen no profit in a regular attack on the treaty. It is past and nothing can undo it except time and the great Mercy which washes away all our poor human follies. Better to be constructive. . . . "

Always optimistic and meliorist about improving the human condition, Keynes felt quite differently. In a previous letter to Smuts, after he had finished his book but before its publication, he had written that "the general condition of Europe at this moment seems to demand some attempt at *éclaircissement* of the situation created by the treaty, even more than when I sat down to write." He noted the growing isolationism in the United States and in Great Britain, as well as the anti-German feeling in the latter, and added, "But perhaps what is most alarming is the lethargy of the European peoples themselves. They seem to have no plan; they take hardly any steps to help themselves; and even their appeals appear halfhearted. It looks as though we were in a slow steady deterioration of the general conditions of human life, rather than for any sudden upheaval or catastrophe. But one can't tell."

It was a condition such as Yeats described in *The Second Coming:*

> Things fall apart; the center cannot hold;
> Mere anarchy is loosed upon the world.
>
> The best lack all conviction, while the worst
> Are full of passionate intensity.

Keynes did not lack conviction; he seized the opportunity—the historical moment—and passionately presented his diagnosis and prescription for Europe's economic and political ills.

There is some confirmation of this interpretation of Keynes's role at the peace conference in the recently published diaries of Professor Felix Frankfurter, who was present at the conclave as the assistant to the United States secretary of war. On July 11, 1919, Frankfurter wrote Walter Lippmann, explaining the reasons, as he saw them, for President Wilson's failure at the conference. He contended that neither the President nor his advisor, Colonel Edward M. House, had an adequate conception of the technique of peacemaking, of the processes which would come into play and the forces that they could rely upon. The effect of the United States and British elections were not taken into account. Arguing that what was lacking was "the directing will on the top," even though there was no dearth of the necessary knowledge and vision to approximate the world order that was attainable, he speculated about the possible causes for the frustration of these aims and "the causes that prevented two or three people from breaking through." Then he added, "If Smuts or Botha [Louis Botha, the other South African soldier and statesman who represented his country at the conference] had shouted aloud months ago what they said in private, if there had been public courage on the part of two or three of our own people, this treaty would never have been. Of course, there were some brave people like Keynes (you may have met him, he was the financial advisor of the British), who resigned because of the utter breach of faith that the treaty involved." Earlier, in reminiscing orally about the conference, Frankfurter said that "there were lots of people in Paris—colleagues of mine from Harvard, Sam Morison, Allyn Young—who felt as Keynes did about the kind of thing that Keynes published, but just didn't think he ought to 'rock the boat,' as the phrase runs."

In his biography of Keynes, Harrod acknowledged, of course, that the publication of *The Economic Consequences of the Peace* was "a turning point in his career," but he failed to recognize the creative elements of that work. Keynes's achievement in writing that powerful polemic was creative in more than one sense. That quality is exhibited in his masterful combination of literary imagination and lucid, logical analysis of the treaty's economic provisions. His psychological portrayal of the Big Three and his allegory of the prince and the maid, with its employment of paleological thinking alongside Aristotelian logic, were original and powerful for a political tract of that kind. Later in his career he further articulated the implications of some of the concepts used in this book. In the field of economics, his imaginative focusing on the future of Europe rather than its past and his insistence on a holistic approach to its problems was innovative in the highest sense. This, plus his grand scheme for the economic rehabilitation of the continent, anticipated, of course, the idea of the Marshall Plan and the European Economic Community. The only reservations that one might legitimately have about these proposals involve questions of political judgment, namely, whether they were premature, too much ahead of the times, and failed to deal with the question of French security.

From the perspective of his life's work as an economist, it is now clear that the most creative aspect of *The Economic Consequences of the Peace* was Keynes's vision of oversaving in that volume. Professor Joseph A. Schumpeter was the first to call attention to that element in his work, contending that it motivated and influenced his later thinking. By the term "vision" Schumpeter meant "that mixture of perceptions and prescientific analysis which shapes and influences the theoretical model of the empirical research that an economist produces." He emphasized the ideological context of such visions and expressed the belief that they gradually lose their bias or slant in the course of scientific development. It is interesting that the psychologists have another, more neutral term than vision; they speak of an "incept" which consists of "a word or phrase, a series of phrases, an overall structure or theme, an image of a visual form" which initiates an investigation. "These," writes Dr. Rothenberg, "are far from completed ideas ready to be spelled out, but they are elements that the creator is interested in exploring. The creative process itself is the means and method of exploring these concepts."

The Keynesian concept of oversaving was such an incept which began a creative process extending over nearly two decades. In *The Economic Consequences of the Peace,* Keynes tentatively broached the possible long-run tendency of savings to outrun investment opportunities in the future. Then in *The End of Laissez-Faire* (1926), he alluded again to the problem of coordinating the volume and direction of savings and investment; the question was still very much on his mind. When later he more fully analyzed the relationship between these two variables in *A Treatise on Money* and *The General Theory,* he couched the problem in short-run terms. In his essay on the treaty he made some general use of dialectical analysis, but in this later work on monetary theory the employment of opposites in the development and elaboration of his ideas is much more conspicuous. In terms of economic methodology, while his analysis of reparations is carried out in a fairly conventional neoclassical style, what is notable is his use of the categories of modern psychology and his grasp of *realpolitik.* His experiences at the conference and earlier in the Treasury were demonstrating that reality was not the realm of reason, but often of dark, mysterious forces whose outcome could not be wholly foreseen. Now he realized more than ever before that the European economic system, rather than being stable and self-regulating as conventional theory might suggest, was "unusual, unstable, complicated, unreliable, temporary." What stability it had was mainly due to man's ability to become "habituated to his surroundings," that is, to the institutional structure of life. These insights, much modified by the passage of time, were to emerge later in the underlying assumptions of *The General Theory.*

In casting himself in the role of a critic capable of pointing out the errors or shortcomings of the leading international statesmen, Keynes not only catapulted himself into world fame, but he made himself almost a powerful political figure in his own right. In retrospect, it is now clear that Harrod exaggerated the degree to which he was ostracized in official circles in Great Britain as a result of the book's publication. As a matter of fact, Keynes kept in touch with Basil Blackett and Sir Robert Chalmers of the Treasury, was asked for advice by Austen Chamberlain, the chancellor of the exchequer, and by Herbert Asquith, the ex-prime minister, and then was invited to stand for election by all three political parties—all this within a year after his book appeared. Later, in the twenties, he became a key advisor to Lloyd George again. It is simply incorrect to say that he remained "an outlaw from British official circles for many years afterwards" as a result of writing his book.

At a critical juncture in world affairs, he saw that political vision was needed, no matter how much it would be annoying to those who had to "keep the machinery of civilization operating" in Herbert Hoover's rather pedestrian conception. He saw that more was needed than an engineering mentality or a completely present-oriented view of reality, and he had the ego strength to project his own vision of the economic future in a most persuasive way. In doing this, he was sustained by significant others, such as Margot Asquith, Lord Robert Cecil, General Smuts, Leonard Woolf, and probably other Bloomsbury friends who had faith and confidence in his ability. Underlying all those conscious influences was his own humanitarian sense and hope for a better world. In all this, one should not overlook what Harrod called "the presuppositions of Harvey Road," the conviction that he was of the political elect who had the responsibility to govern, coupled with a strong, idealized self-image that marked out the course of duty.

As evidence of his public stature and the high esteem in which he was held after the publication of his book, one should recall that in 1923 he was considered for the Nobel Peace Prize. Wilhelm Keilhau, a member of the Norwegian Parliament who investigated certain misrepresentations about Keynes's presence at the peace conference, wrote him to say that he had concluded his report as follows: "However, the ideas of Keynes have not made the same impression upon the statesmen in power as on the public. This is most deplorable, for had those statesmen acted upon his advice, there is every possible reason to believe that we now should have seen happier days and been able to work under the benefits of a real peace."

Thirty names were considered for the Nobel Prize that year, including, besides Keynes, Lord Robert Cecil, who had been chairman of the Supreme Economic Council; Francesco Nitti, former premier of Italy; Charles Evans Hughes, former U.S. secretary of state; Jane Adams, the American social reformer; and President Harding. No one was granted the award for that year, but Keynes did not need it psychologically—he had created a name that was famous all over the world. More important, in writing his tract he had developed a cognitive style or way of looking at economic reality which would eventually lead to his recognition as one of the world's most creative minds.

CHAPTER 9

The Challenge of New Careers

Democracy may have to be jockeyed, humbugged, cajoled along the right road.
                                                                    J. M. Keynes

Even before the success of *The Economic Consequences of the Peace,* Keynes had decided to undertake a new career rather than return to the pattern of his prewar life. In June 1919, he was determined to reduce his university and college teaching, so he informed his superiors that he did not wish to tutor but would lecture once a week only on the "Economic Aspects of the Peace Treaty." He did not want to resume the heavy load of teaching and external examining that he had had before the war; now he believed that he could take an active part in shaping public opinion more directly. His experience in the Treasury had provided him with an expertise which should be valuable not only in public affairs, but in business. Always optimistic and courageous in temperament, he decided to take the risk. Accordingly, he later resigned from his Girdler lectureship at the university. Even before this the authorities at King's began to investigate the possibilities of using his financial knowledge in behalf of the college. Finally, in November 1920, he was appointed second bursar at a stipend of one hundred pounds a year.

In the meanwhile, another offer was made to him involving the chairmanship of a Scandinavian trading bank at a salary of two thousand pounds a year. This post would require him to give only one day a week to his duties so that it would not interfere with his activities at Cambridge. However, after consulting with friends he decided against the offer, believing that in part it might jeopardize his other financial connections in the City.

While he was writing his book on the peace treaty at Charleston, he had, in fact, undertaken another career which was to fascinate him a great deal in future years—that of a speculator. Operating on a margin basis, he began buying and selling foreign exchange, dealing in rupees, the dollar, the French franc, the German mark, and the Dutch florin. On the whole, he took a bull position on the dollar and was bearish on the European currencies. In this sort of enterprise, he was definitely using the knowledge and skills he had acquired in his previous Treasury service; soon he found that he was making big profits. In a letter to his mother, he explained and rationalized his activities: "I haven't lived such a regular life for years and am very well. My diversion, to avoid the possibility of tedium in country life, is speculation in the foreign exchanges, which will shock Father but out of which I hope to do very well."

In September 1920, Oswald Falk, who had worked in the "A" Division of the Treasury with Keynes, was instrumental in his being invited to join the board of the National Mutual Life Insurance Company; subsequently, in 1921, he became chairman of this company and continued in that post until 1938. This was truly the beginning of his financial career.

Shortly after this development, Dr. G. Vissering, the governor of the Bank of the Netherlands, invited him and some other financiers to Amsterdam to draw up a proposal for an international loan; most of these experts believed that carrying out the provisions of the Paris treaty in a literal way would spell economic disaster for Europe. In their view there was a need for additional international credit to ease the situation. Working with Paul Warburg, the American banker, Keynes drafted the document for such a loan and suggested that it should be submitted to the League of Nations for implementation. Nothing came from this initiative, but at least he had a chance for the first time of renewing his friendship with Carl Melchior in Amsterdam and of picking up assorted bits of inside information on the European financial situation. On the basis of this and other facts, he took a bearish position on the German mark, and when the latter temporarily rose, he lost £13,125 between the first of April and the end of May 1920 and also £8,498 belonging to a small syndicate for which he had the moral responsibility. He had come to the very edge of personal bankruptcy, for his brokerage firm had demanded that he pay £7,000 to keep his account open. He was only able to meet it by an opportune loan of £5,000 from a financier who had thought highly of his work at Paris and by an advance royalty of £1,500 from Macmillan.

Despite this close scrape with disaster, in the long run Keynes's multifaceted career was beneficial because his various roles in business, government, and academia contributed to his creativity. Psychologists believe that new roles are conducive to creativity because they enable one to perceive reality from a perspective different from that which is customary. In Keynes's case, as one of his biographers has noted, the interweaving of his different roles fostered his creativity to a marked degree.

While profits from his speculations were piling up, he had taken off with Duncan Grant and Vanessa Bell for a holiday in Italy. In Rome they engaged in an orgy of buying furniture, dresses, pots, and other miscellaneous items, spending three hundred pounds in a month. Duncan and Vanessa painted, while Keynes read and wrote. Later they visited the Berensons at I Tatti near Florence where there occurred the amusing incident in which Keynes was mistaken for "il pittore Grant" and Duncan taken for "l'economisto Keynes" and asked about the European financial situation. Growing bored with the Berensons, they were off to Paris where the painters visited Picasso and Maynard wrote and read. They returned home to the near-financial disaster that lay in store for the latter.

This trip to Rome had another unforeseen consequence. While there Keynes had renewed an acquaintance with an old Kingsman, W. H. Haslam, who when he returned to England a few years later proposed to the Provincial Insurance Company that he and his friend Falk should be asked to serve as economic advisors. In 1923, Keynes joined the board of this company and became president of its finance committee, a position he held throughout the rest of his life.

After he had recovered from his financial setback with the aid of his journalistic earnings, Keynes returned to speculation in commodities and securities. Starting in 1921, he traded heavily in cotton, lead, tin, copper, rubber, wheat, sugar, linseed oil, and jute, all on a margin basis. He also entered into a number of security syndicates, acting as a consultant, and formed a small investment company with his old associates of the "A" Division. Some of this financial decision-making was carried out while he was still in bed in the morning; reports would come to him by phone from his brokers, and he would read the newspapers and make his decisions. This biographical detail reminds one of the story told by Duncan Grant of Margot Asquith's telephone call at 7:00 A.M. to Maynard. When Grant told her that he was still in bed, she replied, "Well, tell Maynard Keynes for me that if he does not get up earlier than this, he will never get on in the world."

During 1920, Keynes was absorbed for most of the year in preparing his *Treatise on Probability*. He had not attended to this subject since the summer of 1914, so he had some difficulty in going over the whole manuscript again with its abstruse mathematics. By the Easter vacation of the following year, he was ready for a holiday. Duncan Grant was not his companion this time, as he had grown closer to Vanessa Bell. Instead he took "Sebastian" Sprott, one of the new Apostles to whom he had taken a fancy. Young Sprott—he was twenty-four at this time— was the son of a country solicitor who, having served in the war, was now studying psychology at the university. "Outwardly," P. N. Furbank writes, "he was almost an 'exquisite'; he fluttered, dressed elegantly, and spoke in very Bloomsbury accents—the voice shooting up and down the scale or suddenly pouncing on some selected word," or so he seemed after he had been introduced to Bloomsbury by Maynard. Beneath the surface, he was "a tenderhearted, loquacious, and impractical young man, facing the world with a frown of pretended truculence. His comic insouciance made [E. M.] Forster laugh a good deal." If this was his nature when he became very friendly with the novelist two years later, one can see his appeal to Maynard. He later became a quite well-known social psychologist. While Maynard and Sebastian were in Africa, an incident occurred that has become part of Keynesiana. It seems that when they had their shoes polished by the native boys, Keynes offered the urchins an insufficient tip, whereupon the boys began stoning them. Sprott urged Maynard to give them more to allay their wrath, but the latter declined firmly, saying, "I will not be a party to debasing the currency." Sprott was probably surprised at Keynes's frugality, but he did not know of his recent financial losses.

While Keynes remained a good friend of Sprott, his sexual interest in him did not last. In June 1922, the latter wrote Lytton Strachey, inquiring whether he knew anything about Keynes's attitude toward him, only to be reassured that he didn't like him any less, but that he was probably more infatuated with a girl called "Janet," as Sprott himself had suggested might be the case. A few months later, Sebastian wrote Keynes, declining an invitation to visit and informing him in a humorous vein that he was reading Hirschfeld's *Sexual Pathologies,* "which is a most dangerous work. I suspect that I am tainted with Transvestitismus, Autonomoussexualitat, and Hermasphioditismus of the inner sex glands, to say nothing of Homosexualitat and Onanie." Despite his own past sexual proclivities, Keynes, as will soon be seen, was showing increased interest in women at this time and, in particular, in one Russian ballerina.

In August 1921, *A Treatise on Probability* was finally published. It was the work of five years, and it was, on the whole, favorably received. This is the one book of Keynes which was "deliberately philosophical," but it is definitely of the quality which puts him in the class of those economists, such as Karl Marx, Alfred Marshall, and Thorstein Veblen, who moved intellectually from philosophy to economics. In its character, the volume is in the great empiricist tradition of British philosophy. As R. B. Braithwaite, emeritus professor of moral philosophy at King's College, has pointed out, empiricists had divided knowledge into that which is "intuitive" and that which is "derivative" and had regarded the latter as being based on the former in the sense of their being a logical relationship between them. Keynes in effect presented a logical theory of probability in this book, contending that a probability statement expresses a logical relationship between proposition p and a proposition h (where the latter is conceived as a conjunction of propositions). "The originality of Keynes's approach," Braithwaite writes, "lay in its insistence that probability, in its fundamental sense, is a logical relation holding between propositions which is similar to, although weaker than, that of logical consequence."

As for its originality, he further states that, apart from an article by Dorothy Wrinch and Harold Jeffreys which Keynes had not seen, his *Treatise* "contains the first publication of the view that a partial belief is to be justified by knowledge of a logical probability relationship, and that these logical relationships form the subject matter of probability theory." From our more psychological standpoint, it is significant that what Keynes was maintaining was that this relationship in suitable cases can be perceived, directly recognized, or intuited. In developing this position he had made an explicit acknowledgment of his indebtedness to G. E. Moore and Bertrand Russell. In his Memoir Club paper ("My Early Beliefs") he had stated: "It was an important object of Moore's book [*Principia Ethica*] to distinguish between goodness as an attribute of states of mind and rightness as an attribute of actions. He also had a section on the justification of general rules of conduct. The large part played by considerations of probability in his theory of right conduct was indeed an important contributory cause to my spending all the leisure of many years on the study of that subject: I was writing under the joint influence of Moore's *Principia Ethica* and Russell's *Principia Mathematica*." It is of some historical interest that in what seems to be some of his Apostle papers, written while he was still an undergraduate, Keynes dissented vigorously and with great subtlety from Moore's concept of probability as set forth in his chapter treating Ethics in Relation to Conduct.

He showed his sensitivity to others and his openness of mind by his willingness to modify his original position on this subject of probability. In 1931, he reviewed an essay by Frank P. Ramsey, the Cambridge logician whom he highly respected, in which certain criticisms were advanced of his own work. He stated that he was prepared "as against the view which I had put forward" to agree with Ramsey that "probability is concerned not with objective relations between propositions but (in some sense) with degrees of belief." That came close to accepting an alternative approach to probability, namely that of the "restricted betting-quotient," in place of that which he had originally adopted. Those who complain of Keynes's shifts of position on economic questions should note that he was equally disposed to do the same in philosophy when the force of argument warranted it.

Even in writing a book on a subject as abstract as inductive inference and probability, Keynes felt that he had to write with force and conviction. Professor Paul Samuelson has called attention to the unusual statement that he made during the close of that work: "In writing a book of this kind, the author must, if he is to put his point of view clearly, pretend sometimes to a little more conviction than he feels. He must give his argument a chance, so to speak, nor be too ready to depress its vitality with a wet cloud of doubt. It is a heavy task to write on these problems; and the reader will perhaps excuse me if I have sometimes pressed on a little faster than the difficulties were overcome, and with decidedly more confidence that I have always felt." This remark is certainly more revealing about the author's psychology than the validity of his logic. But it is quite in character for an author who believed that if a writer is to be successful he must combine thought with feeling.

After its long, drawn-out process of composition, the publication of his treatise was undoubtedly a relief to Keynes, but that year, 1921, was perhaps more significant to him, emotionally at least, for the fact that Lopokova danced! Of course, Lydia Lopokova, the *première danseuse* of Diaghilev's Russian Ballet Company, had danced in previous years at London, and she had been rapturously received almost from the first. Indeed, the British in those last years of the Edwardian era had rather suddenly discovered and become entranced with Russian and French literature and painting, and Russian drama, opera, and ballet. The first season of the Russian Ballet Company opened in June 1911, at the Royal Opera House, Covent Garden, to enthusiastic notices from the critics. The Russian dance troupe which included Nijinsky profoundly affected the English audiences; some were so taken by its beauty that they spoke in terms of religious conversion. Edward Marsh, Winston Churchill's private secretary, who attended a performance in 1913 meaning to dislike it, wrote to Rupert Brooke, "It's a Post-impressionist picture put into motion. . . . It has almost brought me around to Matisse's pictures."

Maynard, as has been seen, was very much an aficionado of the ballet in these prewar years, but when Lopokova appeared on the scene he was completely captivated. In the 1921 season she returned to the company, after an absence of two years, in the role of the cancan dancer in the *Boutique Fantasque* and as the lead in *Les Sylphides.* She had the good will of the audience, but there were some who believed that her previous inactivity would affect her artistic success. No sooner had she made her entrance, drawn in on a low trolley in her character as a doll, the house echoed to the clapping of hands, the stamping of feet, and shouts of "Lopokova!" As soon as she danced, it was manifest that her past technique was unimpaired; "her every gesture, her every action seemed unstudied, spontaneous, an inspiration." Earlier, Cyril Beaumont, in describing her dancing the cancan with Massine, wrote: "Lopokova had an extraordinary resemblance to a doll, for which her rounded limbs, plump features, curved lips, and ingenuous expression were admirably suited. You could easily imagine her squeaking, 'Mama! Pa-pa!'" Maynard made sure that he would see her in these various parts. "He was spellbound by this princess, so light and quick, so charming and piquant, so coy and unexpected. As he watched, his whole being was filled with joy and exhilaration."

He had met her first in 1918 at a party given by the Sitwells. At that time she was captivating Bloomsbury and other Londoners by her performance in *The Good-Humored Ladies,* Massine's ballet inspired by Carlo Goldoni. Now that he met her again at Bloomsbury parties, Keynes was quite smitten by her. What was her appeal? Osbert Sitwell limned some of her qualities in an Italian ballet: "Her face was appealing, inquisitive, birdlike, like that of a mask of comedy, while, being an artist in everything, she comprehended exactly the span and limits of her capacities; the personification of gaiety, of spontaneity, and of that particular pathos which is its complement, she had developed the movements of her hands and arms in a way that hitherto no dancer had attempted, thereby achieving a new step forward in technique. Her wit entered into every gesture, into everything that she did." Yes, these were the qualities that Maynard admired—wit, gaiety, spontaneity, originality. Lydia had them all.

He began paying her attention, escorting her to Bloomsbury parties, advising her on her finances, even negotiating terms for her ballet performances. She kept her money in the safe at the Waldorf Hotel where she lived, earning no interest. That would never do; he must advise her on her finances. About this time he persuaded her to move to a flat at 41 Gordon Square, close to his Bloomsbury friends.

Lydia Lopokova (her name was originally "Lopukhova," but Diaghilev had simplified it to "Lopokova") was the daughter of a Russian who was an usher at the Imperial Alexandrinsky Theatre and of Constanza Douglas, a member of a Scottish-German family who had come to St. Petersburg from the Baltic states as a housekeeper. There Lydia was born on October 21, 1891; two of her brothers and one sister became dancers also; one of the former eventually became known as a choreographer and ballet director. Lydia herself entered the Imperial School of Ballet at the age of nine and underwent the long, arduous education of a ballerina.

When she was nineteen, just a year out of school, she danced Columbine in Fokine's *Carnaval* for Diaghilev in Berlin and Paris, and then in the following year (1911) she signed up with an American impressario to dance in the United States. She made her appearance at the Globe Theatre in New York in *The Echo,* a musical comedy, and in 1915, she joined the Washington Square Players to gain acting experience. That autumn she was playing a part in Percy Mackaye's *The Antic* and captivating Heywood Broun, the ex-sports writer who was then doing drama criticism for the *New York Tribune.* In his review he exulted, "We will continue to maintain that Lydia Lopokova is the most charming young person who has trod the stage in New York this season. But she did not tread. She did not even walk. She skipped, she danced, she pranced, and like as not, she never touched the stage. Or so it seemed."

The very next day Broun arranged a backstage introduction to his enchanter and began to entertain her nightly at Joel's, his favorite bistro, where they had late suppers. It was one of the after-dark sights of Manhattan to see the popular, lumbering giant of a columnist, clad in a raccoon coat which made him appear even more massive, ambling into Joel's with the effervescent little Lopokova beside him, calling up remarks. Very much smitten, Broun invited her to the cocktail hour and dinner table of his well-to-do, Victorian parents in their fashionable

Brooklyn Heights home. In a little less than three months, while Lydia was taking her daily constitutional, running around the Central Park reservoir, he proposed marriage to her, and she accepted. Next morning in "The Diary of a Modern Samuel Pepys," F. P. A. (Franklin P. Adams, Heywood's friend) wrote in the *Tribune*: "H. Broun, the critic, I hear hath become engaged to Mistress Lydia Lopokova, the pretty play-actress and dancer. He did introduce her to me last night, and she seemed a merry elf and modest."

In that same issue of the paper, Lopokova confirmed that the marriage would be in the fall, but meanwhile Diaghilev's Russian Ballet Company had arrived in New York, and she was asked to rejoin the troupe. After a week of mad rehearsals, she scored a smashing personal triumph on the opening night. She had been so busy in the interval that she had seen little of Broun and was, in fact, spending most of her free time with an old acquaintance, Randolpho Barocchi, Diaghilev's secretary. She finally told her crestfallen fiancé that the latter was her true love and that she must break the engagement, after writing a letter of explanation to his mother. Years later she recalled this old romance, saying, "Our brief acquaintance was interrupted by my rejoining the Russian Ballet, and my professional career involved me in a whirl of excitement. I felt that I did not want to be tied up to Heywood—so I broke it off, hurting him very much at the time, I am sorry to say." Fortunately for Broun admirers, the disappointed writer did not take to drink but married Ruth Hale, a feminist intellectual and writer.

Lydia herself went on an extensive tour of the States with the Diaghilev company, dancing in most of the major cities, in the course of which she married Barocchi. Notwithstanding his virtues, by July 1919 the impetuous Lopokova had grown tired of her little dapper husband and ran off with a Russian officer to Saint John's Wood, as the news billboards in London blared the headline: FAMOUS BALLERINA VANISHES. After a few weeks of this escapade, she was back with Diaghilev, but he was never certain of her staying with his company because, in truth, she was "a bit of a bolter."

When Maynard Keynes fell in love with her several years later, there were complications. Apart from some Cambridge eyebrows which were raised at the prospect of a don marrying a "chorus girl," and a Russian one at that, there were criticisms which came from his Bloomsbury friends. Duncan Grant and Vanessa Bell found her somewhat annoying, her remarks on the ballet would interrupt their painting, and Lytton Strachey referred to her unfeelingly as "a half-witted canary."

Bloomsbury, says Milo Keynes, Maynard's nephew, found her unsound on "the eternal verities, morality, religion, the soul, and, particularly, on politics and public affairs." Lydia, in turn, felt that Vanessa despised her.

Virginia Woolf was on very friendly terms with Maynard during this period. In her diary she tells of sitting with him in Gordon Square and talking for an hour and a half. She recalled: "Sometimes I wish that I put down what people say instead of describing them. The difficulty is that they say so little. Maynard said that he loved praise and always wants to boast. He said that many men marry in order to have a wife to boast to. But I said it's odd that one boasts, considering that no one is ever taken in by it. It's odd that you, of all people, should want praise. You and Lytton are passed beyond boasting—which is the supreme triumph. There you sit and say nothing. I love praise, he said. I want it for the things I'm doubtful about."

Virginia, always critical of others, later wrote her sister about Maynard's courting of Lydia. "Seriously, I think you ought to prevent Maynard before it is too late. I can't believe that he realizes what the effects would be. I can foresee only too well Lydia stout, charming, exacting; Maynard in the Cabinet; 46 Gordon Square the resort of dukes and prime ministers. M[aynard] being a simple man, not analytic as we are[!], would sink beyond recall long before he realized his state. Then he would awake to find three children, and his life entirely and forever controlled."

As it turned out, Virginia's anxiety about Lydia's designs on Maynard was groundless because she could not sweep him right off his feet. She was already married to Barocchi, and divorce proceedings would very likely be protracted.

With the *Treatise on Probability* out of the way, Keynes was now free to attend more positively to international economic developments. As it happened, in January 1921, another international conference was being convened, again in Paris, to determine what Germany should pay. C. P. Scott, the editor of the *Manchester Guardian,* telegraphed him, asking for a signed article on the assembly. The very next day Keynes wired back his essay from London and also arranged for its publication in the *New York Evening Post.* In this piece he strongly attacked the proposals emanating from this conference as "absurd and impossible" (they demanded for a normal period more than £400 million per annum, contrasted with his own high estimate of £100 million as to what Germany might conceivably be asked to pay). The former sum, he asserted, was excessive and "fantastic," bringing the world no nearer to settling Europe's problems, and he characterized it as "just a move in the poker party" at Paris.

All through this period he was writing articles on various reparation proposals which were being advanced at a number of international conferences. He was asked for an article by the editor of the *New York World;* he had it ready in a day. He was following international economic developments very closely and charging stiff rates for his published work. His pieces appeared regularly in the *Manchester Guardian,* occasionally in *The Times,* and his articles were translated for foreign newspapers.

In these articles he usually argued that England should renounce her own claims in favor of France, and he urged the latter country to pursue a policy of restraint rather than threatening the occupation of the Ruhr. He thought it wrong for the allies to threaten Germany because she would not promise "fabulous sums of money which they have not got and could not pay, if at all, by developing a vast trade in competition with our own, which we know very well that we have no intention to permit."

In May 1921, he was able to point out in one such article that the estimate that he had made in *The Economic Consequences of the Peace* of Germany's liability under the treaty had been borne out by the just-published figures of the reparations commission. He had calculated that Germany's total liability would be less than £8,000 million. The commission's assessment was £6,850 million, so his judgment as to the general magnitude of the figures was proved to be correct.

Finally, on May 5, 1921, the allies issued a new set of terms for Germany, making it an ultimatum to be accepted or rejected within one week. In articles in the *Manchester Guardian* and the *New York World,* Keynes urged the Germans to accept the proffered terms, "trusting," as he wrote, "that the whole world is not unreasonable and unjust, whatever the newspapers say; that time is a healer, that time is an illuminator, and that we must still await a little before Europe and the United States can accomplish in wisdom and mercy the economic settlement of the war."

The German government accepted this new settlement within the stipulated time. Keynes had undertaken to have his article advising acceptance telegraphed to the German press, so that he was justified in claiming, as he did in a conversation with the British ambassador to Berlin, the credit for the outcome. Nevertheless, he did not believe that Germany could pay the amounts demanded, anticipating that at the beginning of 1922 it would find it impossible to make the required remittances. These developments certainly suggest the crucial importance of his influence on international financial matters at that time.

In August 1921, he wrote a series of five articles for the *Sunday Times,* reviewing the new reparation settlement and appraising Europe's economic outlook generally. These pieces, especially the first, also had remarkable international repercussions both in Europe and the United States. The first of the series appeared most opportunely, just ten days before Germany was to make her first payment under the new London agreement. He calculated that her reparation burden would amount to one-quarter of the German national income—a crushing amount—and he concluded, therefore, that "the new reparation settlement grants a breathing spell until 1922, but contains no more possibility of permanence than its predecessors."

The Paris correspondent of the *Sunday Times,* commenting on this article, stated that "rarely—probably never in the history of international politics—has a single and opinionative article had such far-reaching effects." He believed this to be the case because Keynes's forecast of Germany's bankruptcy might be said to be "the governing factor of the entire French policy toward Germany and the allies, and though the course to be followed had not yet been decided on by the harassed French cabinet, the statements made by Mr. Keynes may be fairly stated to form the base on which policy will be developed."

The French press was at first inclined to think that Keynes was as usual "playing Germany's game." However, as his article was quoted and requoted in the following weeks, even in the provincial press, French opinion changed and came to the view that if Germany was going to fail financially after the payment of the first billion under the new agreement, France would do well to secure a share of the first installment. In Germany at this time Keynes was held in such veneration that some of its citizens were ready to appoint him financial dictator to solve the country's economic problems.

In his second article it is interesting to find him arguing that Germany's payment of reparations would not necessarily be injurious to those receiving it. Following orthodox free trade doctrine, he contended that the recipient country would have less work to do itself in producing the particular commodities in which the conquered country pays its tribute. "But, since in the course of time the displaced labor can find employment in producing other useful objects, the country receiving the indemnity will be, on balance, richer than before." However, this conclusion, he was quick to point out, was subject to two conditions, namely, that the country which suffers a reduction in certain lines of production because of reparations must be the same country which receives the indemnity, and the new state of affairs must be reasonably permanent so as to give time for a new equilibrium to be established. This last condition, the payment of reparations on a permanent basis, he did not think was likely to be accepted by Great Britain. "I do not expect to see Mr. Lloyd George fighting a general election on the issue of maintaining an army to compel Germany at the point of the bayonet to undercut our manufactures. No! He will never forget that in the election of 1918 he gave a pledge to the electors, and this pledge was that 'we are not going to allow her to pay in such a way as to wreck our industries.'"

In the third of his articles he dealt with the 1920–21 economic depression, attributing it to an enormous overordering by merchants and middlemen in all quarters of the world. The banking authorities in Great Britain and the United States, he thought, had acted on correct principles in coping with the boom-bust cycle, but they had acted too slowly and too late. They had been too slow in putting money rates up during the boom, and then in the depression they were too slow in putting them down again.

In the fourth of his *Sunday Times* articles he considered the earnings of labor, especially the increases in wages that had taken place during the 1919–1920 boom and the reductions which had been made in the following year. He expressed the opinion that, having accepted these reductions with good grace and so long as a serious reduction in real wages was avoidable, it was doubtful that the working classes would upset the social structure in the hope of securing an increase. In the postwar world, he wrote, idealisms were at a discount, but in England at least "a rather cynical conservatism is a far greater danger of the near future than a revolutionary socialism." The path to social improvement, he stated, lies in "the ancient doctrine of Liberalism," including such projects as these: (1) a capital levy on idle old-won wealth; (2) general disarmament; (3) a trade union policy that would aim at making the earnings of the individual as nearly approximate as possible to the output and efficiency of the individual; (4) free trade and international cooperation; (5) reduction and control of the birth rate; and (6) the need to improve health and knowledge.

One is struck by the conventional nature of these recommendations. Keynes at this time, it would seem, was no more radical than many of his fellow British economists. Indeed, one of his ex-students, Dennis Robertson, was led to write him, criticizing his analysis of the universality of the 1920–21 slump and his summary of a "Liberal" economic policy, without taking account of the causes of trade union restriction of effort growing out of economic insecurity, as "very jejeune" on its domestic side and almost as divorced from reality as some of the constructions of the socialist G. D. H. Cole. Though Robertson in the close of his letter hailed him as "master all the time," Keynes did not keep a copy of his reply.

The Swedish economist Knut Wicksell also wrote him about his articles, which had been appearing in a Stockholm paper. He agreed with him that Germany would not pay reparations in the near future without some special assistance, but in being noble-minded toward a former enemy, he thought that it had carried him too far. "Somebody must pay for the war, and it would hardly be a moral right if, as the consequences of a too great liberality, France and England were ruined by the war and Germany thriving." He thought that if the German birthrate and population in the longer future would continue to fall, this would make possible the payment of the indemnity, without reducing individual consumption. In his reply, Keynes admitted that his articles had focused on the near future and that from a longer perspective it was necessary to take account of the points that Wicksell had raised.

Finally, in the fifth installment of his series he dealt masterfully with the war debts, pointing out the reversal of the financial roles that the war had produced, with Europe now in the status of debtor and the United States the creditor. He analyzed very clearly the imbalance in the United States's payments position and concluded that, though American loans in the two years since the end of the war had been essential in seeing Europe through the critical postarmistice period, their continuance could not possibly provide a solution for the existing disequilibrium in the balance of indebtedness. The account could not be balanced by only America providing capital for the less developed parts of the world, as England and France had done earlier, but there must be a fundamental adjustment of the balance of exports and imports. "America must buy more and sell less." He was very critical of America's economic foreign policy: "It is useless for the United States to suppose that an equilibrium position can be reached on the basis of her exporting at least as much as at present and at the same time restricting her imports by a tariff. Just as the allies demand vast payments from Germany and then exercise their ingenuity to prevent her paying them, so the American administration devises with one hand schemes for financing exports and with the other tariffs which will make it as difficult as possible for such credits to be repaid. Great nations can often act with a degree of folly which we should not excuse in an individual."

In short, he argued the futility of the United States in amassing all the gold bullion in the world in the settlement of her foreign balances, the "erection of a sky-scraping golden calf," for only a short postponement might thus be gained. He proceeded to make the case for a cancellation of the inter-Allied debts, thus making possible a sensible conclusion of reparation payments.

A revision of *The Economic Consequences of the Peace* had been on his mind for some time, and in June 1921, he proposed a new edition of that book to his publishers. Instead, Alfred Harcourt suggested that he write a sequel to it, and so he set about preparing a book that would bring matters and information about reparations, war debts, and such matters up to date. In the fall he wrote his German friend Melchior, requesting some statistical information. At about the same time he made a short speech at the Economic Recovery Conference, an international meeting in London which was sponsored by the Fight the Famine Council, an organization in which he was active. In this talk he argued that Britain should renounce all reparation claims to pensions and allowances, which together amounted to two-thirds of the reparations total, and should allow Germany to concentrate on reconstruction of the devastated areas of France. The conference adopted a resolution along these lines. Public opinion seemed to be changing somewhat in accordance with his ideas. In November 1921, the Liberal party went on record as favoring the cancelation of war debts and reduction of German reparations to a more sensible level. Even some elements of French society seemed to be veering in his direction, but not President Poincaré. He wrote a letter to *Le Temps* (November 13, 1921) in which he challenged Keynes's professional competence, saying that in his calculations of Germany's capacity to pay, no allowance had been made for the altered value of gold. Keynes promptly took the French President to task, criticizing his rhetoric and showing his intellectual incompetence on monetary matters.

In order to have *A Revision of the Treaty* appear before an approaching conference on reparations at Cannes, he rushed his manuscript to completion. The day after Christmas 1921, he wrote his mother: "In great haste I finished off the last chapter and dispatched it to the printer before Christmas. I shall get the proof back tomorrow and so hope to have the whole thing printed off and the binders got to work by the New Year. But the last chapter is decidedly hurried, and I should have much preferred to be able to revise it at leisure. However, at the present juncture publication seems to me very important." The work was published in January 1922.

His publishers hoped that he had produced another *Economic Consequences,* but this new volume offered instead a sober chronicle of developments since the Versailles conference, lacking the pyrotechnics such as those found in chapter three of its predecessor. By February of the new year, the English edition had sold 6,839 copies, and Harcourt, Brace separately printed and published an American version and had it translated into French, German, Italian, Dutch, Swedish, Japanese, and Russian.

Keynes himself thought that the last chapter of the book, in which he outlined his own proposals for the settlement of Europe, would be the most attractive feature for the book-buying public, but the opening chapter is also very fascinating because it revealed his attitude toward that mysterious entity, public opinion. In one respect this book represents a slight revision of his views about the role of politicians in a democracy. This matter is important because it relates to the accusation that he entertained too rationalistic a conception of human behavior generally.

He began his argument with a provocative jibe against the tribe of politicians: "It is the method of modern statesmen to talk as much folly as the public demands and to practice no more of it than is compatible with what they have said, trusting that such folly in action as must await on folly in word will disclose itself as such, and furnish an opportunity for slipping back into wisdom—the Montessori system for the child, the public. . . . He who contradicts this child will soon give place to other tutors. Praise, therefore, the beauty of the flames he wishes to touch, the music of the breaking toy; even urge him forward; yet waiting with vigilant care, the wise and kindly savior of society, for the right moment to snatch him back, just singed and now attentive."

This is not a complimentary picture of modern democracy. Indeed, writing like a twentieth-century de Tocqueville, Keynes declared that "there are, in present times, two opinions; not, as in former stages, the true and the false, but the outside and the inside; the opinion of the public voiced by the politicians and the newspapers, and the opinion of the politicians, the journalists and the civil servants, upstairs and backstairs and behindstairs, expressed in limited circles." He made a further differentiation of this outside opinion, at least for England (and perhaps elsewhere also). There was, first, that which is expressed in the newspapers and, second, "the living, indefinite belief of the individual man." The modern politician, he asserted, must be accurately aware of all three degrees of opinion; "he must have enough intellect to understand the inside opinion, enough sympathy to detect the inner outside opinion, and enough brass to express the outer outside opinion." It is obvious that by shrewd observation Keynes had acquired an impressive skill as a student of political behavior; his observations on public opinion remind one, of course, of the similar insights of Walter Lippmann or of Graham Wallas, though in some respects they exceed both of them in their cynicism.

These speculations about public opinion and politicians clearly derived in part from his own experience with criticism of *The Economic Consequences of Peace*. He had based that book, as he stated, on a literal interpretation of the Treaty of Versailles and showed the results of carrying it out. Some of his critics, mostly insiders in politics, said that this was naive; politics was the art of the possible, not of the ideal or most rational course of action. In this connection it is significant that in this volume he conceded that Lloyd George's behavior at Paris had a plausible defense, that "the peace of Versailles was the best momentary settlement which the demands of the mob and the characteristics of the chief actors conjoined to permit." Democracy, he now admitted, may have to be "jockeyed, humbugged, cajoled along the right road."

Using his previous definitions of opinion, he insisted that "inside opinion accepted from the beginning many of my main conclusions about the treaty." But then, in the intervening two years since the Paris conference, "the megalomania of war has passed away, and everyone wishes to conform himself with the facts. For these reasons the reparation chapter of the Treaty of Versailles is crumbling. There is little prospect now of the disastrous consequences of its fulfillment." In the past there had been "a large element of injurious make-believe," but the make-believe, he contended, had ceased to be necessary; "outside opinion is now ready for inside opinion to disclose, and act upon, its secret convictions."

After providing a solid, careful narrative of the successive conferences which had followed Versailles, he analyzed the reparation bill again, reviewed the Allied claim for pensions and allowances, and deplored the disruptive effect of reparations and the inter-ally debts on international trade. On pensions and allowances he relied heavily on Bernard Baruch's and Robert Lamont's accounts of the treaty negotiations; he praised the American delegation for its stand against inclusion of pensions in the reparation bill and put the blame on President Wilson who, in his words, "capitulated to the lying exigencies of politics." In his last chapter he noted that "many of the misfortunes which I predicted as attendant on the execution of the chapter of the Versailles Treaty have not occurred, because no serious attempt had been made to execute it."

As to the solution of the debt and reparation problem, he maintained that a good plan must be in the main simple and negative; it must simplify the situation by canceling futile and injurious entanglements. He summarized his plan as follows: "(1) Great Britain, and if possible America too, to cancel all the debts owing them from the governments of Europe and to waive their claims to any share of German reparations; (2) Germany to pay 1,260 gold marks (163 million gold) per annum for thirty years and to hold available a lump sum of 1 billion gold marks for assistance to Poland and Austria; and (3) this annual payment to be assigned in the shares of 1.08 billion gold marks to France and 180 million to Belgium."

France, he argued, would be wise to accept such a just and sensible settlement, expressing the hope that she would forget "her dangerous ambitions in central Europe" and would limit strictly those in the Near East; "for both are based on rubbishy foundations and will bring her no good." Then, prophesying, he asserted: "That she has anything to fear from Germany in the future which we can foresee, except that she may herself provoke, is a delusion. When Germany has recovered her strength and pride, as in due time she will, many years must pass before she again casts her eyes westward. Germany's future now lies to the east, and in that direction her hopes and ambitions, when they revive, will certainly turn." This confident prediction is another example demonstrating that his political judgment was far from infallible.

On the whole, controversy over this new book was slight compared to that of its predecessor. What is notable is the care and conscientiousness with which Keynes sought to answer his critics. He was well equipped to take remarkable pains in the drafting of his original manuscripts as well as in their sturdy defense. At the same time, his personality was such that he could be very aggressive, if not arrogant, in his handling of those whom he regarded as bumbling critics. His tendency to be prejudiced about Americans comes out, too, in one letter where he attributed his critic's blunder as being "just due, I suppose, to his being an American."

In 1921, a project materialized that was much to his liking. C. P. Scott, noting perhaps Keynes's recent series of articles in the *Sunday Times,* proposed that he should be the general editor of a series of special supplements to his newspaper, providing a comprehensive survey of the financial and economic problems of postwar Europe. Keynes accepted this offer and threw himself into this new, complex role with enormous vigor; indeed, he saw it as an opportunity to deal with the world's economic problems, and in particular with reconstruction in Europe, in a sensible and objective fashion rather than in terms of propaganda, such as had recently dominated public opinion. He solicited and secured the assistance of such friends as Melchior in recruiting German contributors; his Dutch banking friends helped; he consulted such notables as Dr. Walter Rathenau, the German minister of foreign affairs, just prior to his tragic assassination; he interviewed G. V. Chicherin, the Russian foreign minister, and secured an article from Maxim Gorki "The Intelligentsia and the Revolution." He had even proposed asking Mahatma Gandhi to write an article explaining why he hated Manchester so much. Securing a representation of the different strands of French political opinion was one of his most ticklish problems. The list of his contributors, and there were more foreign writers than British, was truly an impressive one.

He regarded this journalistic enterprise as providing a forum for Europe. "The intellectual forces of Europe will here assemble in order to reinforce those of generous impulse," he wrote in his editorial foreword to the first supplement. This sentence expressed well his vision and hope of combining intellect and feeling (or "passionate perception," as he expressed it in his youth) in the endeavor to solve the economic problems of the continent. Ever felicitous in his phrasing, he closed the foreward with these words: "With much detail and technical apparatus our contributors will, like Chrysaor in Shelley's *Oedipus,* 'Stand prating here of commerce, public faith,/Economy and unadulterate coin,/And other topics, ultra-radical.'"

A general introduction to the *Reconstruction in Europe* series was written by him for the second number of the supplements. In this essay he showed a good deal of Edwardian optimism about Europe's economic prospects and assured his readers, after the severe 1920–21 depression, that there was no reason why the former prosperity should not be regained soon. In writing of economists, it is significant as compared with his later views that at this time he did not consider them as "trustees of the possibility of civilization" or as "dentists." No, he stated, "the economist is not king, quite true. But he ought to be! He is a better and wiser governor than the general or the diplomatist or the oratorical lawyer. In the modern overpopulated world, which can only live at all by nice adjustment, he is not only useful but necessary." In fact, his social philosophy in these essays was quite conventional in character. As to the economic future, there was a hint of possible economic stagnation after "the magnificent episode of the nineteenth century is over." And, "Progress is a soiled creed, black with coal dust and gunpowder, but we have not discarded it. We believe and disbelieve, and mingle faith with doubt."

He wrote, "If Europe is to suffer a decline, it will be due not to material but to spiritual causes." Striking a note that recurs in his later work, he stated, "We today are the most creedless of men. Every one of our religious and political constructions is moth-eaten, even more moth-eaten than we ordinarily admit to ourselves. Our official religions have about as much practical influence on us as the monarchy or the lord mayor's coach. But we no longer substitute for them the militant skepticism of Voltaire and Hume, or the humanitarian optimism of Bentham and Comte and Mill, or the farfetched abstractions of Hegel." Citing his good friend Ludwig Wittgenstein (his influential *Tractatus Logico-Philosophicus* had just appeared and was stirring Cambridge minds), he concluded that "with religion dead and philosophy dry, the public runs to the witch doctors. In cut and material, our fig leaves have fallen out of fashion, and we find them neither comfortable nor becoming. Freud tells us to strip them off; [Emile] Coue to wear two pairs.

"Capitalism has lost its self-confidence. . . . There has been no common purpose lately between nations or between classes, except for war."

In these popular essays his basic answer to the world's economic and political problems were "the principles of pacifism and population or birth control" which, he asserted, were "the prolegomena to any future scheme of social improvement." This emphasis on Malthusianism is rather marked in his thinking of that period; its relationship, if any, to his own sexual nature poses a difficult question of interpretation. In any case, whatever its mental origin, there will be those who will feel that he showed remarkable prescience in making the following statement: "Indeed, the problem of population is going to be not merely an economist's problem, but in the near future the greatest of all political questions. It will be a question which will arouse some of the deepest instincts and emotions of men, and feeling may run as passionately as in earlier struggles between religions."

The supplements were generally well received by the press. While they were not financially profitable to the *Manchester Guardian,* its editor recognized that they had greatly enhanced his paper's prestige. At their completion he wrote Keynes, saying, "Whatever its merits they are entirely yours, and I hope that you will believe that we are grateful."

In the midst of all this editorial work, Keynes decided to undertake still another role—that of special correspondent of the *Manchester Guardian* at the upcoming Genoa conference which had been called in 1922 to strengthen European economic confidence. He agreed to write eleven major articles over a period of three weeks. The conference was especially important because Germany and, for the first time since the Great War, Russia were to be represented. This was the first occasion since that conflict that the exbelligerents were to negotiate as equals, and great hopes were consequently held as to the outcome. As Keynes himself later wrote, "This is a council of Europe, not of the allies, an assemblage wider-embracing than the League of Nations."

The *Manchester Guardian* paid him three hundred pounds for his articles, and with much effort he arranged to sell the British rights to the series to the *Daily Express,* the *New York World,* and other newspapers, including seven European journals; he was anxious to obtain as wide a circulation as possible. Furthermore, the income from these publications would pleasantly bolster his account with his brokers.

Right off, he scooped the conference by writing an article on "The Stabilization of the European Exchanges"; it was almost immediately the talk of the assembling delegates and a subject of comment in the financial papers and in the City. In it he advocated a return to a gold bullion standard and a stabilization of exchange rates rather than a policy of trying to improve currency values by deflation. In countries where the legal tender money had depreciated more than twenty percent below its prewar values, he advised against any attempt at restoration to the earlier levels. It was desirable, he thought, that all currencies should be made convertible to gold, but at a very cautious valuation. He recommended further that the state banks of Europe permit a difference of five percent between their buying and selling prices for gold, thus allowing small seasonal or temporary fluctuations in the exchanges. He proposed, too, that each of the participating countries should give an unconditional guarantee for five years of redemption of their notes in gold at the rates originally fixed, with certain provisos, and that the Federal Reserve Board of the United States might agree to make temporary gold loans to the participating central banks to facilitate the stabilization process. This article made quite an impression among the delegates at Genoa. Indeed, he no sooner had arrived when he was invited to consult with the British delegation as to whether his proposals should formally be put before the conference. Actually, the ideas of another of his articles, "The Forward

Market in Foreign Exchanges," whereby the state banks should enter the market to buy or sell forward exchange, were included in the financial resolutions of that body.

With his wide and influential friendships among the delegates, his consummate publicist and economic expertise, and his lively, readable style, Keynes was certainly an extraordinary journalist at Genoa. Given his influence, it is little wonder that some regarded him as an almost sinister figure. *Le Temps* even tried to circulate the story that he was at Genoa as a German newspaper correspondent, but this fabrication was easily scotched by publication of the facts. Despite these denials, another French newspaper, *L'Echo National,* represented him as "the doctrinaire agent of a London banking group with German leanings." From a photograph of him at the conference one can see that the once carefree Maynard looked very much like a staid banker with his Homburg hat and cane. Two years later, gossipy Virginia Woolf wrote her sister, "Maynard's an odd fish; weighs thirteen stone, he says, and is somehow respectable."

Keynes showed real curiosity in "the great Russian experiment" and in the financial problems and system of the new Soviet government. G. V. Chicherin, the Russian foreign minister, was also a figure of much interest to the delegates at the conference. Oddly, he also happened to be homosexual and had arrived with two of Keynes's books to read on the journey. The eager journalist lost no time in asking for an interview, stating that whether the conference would be "no better than a bore depends almost entirely on yourself and Mr. Lloyd George between you." Later he prodded other Russian experts with questions, wrote a revealing essay on "The Financial System of the Bolsheviks," and urged *de jure* recognition of their government and a substantial government credit by Britain to Russia to promote reconstruction and trade. He felt that solid foundations could be laid to build a bridge between the two governments. "Revolutions," he reminded his readers, "are not kid-glove affairs, particularly in Russia. But a mere disgust and moral indignation, which has not even the curiosity to discover the facts, is never by itself the right reaction to a great historical event."

The Russians did not disappoint Keynes or the delegates at this conclave; in fact, they stunned them by negotiating the subterranean Rapallo agreement with Germany whereby the two countries mutually wiped out claims arising from the war. The Soviet government also waived claims for compensation over injury done by their legislation to private interests; in addition, Germany granted the Russian regime *de jure* recognition and agreed to resume normal trading relations. Keynes saw little objection to the substance of this pact but thought that the method was open to serious criticism. Signing a document of this kind without any notice to the other members of the conference was hard to justify; "the Germans have undoubtedly done themselves harm," he wrote, "and rearoused old suspicions." Four months later the Russians again surprised the Western world by being the first of the European belligerents to stabilize their currency, a development that Keynes had casually anticipated in one of his articles.

His tendency to employ oppositional concepts in the course of his analysis manifested itself again in his last article of the conference in the figure of two horses. "The political government of the world," he observed, "is dragged along by two horses, equally ill-mated in tandem or in yoke." He referred to "the creation of atmosphere, the development of public sentiment, the precise emotional suggestion of the cant phrases of the hour" as the one horse, and the other as "a right policy of action." In a sense this figure of speech was analogous to his previous distinction between inside and outside opinion. He believed that too much time had been devoted at Genoa to discussion of standards of propriety and not enough to more substantive questions, though he granted that the former had accomplished some good. "The medicine men were busy at Genoa establishing certain necessary taboos among the savage tribes of Europe."

Lloyd George, he stated, could claim to have achieved a modified success at the conference by creating a certain climate of opinion which "made sabotage in Europe a more difficult undertaking than it was before." But if the test is not propaganda but the drawing up of "a well-considered plan for the economic reconstruction of Europe, then the favorable judgment of the world must be accepted." Having completed his contracted three weeks at the meeting, he left before its close, as he had done in a more dramatic way at the more famous assembly four years before.

One of the most serious economic developments of the early twenties was the hyperinflation of the German mark and the social dislocation that it caused. Keynes was drawn into this matter very early. In August 1922, he was invited to Hamburg to take part in an Overseas Week designed to encourage the restoration of trade relations. This was his first visit to Germany since the war. He gave a public address in which he urged the Germans to remain calm and to put their own house in order by checking the insidious inflation in their economy. A moratorium on reparations until 1930 should be declared, he told them, and there was no hope of raising a large international loan. He proposed instead a new reparations plan which would fix Germany's total liability at forty billion gold marks, this to be due in 1930 or thereabouts. He had been introduced to his German audience of businessmen as "the man most responsible for the changed attitude of the English-speaking world toward Germany." Amid cries of "*Hoch!*" he was given prolonged applause. "His remarks," the *Daily Telegraph* stated, "are reported in the German press at a length and with a prominence which is usually reserved for the heads of government."

Yet it is striking fact that his concurrent dispatches to the *Manchester Guardian* altogether lacked the optimistic tone of his speech. He found the German people terrified by the uncertainty caused by inflation; the country seemed to him to be on the verge of civil war. He urged the Allies to declare an unconditional moratorium without delay. At the reparations commission in Paris late in August, the British moved for such a breathing spell until the end of the year, but this was rejected. Adopted instead was a Belgian proposal that Germany should pay her installments in six-month Treasury bills rather than in cash. In September, Keynes was pleading in the *Manchester Guardian Commercial* that a moratorium should be given Germany at least until the end of 1923; reparations in kind should be abolished; the reparations commission should be dissolved and the occupation of the Rhineland terminated. In this long article he continued to assert that the reparation game was not "worth the candle." "The reparation conferences of the past three years between the prime ministers of France and England may seem to the future student among the most frivolous and misguided episodes of history, and those who attended them the blindest of statesmen. We waste our time with nonsense while bigger events are shaping." Lloyd George had proved himself "the least capable of enduring and constructive statesmanship of any man who has held long power in England."

In another article, "Speculation in the Mark and Germany's Balances Abroad," Keynes displayed his usual industry in refuting those such as the Francophile *Times* which claimed that Germany was concealing large amounts of assets abroad. Meanwhile, the German mark, which had been declining steadily, dropped sharply on the exchanges when the government had to make a cash payment for reparations, as he had earlier predicted. In November, as its decline accelerated ominously, the German authorities invited a group of monetary experts, including Keynes, to discuss its possible stabilization. He, R. H. Brand, Gustav Cassel, and J. W. Jenks in a majority report on the subject recommended immediate stabilization of the mark, a reparation moratorium of at least two years, a balanced budget, and some international credits. Keynes felt strongly that the proper course for Germany, after a moratorium, would be budgetary balance, and immediate currency stabilization; in his view intervention in the foreign exchange market to support the mark at varying rates would be of no avail.

Keynes was now vigorously expounding the position that, despite the vagaries of the politicians, it was the duty of the economist to seek to alter public opinion. He firmly believed that with the aid of Pigou's cash-balance version of the quantity theory, if the quantity of a currency was controlled, its value could be stabilized. He approached all these questions of monetary policy and reparations with amazing intensity and a sense of personal involvement. He was very restless and critical of what he regarded as the feebleness and muddleheadedness of Britain's foreign policy, and he showed this even in letters to the newspaper and to friends. He wrote numerous articles for the *Manchester Guardian,* and later in 1923 for the *Nation,* with meticulous care, kept up his correspondence with Melchior and other banking and Treasury friends, and was constantly *au courant* with the developing situation.

When, for example, Lloyd George's coalition government ended in October 1922 and the subsequent general election brought the Conservatives to power, with Bonar Law as the prime minister and Stanley Baldwin as the chancellor of the exchequer, he lost no time in establishing himself "behind the scenes." This was not difficult to do because he had known both men in his Treasury days, and they were all members of the United University Club. The new government was faced with two immediate problems: an approaching conference on reparations and negotiations with the Americans on the British war debt. He had been in correspondence on the former question with Sir John Bradbury, the British delegate to the reparations commission, commented on his proposals, and submitted his own plan for a settlement with Germany. In December he conferred with Bonar Law, presumably on this matter, and later met with the chancellor on the eve of his departure for America to arrange the terms of Britain's debt. The conditions Baldwin secured in his negotiations with the Americans were far less favorable than had been hoped—they required annual payments of $161 million for ten years and $184 million annually for the following fifty-two years.

These provisions were the subject of a heated debate in the Cabinet, with Baldwin defending and the prime minister strongly opposing their acceptance. Keynes earlier had expressed his "passionate objections" to the American settlement to Montagu Norman, the governor of the Bank of England, who had accompanied Baldwin on the United States mission. On the very day of the Cabinet debate, his letter to J. C. Davidson, Bonar Law's private secretary, was given to Baldwin. In it he had stated, "I hope, on the whole, that we refuse the American offer, in order to give them time to discover that they are just as completely at our mercy as we at France's and France's at Germany's; it is the debtor who has the last word in these cases." Later, however after the French had invaded the Ruhr, an action which he strongly deplored, he relented and said that, while he was not satisfied with the justice of the American settlement, "if it helps England and America to feel and act together about the new war with which France is distracting Europe," it was a good thing. "If some joint policy results, that will be worth everything." This was another instance of his ability to change his mind in the face of the shifting kaleidoscope of political events.

He was so intent on solving the reparations problem at this time that he sought to help the Germans as well as the Conservative party on this matter. He viewed the French occupation of the Ruhr with deep concern—"a desperate expedient," he called it, believing that it contributed to further deterioration in economic activity and endangered the balance of political power. He feared that "the combination of economic distress and patriotic rage might at last drive Germany desperate." He wrote, "The extreme docility toward the allies, and even weakness, of recent German governments has been remarkable. It will not help France or Europe," he warned with uncanny insight, "to replace them by more savage material, such material as we know with only too much reason to lie below the surface in Germany."

The Cabinet of Joseph Wirth which had resigned in Germany on November 24, 1922, stating that it could not stabilize the mark without a foreign loan and a moratorium on all payments except to the devastated areas, was succeeded by a coalition government. It was headed by Wilhelm Cuno, the former manager of the Hamburg-Amerika shipping line, who was known to Keynes as a German expert at the peace conference and as a contributor to his supplements. More important, Carl Melchior, Keynes's intimate at Versailles, was very close to Cuno. Keynes's letters to the former were shown to the chancellor and to other German officials as the situation grew more intense. When on January 2, 1923, the reparations commission declared Germany in voluntary default on coal deliveries, the French troops were readied for movement, and nine days later they and their Belgian counterparts entered the Ruhr. The Germans adopted a policy of passive resistance in reaction. All reparations and deliveries stopped, workers and miners quit work, and the French took over factories and mines, banks and customs collection. Soon food became scarce, and within a week of the invasion the mark lost two-thirds of its shrinking value on the exchanges. As Melchior had stated in a letter to Keynes, "the beginning of 1923 smells extremely badly."

The cold, despairing days of the Ruhr occupation dragged on until April 20 when Lord Curzon, the British foreign minister, invited the Germans to submit their own ideas for a settlement. When that was forthcoming the following May 2, it was very disappointing; it was apparently the work of a drafting committee, repeated for the most part proposals submitted earlier, but contained one new element, namely, Germany's willingness to submit the terms of settlement to an international body of experts, thus opening the door to what eventually became the Dawes Plan. This document had been drawn up, however, in the most obnoxious, bureaucratic style, leading Keynes to observe, "From the days of Versailles until now the notes of the German government have lacked both passion and persuasiveness [both cardinal virtues in his mind]. . . . One might suppose that her statesmen, as well as her students, were nourished exclusively on potatoes. Heaven knows that propaganda is a sinful thing! But there is nothing wrong in writing a short sentence."

Keynes found Lord Curzon's reply to the Germans equally lacking, particularly in its ignoring the German offer to submit her capacity to pay to impartial arbitration. To him the British government still drifted and was without a European policy. Meanwhile, he was exchanging inside information with Melchior and writing directly to the German chancellor, even submitting a "suggested German reply to Lord Curzon" for the former's use. Melchior served as intermediary in these exchanges with their "mutual friend"—the chancellor. Keynes gave the Germans economic advice, telling them that a big international loan was illusory, and also appraised the effects of the British Cabinet on the prospects for successful negotiations for their benefit. At this time he also drafted a letter addressed "Dear Prime Minister" in which he stated what Cuno might say to the British head of government, but there is no indication that it was ever sent. He did go on a flying trip to Hamburg and Berlin late in May and early June (1923), during which he breakfasted and dined with the German chancellor and the foreign minister and reviewed the new reply they were preparing on reparations. Before leaving on this mission, he had sought an interview with the new British prime minister, Stanley Baldwin.

He returned from these delicate meetings on June 4, as Melchior stated, "without doubt to prepare public opinion [in England], especially at *The Times*." The Cuno government was afraid that if their offer was rejected, more radical forces would take over the government. "I believe that Keynes convinced himself of the seriousness of the situation," Melchior wrote, "and I can only hope that he will exercise a good influence with the press as well as with Bonar Law and McKenna."

Certainly, he was in an amazingly strategic role at that time; he was both journalist and broker-statesman, suggesting proposals to the Gemans and then returning to London to persuade opinion in their favor. The note that Germany offered on June 7 was conciliatory, restating its willingness to submit to international arbitration the controversial question of her capacity to pay and the amounts and methods of payment. She was willing to pay under a system of annuities, if a large-scale loan was impracticable. These were the very points that Keynes had advocated in prior correspondence with them. It is not surprising, therefore, that his lead in the *Nation* of June 16, 1923, opened with the words, "The new German note affords as fair a basis for the settlement of the economic problem of reparations as it is within the power of the German government to give."

Whatever one may think about the ethics of his dual role in this matter, it was certainly diplomacy in a new style. What we do know is that the German chancellor wrote him on June 16, thanking him for his kind message of June 16 (it is not clear whether this refers to Keynes's editorial in the *Nation* or not) and "all the support you gave our memorandum. You were very successful indeed." Surely, with so persuasive a voice in the fields of journalism and diplomacy, at this time Keynes had the best of both worlds.

CHAPTER 10

The Gold Standard and Monetary Reform

In the field of action, reformers will not be successful until they can steadily pursue a clear and definite object with their intellects and their feelings in tune.

J. M. Keynes

AT A LECTURE at Oxford University in November 1924, Keynes expressed himself as quoted above. It is a fascinating statement because it reflects his psychological nature so well and brings to mind his letter to Swithinbank almost twenty years before in which he stated an almost identical sentiment: "Why is it so difficult to find a true combination of passion and intellect? What is there worth anything except passionate perception?"

In the years 1919–25 he had attacked the Treaty of Paris and the reparation problem with intense intellectual force and passion. Looking back on that period, he wrote that he had "plunged" himself "without reserve" into three great controversies—"the treaty of peace and the war debts, the policy of deflation, and the return to the gold standard." In this same place he expressed the hope and belief that "the day is not far off when the economic problem will take the back seat where it belongs, and that the arena of the head and the heart will be occupied or reoccupied by our real problems—the problems of life and human relations, of creation and behavior and religion." These words and the figure of speech employed suggest the attitude of a passionate reformer who was supremely capable of using both his head and his heart in the espousal of necessary social change.

[201]

In his interest in social reform, Keynes was not so different from the other master economists who had revolutionized British economics in the preceding two centuries. An anatomy of those revolutions in economic theory shows that they emerged in close association with arguments for social reform. Typically, it is true that the reform programs of these British economists were not explicit in their theoretical treatises, but if we look into their contemporaneous pamphlets and correspondence, we can usually find an intimate relation between their theories and their policies. Why is this so?

Fundamentally, the answer is found in the fact, as Professor Dudley Dillard states, that

the principles of economics are always on the road to obsolescence. They become decreasingly relevant to the new problems that emerge with the passage of time. . . . A new system of theory cannot be built on the one it succeeds because they are addressed to different problems. The old theory is not wrong so much as it becomes obsolete or irrelevant to the new problem. In a sense, a successful theory helps to induce its own obsolesence by providing a solution to a major problem, which in time is replaced by a different problem that requires a different theory.

Keynes was very conscious of the new problems that had emerged in Great Britain and in the world economy generally as a result of World War I. His strategic position in the Treasury, handling inter-Allied finances, had made him very aware of the radical change in Britain's creditor position and of the new powerful status of the United States in international finance. He had expressed his misgivings about the possibility of restoring the economic structure of the prewar period in *The Economic Consequences of the Peace.* Then in the immediate postwar years he had watched and studied with concern the unregulated boom and crash of 1919–21, and the destructive inflation in Germany and in some of the other continental countries. In his Christmas 1917 letter to his mother one recalls his opinion that the war probably meant "the disappearance of the social order that we have known hitherto" and his fear of general impoverishment. His perception of the world was very likely transformed, too, by the impact of total war and the economic planning that was tried during the international conflict. That struggle by its very economic nature was a challenge to internationalism and the venerable doctrine of the minimum state.

His penetrating appreciation of the significance of those historic changes was undoubtedly attributable to his conception of the nature of an economist and to his own unusual personality traits. "The economist," he wrote about this time, "must study the present in the light of the past for the purposes of the future." He was, writes one historian, "the historical *amateur* in the best and original meaning of the word," and he adds perceptively that Keynes valued "the added dimension" history affords the imagination.

In terms of economic methodology or schools of thought, Keynes was in part an institutionalist interested in the culture, social structure, and psychological character of the human beings in the economy he was studying. Professor Robert Skidelsky has aptly noted that "the absence in Keynesian theory of any explicit historical dimension should not blind us to the practical and historical roots of Keynes's equations." In this connection it is notable that in arguing that the Western world was in "a perilous age of transition" in the twenties, he cited Professor John R. Commons, the eminent American institutional economist who, he said, "had been one of the first to recognize the nature of the economic transition amidst the early stages of which we are now living." Commons had described three eras: first, that of scarcity, which was the normal state of the world up to about the fifteenth or sixteenth century; second, the era of abundance, which coincided with the expansion of mercantilism and then of individualistic capitalism; and last, the third era which we are now entering, a period of stabilization characterized by increased concerted and collective actions of corporations, trade unions, and government.

That Keynes was a reformer we hardly need demonstrate; he himself said that he was possessed by "the *Verbesserungs* malady." Harrod recognized that "he was keenly alive to the great social evils and sensitive to suffering. He was by nature a progressive and a reformer. He believed that by thought and resolution things could be made better and that quickly." He also attributed Keynes's strong vein of pacificism to the gentleness of his nature and the philosophy of his Bloomsbury friends. However, we would go further and relate these attributes in both Keynes and among the Bloomsberries to the elements of androgyny in their respective natures. Keynes's homosexuality or bisexuality was also an independent element in his reformist tendency; as such, he was an outsider in a heterosexual world that he had never made. In a speech at the Manchester Reform Club in February 1926, he delightfully said that he fancied he had played with "the possibilities of greater social changes than come within the present social philosophies of, let us say, Mr. Sidney Webb, Mr. [James H.] Thomas, or Mr.

[John] Wheatley." Borrowing a phrase from the writings of the homoerotic Walt Whitman, he added, "The republic of my imagination lies on the extreme left of celestial space."

From his university days he had been sympathetic to the Liberal party and indeed had spoken at several elections in its behalf. Now, in the twenties with the problems of postwar reconstruction so pressing, he began to take a more active part in its activities. In 1921, he met at Grasmere with such Liberals as Ramsay Muir, E. D. Simon, Walter Layton, William Beveridge, and Ted Scott to discuss the future of the party. One result of this meeting was the establishment of the annual Liberal Summer Schools which had as their purpose the education of the membership on current problems. This school, which met alternately at Cambridge and Oxford for a week in August, provided a valuable forum for political discussion in the following years. In the October 1922 election, Keynes spoke publicly for the Liberal party and at the same time, as we have seen, sought to influence the policies of the Conservative party through his acquaintance with Bonar Law and Stanley Baldwin. Then, in April 1923, he involved himself even more deeply in the Liberal party's fortunes by acquiring, with a group of Liberal friends, a controlling interest in the liberal weekly periodical, the *Nation and Athenaeum*. Since its founding in 1907, this journal had been edited by W. H. Massingham, a distinguished figure in Liberal party circles; it was owned by the Rowntree family, and though it provided a valuable forum for social criticism, its liberalism was oriented somewhat toward the past—it lacked the "new look" and, in addition, it was not financially profitable. Keynes vigorously assumed the post of chairman of the editorial board, and he and his colleagues persuaded Hubert Henderson, a Cambridge economist who had studied under Marshall, to take the position of editor. The new management sought to give their magazine wider circulation; they cut the price from nine pence to six pence and brought in Bloomsbury and Cambridge friends to enliven its pages. Leonard Woolf became literary editor, and not surprisingly, the first issue featured essays by practically a roster of Bloomsbury's best writers, and Keynes himself wrote a weekly page in finance and investment. The first issue appeared on May 5, 1923, after *Punch* had hailed it a week or so before in a bit of verse which concluded:

> And hope of salvation
> Revives and remains,
> For the rule of the *Nation*
> Is passing to Keynes.

In statements to the press and in an editorial foreword to the renovated organ, Keynes left his readers with no doubt as to where it would stand—"We shall be very Liberal and Labor"—and went on to say that there would be no commerce whatever with Conservative opinion, however moderate, and "the doctrinaire part of the Labor party is completely inadequate for the solution of our present troubles. . . . Our own sympathies are for a Liberal party which has its center well to the left, a party definitely of change and progress, disconnected with the world, striving after many things, but with a bolder, freer, more disinterested mind than Labor has, and quit of their out-of-date dogmas." The great dividing questions of the future were seen to fall into two groups; peace and disarmament, and the economic structure. In the succeeding years, Keynes wrote many cogent and witty editorials on a wide range of public problems for the new journal.

He had spent considerable time and effort in getting this periodical off to an auspicious start, but within a month or so after its inaugural issue, he was writing to his mother: "For the last week or two and for the next week or two I am doing very little for the *Nation* so as to be able to get on with my book, the scope of which, as usual, tends to grow a little under my hands." He was referring to his *Tract on Monetary Reform,* which dealt with an aspect of economic policy that was to occupy him increasingly after this date. The volume which appeared in the bookshops in December 1923 represents an important work in Keynesian literature because in it he launched for the first time a strong attack on that venerable institution of capitalism, the gold standard. Its analysis had considerable impact on professional as well as lay opinion; it was published in American, French, German, Italian, Danish, and Japanese editions.

The Tract starts off quite mildly and soberly in its early chapters, but in its latter part Keynes "zeroes in" on the conventional monetary wisdom. The first chapters were, in fact, a reworking of three articles he had written for the *Manchester Guardian Supplements* the year before. In the former chapters, he lucidly explored the evils resulting from the instability in the purchasing power of money, the effects of the exigencies of public finance on money's value, and the theory of money and the foreign exchanges. On the first topic he concluded that "inflation is unjust and deflation is inexpedient. Of the two, perhaps deflation is, if we rule out the exaggerated inflations such as that of Germany, the worse, because it is worse, in an impoverished world, to provoke unemployment than to disappoint the rentier. But it is not necessary that we should weigh one evil against the other. It is easier to agree that both are evils and should be shunned. The individualistic capitalism of today, precisely because it entrusts saving to the individual investor and production to the individual employer, presumes a stable measuring rod of value, and cannot be efficient—perhaps cannot survive—without one."

In the second chapter he examined how governments have employed inflation of the currency or of credit as a method of taxation, describing the catastrophic hyperinflation in Germany and in eastern Europe in the early twenties. He weighed the relative merits of currency depreciation against a capital levy as alternatives in moderating the claims of the state's bondholders when they have reached, in terms of money, an excessive proportion of the national income.

In his third chapter he expounded the Pigou (or Cambridge) version of the quantity theory of money rather than the one familiar to American students of economics in that generation, that of Professor Irving Fisher. He demonstrated how the basic value of money was dependent on two crucial decisions—the decision of the central bank concerning the quantity of credit to create, and the decisions the public makes as to how much real value it wishes to hold in the form of currency or bank balances. Using the equation $n = p(k - rk')$, he stated that so long as K, k' and r remain unchanged, there is a direct relation between the quantity of cash (n) and the level of prices (p). Expressing the opinion that the cruder form of the quantity theory was valid only in the long run, he then sharply and quite authoritatively added a thought which has become one of the most quoted bits of Keynesiana: "But this long run is a misleading guide to current affairs. *In the long run* we are all dead. Economists set themselves too easy, too useless a task if in the tempestuous seasons they can only tell us that when the storm is long past the ocean is flat again."

He felt very strongly about currency reform at that time. We can note, for example, his remark in the book's preface and in other places that "nowhere do conservative notions consider themselves more in place than in currency; yet nowhere is the need of innovation more urgent." In the next chapter of the *Tract* he set out the case for an active management of currency with unusual force and confidence; there is a noticeable increased use of the personal pronoun *I* as contrasted with the earlier exposition. He distinguished between devaluation of the currency, by which he stated that he meant a policy of stabilizing the value of the currency somewhere near its present value, and a policy of deflation, that is, increasing the value of the currency in terms of gold or commodities. Next he discussed the alternative goals of stability of prices versus stability of exchange rates, namely the internal value of the currency versus its external value as measured in terms of foreign currencies. And last, he raised the question of the restoration of the gold standard—is it, "however imperfect in theory, the best available method for attaining our ends in practice"?

On this last question he asserted very confidently that World War I had effected a great change: gold itself had become a "managed" currency. "In the modern postwar world of paper currency and bank credit there is no escape from a 'managed' currency, whether we wish it or not; convertibility into gold will not alter the fact that the value of gold itself depends on the policy of the central banks."

In his mind the advocates of a return to gold were suffering from a form of cultural lag in that they disregarded the significant changes in the contemporary context in which the gold standard would have to function as contrasted with the conditions which prevailed in the prewar period. "In truth, the gold standard is already a barbarous relic. ... A regulated nonmetallic standard has slipped in unnoticed. It *exists*. While the economists dozed, the academic dream of a hundred years, doffing its cap and gown, clad in paper rags, has crept into the real world by means of the bad fairies—always so much more potent than the good—the wicked ministers of finance." Here he reverts to figures of speech and images which remind us of his *Economic Consequences of the Peace*.

Using a ploy that he used quite often, he next cited his friend and ex-Treasury colleague Ralph G. Hawtrey as advocating a managed gold standard with international cooperation. Differentiating his stand from Hawtrey's, he remarked that he saw "grave objections to reinstating gold in the pious hope that international cooperation will keep it in order." No, with the existing maldistribution of the world's gold, with the United States holding the bulk of it, "the reinstatement of the gold standard means, inevitably, that we surrender the regulation of our price level and the handling of the credit cycle to the Federal Reserve Board of the United States." Even with the best of cooperation between that board and the Bank of England, he argued, the balance of power would still lie with the former. "Moreover"—and here he added a provocative generalization—"we can be confident beforehand that there will be much suspicion amongst Americans (for that is their disposition) of any supposed attempt on the part of the Bank of England to dictate their policy or to influence American discount rates in the interests of Great Britain."

In his last chapter he offered his own positive suggestions for the future regulation of money, showing that the system which had grown up "half-haphazard" since the war was one in which the level of prices depended fundamentally on the deliberate policies of the Bank of England and the Treasury. These agencies, he declared, tend to watch and control the creation of bank credit and let the creation of currency follow suit, rather than the reverse which was the policy followed formerly. In this new system, gold really played no part, except for occasional shipments to the United States to settle Treasury obligations, and the foreign exchanges were unregulated and allowed to look after themselves.

At that time Great Britain was not on the gold standard, though there was considerable aspiration to return to a fixed dollar exchange at the prewar parity. Keynes held that the managing authorities should adopt the stability of sterling prices as their primary objective with exchange stability as a secondary aim, to be achieved through cooperation with the American authorities. The trend of the general price level, he suggested, might be measured by an index number of the price of a standard composite commodity similar to the plan of Professor Irving Fisher's celebrated "compensated dollar." As to foreign exchange rates, he would permit sterling to float and have the Bank of England regulate or change the price of gold daily both for immediate delivery and for delivery three months forward, with the above objective in mind. Shocking as it may seem to some, as he said, he would separate entirely the gold reserve from the note issue and use the former only for the purpose of avoiding short-period fluctuations in the exchange.

From this summary of his views it can be seen that he was a wholehearted believer in managed money, and his bold advocacy of such a policy represented at that time an innovative departure from monetary orthodoxy. *"The Tract,"* writes Professor Donald Moggridge, "represented a distinct break from the Cambridge tradition of Marshall, Pigou, and most of their pupils in its activism and its emphasis on positive management rather than changes in such things as the rules regarding bank behavior."

In the years that followed, Keynes continued to urge a policy of active monetary management rather than a return to the "automatic" gold standard. He did so because he believed that actual practice had already seriously departed from the traditional assumptions and principles of the gold standard. In the United States, as in Great Britain, the objectives and the methods that were being pursued, "half consciously and half unconsciously," were in accordance with what he was advocating. "The theory," he wrote, "on which the Federal Reserve is supposed

John Neville Keynes, 1905

Florence Ada Keynes, 1905

The three Keynes children in 1889, *left to right*, Margaret
(later Mrs. A. V. Hill) age four; Geoffrey, age two; and Maynard, age six

Maynard Keynes, age 12

Keynes as an Eton graduate in 1902

John Maynard Keynes in London,
1912

Lytton Strachey, *left*, and
Duncan Grant, 1922

Left, Lydia Lopokova as the ballerina in the ballet *Petrushka*, and dancing in the open air at Garsington, 1925 *(right)*

Lydia and Maynard Keynes, 1929

Keynes, Mrs. Karl Melchior,
Lydia, and Karl Melchior

Harry D. White
and John Maynard Keynes at
Bretton Woods, N.H., 1944

Virginia Woolf and Maynard Keynes at Monk's House, Sussex, 1932

George Bernard Shaw and Keynes on the steps of the Fitzwilliam Museum, Cambridge, 1935

Lady and Lord Keynes at the time of the British loan negotiations
(Courtesy of the New York *Daily News*)

John Maynard Keynes in the
library of his London home

to govern its discount policy, by reference to the influx and efflux of gold and the proportion of gold to liabilities, is as dead as mutton." It perished, he maintained, because the Federal Reserve Board in effect demonetized gold in the sense that "gold was not allowed to exercise the multiplied influence which the prewar system presumed." Though the United States continued to give lip service to the gold standard, "a dollar standard was set up on the pedestal of the Golden Calf. For the past two years the United States has *pretended* to maintain a gold standard. In fact it has established a dollar standard; and, instead of ensuring that the value of the dollar shall conform to that of gold, it makes provision, at great expense, that the value of gold shall conform to that of the dollar. This is the way by which a rich country is able to combine new wisdom with old prejudice."

The United States, he concluded, like Great Britain, should "aim at the stability of the commodity value of the dollar rather than at the stability of the gold value of the dollar." The foreign exchanges of the two countries should be stabilized through an intimate cooperation between the Federal Reserve Board and the Bank of England. So there would be two managed currencies instead of one, which was the best that the evolution of money currently permitted up to that time.

Upon its publication, Keynes's *Tract* created quite a stir and a lot of controversy, expecially among Liberals, many of whom were not convinced that the central authorities should be given extended discretion over the supply of money. The reaction of many others was also hostile, the feeling being that inflation might well become runaway under managed currency without the check provided by the gold standard. Keynes was not impressed by these criticisms, believing that the Treasury and bank officials were not "so irresponsible that, if only they were given the power, they would embark on a career of squander-mania by printing bank notes." He believed that the "old boys were fundamentally trustworthy and well meaning, but they were blind and complacent, and greatly needed prodding." These philosophical differences over monetary policy have persisted to some degree even to the present, but in the meantime many of the innovations which he argued for have become commonplace. Currency reform was very important to him at that time, but he soon came to realize that even more far-reaching changes would be necessary if a middle way was to be found between socialism and unregulated capitalism.

In April 1924, Keynes's attention was drawn from monetary reform to the problem of unemployment when Lloyd George proposed a large-scale program of public works as a solution in an article in the *Nation*.

The question aroused a good deal of interest because about a million workers were then unemployed in Great Britain. A month later in the same journal, Keynes asked, "Does unemployment need a drastic remedy?" He answered with a decided affirmative and proposed that the Treasury should use the sinking fund to spend as much as £100 million per year on capital projects, such as mass-produced housing, road modernization, and electric power transmission. In this piece he looked for "the ultimate cure of unemployment and for the stimulus which shall initiate a cumulative prosperity to monetary reform— which will remove fear—and the diversion of the National Savings from relatively barren foreign investment into state-encouraged constructive enterprise at home, which will inspire confidence." He was increasingly critical of the rate of foreign investment, holding that much of it was excessive and undesirable and that it did not promote exports and employment as much as *laissez-faire* theorizing would suggest. He returned to the subject of foreign investment again at the Liberal Summer School that year, arguing that many such past investments had turned out badly. On the whole, however, he was not successful in these efforts at persuasion; his advocacy of these policies lacked a solid foundation of economic theory that would explain the causes of depression and unemployment. In the next half dozen years, he sought to overcome this grave deficiency in economic thought.

In 1924, Keynes also sought to help his old friend Wittgenstein, who had fought on the Eastern front during the war and had been taken prisoner in 1918. When the young philosopher was captured, he was carrying in his knapsack the manuscript of a book that was to make him famous, *Logisch Philosophische Abhandlung*. He had sent copies of it to Bertrand Russell, Keynes, and Gottlob Frege, and in 1922 Russell published an English translation with the ponderous title *Tractatus Logico-Philosophicus*.

Keynes had been anxious to keep in touch with Wittgenstein during the war, even to the extent of lending him money, exchanging books, and intervening to secure his release from the prison camp at Monte Cassino. Once secured, the difficult philosopher refused to take advantage of it. Upon his release in 1919, one of the first things he did was to give away all his money, his father having left him a considerable fortune. He then decided to become a schoolmaster in the remote Austrian villages of Simmering, and there he remained for the eight years 1921–29. This dark period, the mystery years of Wittgenstein's life, was finally illuminated as a result of the extraordinary research of an

American philosopher, William W. Bartley III, who went up to these villages, spoke to the people who had known the peculiar Austrian as a teacher, and thus discovered the explanation of his mysterious behavior. Wittgenstein had decided to live in such out-of-the-way places to remove himself from homosexual temptation in more congested areas. In 1921, he was in a state of despair because he felt that he had not realized himself intellectually. In a letter to a friend, he wrote, "I have been morally dead for more than a year. . . . I ought to have become a star in the sky." Apparently he had become convinced that the high spiritual and intellectual creativity he wanted was incompatible with sexual activity. Wittgenstein's later friendships with students in Cambridge, says Bartley, were seen by him as "moral encounters; within them he became creative, intimate, even playful. Sex was immoral; by and large it was not for friends."

In March 1924, Keynes wrote Wittgenstein, "I would do anything in my power which could make it easier for you to do further work." He went on to tell him that his book was "a work of extraordinary importance and peculiar genius. [Keynes crossed out the word *peculiar*.] Right or wrong, it dominates all fundamental discussions at Cambridge since it was written." Frank Ramsey had suggested that Wittgenstein might stay with Keynes in the country, if he came to England. Maynard was altogether willing to have him as a guest, but he had to read fantastic letters such as the following to determine whether his friend would come:

I mean to say, shall I just come to be nice? Now I don't think at all that it isn't worthwhile being nice—if only I could be *really* nice—or having a nice time— if it were a *very* nice time indeed. But staying in rooms and having tea with you every other day or so would not be nice enough. But then I should pay for this niceness with the great disadvantage of seeing my short holladaies [*sic*] vanish like a phantom without having the least profit—I don't mean money—or getting any satisfaction from them. Of course staying in Cambridge with you is much nicer than staying in Vienna alone. But in Vienna I can collect my thoughts a little, and although they are not worth collecting, they are better than mere distraction. Now it wouldn't seem impossible that I could get more out of you than a cup of tea every other day, that's to say that I could really profit from hearing you, and in this case it would be worth while coming and talking to you. But here again there are great difficulties. [He mentioned next that they had not met for eleven years. Since they met] I have changed tremendously. I am sorry to say I am no better than I was but I am different, and therefore if we shall meet you may find that the man who has come to see you isn't really the one you meant to invite.

All one can say is that a man who could read such letters would lay down his life for his friend.

Even Keynes's patience was tried by Wittgenstein's thinking that the money he had lent him had come between them. In a letter of May 26, 1929, he finally burst out:

What a maniac you are! Of course there is not a particle of truth in anything that you say about money. . . .

The truth is that I alternate between loving and enjoying you and your conversation and having my nerves worn to death by it. It's no new thing. I always have—any time these twenty years. But "grudge" and "unkindness"— if only you could look into my heart, you'd see something quite different.

Well, if you can forgive me sufficiently, will you come and dine with me in hall tonight (I shall be away nearly all next week)? Then you can talk or not talk about cash, just as you feel inclined. Yours ever.

Keynes's interest and solicitude for his brilliant friend was justified by the subsequent course of events, at least in terms of scholarly achievement. The charismatic Ludwig, after returning to Cambridge in 1929, was soon awarded the doctorate and elected a fellow of Trinity College. Ten years later he succeeded Moore as professor of philosophy and held his chair until 1947. In the thirties he got the idea that he wanted to settle in Russia; he asked Keynes to introduce him to Ambassador Ivan Maisky to facilitate the matter. Again Maynard obliged, but nothing came of this strange request, although Wittgenstein later went to that country, but he did not stay. Wittgenstein was eccentric, to say the least, but then he was "a star in the sky."

In the summer of 1924, Keynes had another task to perform—a sad one, in this case. Alfred Marshall, his old Cambridge mentor, had died on July 13 just short of his eighty-second birthday. Keynes had written portraits before, such as those of the Big Three at Versailles, but now he put his hand to drawing a sketch of the life history of one whom he knew well and respected. The memoir which he composed ran to sixty-two heavily annotated pages and provided a fascinating intellectual history of the period as well as a penetrating psychological analysis of Marshall's personality. He described the highlights of his early development—his father's hope for a clerical career, his switch to mathematics and physics at Cambridge, and his mental crisis, brought on by religious debates of the 1860s and the publication of Darwin's *On the Origin of Species*. Thereafter, he turned to metaphysics, then to ethics, and finally to the study of the moral sciences and, in particular, to political economy.

He insisted that Marshall's "peculiar genius" contributed to his scientific creativity, describing seven or so of his original contributions to the discipline. The greatest of Marshall's creative accomplishments, in Keynes's mind, was the technique of static equilibrium analysis: Economics in this light, as Marshall himself said, "is not a body of concrete truth, but an engine for the discovery of concrete truth. This engine, as we employ it today, is largely Marshall's creation. He put it in the hands of his pupils long before he offered it to the world. The building of this engine was the essential achievement of Marshall's peculiar genius."

He then outlined what he saw as his teacher's main shortcomings: He suffered, in a sense, from the defects of his virtues, as the French say. He hankered after "concrete truth," for the discovery of which he was not especially qualified, and he was too much afraid of being wrong, too sensitive about criticism, and too anxious to "do good."

There was a side of Marshall of which Keynes was not at all admiring, namely, his stiff, unyielding Victorian attitude toward the intellectual possibilities and potentialities of women and his treatment of his wife. When she died in 1944, Keynes thought that she was deserving of a record of piety and remembrance, so he wrote her obituary for the *Economic Journal.* He called attention, of course, to the fact that she came of a high lineage—her great-grandfather was William Paley, fellow and tutor of Christ College and author of a famous theological book generally known as Paley's *Evidences;* her father was "an evangelical clergyman of the straitest Simeonite sect." She was a distinguished person in her own right, one of the earliest graduates of Newnham, the first woman lecturer on economics at Cambridge, and the loyal supporter of the Marshall Library for the last twenty years of her long life. Maynard obviously had a soft spot in his heart for Mary Marshall. His sensitive nature recognized her talent as an amateur watercolorist as well as her qualities as an intelligent, devoted woman. On the other hand, her husband did not always appreciate her intellect and her other virtues as a woman. For example, in their years of teaching she had prepared a textbook, with his aid, for some extension lectures. Keynes said that it was "an extremely good book; nothing more serviceable was produced for many years, if ever." Yet Professor Marshall, disliking it because it was too short and simple, allowed it to go out of print, even though there was a strong demand for it. Keynes stated that his father always felt that there was something ungenerous in Marshall's attitude toward that little book, and obviously he agreed with him.

With poignant nostalgia, he described this extraordinary woman who lived for ninety-four years "without decay of the grace and dignity and honor of character and sensibility which nature as well as nurture had given her." To him she represented "the beauty, the behavior, and the reserve of an age of civilization" which had departed.

In November 1924, Keynes was at Oxford lecturing on economic philosophy. He had chosen this subject even though he was in the midst of advocating practical currency reforms, because he had encountered opposition to his proposals for managed currency and the broadened role that it entailed for government. He sought to answer those who rejected his ideas on ideological grounds by showing that their orthodox philosophy rested on archaic concepts and that these principles of individualism and *laissez-faire* ruled over us by hereditary right rather than on their personal merits. After tracing the intellectual origins of individualism and *laissez-faire* back to the famous eighteenth- and nineteenth-century thinkers, he explained that the economists had developed their discipline by starting with the simplest provisional hypotheses, that the most efficient use of resources would be attained by encouraging the pursuit of maximum profit and ideal consumption by allowing competitive bidding for what is produced. He described these social arrangements as embodying "a ruthless struggle for survival" and parodied the theory of *laissez-faire* with a vivid animal metaphor of giraffes at mealtime. This simple theory that "individuals acting independently for their own advantage will produce the greatest aggregate of wealth" was based, he explained, on several unreal assumptions, namely, "that the processes of production and consumption are in no way organic" and that there are adequate opportunities for obtaining the foreknowledge necessary for rational decisions. The principles of *laissez-faire,* he contended, had won the day and dominated conventional thinking in the nineteenth century, in part because of the weaknesses of the opposing proposals, such as protectionism and Marxian socialism. They had gained dominance, too, because they gave full scope to "our erstwhile heroes, the great businessmen. But with the spread of corporate enterprise and separation of ownership and management, the master individualist, the great captain of industry, was fast becoming "a tarnished idol. We grow more doubtful whether it is he who will lead us into paradise by the hand."

Rather than depending upon the beneficence of natural economic forces and competition, with a limited role for government, the chief task of the modern economist must be to distinguish afresh the *Agenda* of government from the *Non-Agenda;* the former would embrace functions which fall outside the sphere of the individual and would consist of decisions which no one would make if the state does not make them. The cure for society's economic ills, he felt, lay outside the scope of the individual; it lay in developing semi-autonomous organizations, such as the Bank of England and other corporations, where the separation of management and ownership permits a more socialized view of the enterprise's goals. His vision, in short, was that of a managed capitalism, but he admitted that the necessary degree of management had been difficult to attain because the nation's sympathies and judgment had tended to be on opposite sides, and thus action had been paralyzed.

In the mid-twenties the United Kingdom was faced with many difficult decisions, but perhaps the most important financial one it had to make was whether it should return to the gold standard at the old prewar parity with the dollar. The question was a momentous one because the nation had been on that type of monetary standard *de facto* or *de jure* since Sir Isaac Newton had set the mint price in 1717, with the exception of a period during and after the Napoleonic Wars. It had become associated with the general prosperity and economic expansion of the Victorian era, with the consequence that it had become practically an article of faith to most economists and bankers. The prewar standard had worked well for Britain; the conditions were favorable— trade was relatively free, competition was quite widespread, and most of the advanced countries of the world adhered to the same standard so that the adjustment mechanisms kept their cost-price structures in a reasonable relationship. The whole process of adjustment was made easier by the fact that London was the premier money capital and commodity capital of the world. Official thinking after the war was colored by a sort of idealized picture of the standard's functioning in those years.

In line with these conceptions, the Cunliffe commission, which had been appointed in 1918 to consider the transition from war to peace, simply assumed that Britain would return to the gold standard at the prewar parity. Its attention was focused instead on the timing and the process of deflation which it was assumed would be necessary to make the transition. Even in the course of the adjustment to peace in 1919 when Britain placed an embargo on gold and thus formally departed from the standard, it was taken for granted that the primary aim was to return to gold. The process of adjustment was aided somewhat by the deflation accompanying the depression of 1920–21. When the Conservatives came to power in October 1924, sterling rose on the foreign exchanges and the move to restore the gold standard more quickly was strengthened. As a matter of fact, the matter had been under consideration by the Chamberlain-Bradbury Committee for more than a year. Most of the expert witnesses who appeared before that body favored resumption; only Keynes and Reginald McKenna, the chairman of the Midland Bank, were opposed. The former argued that the embargo on gold should be permanent, since in his mind domestic price stability should be England's main concern; he feared American financial instability and foresaw inflation as inevitable there, with the result that gold would flow back to Britain and destabilize her price level.

Keynes carried on his campaign against the restoration of the gold standard strenuously in public speeches, testimony before government committees, and in the columns of the *Nation.* He analyzed the speeches of the bank chairmen, calling two of the more conservative ones "impeccable spinsters." Marriage was obviously very much on his mind. He ridiculed those who advocated "marriage with the gold standard" as the most blessed of all possible states. He wrote that they "had better not be too precipitate" because "Miss G[old standard] happens to be an American, so that in the future the prices of grapefruit and popcorn are likely to be more important to him than those of eggs and bacon."

Later in the same article he pointed out that in the prewar period Britain had been "the predominant partner in the gold standard alliance" and that those who thought that a return to the gold standard meant a return to those conditions were "fools and blind." He was very wary of the American bankers, noting that "it suits the United States that we should return to gold," but he did not believe that it would or ought to manage its affairs to suit Britain's convenience. A gold standard would mean, in practice, that Britain would have the same price level and the same money rates (broadly speaking) as the United States, and he warned the monetary authorities that this might be a "dangerous proceeding."

When Keynes's piece, "The Return to Gold," appeared in the *Nation,* Otto Niemeyer of the Treasury, taking him very seriously as a critic of official thought, answered his argument point by point. Churchill, having read the original article and Niemeyer's comments, was much impressed by Keynes's argument. He wrote:

The Treasury has never, it seems to me, faced the profound significance of what Mr. Keynes calls "the paradox of unemployment amidst dearth." The governor of the Bank of England shows himself perfectly happy in the spectacle of Britain possessing the finest credit in the world simultaneously with a million and a quarter unemployed. . . . The community lacks goods, and a million and a quarter people lack work. It is certainly one of the highest functions of national finance and credit to bridge the gulf between the two. This is the only country in the world where this condition exists. . . . At any rate while that unemployment exists, no one is entitled to plume himself on the financial or credit policy we have employed.

Granting the risk of danger in a more experimental policy, he still felt that if he saw a way, he would rather follow it than any other. "I would rather see Finance less proud and Industry more content." Niemeyer answered these remarks by stressing the danger of inflation arising from unconventional policies and attributed the deficiency of effective demand to the economic losses of the war.

Churchill was the chancellor of the exchequer in the new Conservative government, but he had a limited understanding of technical monetary matters. As an aid to his decision-making, he had submitted a memorandum to the top Treasury and Bank of England officials which seems to have been based in part on Keynes's ideas; the memo proposed that Britain should renounce efforts to reestablish the gold standard, should ship £100 million in gold to the United States, and thus reduce its war debt and "congest" the Americans with the metal, causing their price level to rise and sterling to grow stronger.

However, Churchill's advisors answered his memo to his satisfaction, and so on April 28, 1925, Britain returned formally to gold; the "Norman Conquest of $4.86" was a reality. Montagu Norman, as governor of the Bank of England, had strongly favored such a course; in his words, the "golden age" was resumed.

While the return to gold at the prewar parity stabilized Britain's exchanges, from all accounts it resulted in an overvaluation of sterling by at least ten percent. Prior to this decision, Keynes had warned of the dire deflationary consequences of returning gold at too high a rate. Theoretically, such a policy would tend to reduce exports and increase imports and thus lead to a deterioration in Britain's trade account. Support of such action had generally been premised on an expectation of rising prices in the United States and monetary policies in other European countries which would be favorable to the pound; but neither of these happened. The United States "sterilized" the excess gold it received and managed to stabilize its domestic price level. France stabilized *de facto* at a rate which undervalued the franc relative to sterling by approximately twenty percent. In general, though the monetary authorities made the best of a bad situation, unemployment remained high after restoration; sterling was continually under pressure, and London's financial position steadily deteriorated. Britain was poorly prepared to cope with the even more adverse conditions which developed with the advent of the Great Depression.

Keynes quickly reacted to these troublous developments with a pamphlet cleverly entitled *The Economic Consequences of Mr. Churchill.* The chancellor, he wrote, in returning to gold at $4.86 "was just asking for trouble, for he was committing himself to force down money wages and all money value without any idea how it was to be done." Rhetorically, he asked, "Why did he do such a silly thing?"

Churchill, he answered, lacking instinctive judgment in money matters, had been deafened by "the clamorous voices of conventional finance" and had been "gravely misled by his experts." He went on to argue that to sustain sterling at parity the monetary authorities would have to raise short-term rates, restrict credit, and intensify unemployment, in the hope of thereby reducing costs. He showed the hardships this policy was imposing on the coal industry. British coal with sterling at $4.86 was competitively overpriced, with the result that the colliery owners proposed that wages should be reduced, regardless of the cost of living, to make them competitive.

But, argued Keynes, "on grounds of social justice no case can be made out for reducing the wages of the miners. They are the victims of the economic juggernaut. They represent in the flesh the 'fundamental adjustments' engineered by the Treasury and the Bank of England to satisfy the city fathers to bridge the 'moderate gap' between $4.40 and $4.86. They (and others to follow) are the 'moderate sacrifice' still necessary to ensure the stability of the gold standard. The plight of the coal miners is the first, but not—unless we are very lucky—the last of the economic consequences of Mr. Churchill."

Then, directing his verbal shafts at the Establishment and conventional principles, he asserted that "the gold standard, with its dependence on pure chance, its faith in 'automatic adjustments,' and its general regardlessness of social detail, is an essential emblem and idol of those who sit in the top tier of the machine. I think that they are essentially rash in their regardlessness, in their vague optimism and comfortable belief that nothing really serious ever happens. Nine times out of ten, nothing really serious does happen—merely little distress to individuals or to groups. But we run a risk of the tenth time (and are stupid into the bargain) if we continue to apply the principles of an economics which was worked out on the hypotheses of *laissez-faire* and free competition to a society which is rapidly abandoning these hypotheses."

In understanding Keynes's penetrating economic criticism of the current monetary policy, one needs to remember that he looked at Britain's economic arrangements as a marginal man. Several economists have been puzzled at his critical stance toward English society— how could an elitist such as he, the precious product of upper-middle-class society, the aristocrat of Eton and Cambridge, take so critical a view of the Establishment? It seems to defy the Marxian analysis of the social class structure and of class consciousness. What such a view overlooks was that as a homosexual he was an outsider, or rather considering his access to those in power, he was an outsider insider. When he later wrote in his *Treatise on Money* about the *auri sacra fames,* one can detect the overtone of alienation and sharp criticism of a homosexual in a hostile world. "Of late years the *auri sacra fames* [the accursed lust for gold] has sought to envelop itself in a garment of respectability as densely respectable as was ever met with, even in the realms of sex or religion." In short, Keynes's skepticism of conventional belief and practice in the two latter areas of life probably contributed to his questioning attitude toward the respectable and accepted in the economic and political realms; as social psychologists have noted, there is a strain or tendency toward consistency in human attitudes.

And, in retrospect, when one examines the decision-making process underlying Britain's return to gold, one finds much reason to agree with Keynes's questioning attitude about the respectable conventions of those in the top tier of the economic machine. Professor Moggridge and others have shown that the attitude of mind permeating that decision was akin to "an act of faith" and that the step was taken more for moral than for economic reasons. Rather then probing carefully into the problems of economic adjustment attendant on gold's restoration, there was a reliance on irrelevant long-run analysis, little quantitative inquiry, but the use instead of *ad hoc* expedients and rules of thumb. The former author was amazed that "recognition of the weakness of Britain's international financial position at $4.86 in any vaguely comprehensive form took over five years." Basic to all the confusion in the policy-making was the lack of knowledge. The Bank of England, for example, did not hire a specialist in economic research and statistics until 1928, and as late as that year Governor Norman privately admitted that ten or fifteen years would elapse before the bank had a professional staff "with the knowledge of the problems with which we are dealing." The secrecy surrounding the operations of the bank, which Keynes frequently denounced, simply covered over in some instances gross, irresponsible ignorance.

As has been already noted, Keynes was very sensitive and conscious of the changed environment in which capitalism was operating in the postwar years. Concurrently, the Communist attainment of power in Russia and the beginnings of fascism on the Continent had made controversy over the alternatives of political philosophy more intense and heated. With Britain's economy lagging and unemployment persisting, as a Liberal activist he had to consider the adequacy of his party's platform to the pressing issue of the day. We know that he was dissatisfied with the old answers; there were Liberals who felt that there was no need for new fundamental thinking, but he thought that an innovative program would have to be devised, almost from the beginning. What should be its nature and, most important, what touchstone should be employed in deciding one's allegiance to the existing parties? Like many others in those changing times, he was thinking and reading widely to find an answer to these questions. Among those whom he read was H. G. Wells whose mind, he said, "seems to have grown up alongside his readers, so that, in successive phases, he has delighted us and guided our imaginations from boyhood to maturity." (We know that he was fond of reading Wells in his youth; this is undoubtedly a frank expression of his debt to his famous contemporary.) In a review of Wells's novel *Clissold*, written in 1927, he made his criterion of political allegiance very clear when he said, "The remolding of the world needs the touch of the creative Brahma. But at present the Brahma is serving Science and Business, not Politics and Government. The extreme danger of the world is, in Clissold's words, least 'before the creative Brahma can get to work. Siva, in other words the passionate destructiveness of Labor awakening to its now needless limitations and privations, may make Brahma's task impossible.' We all feel this, I think. We know that we need urgently to create a milieu in which Brahma can get to work before it is too late."

In an address to the Liberal Summer School at Cambridge in 1925, Keynes had an opportunity to assess the relative merits of the major parties in providing such an environment for creative political change. The Conservative party, he remarked, had no attractions for him, either intellectual or spiritual. While it offered a home for the diehard, it was still oriented for the most part to the historic party questions of the past. The Capitalist leaders in the City and in Parliament who were associated with that party were "incapable of distinguishing novel measures for safeguarding Capitalism from what they call Bolshevism."

The Labor party likewise had its difficulties in claiming his allegiance. While it was superficially more attractive, the first difficulty was that it was a class party and did not represent his class; he felt that he could be influenced by justice and good sense, but "the class war will find me on the side of the educated bourgeoisie." It was not a matter of culture, but of the possibilities of intelligence shaping the direction of political change. He did not believe that the "intellectual elements in the Labor party" would ever exercise adequate control. It seemed more likely that the control of the party might be seized by "an autocratic inner ring"—the Communists—whom he termed the Party of Catastrophe.

On the negative test of being least repulsive to his beliefs, he felt that the Liberal party was "the best instrument of future progress," provided it had a strong leadership and the right program. Such a party, he thought, would or should be able to cope with the questions of the future which cut across the old party lines. In other words, there was room for a party which would be disinterested in classes and would be able to build the future free from the influences of diehardism and of catastrophism.

Turning to the program, he contended that such a party should not deal with the historic questions of Liberalism but, taking the risks of unpopularity and derision, should confront matters which were of living interest and urgent importance. He divided those questions into five headings in this order: (1) peace questions; (2) questions of government; (3) sex questions; (4) drug questions; and (5) economic questions. The surprising thing about this agenda was the high position and prominence which he gave to sex questions. Harrod, who was in the audience, thought that Keynes had been prodded into speaking on this topic by his Bloomsbury friends, but knowing of his homosexual nature, one can appreciate his interest in what has come to be called "gay liberation." He boldly stated that sex questions were about to enter the political arena, that the suffrage movement was only the beginning.

"Birth control and the use of contraceptives, marriage laws, the treatment of sexual offenses and abnormalities, the economic position of women, the economic position of the family—in all these matters the existing state of the law and of orthodoxy is still medieval—altogether out of touch with civilized opinion and civilized practice and with what individuals, educated and uneducated, say to one another in private. . . . A party which would discuss these things openly and wisely at its meetings would discover a new and living interest in the electorate because politics would be dealing once more with matters about which everyone wants to know and which deeply affect everyone's own life." He showed, too, how these sexual questions related to the economic issues, but the party managers could not be persuaded that this was the way to restore the fortunes of their organization. In retrospect, of course, we now can see how far ahead of his time he was and can only marvel at his prescience.

On economic matters generally, he was a political gradualist. In this speech and others at that time he affirmed his faith in "the creative possibilities of freedom and in the technical possibilities of a middle way between the anarchy of *laissez-faire* and the tyranny of totalitarianism." He admitted that constructive Liberal thinkers such as himself who were trying to formulate the economics of the middle way were "a bit foggy as yet." His theory of employment, which would provide the means to implement that vision, was still in the future. Whatever form it would take, he would persist in defending the moral principles of liberty.

Maynard's marriage to Lydia Lopokova, it has been previously explained, had been put off until divorce proceedings could release her from her marriage to Randolpho Barocchi. Lydia's dancing and her earlier romantic affairs have been sufficiently described, but what was she like off stage? Cyril Beaumont, who knew her shortly after the Great War, has given us a vivid impression of her as a person: "Her hair was fair, fluffed out at the forehead, and gathered in a little bun at the nape of her neck. She had small blue eyes, pale plump cheeks, and a curious nose, something like a hummingbird's beak, which gave a rare piquancy to her expression. She had a vivacious manner, alternating with moods of sadness. She spoke English well, with an attractive accent, and had a habit of making a profound remark as though it were the merest badinage. And I must not forget her silvery laugh."

The *New York Times* in 1921 also noted her exuberant gaiety and comic gifts, both on and off stage: "To publish an interview with Lydia Lopokova, will-o'-the-wisp dancer, without recording the charm of her Russian plus French plus Italian version of the English tongue is as futile as an attempt to paint a convincing sunset in India ink. Miss Lopokova says many interesting things, it is true, but no one would care if she didn't. Her utter lack of self-consciousness, her swift-moving grace, her rippling voice with its piquant inflections, her mobile face and hands, and the aura of light and movement that surrounds her give such an amount of esthetic pleasure that mere ideas lose caste by comparison."* Lopokova, Beaumont informs us, did not have an exalted idea of her position. "As soon as she had taken leave of those who came to pay her homage, she would wipe off her makeup—she never put much on—and change into a simple short skirt, wooly jumper, and tam-o-shanter, skipping home like a schoolgirl let out of school. She had an ingenuous manner of talking, but she was very intelligent and witty, and unlike some dancers, her conversation was not limited to herself and the ballet." Bloomsbury, too, as has been noted, was at first charmed by her jokes and sallies, such as the famous one which revealed her uncertain grasp of the King's English: "I dislike being in the country in August, because my legs get so bitten by barristers."

Beaumont's image of the charming Lydia is in striking contrast to the glimpses that we get of her in Virginia Woolf's catty letters; the Woolfs were seeing more of Lydia in 1922–24 as Maynard escorted her to their home quite frequently. Virginia wrote to Jacques Raverat in this fashion in the latter year: "Maynard is very heavy and rather portentous; Maynard is passionately in love, because he sees very well that he's dished if he marries her and she has him by the snout. You can't argue solidly when Lydia's there, and as we set now to the decline, and prefer reason to any amount of high spirits, Lydia's pranks put us all on edge; and Bloomsbury steals off to its den, leaving Maynard with Lydia on his knee, a sublime but heartrending spectacle."

Three months later the novelist returned to the subject with the same correspondent:

Why will Maynard be dished if he marries her [Lydia Lopokova]? Because she has the nicest nature in the world and a very limited headpiece. She came to tea on Sunday with your brother-in-law Geoffrey Keynes, and really I had the hardest time in the world. Her contribution is one shriek, two dances, then silence, like a submissive child, with her hands crossed. At thirty this is pathetic. Soon she will be plaintive. And they say you can only talk to Maynard now in words of one syllable. This he will soon tire of. She will cry, and the great ladies won't ask her to their parties; you old married couples can fill it in at your leisure. (I get this largely from other sources.)

Why should he marry her? She wants her sons to go to Eton.

I agree that Maynard's fallibility endears him to me.

---

*This description of Lydia Lopokova was quoted in the obituary of the *New York Times,* June 30, 1981, which reported her death in England on June 8 at the age of eighty-eight. If the birth date given in the text is correct, she would have been over ninety.

Despite all Virginia Woolf's misgivings about the event, Maynard and Lydia were married on August 4, 1925, at the Saint Pancras Central Register Office. Present at the happy occasion were his mother and father, Mrs. A. V. Hill (his sister), Duncan Grant, and Mrs. Harold Bowen, a good friend of Lydia's. Maynard received thirteen written notes of congratulations, including one from Carl Melchior and some from his intimates of the old days. If a homosexual inclination indicates a failure of maturation, as many psychoanalysts believe, he had apparently undergone a transformation in the war and early postwar years. The perceptive Virginia Woolf had observed that he had put on weight compared to his prewar years and looked "portentous" and "somehow respectable." Many were made happy by his marriage. His old friend Mary Marshall, years after, remarked to Roy Harrod that it was "the best thing that Maynard ever did." Even popular opinion seemed to endorse the union with a verse which circulated at the time, "Was e'er such a union of beauty and brains, as the fair Lopokova and John Maynard Keynes?"

The newlyweds went off to Russia to visit Lydia's relations. Upon their return, Maynard wrote three articles on that country for the *Nation,* which were also published by the Woolfs' Hogarth Press under the title *A Short View of Russia.* In this brief publication he discussed the new Soviet order and in so doing gave us further insight on his own social values at that time. Leninism fascinated him because, as he said, it combined two things which Europeans for some centuries had kept in different compartments of the soul—religion and business. He was curious about a new religion and willing to sympathize with those who sought for something good in the new Soviet regime, but rejected its creed as destructive of liberty and security in life. "How can I adopt a creed which, preferring the mud to the fish, exalts the boorish proletariat above the bourgeoisie and the intelligentsia who, with whatever faults, are the quality in life and surely carry the seeds of all human advancement? Even if we need a religion, how can we find it in the turbid rubbish of the Red bookshops?"

The essence of the new religion, he felt, was that it was absolutely and defiantly nonsupernatural, and it centered about the individual's and the community's attitude toward the love of money. It had constructed a social framework which changed pecuniary motivation, social status, and power based on money. "A society," he wrote, "of which this is even partially true is a tremendous innovation."

While he did not expect any contribution from Russian communism to scientific understanding of economics, nevertheless he thought that as a religion it might have a significance because religion provides a social bond among people. Whereas—and here he invoked Coleridge again—"modern capitalism is absolutely irreligious, without internal union, without much public spirit, often, though not always, a mere congeries of possessors and pursuers. Such a system has to be immensely, not merely moderately, successful to survive." Assuming something of a prophetic role, he stated that "if irreligious capitalism is ultimately to defeat religious communism, it is not enough that it should be economically more efficient—it must be many times more efficient."

In this essay he philosophized in a broad manner on the decay of religion and upon the advisability of keeping business and religion in separate compartments of the soul. These thoughts led him to conclude that perhaps Russian communism did represent "the first confused stirrings of a great religion."

For some his speculations on these topics may be invalidated or at least vitiated by his tendency to make illegitimate comparisons between communist doctrine and capitalist practice. Still, his ruminations, closely studied, make clear his own reservations about capitalist affluence and capitalist ethics as revolving unduly about the love of money. They reveal, too, a moral sensitivity and a contempt for respectability that probably derived in part from his own unconventional, homosexual outlook on the world.

There is more on this subject of the love of money in a brief, unpublished sketch of Einstein which he wrote in June 1926 while on a visit to Berlin. He had gone there on a lecture engagement to speak at the university on The End of Laissez-Faire, a repeat of the talk which we have discussed above. Einstein, he tells us, had attended the lecture and also the official dinner that followed. At first sight he did not recognize the famous physicist but mistook him for Aristide Briand, the French statesman. When he moved nearer he saw that "the true comparison was Charlie Chaplin. Charlie Chaplin with the forehead of Shakespeare is the best description of Einstein. The spirit and the impish sidelong glances of Charlie are just the same. He is that kind of Jew—the kind which rarely has its head above water, the sweet tender imps who have not sublimated immortality into compound interest."

He conversed with Einstein briefly and asked whether he agreed with a passage in his lecture in which he had hinted a kind of sympathy with communism. "Yes," he answered, "I am Red at heart, but my mind does not yet follow." Before he left the dinner, Keynes says, Einstein gave him a sympathetic look and a little compliment for his speech, adding a remark which reminds us of his bisexual temperament, "I had indeed had a little flirt with him."

The German scientist had impressed him as the nicest and only talented person he had met in all Berlin, with a few exceptions, and he was a Jew like his dear friend Melchior. He added, "Yet, if I lived there, I felt I might turn anti-Semite. For the poor Prussian is too slow and heavy on his legs for the other kind of Jews, the ones who are not imps but serving devils, with small horns, pitchforks, and oily tails. It is not agreeable to see a civilization so under the impure thumbs of its impure Jews, who have all the money and the power and the brains. I vote rather for the plump hausfraus and thick-fingered Wandering Birds. . . . But I'm not sure that I wouldn't even rather be mixed up with Lloyd George than with the German political Jews."

These remarks and others which could and will be quoted definitely indicate an anti-Jewish bias in Keynes which he apparently shared with persons like Lytton Strachey. Nevertheless, his thoughts along these lines should not be lifted out of the context in which they were written, for he later did show true sympathy and concern for the Jews who suffered under the hateful persecution of Hitler. The essay does reflect some of the idealism of the Apostles and that love of the sweet imps of mankind without which one cannot understand Maynard Keynes.

CHAPTER 11

The British Economic Malaise and
A Treatise on Money

> The love of money as a possession ... will be recognized for what it is, a somewhat disgusting morbidity, one of those semicriminal, semipathological propensities which one hands over with a shudder to the specialists in mental disease.
>
> J. M. Keynes

UPON HIS MARRIAGE to Lydia, Keynes arranged a lease of an old country house called Tilton which was located near Lewes in Sussex, just a few hundred yards from Charleston, the home of his good friends Vanessa Bell and Duncan Grant. At the time of its acquisition he did not realize that this estate had once belonged to his father's branch of the family. In 1937, he rented 300 additional acres of land nearby and during World War II increased his holding to 570, undertaking to farm the property with the aid of Logan Thompson, a farmer from the King's College holdings in Lincolnshire.

Tilton, with its picturesque house and garden, had fine views of the surrounding countryside. It was a commodious dwelling with a long, sunny drawing room, a connected loggia in which Keynes loved to read, and a west wing furnished for the comfort of guests. It was a very restful place, and now that Maynard was over forty and Lydia thirty-four, they appreciated its quiet and beauty. They spent many happy years there on vacations and at other times when they could get away from their many activities.

Both of them were still very busy, Maynard with his college bursar duties, editing the *Economic Journal,* testifying before government bodies, and writing, and Lydia with her dancing. She appeared with the Diaghilev Ballet in 1925 and 1926, but she could not play a full role in the company. In 1927, she danced only once, before the king of Spain. In all this, Maynard was the manager behind the scenes who wrote the letters and negotiated with theatrical agencies for her. He was the spirit also behind the scenes in her debut as an actress; she had a talent for character acting, and he arranged for her to participate in some private performances—in 1926, she played the principal part in Merimee's *L'Amour Africaine* and later did *Comus* opposite George ("Dadie") Rylands. She made her public debut in Calderón's *Life's a Dream* at the Cambridge Amateur Dramatic Club. While she was a good character actress, there was still difficulty with her accent; Maynard coached her in pronunciation and in the delivery of her lines. She performed in other plays to good reviews, and then in 1930, she and Maynard launched the Camargo Ballet Society at a big dinner party; later in that year, at its first production in London, she hailed it as "the birth of British Ballet." Maynard continued to be an enthusiast for the art, writing in a letter to Viscount Rothmere a few years later that "ballet is above and beyond language." His dedication to it is also shown by the pains he took in demanding perfection from the British motion picture companies in the filming of ballet productions.

He was, in fact, helping the arts in several ways in these years. Apart from the purchase of paintings for his private collection, he was instrumental in forming the London Artists Association. The purpose of this group was to provide worthy artists with a guaranteed income from the proceeds of exhibitions of their works. He made a substantial contribution to the original fund and got his wealthy friend Samuel Courtauld and others to join. Duncan Grant, Vanessa Bell, Keith Baines, and other artists were members, and the organization at first did well, but in time there was a noticeable tendency for the better painters to withdraw, leading toward a "survival of the unfit." Keynes's interest in painting was not only for his own pleasure for he loaned many of his best possessions to the famous British galleries and to those in foreign countries, including the United States.

The Keyneses when in London were usually at 46 Gordon Square, and there they had many parties and dinner affairs. Bloomsbury was often represented, but now others from London society joined in the festivities. Lydia was still on friendly terms with some of the Blooms-berries, and she made many new friends in addition. Socially, Lydia and Maynard continued to mix and dine with the Woolfs and other Charlestonians, as one notes from the malicious comments that Virginia Woolf made on their hospitality in her letters and diary. On March

20, 1927, she wrote to her sister Vanessa: "Maynard is apparently conscience stricken about luxury and gave us no wine, a poor dinner, and only broken springed lodging chairs to sit in." In the same letter she ridiculed Lydia's decorations at Tilton, and two months later in another letter was still complaining that Maynard had not given them a drop to drink. Still, says Virginia, "he had a 'doglike affection' for you [Vanessa], and I remain convinced that he feels at his heart your malicious ways, and yet can't overcome his superstition [*sic*] that you and Duncan are the soul and salt of the world." In August, she wrote a "Tiltoniad" which contained so many indiscretions, not to say indecencies and vulgarities, that she thought to keep it for the Bells' eyes alone. On September 3, 1927, in another note to Lytton Strachey, she described another party at Tilton at which Maynard was crapulous and obscene beyond words, lifting his left leg and singing a song about women. At this party she reported that three to eleven people "picked the bones of Maynard's grouse. . . . This stinginess is a constant source of delight to Nessa—her eyes gleamed as the bones went around." While Virginia Woolf could be ultracritical of others, it is to be noted that the editors of her *Letters* state that "it was the common opinion of Bloomsbury that the Keyneses were remarkably economic in their hospitality."

Still, to keep the record straight and give the novelist her due, there is another diary entry which is much more complimentary. On April 19, 1928, she and Leonard dined with the Keyneses, and later she noted, "two couples, elderly, childless, distinguished. He and she both urbane and admirable. Grey comes at Maynard's temples. He is finer looking now: not with us pompous or great; simple, with his mind working always, on Russian, Bolsheviks, glands, genealogies; always the proof of a remarkable mind when it overflows thus vigorously into bypaths. There are two royal stocks in England, he says, from which all intellect descends. He will work this out as if his fortune depended on it. Lydia is composed and controlled. She says very sensible things."

In the meantime, during what Americans were calling the golden twenties, Britain's economy continued to stagnate "in the doldrums," as Professor Pigou expressed it. Unemployment, a key symptom of its malaise, persisted at over a million (or more than ten percent of the available labor force) over the years 1924 to 1929, when other industrial countries were enjoying fairly substantial prosperity. The income and profit deflation, which, as Keynes saw it, the return to gold had forced on Britain, had caused wholesale prices to decline. He believed that the Treasury and the Bank of England, which had often used the traditional weapons of credit restriction and bank rate against a profit inflation, were now imposing "a cold-blooded income deflation" on the nation. The withdrawal of credit from entrepreneurs reduced their ability to offer employment and, further, the increased cost of credit together with the concomitant fall in wholesale prices and the contraction of domestic purchasing power reduced profits and thereby the incentive to produce. In these circumstances the businessmen, Keynes argued, had only three alternatives: to let their losses run, to curtail their less profitable activities, or to seek to reduce the money earnings of labor. The first two were tried with little beneficial results—"Five years after the consummation of the return to gold, the curtailment of employment was still in operation in unabated degree." And when the businessmen sought to use the third expedient—that of reducing the money earnings per unit of output—they brought on the general strike of 1926. While wage rates in particular industries fell heavily, the general index of weekly wage rates was practically as high in 1930 as it had been in 1924.

Unemployment in these years, 1926–30, was extremely severe in coal, textiles, and the dock and harbor services which were hurt by the shrinkage of export trade. The dismal term "depressed area" came into use to characterize such hard-hit regions as Lancashire, south Wales the northeast coast, and the Scottish Lowlands.

As an active Liberal, Keynes played an important part in the formulation of public policies to cope with these problems. During 1927 he often met at Lloyd George's country home to work on what was called the "Liberal Yellow Book." Following the ex-prime minister's 1924 article in the *Nation,* a committee of the Liberal Summer School had set up an Industrial Inquiry and this group, working with economists and leading businessmen, had explored Britain's industrial situation in the greatest detail over a period of two years. Keynes was especially interested in the sections of its report "The Organization of Business" and "Currency and Banking." He got committees working on these subjects to adopt his ideas on currency management, public investment and its control, and on greater publicity about the financing of large firms above a certain size. He discussed some of these proposals at the Liberal Summer School at Cambridge in July 1927. The complete study of the Liberals, entitled *Britain's Industrial Future,* appeared the following January. What is most striking about this inquiry is that so many of the policies we associate with Keynes were so clearly adumbrated in its analysis. In other words, the Keynesian policies came first; the underlying economic theory to support them was the work of later years.

Throughout the next year, 1928, he was carefully following economic developments in Europe and the United States. At the close of 1927, he had anxiously analyzed Britain's balance of trade and was keeping close tabs on the banking and stock market situations in the United States as the economic boom there rose to a crescendo. He watched enviously as the French stabilized the franc at about one-fifth of its prewar gold value; having written down her war debts four-fifths, she persuaded her allies to let her off more than half her external debt and was avoiding inflation. France, he observed, had abandoned principle and consistency alike and obeyed the teachings of experience, but "we in England have not submitted either to the warnings of theory or to the pressure of facts, obstinately obedient to conventions."

In these mid-twenties his main intellectual preoccupation continued to be the persistent slump in Great Britain with its grievous burden of unemployment. He was still a political activist and indeed, in the winter of 1928, preparing for the general election which was expected in the following spring, the Liberal party asked him to be its candidate for the university, but he did not think it wise to do so. Instead, he wrote two articles for the *Evening Standard* in support of Lloyd George and then in May, collaborating with Hubert Henderson, wrote a long pamphlet, *Can Lloyd George Do It—The Pledge Examined.* The pledge had been made by the Liberal politician the previous March in which he promised to reduce unemployment to normal proportions by a program of public spending and to do it within the course of a single year without adding to the national debt or to local taxation.

Keynes and Henderson made a popular, vigorous argument for their position representing common sense, while the objections of their critics were condemned for being based on highly abstract theories, and venerable and academic ones at that. The pamphlet practically exuded optimism and patriotism, urging the "push and drive, which tackled more formidable tasks in the war and delivered the goods to us on the scheduled date." After reviewing the facts of British unemployment, it contended that a program of spending £100 million a year would employ five hundred thousand men. Citing the waste that unemployment involved, it insisted in Keynesian fashion and spirit that such a modest effort was "a negligible risk to cure a monstrous anomaly." A policy of inaction was deplored—"every puff of Mr. Baldwin's pipe costs us thousands of pounds."

The Keynes-Henderson program of national development consisted mainly of improving and modernizing the nation's roads and railways, building two hundred thousand houses each year, projects of telephone and electrical construction, and land drainage. The pamphlet claimed that each million pounds spent, for example, on road improvements would employ five thousand workers. The authors did not cite a precise "multiplier" but did show that their critics ignored the indirect employment that public projects would generate. As to cost, it was argued that the extra revenue such spending would create, plus economies on armaments, would make it virtually costless, at least in relative terms. Nor was such a program of public works to be considered socialism because these activities were already in the public sector, the choice having been made by the electorate. As to the contention that public spending financed by loans would merely divert and diminish the capital available for ordinary industry, Keynes and Henderson would only say that the current savings were being spent on the unemployed and that savings were running to waste because of lack of credit. They came close to a theory of employment when they wrote, "So far from the total of investment, as determined by these factors, being necessarily equal to the total of saving, disequilibrium between two is at the root of our troubles." Unfortunately, they did not have a developed theory of effective demand or a precise multiplier to bolster their argument at this point.

Blasting the policy of the Conservatives as a policy of negation, restriction, and inactivity, they concluded on a characteristic Keynesian note, "There is no reason why we should not feel ourselves free to be bold, to be open, to experiment, to take action, to try the possibilities of things. And over against us, standing in the path, there is nothing but a few old gentlemen tightly buttoned up in their frock coats, who only need to be treated with a little friendly disrespect and bowled over like ninepins.

"Quite likely they will enjoy it themselves, when once they have got over the shock."

There is a decided self-confidence in this essay because Keynes probably believed that the work he was doing on his *Treatise on Money* had enabled him to diagnose the fundamental cause of depression and unemployment. To understand the nature of that effort, it is necessary to consider the state of economic theory at that time.

In the twenties there was a growing sense of crisis in economic theory as the anomaly, as Keynes phrased it, of "unemployment amidst dearth" made a number of authors question orthodox reasoning on the subject. In the previous century, the view that individualistic capitalism was self-regulating and that permanent unemployment was impossible had been challenged by the Reverend Thomas R. Malthus, Karl Marx, and other dissenters from orthodoxy. These dissenters generally questioned the "law" or principle of a French economist, Jean Baptiste Say, that "supply creates its own demand"; namely, that increases in production automatically generate the purchasing power to buy the increased supply.

Keynes, as already noted, had studied under Alfred Marshall at Cambridge, and it was the latter's *Principles of Economics,* published in 1890, that constituted the "normal science" of the period. The Marshallian conceptual framework provided the prism through which most orthodox economists in Great Britain and the United States viewed economic phenomena. His intellectual dominance was so pronounced as to lead one recent authoritative student of the subject to state that this work [*Principles*] "cemented his lasting reputation and held Anglo-Saxon economics in its thrall for almost half a century." Indeed, even before the publication of that work, Marshall's influence on British economics was pervasive; one contemporary, H. S. Foxwell, observed in 1887 that "half the economic chairs in the United Kingdom are occupied by his pupils, and the share taken by them in general economic instruction is even larger than this." Without doubt, Marshall was "the great father figure of English economics, firmly upholding the virtue of respect for one's elders and betters in the family of economists."

The main concerns of Marshallian economics were the questions of value, distribution, and the efficient allocation of resources, and for the purposes of such analysis it was usually assumed that, barring exceptional circumstances, there would be adequate demand to employ all the factors of production. In short, much of this type of economics was based on the assumption of full employment. Further, by its development of the marginal productivity theory of distribution under the assumption of wage and price flexibility, Marshallian economics strengthened the apparent validity of Say's Law. Price flexibility included flexibility in interest rates, and it could be demonstrated by supply and demand analysis that the variations of the interest rate would ensure an equality between savings and investments so that those variables could not be a cause of persistent unemployment. As to wages, Professor Pigou, Marshall's successor in the chair of political economy at Cambridge, proved that only frictional, temporary unemployment could exist in a world of perfectly flexible wages. Consequently, as he stated, "With perfectly free competition ... there will always be at work a strong tendency for wage rates to be so related to demand that everybody is employed."

In writing his influential *Principles,* Marshall had intended it to be merely the first volume of a trilogy in which he would analyze comprehensively the functioning of the economy. Unfortunately, he was never able to carry out his project as he had originally planned; his *Money, Credit and Commerce* (1923) was, as Joan Robinson remarks, but "a pale ghost of the third volume of the *Principles* which he originally intended it to be." Nevertheless, he saw, as did Marx, the weakness in his theoretical system and in a sense anticipated Keynes's exposure of it. He conceded that in times of commercial disorganization, when business confidence is shaken, "though men have the power to purchase, they may not choose to use it."

On the basis of his knowledge of Marshall's written work as well as of the Cambridge "oral tradition," Keynes, as we have seen, espoused the quantity theory of money. Indeed, in his *Tract on Monetary Reform* he had asserted that the quantity theory was fundamental. "Its correspondence with fact is not open to question." Now it should be recognized that when quantity theorists stated that changes in the quantity of money had a proportional effect on the price level, they were assuming that the level of output was already at full employment. It followed that Irving Fisher's version of the quantity theory depended for its validity on the assumption of Say's Law. In so-called transitional periods, when output was below full employment, the theory's conclusions did not follow, as Fisher himself admitted. These shortcomings of the conventional quantity theory were some of Keynes's main concerns in the *Treatise on Money.*

In summary, it can be said that the dominant paradigm of Marshallian economics held that the economy was automatically self-regulating and tended toward full employment in accordance with Say's Law. In consequence, the normal scientists of this tradition or school of thought, with their strong faith in the ruling paradigm, could not believe that any alternative perception of economic reality was necessary or valid. For example, economists such as Gunnar Myrdal and Dennis Robertson argued that unemployment could be explained by the classical paradigm if it was suitably extended.

But not all who were writing on economic problems in the twenties were of this "normal" persuasion; in fact, there were a considerable number of heretics or "cranks" who questioned economic orthodoxy. In this connection, Joan Robinson has remarked that a "sure sign of crisis in economic theory is the prevalence of 'cranks' and in her opinion they "are to be preferred to the orthodox because they see that there is a problem." In the twenties several such cranks were analyzing the anomaly of unemployment in complete disregard of the classical paradigm. It is noteworthy that most of those who initiated the attack on orthodox thinking were definitely from outside the economics profession. One economist was so upset apparently by the intruders that he later talked about "the invasion of economic theory by the barbarians." "The brave army of heretics," as Keynes called them, included John A. Hobson, Major Joseph Douglas, Silvio Gesell, Frederick Soddy, and others. Soddy was a Nobel Prize winner who was so disturbed by economic conditions in Great Britain and in the world generally that he turned from nuclear physics to explore the mysteries of money. In the United States, the most notable dissenters from orthodoxy were William T. Foster, former president of Reed College, and Wadill Catchings, an iron manufacturer and later a partner in the investment firm of Goldman, Sachs. Within the economics profession there were institutional economists, such as Wesley C. Mitchell, John M. Clark, and Rexford G. Tugwell, who were highly critical of received theory, but they failed to provide an alternative theoretical framework acceptable to the majority. And, as James Conant has stated, "it takes a new conceptual scheme to cause the abandonment of an old one."

Disproof of the neoclassical tenets was difficult because the Cambridge school was more than an intellectual phenomenon, it was a sociological group whose members shared attitudes to political and social questions on the basis of nonscientific grounds. There were subtle factors at work sustaining orthodoxy. For example, Marshall, having established economics as an independent field of study at Cambridge and published his prestigious *Principles,* had a canny way of being "all things to all men," and this inhibited criticism of his ideas. At the same time, he stressed deference and respect for the Ricardo-Mill tradition, and this exerted a strong conservative influence. The "oral tradition" at Cambridge, whereby only the initiated could explain what the master really meant, also sustained the accepted pattern of thought. The examination system and the appointment process, both of which were under strong Marshallian influence, tended in the same way to eliminate or minimize dissent. While Marshallian economics was criticized from within by such men as H. S. Foxwell and Cunningham, even Maynard Keynes as late as 1927 criticized his colleague Dennis Robertson for commending the heretic Hobson's ideas in the same breath with the master's.

The difficulties that Hobson encountered in trying to teach

heterodox ideas demonstrate how difficult it was for dissenting thought to find expression. As an Oxford graduate and a close student of Ruskin's writings, he had entered into a collaboration with a free-thinking businessman named Albert F. Mummery in writing a book, *The Psychology of Industry* (1889), in which he elaborated the thesis that unemployment was due to the economy's tendency to generate an excess of savings. At about the same time he sought to teach political economy as a university extension lecturer, but was refused permission by the licensing authority because Professor Edgeworth of Cambridge, having read his book, considered it "equivalent in rationality to an attempt to prove the flatness of the earth. How could there be any limit to the amount of useful saving when every item of saving went to increase the capital structure and the fund for paying wages?" Later, Hobson sought to give some lectures on economics for the Charity Organization Society when suddenly the invitation was withdrawn. He was permitted only to address audiences in the provinces so long as he confined himself to practical aspects of working-class life. As he himself concluded, "Even then I hardly realized that in appearing to question the virtue of unlimited thrift I had committed the unpardonable sin."

Keynes was reading the publications of these monetary cranks or outsiders while he was preparing his *Treatise on Money*. In it he mentioned the work of Abbati, N. Johannsen, and Colonel Rorty in footnotes, and referred to the "oversaving" or "underconsumption" theories of Bouniatin, Hobson, Foster, and Catchings as having "at bottom ... some affinity" to his own. Despite his earlier reproof of Robertson for his dallying with Hobson or mentioning him alongside Marshall, he now had a complimentary paragraph for the heretic: "Mr. J. A. Hobson and others deserve recognition for trying to analyze the influence of savings and investment of the price level and on the credit cycle, at a time when orthodox economists were content to neglect almost entirely this very real problem. But I do not think they have succeeded in linking up their conclusions with the theory of money or with the part played by the rate of interest."

Meanwhile, he was working closely with another brilliant colleague and ex-student, Dennis H. Robertson, whose ideas as expressed in his almost unreadable book, *Banking Policy and the Price Level,* had a crucial influence on the older man. They collaborated so closely on chapters five and six of that volume that Robertson wrote that "neither of us now knows how much of the ideas therein contained are his and how much mine." Ten years later Keynes paid a handsome tribute to his friend when he wrote, "I certainly date all my emancipation from the discussion between us which preceded your *Banking Policy and the Price Level.*"

Robertson was the sixth and youngest son of a clergyman headmaster of Scottish descent. His father had taught him his classics, and when he went to Eton, he had a very successful career, being elected captain of the school and awarded a classical scholarship to Trinity. At Cambridge, he shifted from the classics to economics and under the supervision of Pigou and Keynes won the highest honors for his work. He was given a Trinity fellowship in 1924 for his pioneer study of industrial fluctuations, and from then on Cambridge was his home. A confirmed bachelor, he too was homosexually inclined. According to Lord Annan, by the end of World War I there was a saying about Trinity men: "There were 'good Trinity' (those who didn't) and 'bad Trinity' (those who did), and the best known of the latter was Dennis Robertson." It is a striking fact that he shared with Keynes an interest in economics as well as a taste for poetry and a lifelong love of acting. In the twenties he was at times ahead of Keynes in his appreciation of the insights of some of the heretics; for example, in 1929 he wrote a quite respectful review of a volume of Foster and Catchings, criticizing their "pseudoscientific apparatus" but enforcing their plea for public works in time of unemployment. However, after 1931 Keynes outdid him in this respect. In general, one can see that the crisis in economic theory was coming to a head; there was dissension and criticism of orthodoxy even within the citadel of Cambridge economics. The economists were awakening from their Marshallian slumber, but it would take the Great Depression itself to shatter the old way of seeing economic reality and prepare the ground for a new paradigm.

As early as the middle of 1924, Keynes had started work on a new book which he tentatively entitled *The Standard of Value,* but his progress at first was slow. He made three different draft tables of content in that year, but then in the summer things went somewhat better. In mid-September he urged Robertson to come down to Tilton for a few days to discuss credit cycle theories, but he didn't accept the invitation, possibly because he was busy with his own book. Keynes gave him much candid criticism on his manuscript, but the two remained good friends. The younger man was very undecided about the merits of his own work, as the following bit of correspondence shows: "I am afraid of being swayed into publishing by the desire to avoid disappointment and loss; but I am also afraid of being swayed against publishing by my tendency to believe that you are always right!

Sometimes when I have stood out against this weakness, I have been justified! ... In any case I feel the truth about the whole matter of monetary theory is so obscure and uncertain that it isn't wicked to publish what doesn't pretend to be final truth. I am so unconfident that I should always like to put at the top of everything that I write 'Nobody must believe a word of what follows'; and I think that va sans dire in books on the trade cycle, and that I would rather write a preface to that effect than not publish at all! Is that a hopeless frame of mind?" Keynes didn't answer this last query, but the attitude expressed in the letter was far different from his own breezy self-confidence.

In 1925, Keynes made only slow progress on his own manuscript mainly because of his marriage and the subsequent trip to the Soviet Republic. He wrote A Short View of Russia and about five chapters of a history of ancient monetary standards, but worked only intermittently on what he now called The Theory of Money and Credit. In July, however, he signed a contract with Harcourt, Brace for a book of this title, and during the course of the year developed three more versions of its table of contents.

In the spring of the following year he did much better, finishing over fifty-five thousand words of book one of what he now for the first time entitled A Treatise on Money. He prepared five more tables of contents for the book as a whole and was hoping to publish the following year. Instead, he revised the table of contents three more times; the volume was obviously growing into a much more substantial affair than he had originally planned. In the meantime, he was helping Robertson with his 1928 edition of Money, a volume in the highly regarded Cambridge Economic Handbooks which he edited. Robertson modestly stated in the preface, "There is much in this book, especially in Chapter VIII— The Question of the Cycle, which ought scarcely, even in a book such as this, to see the light of day over any other signature than his [that is, Keynes's] until his forthcoming work on the theory of money is published." Finally, by devoting the whole of the summer of 1928 to writing, Keynes was able to complete about four-fifths of his book by September. Roy Harrod commented on portions of the manuscript, as well as Robertson and Professor Pigou.

Across the Atlantic at this time, the American boom was manifesting itself in a huge rise in security prices on Wall Street, and this posed a serious problem for the National Mutual Life Insurance Company of which Keynes was the chairman. His old Treasury colleague Oswald Falk, who served with him on the company's board of directors, thought there was a dangerous inflation in the United States and that

National Mutual should liquidate the bulk of its American securities before it was too late. In response to this view, Keynes wrote two papers on the American economic situation in July and September in which he disagreed sharply with Falk's position. In one, entitled "Is There Inflation in the United States?" he concluded, after reviewing trends in the cost of living and business credit, that there was "nothing which can be called inflation yet in sight." In this paper he employed the mode of analysis which he was then developing in the *Treatise*. He thought that the Federal Reserve should be watchful for the possibility of overinvestment, but that it should be equally careful not to produce the opposite, a business slump. He circulated his analysis among the members of the National Mutual's board as well as to several economists, bankers, and officials.

It is evident from this paper and other material that he was most knowledgeable about monetary conditions in the United States and that he was in correspondence with such Federal Reserve officials as Benjamin Strong, W. R. Burgess, and Carl Snyder as well as with American academic economists. Several of the former rejected his analysis, and Charles J. Bullock, president of the Harvard Economic Society, pointedly stated in one letter to him that he did not see "the propriety of limiting the word 'inflation' to commodity price inflation." But Keynes, fearing the dear money policy of the Federal Reserve System, could not help feeling that "the risk just now is all on the side of a business depression and a deflation rather than otherwise."

In one of his letters, Bullock informed him that Harvard University was considering inviting him to lecture sometime for half a year. He assured him—truthful man that he was—that he would find it "an interesting experience, even in these days of partially enforced prohibition, which is more effective in academic communities than in some other places. Of course, if you should come we should, in this organization, do all that we could to make your stay pleasant." Unfortunately, Keynes was unable to accept this hospitable but rather "dry" invitation.

He was still busy with the *Treatise,* having committed himself to publication by the autumn of 1929. In August of that year, he began proof corrections and final rewriting, only to discover that this was so extensive that he would have to divide the book into two volumes and postpone publication another year. At the same time there was some bad news in the political arena. In the spring, despite his and others' efforts in its behalf, the Liberal party suffered a bad defeat in the general elections, winning only fifty-nine seats. This setback marked the end of his active role in Liberal party politics. At the time he was "up to his eyes" in editorial work for the *Economic Journal* and in his duties as bursar at King's College. Nevertheless, he returned to a subject which had intrigued him in years past—the German transfer problem—and engaged in a famous debate with Professor Bertil Ohlin of Sweden which ran over several issues of the above-mentioned periodical. In these articles he continued to insist that the burden of reparations lay in their tendency to turn the terms of trade against the paying country. Other experts, such as his admirer the late Professor Seymour Harris, have felt that he exaggerated the difficulties of transfer and that Germany might have been able to increase her exports much more than she did and, therefore, have paid more reparations. Professor Samuelson, too, expressed the view later that he was "right in his reparations controversy with Ohlin; it is in part for the wrong reasons—reasons which in terms of his later system are seen to be classical as compared with the arguments of Ohlin."

In the summer of 1929, Keynes was honored by being made a fellow of the British Academy, and about the same time he gave some lectures to the Geneva School of International Studies. In November of that same year, as the gathering economic storm broke with the disastrous slide of stock prices on the New York Stock Exchange, he was appointed a member of the Macmillan Committee. This body, officially entitled a Committee of Inquiry into Finance and Industry, was to take much of his time; as with his earlier service on the Indian Currency Commission, the timing was excellent—he was superbly trained and equipped for the post, having just completed his monetary treatise. He played a leading role in its deliberations, and then in January 1930, he was appointed to still another governmental agency, the Economic Advisory Council, which had been established to advise the Cabinet on economic policy. It will be necessary to come back to take a closer look at these activities.

While Keynes was composing *A Treatise on Money,* he was also working out his social philosophy and his vision of the future as has been partially seen above in his 1926 essay, "The End of Laissez-Faire." In the *Treatise* he was mainly concerned with the short period, but in the essays now under consideration he was examining and speculating about the long future of capitalism. In monetary theory he had written and argued against economic orthodoxy; his writing on social philosophy, on the other hand, has led some to view him as essentially a "moderate conservative." His upper-middle-class background and what Harrod called "the presuppositions of Harvey Road" would lead one to think that he was fundamentally conventional in his defense of individualism. However, it is important to understand, as Joan Robinson has pointed out, that he was morally and esthetically disillusioned with capitalism. One certainly can see this in his review of H. G. Wells's *Clissold* that he wrote for the *Nation* in 1927.

In that piece Keynes discussed the idea that our era is an "unsatisfactory age of immensely rapid transition" in which many, particularly the businessmen, are ill-adapted to their environment and bored with their social lives. "What a bore for the modern man whose mind in his active career moves with the times, to stand still in his observances and way of life! What a bore are the feasts and celebrations with which London crowns success! What a bore to go through the social contortions which have lost significance and conventional pleasures which no longer please! The contrast between the exuberant activity of a prince of modern commerce and the lack of an appropriate environment for him out of office is acute. Moreover, there are wide stretches in the career of money-making which are entirely barren and nonconstructive. There is a fine passage in the first volume of *Clissold* about the profound, ultimate boredom of city men." From the tone of these remarks it seems that on the basis of his experience in the City Keynes was very much inclined to agree with Wells.

With evident approval he describes the "Open Conspiracy" which Wells's hero is forming with the intention of moving to the political Left, "far, far to the Left; but he seeks to summon from the Right the creative force and constructive will which is to carry him there." But the practical men to whom Clissold would appeal, says Keynes, "find it more amusing to make money than to join the Open Conspiracy." Why? Because "they have no creed, these potential open conspirators, no creed whatsoever. That is why, unless they have the luck to be scientists or artists, they fall back on the grand substitute motive, the perfect Ersatz, the anodyne for those who, in fact, want nothing at all— Money." And so "Clissold and his brother Dickon, the advertising expert, flutter about the world seeking for something to which they can attach their abundant *libido*. But they have not found it. They would so like to be Apostles. But they cannot. They remain businessmen." The employment of the Freudian terminology and the reference to the Apostles tell us something about Keynes's tacit psychology and social philosophy. In a sense he is saying that the businessmen, not being Apostles, fail to develop a compelling value system, to live "a life of passionate contemplation and communion," so they seek money instead. He closes on a note which is clearly autobiographical, judging from what we know of his early reading: "What a debt every intelligent being owes to Bernard Shaw! What a debt also to H. G. Wells, whose mind seems to have grown up alongside his readers, so that in successive phases he had delighted us and guided our imaginations from boyhood to maturity."

In March 1928, he prepared a speech for the Manchester schoolboys entitled "Economic Possibilities for Our Grandchildren" which is even more revealing about his evolving ideology; he repeated it before an audience in Madrid in the summer of 1930 as the world slump grew more severe. Harrod says that he gave the talk at that time to "lift his audience out of the prevailing depression," but one can see that it represents more than that—it is an important statement of his personal philosophy or *Weltanschauung*. Some have seen it as a mere *jeu d'esprit* or as a light Utopian essay composed in an idle hour; Joan Robinson refers to it as Keynes's "daydream of future civilization." From a psychological standpoint it can be insisted that daydreams—fantasies—are as important to interpret and understand as night dreams. Indeed, this essay may be regarded as analogous to Marshall's "Possibilities of Economic Chivalry" or to John Stuart Mill's speculations on the Stationary State, both well-known examinations of the future of Western society.

At the outset of his talk, Keynes sought to reassure his listeners that pessimism was not warranted, neither the pessimism of the revolutionaries who were preaching that things were so bad that nothing could save society but violent change, nor that of the reactionaries who believed that the economic situation was so precarious that experiments could not be risked. Society was not suffering from the rheumatics of old age, he said, but from the painfulness of a rapid readjustment to new technologies. Drawing from his diagnosis in the *Treatise,* he argued that the banking and monetary system had prevented the rate of interest from falling as fast as economic equilibrium required. He described the enormous accumulation of capital made possible by compound interest over the last three centuries, which combined with the equally fantastic rate of technological change meant that "in the long run" mankind was solving its economic problem, despite the concomitant technological unemployment. He speculated that one hundred years hence the standard of life in progressive countries might be four to eight times higher than it was currently; in short, such countries would be on the verge of an economy of abundance and leisure.

Drawing a distinction between basic needs and those which derived from social emulation—"keeping up with the Joneses"—he contended that the former were not insatiable. Therefore, if important wars could be avoided and population growth held down, the economic problem might be solved, or be within sight of solution, within one hundred years. There would be difficult problems of human adaptation to the new abundance and leisure—Keynes was not assured by the contemporary behavior of the wealthy in this respect, but the strenuous, purposeful money-makers might be carrying us toward a society of abundance nevertheless. Consequently, it behooves us to cultivate the arts of life itself rather than concentrating always on the means. The purposive man who is wed to the Protestant ethic seeks, he said, "a spurious and elusive immortality" for his acts by always pushing his interest in them forward in time. "He does not love his cat, but his cat's kittens; nor, in truth, the kittens, but only the kittens' kittens, and so on forward to the end of catdom."

It is indicative of the trend of his thinking at this time that he added almost incidentally a seeming allusion to those of the Jewish race when he said: "Perhaps it is not an accident that the race which did the most to bring the promise of immortality into the heart and essence of our religions has also done the most for the principle of compound interest and particularly loves this most purposive of human institutions."

He goes on in his essay to describe the changes that will come with the age of leisure and abundance. When capital accumulation is no longer so important socially, he predicted that we shall see major changes in the moral code. "We shall be able to rid ourselves of many of the pseudo-moral principles which have hag-ridden us for two hundred years, by which we have exalted some of the most distasteful of human qualities into the position of the highest virtues. We shall be able to afford to dare to assess the money-motive at its true value. The love of money as a possession—as distinguished from the love of money as a means to the enjoyments and realities of life—will be recognized for what it is, a somewhat disgusting morbidity, one of those semicriminal, semipathological propensities which one hands over with a shudder to the specialists in mental disease." Though he had accumulated a fair fortune himself, it is evident that he was no lover of the acquisitive society. The possible sources of these remarkable views and animadversions on the love of money will be considered later.

But, said Keynes, the time for all these sweeping changes was not yet; we still need the purposeful men to lead us out of "the tunnel of economic necessity into the daylight." For those who have overcome economic necessity already, it will still be reasonable that they should concern themselves and be purposeful in economic effort for those who were not so fortunate. "Meanwhile, there will be no harm in making mild preparations for our destiny, in encouraging and experimenting in the arts of life as well as the activities of purpose."

What are the sources and significance of these values with their vision of abundance which are asserted so vigorously and confidently in this essay? It has been contended that his optimistic hypothesis of abundance with its corollary that poverty is unnecessary derives from his rejection of "the pessimistic hypothesis of scarcity, frugality, abstinence, and hard work" which underlies classical economics. He was holding, in effect, that rather than poverty being due to the limitations of human and material nature, it was attributable to faulty social and economic institutions. Others see it as a reaction to the Victorian value system, especially to G. E. Moore's philosophy of living in the present, that the highest goods of life were certain states of consciousness—"the pleasures of human intercourse and the enjoyment of beautiful objects." Keynes himself, speaking of Moore, said that "his highest states of mind are largely unattached to 'before' or 'after.'" Thus, in shifting the basis of economic speculation from the long run to the short, he was being true to Moore's credo. The trouble with this interpretation is that Keynes, after leaving Cambridge, came to reject the rationalism of Moore's philosophy as being too narrow and limited, though he was very much a believer in the importance of love, beauty, and the pursuit of knowledge. Still another explanation would lead us to trace his outlook back to his homosexual nature, especially his remarks above about the love of money, "a somewhat disgusting morbidity." The homosexual familiar with the writings of Edward Carpenter would be likely to react strongly to that word "morbidity," which was used very often to characterize their sexual orientation. Some homosexuals of that period regarded themselves as more idealistic than the money-minded, materialistic heterosexuals, so there might have been an element of reaction formation in Keynes's denunciation of the morbidity involved in the love of money. However one explains his sentiments on this occasion, it is remarkable how much of his future interests and activities in the way of "encouraging and experimenting in the arts of life" were foreshadowed by this speech.

Incidentally, he returned briefly to these ideas in an article in *The Times* seven years later which suggests that they were not passing thoughts or daydreams. Arguing for a policy of planned investment, he wrote that "the natural evolution should be toward a decent level of consumption for everyone; and, when that is high enough, toward the occupation of our energies in the noneconomic interests of our lives. Thus we need to be slowly reconstructing our social system with those ends in view. This is a large matter, not to be embarked upon here."

Critics of Keynes's distaste of industrial-capitalist values have pointed out that his outlook stems from and is related historically to a long tradition of hostility toward the "acquisitive society." They can trace it back to John Stuart Mill, John Ruskin and his disciple Hobson, and to Matthew Arnold who was so critical of the philistine way of life in Great Britain and the United States. In this view, the fondness for gentry tastes and standards, coupled with this intellectual skepticism, served to contain the cultural revolution of industrialism in Great Britain and to obstruct the modernization of its economy, thus leading or contributing seriously to its present economic malaise.

In December 1930, after many delays, Keynes's *Treatise on Money* was finally published. It was the most formal and least readable of his books on monetary theory; the style was heavier and more professorial than was his wont and seemed to reflect the austerity that one might expect in a treatise. "Indeed," writes Professor Patinkin, "when one reads the *Treatise* against the background of Keynes's other writings, one cannot escape the feeling that it represents a Keynes out of character, a Keynes attempting to act the role of a professor, and a Germanic one at that."

In fact, the *Treatise* is one of Keynes's most ambitious and large-scale works, a comprehensive, two-volume treatment of money in both its pure and applied aspects. It was not designed for the general public, as with some of his journalistic publications, but for a professional audience; presumably, it would serve to establish his academic reputation as a leading thinker in his chosen field. In writing it he proceeded slowly and methodically through its seven books to define the nature, history, and value of money. In the second volume—*The Applied Theory of Money*—he analyzed statistically the key variables of his theory and described the financial institutions which were involved in their fluctuation. Finally, in book seven, he discussed monetary policy, domestic and international, in the light of his theory.

His analysis in this work is close to what economists refer to as dynamic economics. He stated that his purpose was "to find a method which is useful in describing not merely the characteristics of static equilibrium, but also those of disequilibrium, and to discover the dynamical laws governing the passage of a monetary system from one position of equilibrium to another." A related purpose was to extend the so-called quantity theory of money to an economy with a developed banking system.

The primary focus of this book, it must be emphasized, was on price levels rather than on fluctuations in output or employment. Like most orthodox economists in the twenties, Keynes fundamentally presupposed that if stability in the general price level could be achieved, the trade or business cycle would be greatly moderated. The idea was popularly expressed in the saying of Professor Irving Fisher, the most famous American monetary expert of that period, that the variations in the volume of output and employment were basically due to "the dance of the dollar," that is, to fluctuations in its value.

The somewhat heavy, ponderous quality of this book derives in part from the fact that it was written over several years—it was started in 1924, revised in 1929, and finally published in September 1930. During the course of writing it, Keynes's ideas had been developing and changing, with the consequence, as he said, that there was "a good deal in this book that represents the process of getting rid of the ideas which I used to have and of finding my way to those which I now have. There are many skins which I have sloughed still littering these pages. . . . I feel like someone who has been forcing his way through a confused jungle."

In spite of these shortcomings, the volumes are very valuable because, among other reasons, they reveal how the freedom and flexibility of his mind and his receptivity to new ideas made possible his remarkable creativity. Professor Patinkin has expressed the view that the *Treatise on Money* is not important "as a key to an understanding of the major innovation of *The General Theory,* namely, the theory of effective demand" and that "it contributes little toward an understanding of the theory itself, which differs so fundamentally from that of the *Treatise."* Still, from the broader perspective of the evolution of Keynes's ideas, it represents a major step, as Patinkin himself recognizes, in "the Saga of Man's Struggle for Freedom from the Quantity Theory." It is significant also that in the Japanese edition's preface, written in April 1932, Keynes indicated that he would not revise the *Treatise,* but instead "publish a short book of a purely theoretical character," extending and correcting the theoretical basis of his views as set forth in books three and four of the former.

In this work Keynes thought that he was proposing "a novel means of approach to the fundamental problems of monetary theory." Late in June 1931, in his Harris Foundation lectures in Chicago, he spoke of these ideas as being his "secret, the clue to the scientific explanation of booms and slumps (and of much else, as I should claim)." But his fundamental equations did not constitute the conceptual breakthrough that he hoped they would, and they were replaced in time by the more powerful theoretical innovation, the theory of effective demand. What explains this initial failure? Did his creativity as a theorist in the *Treatise* fail him because he lacked the passionate perception (the combination of thought and feeling) that had infused some of his earlier work? The book, it is clear, was not written in the "white heat" of commitment and involvement that had manifested itself in some of his previous efforts. Nevertheless, one can detect some of the passionate dedication to the problems that it addressed in his prefatory statement that "a right understanding of the topics of this book is of enormous practical importance to the well-being of the world." Nor had his character changed between the writing of the *Treatise* and *The General Theory,* but circumstances had. Professor G. L. S. Shackle feels that the former was "a far more relaxed and genial book" than the latter because, while the twenties were not exactly good times for Great Britain, they were "a time of confidence in a peaceful future" and certainly "they were not the grim and menacing 1930s." When the world depression deepened after 1931 and the theoretical crisis of economics became more acute as a consequence, Keynes really believed that he had "the answer" to the enigma of mass unemployment. His stirring, polemical voice was heard once more.

In volume one, as already noted, Keynes reviewed the evolution of the forms of money in most scholarly fashion, citing fascinating illustrations from history and making provocative remarks such as, "The Semitic races, whose instincts are keenest for the essential qualities of money, have never paid much attention to the deceptive signatures of mints, which content the financial amateurs of the North, and have cared only for the touch and weight of the metal." He described the evolution of managed currency from David Ricardo's ingot proposals to the Federal Reserve System of the United States which he considered "the greatest managed system the world has yet seen." Bank money is next discussed, taking note of the distinction between demand and time deposits (in Britain called current and deposit accounts, respectively). The evolution from bank notes to the use of checks, including overdrafts, is carefully described, leading to the conclusion that in modern monetary systems bank credit is more typical than other forms and drawing a vital distinction between the industrial and financial circulation. The former, composed of business deposits held for transaction purposes plus income deposits are governed, Keynes held, by the volume of current output; the latter is not. Digressing from his main theme, he devoted book two to a discussion of the purchasing power of money and index numbers.

In book three, we come to the fundamental equations which were the central theoretical innovation of the *Treatise*. To understand them one must realize that Keynes was in a sense reformulating the quantity theory of money in order to clarify the causal process by which the price level was determined. Instead of focusing on the total amount of money regardless of how it was employed (as in the quantity theory), he analyzed the flow of the community's earnings or money income into (1) the parts earned by the production of consumption goods and of investment goods, respectively; and (2) into the parts which are expended on consumption goods and savings. (In the *Treatise* he defined savings as the difference between income and consumption expenditure, and investment as "the net addition to wealth whether in the form of fixed capital, working capital, or liquid capital.") It was his view, following Robertson's thinking, that these two distinct processes were carried out by different groups of people with no assurance that the total would be equal. On the basis of his equations, he states that the price level of consumption goods "exceeds or falls short of their cost of production, according as the volume of savings falls short of or exceeds the cost of production of new investment. . . . Hence, if the volume of savings exceeds the cost of investment, the producers of the goods which are being consumed take a loss; and if the cost of investment exceeds the volume of savings, they make a profit."

On the other hand, whether the producers of investment goods make a profit or loss depends on whether the expectations of the market about future prices and the prevailing rate of interest are changing favorably or adversely for such producers. In his definition of terms, he included the normal remuneration of entrepreneurs as a cost and focused his analysis on the windfall profits or losses arising from the discrepancies between earnings and cost of production. He made much of the distinction between a "profit inflation" (when rising prices cause windfall profits) and an "income inflation" caused by changes in the costs of the other factors of production. The two types of inflation are related because a profit inflation may lead firms to expand their output and demand for such factors and thus induce an income inflation.

In all this, Keynes emphasized that his equations were purely formal; they were mere identities or truisms. Their value lies, however, in enabling one to trace cause and effect when operated on by the extraneous facts of the actual world. Now, in his view the most important factor subject to control in the actual world was the bank rate. Borrowing from Swedish economist Knut Wicksell, but using different definitions, he concluded that if the market or prevailing rate of interest equalled the natural rate (the latter being defined as the rate which would exactly balance current savings and the value of investment), the economy would be in equilibrium. When the market rate deviates from the natural rate, it causes fluctuations in the savings-investment ratio that leads to booms or slumps. In short, in his mind the banking system has a crucial role as a balancing factor in a capitalistic system. If it controls the terms of credit in such a way that savings equal the value of new investment, then the general price level will tend to be stable, whereas if credit terms are easier than this equilibrium level, prices and profits will rise as investment exceeds the current rate of savings; and vice versa, if credit is more expensive than the equilibrium rate.

The analysis that has been summarized thus far assumes a closed economy, that is, one that does no trading or borrowing or lending with other nations. What are the conditions of equilibrium if a nation is trading or lending to the outside world? He also dealt with this situation, arguing that external equilibrium requires that the foreign balance (defined as the balance of trade on income account, exports over imports) be equal to net foreign lending (the excess of foreign lending over foreign borrowing). Thus, the conditions for equilibrium in an international system are that simultaneously $I = S$ and $B = L$. Complications arise because the bank rate that will promote the latter equality may disturb the conditions of internal equilibrium, namely, $I = S$.

Keynes discussed the alternatives to his fundamental equations in considerable detail, such as the "real balances" or Cambridge equation and Irving Fisher's formula. He preferred his equations because in his opinion the latter dealt with a hodgepodge price level, whereas his formulation singled out more strategic price variables.

Turning to monetary policy, he analyzed the difficult issues confronting the American authorities as the stock market boom reached gigantic proportions in the late twenties, posing an agonizing dilemma for the Federal Reserve System. As security speculation mounted, based largely on margin buying financed by brokers' loans, the Federal Reserve Board was reluctant to raise the rediscount rate because it would probably discourage legitimate commercial and industrial borrowing. Keynes's analysis was very relevant to this problem because it distinguished between the financial and the industrial circulation of money. The latter, in his terminology, refers to the deposits used for the purposes of industry; the former, for the purchases of stock exchange or money market transactions. He analyzed the determinants of each circulation, treating the respective velocity of such deposits and particularly how "bull-bear" opinion affected the financial circulation. The solution of the above-mentioned dilemma, he concluded, if stability of the price level is the objective, lay in "letting both finance and industry have all the money they want, but at a rate of interest which in its effect on the rate of new investment (relative to saving) exactly balances the effect of bullish sentiment." He admitted, however, that "to diagnose the position precisely at every stage and to achieve this exact balance may sometimes be beyond the wit of man." The main criterion, he declared, in interfering with a bull or bear market should be the probable effect on the prospective equilibrium between savings and new investment.

Basically, he was concerned in the *Treatise* with the credit cycle, as the British term business cycle fluctuations. He extensively discussed the causes of disequilibrium in the price level under the heads of monetary, investment, and industrial factors in the light of his fundamental equations. He also considered the changes due to international disequilibrium (chapter twenty-one). Some critics feel that in his enthusiasm for his monetary equations the analysis became overly mechanical and exhibited a sort of magic-formula mentality. Particularly glaring was his failure to distinguish adequately between planned and actual quantities, though he later admitted this shortcoming. Expectations do not receive as much attention as they were to receive in the *General Theory,* but in general one can discern the outlines in this longer book of some basic features of the latter, such as the paradox of saving. Throughout one is impressed by the lucidity of the exposition and the masterful use of metaphor, as in the imaginative parable of the banana plantation which illustrates the paradox of saving.

The second volume of the *Treatise* on the applied theory of money is so rich in detail and complex analyses that it practically defies summarization. In it he exhibited his massive knowledge of the British, continental, and American banking systems. Undertaking detailed statistical investigations of bank deposits, their velocities of circulation, and of business activity, he emphasized the fluctuations of working capital as causes of credit cycles. Most fascinating, perhaps, is his longer chapter on historical illustrations where he imaginatively applied his new ideas to a review of some episodes in economic history. Drawing heavily upon the recently published research of Professor Earl J.

Hamilton on the influence of Spanish treasure on European price levels in the sixteenth and seventeenth centuries, he demonstrated how the inflation that swept through the Continent's economies in those eras redistributed income, weakening the landholding class, strengthening the emerging bourgeoisie, and impoverishing the peasant and working classes. In effect, he was presenting a dynamic theory of income distribution and showing inflation's pervasive effect by boldly asserting, with respect to English conditions, that "we were just in a financial position to afford Shakespeare at the moment he presented himself."

Next, he probed the causes of the depression of the 1890s, a perfect example in his opinion of a prolonged commodity deflation; he considered the war boom of 1914–18, which generated a profit and income inflation and riveted a heavy burden upon British taxpayers. He claimed that by following a relatively virtuous tax policy, Britain emerged from that war with heavy obligations to her rentiers. The postwar boom of 1919–20 was a continuation of the income and profit inflation of the war years, and while the subsequent slump canceled some part of that inflation, from the standpoint of national prosperity it was in his view a mistake. "We might have avoided most of the troubles of the last ten years—and been, perhaps, just as rich as the United States—if we had endeavored to stabilize our monetary position on the basis of the degree of income inflation existing at the end of 1920, i.e., about 175 percent up, as compared with prewar." The policies adopted instead increased the real burden of the debt and gave Britain a decade of unemployment.

He dealt equally forcibly with Britain's return to the gold standard, terming it "a cold-blooded income deflation." Five years after the return to gold, the curtailment of employment was still in operation in "an unabated degree," he solemnly wrote. He argued cogently that the British plight grew out of returning to gold at the prewar parity, thus increasing the gold costs of production relative to what they were elsewhere. At the same time, foreign investment became more attractive than home investment, pushing the amount of foreign lending ahead of the foreign balance. To check the former, the market rate was raised above the natural rate with adverse effects on domestic investment and employment.

Finally, he discussed the boom and slump in the United States over the years 1925–30, admitting that while he had previously stated there was no inflation in the American economy in that period, on the basis of the price indexes, a genuine profit inflation had developed in 1928 and 1929. With the Wall Street collapse in the autumn of the latter year, he

stated that "one of the greatest 'bull' markets in history came to an end."
He attributed the slump of 1930 primarily to "the deterrent effects on
investment of the long period of dear money which preceded the market
collapse, and only secondarily to the collapse itself." The decline of
economic activity caused a disinvestment in working capital, and the
profit deflation discouraged investment while the "psychological" poverty accompanying the fall of paper values probably increased saving.
Thus, he invoked his new saving-investment theory to explain the
onset of the Great Depression.

In book seven, the closing book of the *Treatise,* he exhaustively
examined the methods and problems of the national and international
management of money; he offered a rich feast for the student of central
banking, which unfortunately cannot be sampled here. Still, one cannot
reasonably pass over his famous essay, *Auri Sacra Fames,* in which he
cited Freud and other psychoanalysts as holding that there are "peculiar
reasons deep in our subconscious why gold in particular should satisfy
strong instincts and serve as a symbol." Writing of gold's "garment of
respectability," he speculated whether this respectability was first
assumed because, as the gold advocates alleged, it was "the sole
prophylactic against the plague of fiat moneys" or whether it was "a
furtive Freudian cloak." However, one cannot forbear inquiring
whether these ideas, or at least the phraseology employed, do not reflect
his own past furtive existence as a homosexual.

In the course of his argument about the "accursed love of gold,"
Keynes cited Freud's *Collected Papers,* Sándor Ferenczi, and the British
analyst Ernest Jones. One is not surprised at his knowledge of the
Freudian literature because, thanks to the industry of Professor Moggridge in editing Keynes's *Collected Writings,* it is now known that the
latter closely followed the discussion in the June 13, 1925 issue of the
Nation of the third volume of Freud's *Collected Papers.* In fact, he ended
that discussion with an anonymous letter to the editor of the journal
with the following fascinating appraisal of the Viennese psychiatrist's
genius. Though it is a substantial digression from the topic of money, it
is so revelatory concerning Keynes's epistemology or cognitive style
that it is quoted here almost *verbatim:*

"Professor Freud seems to me to be endowed to the degree of genius
with the scientific imagination which can body forth an abundance of
innovating ideas, shattering possibilities, working hypotheses, which
have sufficient foundation in intuition and common experience to
deserve the most patient and unprejudiced examination and which
contain, in all probability, both theories which will have to be discarded

or altered out of existence and also theories of great and permanent significance." Pointing out that the empirical or inductive proof that had been offered in print for Freud's theories were "hopelessly inadequate to the case," he nevertheless argued that "the case for considering them seriously mainly depends at present on the appeal which they make to our own intuitions as containing something new and true about the way in which human psychology works" and very little on inductive verifications such as had been published up to that time. He closed by saying that Freud's partisans as well as his critics would do well to admit this and to give him "exceptionally serious and entirely unpartisan consideration" because, whether one liked him or not, he was "one of the great disturbing, innovating geniuses of our age, that is to say, a sort of devil."

To return to Keynes's examination of monetary management in his *Treatise,* it should be noted that he discussed the 1930 slump and predicted that the nations could not hope for "a complete and lasting recovery until there has been a great fall in the long-term rate of interest throughout the world toward something nearer prewar levels. Failing this, there will be a steady pressure toward profit deflation and a sagging price level." He thought there was the risk, in fact, that the market rate of interest in falling would never catch up with the natural rate, resulting in continued income deflation and a declining price level. "If this occurs," he further prophesized, "our present regime of capitalistic individualism will assuredly be replaced by a far-reaching socialism."

His hope for avoiding such an outcome lay mainly through international cooperation in the form of the recently established Bank for International Settlements and through supranational management of the value of gold in conformity with an international tabular standard which he proposed. All this was in line with his further hope that monetary theory was now ready to make a critical leap forward which would bring it into effective contact with the real world, with the result that there would be a "better understanding of the detailed behavior of an economic system which is not in static equilibrium." He did not fully realize the extent of the intellectual effort which he in cooperation with others would have to make before this aspiration would be fulfilled.

In completing this massive monetary treatise, Keynes had had the benefit of detailed comments from Professor Pigou, Dennis Robertson, and especially from his old acquaintance and Treasury colleague R. G. Hawtrey. In response to the criticism of Pigou and Robertson, he had drastically rewritten his chapter dealing with the fundamental equations, but his differences with Hawtrey over the meaning of the term "consumer's outlay" and the press of other activities prevented him from fully digesting his comments until after the publication of the book. He had lectured in 1929 from its proofs, but in general it did not receive as close a critical scrutiny prior to its publication as *The General Theory*. Perhaps it was with this in mind that in the latter's preface, he wrote, "It is astonishing what foolish things one can temporarily believe if one thinks too long alone, particularly in economics (along with other moral sciences), where it is often impossible to bring one's ideas to a conclusive test either formal or experimental."

Certainly he had reason to expect a favorable reaction from the reviewers, judging from prepublication comments. Though he had reservations, Dennis Robertson had written that it would be "a noble book," and Joseph Schumpeter wrote to say how much he must feel relieved, adding, "I do not think any scientific book has been looked for with so universal impatience—in our time at least—as yours is." The reviews, as it turned out, were overwhelmingly favorable. Professor Pigou spoke of it as "an ambitious, elaborate, and important book," and Charles O. Hardy in the *American Economic Review* hailed it as "a masterly analysis, comprehensive and extraordinarily free of errors." Six out of the nine reviews reported in the *Book Review Digest* in the United States were favorable; only H. Parker Willis, a professor at Columbia University, dissented, saying that the book was "hasty, not consistent with itself, and largely lacking the judiciousness and balance which must be the outstanding qualities of any permanent contribution to finance."

As has been seen already, Keynes knew the book's limitations—for him it was but a halfway house to a more creative effort in writing its sequel, the classic *The General Theory of Employment Interest and Money*.

CHAPTER 12

The Great Depression and
The General Theory

What is now proved was once only imagined.
William Blake

I N HIS CHARACTERISTIC, provocative style, Paul Samuelson has written that "while Keynes did much for the Great Depression, it is no less true that the Great Depression did much for him. It provided challenge, drama, experimental confirmation. He entered it the sort of man who might be expected to embrace *The General Theory* if it was explained to him. From the previous record one cannot say more. Before it was over, he had emerged with the prize in hand, the system of thought for which he will be remembered." While not everyone will agree with this statement, certainly none can question that the writing of *The General Theory* came at a critical juncture in the history of Western civilization. As the depression deepened and it became evident that it was the greatest economic contraction that the modern West had known, fear and darkness descended on the millions who were thrown out of work and often, as a consequence, into the utmost privation. The depression seemed like some mysterious evil force which no one knew how to overcome. The democracies improvised as best they could, while some countries succumbed to totalitarianism in the attempt to deal with the evil. In the United States, where the new era of high-level mass consumption in the twenties had fostered the illusion of economic stability, cures and panaceas to end the slump multiplied, and economists intensified their efforts to acheive a scientific understanding of the business cycle. Some insisted that recovery should be sought through retrenchment and economy, but these, said Keynes with contempt, were "the voices of fools and madmen." In his own struggle to develop an acceptable theory and policy to cope with the crisis, he was, in Harrod's words, engaged in "a race with time. In his own mind he was quite sure that it [*The General Theory*] would revolutionize thinking. But if this was to be so, he must state his position with absolute clarity; he must hear all objections; he must revise, rewrite. It was a herculean labor, making a greater call upon the vital energies than his more spectacular work in the second war. It was only achieved in the nick of time." It is true that at the time Keynes confidently believed that the West was at "one of those uncommon junctures of human affairs where we can be saved by the solution of an intellectual problem, and in no other way." Yet, as will be seen, the road from the *Treatise on Money* to *The General Theory* was to be a long and controversial one.

The year 1930 was a very busy one for Keynes, what with his membership on the Committee on Finance and Industry, headed by Lord Macmillan, and his chairmanship of the Economic Advisory Council, which the MacDonald government set up in July to review the causes of the deteriorating economic situation and to suggest possible routes to recovery. This former committee was composed of some very able men, including the progressive Reginald McKenna, Professor T. E. Gregory, and the experienced politician Ernest Bevin, and its members were very interested in Keynes's new ideas on money and monetary policy. He testified for no fewer than eight days, wrote numerous memoranda, and played a major part in shaping the committee's final report. A long list of witnesses was heard, among them Montagu Norman of the Bank of England, Sir Richard Hopkins of the Treasury, and the chairmen of the joint stock banks and other experts. Keynes insistently interrogated them all in the course of exploring the limits of orthodox policy. It was clear that Britain was in a very awkward economic position because as a leading banking center, recently returned to the gold standard at a high parity, her interest rates could not fall below the world level. If she reduced her rates, more capital would flow abroad than could be financed by the excess of exports over imports, and the consequent outflow of gold would threaten the maintenance of the gold standard. To maintain external equilibrium, a higher rate of interest was required than was necessary to induce domestic investment; this was the basic dilemma which the committee faced.

Since the *Treatise on Money* had not yet been published, Keynes distributed proofs of the volume among the committee members in order to familiarize them with his new approach and to get their reaction. In some ways the committee's meetings were like a university seminar, and Keynes benefitted from the intellectual exchange as much as anyone else. The climax of it all came in the debate he had with Sir Richard Hopkins of the Treasury who was skeptical, among other things, about the wisdom of a large-scale program of public expenditure; he very capably raised many objections, the principal one being, if these works were not to divert capital from the private sector, where was the additional capital to come from? This question, it can be seen, leads inevitably to the matter of the secondary effects of public spending and the idea of the multiplier, which Richard Kahn was to expound in his important article, "Home Investment and Unemployment" in June 1931. Thus, it is evident that Keynes's participation in the deliberations of the Macmillan Committee provided him with some very valuable ideas and experience which went into the composition of *The General Theory*. The committee's report itself had somewhat of a Keynesian character in its commitment to currency management to achieve stability of output and employment at a high level, though the majority did not go along with him on a public works program which was advocated in a supplement supported by five members. Even more controversial was his suggestion, in the course of private testimony, that a degree of tariff protection might be desirable, principally because it would bolster business confidence and stimulate a higher level of domestic investment. This was certainly a *volte-face* for one who had been such a staunch defender of free trade for so long. In March 1931, in a *New Statesman* article, he came out publicly for a modified revenue tariff with provisions for subsidies for certain industries, again to much protest against his inconsistency. He was very intent at this time in bringing the determination of the level of employment under national control rather than let it remain subject to the unpredictable forces of internationalism and domestic *laissez-faire*.

This issue of protectionism became a sore spot again in the discussions of the Economic Advisory Council, a small group consisting of Hubert Henderson, Professors Pigou and Lionel Robbins, Lord Stamp, and Keynes. In the course of the council's deliberations, the latter advocated increased public expenditures during the slump and abandonment of free imports, in other words, a protective tariff. Young Robbins—he was then just thirty-one, the youngest professor of economics in the country at the time—opposed him on both proposals and threatened to write a minority report. At this Keynes was furious.

"Then, as always," writes Robbins in his autobiography, "he was capable of fits of almost ungovernable anger." But the younger man made it clear that he was ready to carry the matter to higher authorities or, if necessary, to the public. At this Keynes caved in, though he commented adversely to the other members on Robbins's emotional state and suggested that he not attend the council's last meeting. Looking back in 1970 on these far-off events, Lord Robbins held that he was right about the inadvisability of abandoning free trade, but admitted that his opposition to an expansionist fiscal policy in the thirties was "the greatest mistake" of his professional career. To balance the ledger, he thought that Keynes was extraordinarily naive to think that a tariff, once imposed, could be lifted. "How can you say that the public will show such reluctance?" he stated in the course of one of their disputes. "*I have never yet spoken on the problem.*" Another instance of his cocksureness and confidence in his persuasive powers; still, it is the impression of close students of the advisory council that his disputes with Pigou and Robbins and their relative incomprehension of his ideas convinced him of the need to restate them in a new form.

These professional disagreements over protectionism soon became academic because, with Britain's historic suspension of the gold standard in September 1931, the nation's gold fetters were broken, as he expressed it, exulting, "We feel that we have at last a free hand to do what is sensible." The subsequent decline of sterling on the exchanges put British exports at an advantage, so he retracted his stand on the issue of protection, though he returned to the subject two years later.

In 1933, he was still absorbed with this difficult question as to how Britain could achieve domestic full employment in the context of the unpredictable fluctuations associated with a free trade, *laissez-faire* economic system. In his view the latter posed the threat of not only periodic depression but of world war because of international rivalry for trade. In a strongly worded essay entitled "National Self-Sufficiency," published simultaneously in Great Britain and in the United States in June 1933, he indicted that system in no uncertain terms: "The decadent international but individualistic capitalism, in the hands of which we found ourselves after the war, is not a success. It is not intelligent, it is not beautiful, it is not just, it is not virtuous—and it doesn't deliver the goods. In short, we dislike it and are beginning to despise it. But when we wonder what to put in its place, we are perplexed." Believing that the attainment of peace and prosperity required the creation of alternative economic institutions, he proposed that freedom from war and depression could be reached by an experimental, evolutionary process of social transformation, a transition toward greater national self-sufficiency, and a planned domestic economy. His advocacy of national self-sufficiency was deliberately designed to facilitate the reduction of domestic interest rates toward the vanishing point and thus accomplish the "euthanasia of the rentier"; foreign exchange controls would prevent any flight of capital resulting from the latter policy. He argued that Britain had to be as free as possible from "interference from economic changes elsewhere, in order to make our own favorite experiments toward the ideal social republic of the future." Ten years later, when he was already involved in the negotiations that led to the International Monetary Fund, he stated in a letter that he was still "a hopeless skeptic about this return to nineteenth-century *laissez-faire,*" and asserted that "the future would lie with (i) state trading for commodities; (ii) international cartels for necessary manufactures; and (iii) quantitative import restrictions for nonessential manufactures." At that time, with Britain closer to financial insolvency, the circumstances necessitated other means, but one can still perceive in his International Clearing Union proposals (to be discussed later) the old objective of greater autonomy for domestic economic policy.

In discussions of the history of science, it has recently been observed that we appear to be passing from the phase of justification or validation of theories to a phase in which the logic and context of discovery will be the chief concern of historians and other scholars. If this proves to be so, the analysis of Keynes's composition of *The General Theory* could well become a major focus of interest because, thanks to the splendid editorial work of Professor Donald Moggridge, a superb collection of documents is available concerning the creative process involved in the writing of that work. In what follows, both these sources have been intensively drawn upon; the interested reader is referred to them for further detail.

The General Theory evolved from the *Treatise,* as has been previously explained, and therefore, to follow the thread of its development, it is necessary to return to the latter's treatment at the hands of reviewers. Certainly it must be agreed that the intellectual reaction to it was prompt; even before its publication, Joseph Schumpeter had hailed it in a private letter to Keynes as "truly a Ricardian *tour de force*" and expressed the belief that it would ever stand as "a landmark in its field." (That reference to Ricardo was unfortunate and badly chosen; Keynes had a much higher opinion of his more intuitive contemporary, the Reverend Thomas Malthus.) In the following spring a real discussion of the book started within Cambridge itself, and it was much more critical. As has been already noted, Keynes had remarked in the *Treatise*'s preface, "I could do it better and much shorter if I were to start over again." What led him to become dissatisfied with what he had regarded as his *magnum opus*? The meetings of the Macmillan Committee and of the Economic Advisory Council had raised some questions, but now even more cogent objections began to be raised within Cambridge itself.

Dennis Robertson, his old friend and colleague, who had at first praised the book, wrote in May 1931 that he "should like to have been able to subscribe to the fundamental analysis of your *Treatise*, but the more I studied it, the more obstacles I find in the way of doing so." Robertson developed the argument that, contrary to Keynes's view, when the price level of consumer goods fell in response to an excess of savings over investment, the price level of investment goods would rise, moving in the opposite direction, like buckets in a well. He put this and other objections in an article in the *Economic Journal,* to which Keynes replied with the assistance of Richard Kahn, a former student. At times in his proposed rejoinder Keynes lost his temper, writing, "Mr. Robertson's last paragraph of all—yes! a mere relic of sadistic—well, not so much barbarism as puritanism. But at this point psychoanalysis must take charge and economic analysis withdraw discreetly." Kahn had commented on this passage, "I hope that you will decide to omit." Keynes did so.

Another critical review of the *Treatise* appeared in midyear from the pen of Friedrich A. von Hayek, then but thirty-two years of age and director of the Austrian Institute of Economic Research. Keynes was so unhappy with the first installment of his criticism that he marked no fewer than thirty-four comments on it and then concluded, "Hayek has not read my book with that measure of 'good will' which an author is entitled to expect of a reader. Until he can do so, he will not see what I mean or know whether I am right. He evidently has a passion which leads him to pick on me, but I am left wondering what this passion is." Later, in a combative "Reply to Dr. Hayek" in the same journal (November 1931), he complained that the Austrian had seriously misunderstood his conclusion and central contention. Hayek was holding, according to Keynes, that the disequilibrium between savings and investment was caused by the banking system departing from a position of neutrality, but this was not his position at all. "Thus, those who are sufficiently steeped in the old point of view cannot bring themselves to believe that I am asking them to step into a new pair of trousers, and will insist on regarding it as nothing but an embroidered version of the old pair which they have been wearing for years." Turning to Hayek's own volume, *Prices and Production,* he attacked it unmercifully, saying that it seemed to him to be "one of the most frightful muddles" that he had ever read, yet he conceded that it was likely to leave its mark on the reader. "Yet it is an extraordinary example of how, starting with a mistake, a remorseless logician can end up in Bedlam. Yet Dr. Hayek has seen a vision, and though when he woke up he had made nonsense of his story by giving wrong names to the objects which occur in it, his Kubla Khan is not without inspiration and must set the reader thinking with the germs of an idea in his head."

Concluding that their respective theories occupied different terrains, Keynes admitted that Hayek was right in saying that he did not have a clear account of the factors determining the natural rate of interest and that he would endeavor to make good this deficiency. He agreed with Hayek, too, in his rejection of John Stuart Mill's dictum that "there cannot, in short, be intrinsically a more insignificant thing, in the economy of society, than money," and in his view that monetary theory needed to investigate the changes in pure theory necessitated by the shift of assumption from barter to indirect exchange. This last point is very important because, as will be seen, Keynes later sought to develop a monetary theory of production.

This long exchange of ideas with Robertson and Hayek led a research student (later to become famous as Professor Nicholas Kaldor) at the London School of Economics to write Keynes, raising very politely some subtle points of argument and terminology. In his reply, the latter admitted that he needed to be more lucid and added, "I am now endeavoring to express the whole thing over again more clearly and *from a different angle.*"

About this time Keynes also received a comment on his book from Professor Frank W. Taussig of Harvard University which he "appreciated immensely." The latter wrote of "the masterly character" of his volume and expressed the opinion that, while it would have plenty of reviews, "you must be prepared to have very few that show a real following of your work. It will probably take years before it is fully understood and before critical comment will be made deserving your careful attention."

Meanwhile, Keynes was receiving more sympathetic criticism from another quarter that was to lead him to do it all over "from a different angle." Shortly after its publication, a remarkable group of younger economists in Cambridge began meeting to discuss and criticize the

Treatise; this was during the period January–May 1931. The "Circus" or, as we would say today, the seminar held its meetings first in Richard Kahn's rooms in the Gibbs building and later in the Old Combination Room at Trinity. Sometimes some of the ablest undergraduates and even members of the faculty would participate, but the discussion was mainly carried on by these five: Richard Kahn, James Meade, Piero Sraffa, and Joan and Austin Robinson. Neither Keynes nor Pigou took part in this seminar, so Kahn would usually give an oral report of the argument to Keynes in his rooms. Meade later gave his impression of this strange procedure: "From the point of view of a humble mortal like myself, Keynes seemed to play the role of God in a morality play; he dominated the play but rarely appeared himself on the stage. Kahn was the Messenger Angel who brought messages and problems from Keynes to the 'Circus' and who went back to Heaven with the result of our deliberations."

One focus of the group's debate had to do with what became known as the "widow's cruse fallacy" which grew out of a passage in the *Treatise* in which Keynes tacitly assumed a fixed output with the adjustment taking place through prices rather than through changes in production or employment.* The young economists held that this would never do as a general theory. Another modification grew out of Kahn's article on the multiplier which he had worked out in the summer of 1930; Keynes had read it then, but it was too late to incorporate its implications in the *Treatise.* In the latter he had theorized how a change in savings-investment would affect the prices of consumer and investment goods, but did so again on the assumption of full employment. Kahn's article had pointed out that in time of depression, when there is idle plant and labor, the supply curve of consumption and investment goods was likely to be very elastic, and therefore the amount of secondary employment created by public works spending would be very large and the rise of prices small. He argued, in effect, that Keynes's fundamental equations applied only on the assumption of full employment, that this was a particularly unrealistic assumption in the face of 1931 conditions, and that it was probable that "under certain circumstances employment can be increased without any significant alteration in the difference between savings and investment."

In the *Treatise,* Keynes had ascribed the movement of the price level of consumption and investment goods to different causes, but Kahn

---

*Keynes called this the "widow's cruse" after the story of Elijah (Kings 17:13–16) because the more profits are paid out, the more they return to be paid out.

argued that actually the difference was only a matter of degree, except in the extreme case when no profits were spent on consumption goods. This line of argument showed another limitation in the *Treatise* and probably increased Keynes's dissatisfaction with its formulations.

In the summer of 1931, another form of dissent appeared when Joan Robinson worked out her "Parable on Savings and Investment" by way of answering Hayek from a Keynesian point of view. In the course of her piece, however, she too emphasized the *Treatise*'s assumption of unchanging output and sided with Kahn on the matter of the relative price levels of consumption and investment goods. In the spring of that year, Piero Sraffa, the brilliant Italian economist whom Keynes had been instrumental in bringing to Cambridge in 1927 after he had translated *The Tract on Monetary Reform,* had also challenged his benefactor on some points, and the latter had replied at some length. Professor Pigou likewise wrote some deferential criticism, and Hayek returned to the offensive in an exchange of letters with Keynes in late 1931 and 1932. Keynes then wrote a memo to Kahn and Sraffa about this correspondence: "What is the next move? I feel that the abyss yawns—and so do I. Yet I can't help feeling that there is something interesting in it." It is evident from this material that Keynes had a coterie made up largely of ex-students who, while critical of his work, were ready to go to his defense. Richard Kahn and Joan Robinson were the most important in this respect, though there were others. One needs to know these friends of Keynes, for they played a crucial part in the development of his ideas in these years.

Richard Kahn had been educated at Saint Paul's School and then went to King's College where he specialized first in mathematics and physics; he received his B. A. in 1927. In June 1928, Keynes wrote Professor Pigou, then serving as head of the economics faculty, supporting Kahn for a Wrenbury scholarship and stating that up to a year earlier he had been working at physics. He continued, "Kahn has as much natural aptitude for economics as anyone whom I have taught since the war. . . . He has, I think an exceptionally good head for the essential difficulties of the subject." (As subsequent developments were to prove, this was a very shrewd assessment indeed.) In 1930, Kahn completed his fellowship dissertation on "The Short Period" and in recognition was made a fellow of King's where he has remained since, except for his service on the Board of Trade during World War II. He also served as one of the secretaries of the Committee of Economists under Keynes's chairmanship in the early thirties, and after the war, apart from his professional economics work, he served as bursar of

King's College. He was a very good friend of Maynard and Lydia for many years, and while "Alexander," as he was familiarly known for a period, was somewhat self-effacing, with his sharp, almost Talmudic mind, he was a "perfect foil" for his more intuitive colleague.

Joan Robinson was also educated at Saint Paul's Girls' School in London, having been reared in a distinguished family—she is the great-granddaughter of Frederic D. Maurice, one of the founders of the Apostles. After matriculating at Girton College (Cambridge), she shifted from her original major, history, to economics because, as she said, the latter offered more scope for rational argument. Under Keynes and other Cambridge professors, she quickly proved that she had a remarkable talent for that subject and was appointed an assistant lecturer in economics in 1931. Two years later she published *The Economics of Imperfect Competition* which, along with Edward Chamberlin's somewhat similar work the same year, revolutionized the subject of price theory and established her reputation worldwide as a theorist. A prolific, witty, and lucid author, she has written many books and articles in a long, distinguished career. While Keynes was alive she was his affectionate friend; she had married another member of the Circus, E. A. G. (Austin) Robinson, a fellow of Corpus Christi College who had been appointed university lecturer in 1929. Author himself of numerous, well-known articles on economics, he too was especially close to Maynard as assistant editor of the *Economic Journal* (1934–44), and as his confidant during the British-American loan negotiations.

The scholarly achievements of his young colleagues must have been a real source of satisfaction to Keynes in these years, but as the depression deepened there was another development that gave him much concern. Communism was becoming a popular cult among the politically conscious undergraduates at Cambridge; a cell was established at Trinity College in 1931, and soon there were others at similar institutions. Some of the radical youth saw Russian Communism as a theoretical antithesis to fascism or Nazism or were attracted to it by the government's failure to find jobs for the growing numbers of unemployed. Others were drawn into the Marxist net by the busy agents of the Comintern who found recruits most readily among the "choice spirits" of the Apostles. Keynes discovered that the sacred enclave of the Society was penetrated by such Marxists as Anthony Blunt, Guy Burgess, and Julian Bell, the militant son of his friends Vanessa and Clive. He was so shocked by this development that, at his suggestion, the meetings of the group were officially suspended, but its members continued to meet unofficially. He attributed the appeal of Communism to a revival of the strain of Puritanism in English culture, a desire to adopt a painful solution because of its painfulness. In 1934, in a *New Statesman* article, he wrote, "When Cambridge undergraduates take their inevitable trip to Bolshiedom, are they disillusioned when they find it all dreadfully uncomfortable? Of course not. That is what they are looking for."

Unbeknown to him, some of these disillusioned sons of the Establishment later became Soviet agents, burrowing within the British Secret Service or other government bodies, to the grave detriment of the free world before and during World War II. Keynes had probably known Guy Burgess, Donald MacLean, and "Kim" Philby when they were at Cambridge, but he could hardly have comprehended the depth of their secret commitments. Still, he was attracted by some of these bright young men, as was shown by his interview with Kingsley Martin, the editor of the *New Statesmen,* in January 1939:

"There is no one in politics today worth sixpence outside the ranks of liberals except the postwar generation of intellectual Communists under thirty-five. Them, too, I like and respect. Perhaps in their feelings and instincts they are the nearest thing we now have to the typical nonconformist English gentlemen who went to the Crusades, made the Reformation, fought the Great Rebellion, won us our civil and religious liberties, and humanized the working classes last century." A controversial statement, surely, that merely serves to underline the depth of his own nonconformity. Impatient with the policies of the incumbent government, he himself had flirted with the ideas of Sir Oswald Moseley's new party in 1933 to such a degree that Virginia Woolf feared on one occasion that she might be converted by him to what she suspected was "a form of fascism."

These years when he was framing *The General Theory* were difficult and trying times for Keynes. His old friend Lytton Strachey died of cancer on January 21, 1932, and a few months later the bereft Carrington committed suicide. Actually, after Maynard and Lydia married, their relations with Strachey had become somewhat distant, though Lytton still remained "very kindly and amiable." In 1925, he had visited Tilton but found Maynard "rather far off" and hard to communicate with. "Would you believe it?" he later wrote Carrington. "Not one drop of alcohol appeared. The Charlestonians declare that *il gran* Pozzo is now immensely rich—probably £10,000 a year.* I can believe it—and water, water everywhere! Such is the result of wealth."

---

*Strachey had nicknamed Keynes Pozzo after a Corsican diplomat, Pozzo di Borgo, who was, according to Harrod, "not a diplomat of evil motive or base conduct, but certainly a schemer and man of many facets."

Some insight into the frayed relationship between Maynard and Lytton is gained from Virginia Woolf's diary notes about a luncheon with the Keyneses in December 1931, when Strachey was already dying. Maynard said, according to the novelist, that "Lytton's last relations [at Ham Spray] had been very thin. He was not sure when he had seen him last. He [Lytton] had not really changed; nothing of importance had happened. They [the Keyneses] did not go to Ham Spray because Lydia disapproves of the immorality of Carrington. She is the dog in the manger. The relationships are hypocritical."

During this time of hard work and sorrow there was one consolation for Maynard—under his tutelage, Lydia was making progress as an actress. While her *Comus* with "Dadie" Rylands was received lukewarmly, her appearance in Ibsen's *A Doll's House* at the Arts Theatre in London on March 4, 1934, was "a triumphant success." So Virginia Woolf later reported in describing Keynes's reaction at the performance: "Dear Old Maynard was—this is exactly true—streaming tears; and I kissed him in the stalls between the acts; really, she was a marvel, not only a light leaf in the wind, but edged, profound, and her English was exactly what Ibsen meant—it gave the right aroma. So she's in the Seventh Heaven and runs about kissing and crying. Whether it means business, I don't know."

At the end of May 1931, the Macmillan Committee having completed its hearings, Keynes embarked for the United States on his first visit since the war years. He had been invited by the University of Chicago to give some lectures for the Harris Foundation on the subject of Unemployment as a World Problem. While abroad he also visited with some New York businessmen, officials of the Federal Reserve System, and had a meeting with President Hoover who had just declared a moratorium on the war debts.

In his three lectures on unemployment at Chicago, he emphasized that the world was in the midst of the greatest economic catastrophe of modern times and thought it possible that economic historians of the future would regard this crisis as a major turning point. He analyzed the causes of the slump in terms of his *Treatise* concepts, admitting that in the late twenties there was a profit inflation in the United States. He gave a very lucid exposition of the *Treatise*'s argument, stating that business contraction in a depression would eventually reach "a sufficiently low level of output which represents a kind of spurious equilibrium." Some have thought that this passage represents an adumbration of the idea of equilibrium at less than full employment, but from the context it is clear that he was describing merely a turning point in the trade cycle. The road to recovery, he contended, would be found not by deflating costs and prices, but by raising the level of investment by restoring business confidence, undertaking public works, and reducing the long-term rate of interest. While he gave more attention in these lectures to changes in output than to price changes, he was still working with the conceptual framework of the *Treatise*.

However, by the fall of that year from his correspondence with Richard Kahn one can see that he was moving forward from the *Treatise* formulations; thus, in a letter dated September 24, he very definitely analyzed changes in output and described a position of "long-period unemployment, namely, an equilibrium position short of full employment." Maximum output, he wrote, would not be achieved "without management." In his Easter term lectures in 1932, he broke more new ground and elicited interested comment from Dennis Robertson and Joan Robinson, though he still spoke of his "half-forged weapons." In the summer he had made further progress so that by September 18, 1932, he was able to inform his mother that he had written nearly a third of his new book on monetary theory.

Fragments of chapters written during this period, entitled "The Monetary Theory of Production," show him writing of "the vital generalization that increases and decreases in the volume of output and employment depend upon changes in disbursements relative to earnings"; it is evident that he was shifting to this mode of expression and analysis rather than the savings-investment terminology of the *Treatise*. He was emphasizing, too, that "the volume of employment must be expected to move in the same direction as the volume of capital development." There are other passages clearly foreshadowing *The General Theory* in these early drafts in which he analyzed the "stoppers" or turning points in the business cycle: "There is no presumption whatever that the equilibrium output will be anywhere near the optimum output . . . ; an active policy of stimulating investment renders a greater volume of savings consistent with a greater volume of output. Thus, it might be truer to say that the amount of saving over a period of time depends upon the amount of investment, than the other way round." In another place he argued against wage reductions as a way out of the vicious circle of declining profits and deflation, calling it "a competitive remedy" in that it benefitted the entrepreneurs who cut but did not improve the economic situation in the aggregate. He treated unemployment insurance as an automatic stabilizer of the economy and introduced a concept of quasi-rent to stand for the expectation of the productivity of capital; it is apparent that he was in the process of meeting Hayek's previous criticism on this matter. There is also a discussion of liquidity preference in this draft.

In a note entitled "Historical Retrospect," probably written in 1932, he criticized the orthodox equilibrium theory of economics, saying that "the economists in their devotion to a theory of self-adjusting equilibrium have been, on the whole, wrong in their practical advice and ... the instincts of practical men have been, on the whole, the sounder." Mercantilists, anti-usury laws, and cheap money policies were all approved in this draft as increasing investment, anticipating the position of *The General Theory*.

The unexpected discovery of additional Keynes papers at Tilton in the winter of 1975–76 now enables us to reconstruct more clearly the steps in the creative process which lead to the writing of that book. These materials reveal the important part which oppositional contructs played in the development of its argument and suggest some of the passionate enthusiasm and creative joy with which Keynes expounded the new ideas. For example, in his lectures in the spring of 1932, he wrote of "the remarkable generalization that, in all ordinary circumstances, the volume of employment depends on the amount of investment." And then, having cited examples in mathematical terms of his thought, he exclaimed, "We can galvanize our truisms in being generalizations of far-reaching practical importance. Indeed, I believe, that any man who has thoroughly grasped the truism $\Delta Q = \Delta I - \Delta F - \Delta E$ and has allowed this colorless and in itself inoperative liquid to enter his marrowbones, will never be, in his outlook on the practical man, quite the same man again!"*

The overtone of an "eureka" or exclamation of triumphant achievement in that sentence is unmistakable, but the allusion to "marrowbones" is puzzling until one recalls Keynes's love of poetry and his probable reading of W. B. Yeats's *A Prayer for Old Age*:

> God guard me from those thoughts men think
> In the mind alone;
> He that sings a lasting song
> Thinks in a marrow-bone.

Like Yeats, Keynes did not think "in the mind alone"; he believed that creative work required passionate perception, the combination of

---

*Professor Moggridge, the editor of Keynes's writings from which this is drawn, states that "we have no means of telling directly the exact meaning attached to the symbols used in this lecture," but their definition is not necessary for the use of them made in the text.

the mind with feeling, and consequently, projecting his own cognitive style upon "any man," assumed that he too could allow new insights to permeate his "marrow-bones" as well as his mind.

There is further evidence in these newly found papers of the thoroughness with which his colleagues, especially Joan and Austin Robinson and Richard Kahn, debated aspects of the evolving work, issuing a "manifesto" against certain of its contentions, which Keynes sought to answer point by point. We learn, for example, that one day in May 1932, he talked with Joan Robinson and Kahn "all day," but fortunately they "solved the problem amicably in the end." The intensity with which he worked at times comes out, too, in a letter in which he reported (to Lydia) "a tremendous burst of activity of writing- ... scribble, scribble, scribble for three and a half hours, nineteen pages." His willingness to take criticism is illustrated in his lecture notes: "I hope that in these lectures I shall show that I am not obstinate and can take advantage of criticism on substantial points of argument and exposition." That this was more than good intention is disclosed in another remark, "Alexander [Kahn] has proved to me that 'my important discovery' last week is all a mistake." But enough of such instances of his method of work; it is necessary to turn to the more fundamental aspect, the underlying structure of his thought.

The distinguished historian of science, Gerald Holton, has pointed out that the formulation of opposites and antitheses has played a crucial role in the development of scientific creations. "Science," he writes, "has always been propelled and buffeted by such contrary and antithetical forces. Like vessels with draft deep enough to catch more than merely the surface current, scientists of genius are those who are doomed, or privileged to special sensitivity to contraries that has made possible for them to do so, and it is an inner necessity that has made them demand nothing less from themselves." The historical account of the structure of scientific revolutions given by Thomas S. Kuhn also demonstrated that the formulation of antitheses and oppositions, and their resolution, has been a salient feature of scientific advance. From this standpoint it is most illuminating to analyze the oppositional categories that Keynes employed in the process of writing *The General Theory*.

In his first draft table of contents in 1933, he entitled the work *The Monetary Theory of Employment,* but he did not utilize any explicit oppositional categories. In the second draft that same year, he now called his book *The General Theory of Employment,* and in chapter one he planned to discuss "the nature and significance of the contrast between a cooperative and an entrepreneurial economy." He used this conceptual opposition to explore the tacit postulates of the classical economics. In the first type of society he set up, the real-wage or cooperative economy, the factors of production were rewarded by dividing up in agreed proportions the actual output of their cooperative efforts; in this model the presuppositions of the classical theory were fulfilled, in his opinion. A second type of economy, called a neutral entrepreneur or neutral economy for short, envisions that the productive factors are hired for money, but there is a mechanism which ensures that the exchange value of their incomes is always equal to their share in the cooperative economy. In the third he described the money-wage or entrepreneur economy as one in which the entrepreneurs hire the factors for money, but lacks a mechanism to assure an equality between aggregate disbursements and earnings. On the basis of these definitions, he asserted that the contemporary economic organization (as of the early thirties) had the characteristics of the latter type of economy.

In his 1933 manuscript he remarked that the distinction between a cooperative and an entrepreneur economy bore some relation to "pregnant observation made by Karl Marx—though the subsequent use to which he put this observation was highly illogical." (Incidentally, he did not comment at this point on the dialectical background of Marxian thought.) In volume one of *Das Kapital,* Marx had pointed out that capitalist production is not a case of $C - M - C'$, that is, a matter of exchanging commodity or effort for money in order to obtain another commodity. In the capitalist economy, he insisted business is interested in the case of $M - C - M'$; in short, it parts with money for a commodity or effort in order to make more money. By exploring the implications of these contrasting polar types of economy, Keynes was able to formulate his theory of effective demand and to suggest the sort of public policies which could be adopted to keep the entrepreneur economy in a neutral condition.

Institutional economists such as Professor Dudley Dillard have emphasized the resemblance between Thorstein Veblen's polar categories of finance and industry (or making money versus making goods) and those which Keynes developed, though it must be admitted that the latter provided a more integrated theoretical analysis of the functioning of capitalism than the American economist. That both these creative social scientists employed oppositional or polar (Janus-like) constructs in a fruitful way is indisputable. It is curious too that Keynes, in expounding what he called "a theory of involuntary unemployment," at one stage wrote of it as "a theory of chronic unemployment," a phrase which reminds one of Veblen's view that depression was a chronic condition in an advanced capitalist system.

In the published version of *The General Theory* one finds Keynes still examining possible oppositional categories. He refers to the gulf in existing economic theory between the Theory of Value and what was taught under the Theory of Money and Prices about such subjects as inflation and deflation. Reflecting upon the intellectual ambivalence or conflict the conventional approach produced, he wrote, "We have all of us become used to finding ourselves sometimes on one side of the moon and sometimes on the other, without knowing what route or journey connects them, related, apparently, after the fashion of our waking and dreaming lives."

One of the objects of his book, he wrote, was "to escape from this double life," and he went on to argue that the present division of economics between the Theory of Value and Distribution and the Theory of Money was a false division. The right dichotomy, he suggested, was between the Theory of the Individual Firm or Industry and the Theory of Output and Employment *as a whole.* (This distinction is what is now recognized as the difference between micro- and macroeconomics.) Then, as if demonstrating that his concepts were not frozen, he added, "Or perhaps we might make our line of division between the theory of stationary equilibrium and the theory of shifting equilibrium—meaning by the latter the theory of a system in which changing views about the future are capable of influencing the present situation. For the importance of money essentially flows from its being a link between the present and the future." These speculations about possible conceptual antitheses strikingly illustrate the role of such polar or Janusian thinking in Keynes's last work and serve to support Holton's view that opposition is "a concern and a central preoccupation of creative scientists."

The completed structure of the theory of demand in *The General Theory* did not consist simply of these ideas for the practical functioning of the economy. As Dr. Rothenberg has emphasized, "The creative process progresses from the formulation and specification of polarities, dichotomies, and extremes toward moderation. Rather than using diffuse or moderate elements and relationships at the start, and for some distance along the way, the creator is willing to deal with the risks of contradiction and conflict. He modifies and shapes the conflicting extremes in forming a creation." In similar fashion, Keynes moved from these preliminary antitheses to conceive how the entrepreneur economy could be stabilized by variations in government loan expenditure, changes in the rate of interest, or by redistribution of income so as to affect the propensity to consume. These thoughts finally resulted in a Janusian conception of a mixed economy in which the seemingly opposed private and public sectors could be stimulated to supplement each other in their simultaneous functioning.

These evolving ideas soon began to appear in Keynes's published writings. Late in 1932, he contributed to a *Festschrift* for Professor Arthur Spiethoff another essay on "A Monetary Theory of Production" which is obviously an outgrowth of his earlier exchange with Hayek. In it he made the distinction between a real-exchange and a monetary economy and contended that business cycle theory was in an unsatisfactory state because of a lack of a monetary theory of production. Most treatises on economic principles, including Marshall's, he asserted, were concerned mainly, if not entirely, with a real-exchange economy and not with the monetary economy in which we actually lived. The idea that it is easy to adapt the hypothetical conclusions of the former to the latter was a mistake. The abstract economies of the real-exchange economy on which most had been brought up was "a singularly blunt weapon for dealing with the problem of booms and depressions. For it assumed away the very matter under investigation." In other words, he insisted that booms and depressions were peculiar to an economy in which money, in some significant sense, was not neutral. And he concluded that the next step of economics was to work out a detailed monetary theory of production, adding, "At any rate, that is the task on which I am now occupying myself, in some confidence that I am not wasting my time."

In his lectures that year he developed this distinction between a neutral or real-exchange economy and a monetary economy and argued that there was no long-period tendency toward full employment in the latter. Meanwhile, though there were some signs of economic recovery in the United Kingdom, the international economy was still badly depressed—exchange restrictions, tariffs, and quotas were steadily drying up the flow of international trade and investment. The statesmen of the West consequently decided to hold a World Economic Conference in London in 1933 to consider a collective strategy to cope with the spreading depression. Partly with this in mind, at this time Keynes prepared a series of four articles for *The Times* which were later reprinted under the title *The Means to Prosperity*. In them he made a careful, persuasive case for loan expenditure to end the slump, including a popular exposition of the multiplier, and closed with a plea for a reflation of world prices via increased loan expenditure and the issuance of $5 billion in gold notes by the major countries to bolster the "gold" reserves of the different central banks. He wrote Richard Kahn, who was in the United States, about his preparation of these articles, saying, "I hope I don't make any bloopers—I wish you were here to look over my shoulder."

At the same time he was writing these articles, he was readying his *Essays in Biography* for publication. In the latter he included a rewritten essay on Malthus which he had read to the Cambridge Political Economy Club as far back as 1922. In this revision he took advantage of the contemporaneous research of his friend Piero Sraffa on Ricardo and worked in some controversial passages about Malthus's ideas on effective demand and the rate of interest. He later used this material in *The General Theory* to give a provocative historical perspective on his own theory of effective demand.

During the rest of 1933, he worked strenuously on his new book, analyzing the characteristics of the entrepreneur economy in order, as he said, to "bring home the essential features to the reader's intuition." Some of this writing on the meaning of savings, quasi-rents, and the so-called marginal efficiency of capital was so extremely lucid that it is a pity it was not used in the final version of the book, which is much more complicated and tortuous in its exposition. In these chapters he was exploring the difficult paradox of saving, concluding, for example, that "voluntary" saving was detrimental whenever employment was suboptimal. "An increment of 'voluntary' saving, i.e., economizing," he wrote, "is only to be welcomed as socially beneficial when employment is supraoptimal and earners are finding themselves tricked by the industrial machine into exerting themselves on a scale, the marginal disutility of which is not adequately rewarded by their marginal product—[a] state of affairs which actually in the modern world is very infrequent." But perhaps this passage contains such subtleties and technical terms that it will not be very apparent to the general reader's intuition.

Keynes himself was so completely absorbed in his writing at this period that he refused, in a letter to his publishers, "to spend time revising my *Treatise on Money,* even in minor particulars." In October of that year, Joan Robinson published an article in the first issue of a new journal in which she forthrightly summed up the significance of the novel Keynesian ideas which were already in circulation. She wrote: "The plain man has always found the Theory of Money a bewildering subject, but at the present time many academic economists are as much bewildered as the plain man. The reasons for this state of affairs is that the Theory of Money has recently undergone a violent revolution. It had ceased to be the Theory of Money and became the Analysis of Output." In her prescient essay, Robinson declared that in his *Treatise on Money* Keynes had failed "to realize the nature of the revolution that he was carrying through," but the criticisms of the Circus had finally put him on the right trail and that he had now shown economists "how to crack the egg," namely, to approach the problem not through the quantity theory of money but in terms of the demand for output as a whole.

Whether one accepts the Robinson claims as valid or not, it is clear that when Keynes gave his Michaelmas lectures in 1933, under the title "The Monetary Theory of Production," his exposition of the subject was distinctly different from that of the year before. He differentiated the classical theory (the real-exchange economy) from his own approach, which he labelled "the entrepreneur economy," introduced his definition of "involuntary" unemployment, and took Professor Pigou's book on that subject as his point of departure, as he did in the finished volume, *The General Theory*. By December 1933, he had drawn up his first table of contents of a book which he now called *The General Theory of Employment*. He continued working on it into 1934, and by the spring wrote Joan Robinson, "I am going through a stiff week's supervision from R. F. K.[ahn] on my ms. He is a marvelous critic and suggester and improver—there never was anyone in the world to whom it is so helpful to submit one's stuff." Four days earlier he had informed his mother that his book "was now nearing completion."

In May, Keynes paid another visit to the United States where he gave a paper to the American Political Economy Club which included in its membership some of the leading economists specializing in business cycles. In his presentation he gave a brief economic analysis of the American business situation, discussing it in terms of his theory of effective demand, estimating the multiplier for the United States as compared to that for Great Britain, and prophesying cautiously an autumn recovery, but warned that unless government loan expenditure were undertaken after that, he was not hopeful. "The difference between $200 million a month and $400 million a month will be the difference between depression and recovery," he told his select audience.

This paper had been written before he went to Washington, where he met a number of high New Deal officials and had his disappointing visit with President Roosevelt. The President had known him from the World War I period and had not exactly cherished him because of his critical portrait of Wilson in *The Economic Consequences of the Peace.* Nevertheless, at the end of 1933 he had addressed an open letter to the President in the *New York Times* in which he stated:

"You have made yourself the trustee for those in every country who seek to end the evils of our condition by reasoned experiment within the framework of the existing social system. If you fail, rational change will be gravely prejudiced throughout the world, leaving orthodoxy and revolution to fight it out. But if you succeed, new and bolder methods will be tried everywhere, and we may date the first chapter of a new economic era from your accession to office."

After this 1934 meeting, the President wrote Felix Frankfurter, "I had a grand talk with Keynes and liked him immensely." The other reports that we have of their conversation hardly suggest that Keynes was very persuasive on that occasion. Roosevelt later remarked to his secretary of labor, Mrs. Frances Perkins, "I saw your friend Keynes. He left a whole rigmarole of figures. He must be a mathematician rather than a political economist," and Keynes, obviously equally disappointed, told Secretary Perkins that he "supposed the President was more literate, economically speaking." Perhaps he was so preoccupied with the President's hands, an old Keynesian obsession, that he was not at his best that day as his own description of the interview suggests:

But at first, of course, I did not look closely at these things. For naturally my concentrated attention was on his hands. Rather disappointing. Firm and fairly strong, but not clever or with finesse, shortish round nails like those at the end of a businessman's fingers. I cannot draw them right, yet while not distinguished (to my eye) they are not of a common type. All the same, they were oddly familiar. Where had I seen them before? I spent ten minutes at least searching my memory as for a forgotten name, hardly knowing what I was saying about silver and balanced budgets and public works. At last it came to me. Sir Edward Grey. A more solid and Americanized Sir Edward Grey. The idea will probably mislead you, but there is a grain of significant truth in it. Much cleverer, much more fertile, sensitive and permeable, but something all the same, which corresponded to those fingernails and carried me back to Sir Edward Grey.

Whatever opinion others might have had of Keynes's persuasiveness with the president, Walter Lippmann, with whom he had been on friendly terms since 1919, thought that his open letter to the *New York Times* of December 31, 1933, had had considerable influence on the government's policy. He wrote him: "I don't know whether you realize how great an effect that letter had, but I am told that it was chiefly responsible for the policy which the Treasury is now quietly but effectively pursuing of purchasing long-term government bonds with a view to making a strong bond market and to reducing the long-term rate of interest." Lippmann, who was critical of the National Recovery Administration, continued, "Nobody could make so great an impression upon the president as you could, if you undertook to show him the meaning of that part of his policy."

Before leaving the United States and in apparent response to Lippmann's plea, Keynes wrote another statement on American economic policy, which he entitled "Agenda for the President," and sent it again to the *New York Times*. In it he criticized the restrictionist philosophy of the NRA, supported the AAA (Agricultural Adjustment Aministration) for "organizing the advisable measure of restriction which industry long ago organized for itself," and endorsed the administration's "excellent currency policy" at which it had arrived "either by skill or by good fortune." His main emphasis, however, was on the government's emergency spending, which he thought might have to be continued for a full year to stimulate economic recovery. In January 1935, in another letter to Keynes, Lippmann expressed the view that the President's new policy was more in accord with his advice.

Upon his return from America, Keynes worked hard at revising the manuscript of *The General Theory,* a task which he had undertaken partly at the suggestion of Richard Kahn. The latter had a long visit with him at Tilton in September in which he went over difficult points; Keynes later wrote his mother, "As usual he [Kahn] was extraordinarily helpful." In the autumn he lectured from the proofs of his book, and during the Michaelmas term he gave a radio broadcast in a series on "Poverty in Plenty" in which he addressed himself to the question, "Is the economic system self-adjusting?" His answer, of course, was that it was not, and he went on to say that "without purposive direction, it is incapable of/translating our actual poverty into our potential plenty." The self-adjusting school of thought, he stated, had behind it almost the whole body of organized economic thinking and the doctrine of the last hundred years; it had the prestige and influence in business and government. On the other side of this gulf of opinion were those who rejected the idea that the existing economic system was self-adjusting, such as John A. Hobson and others. But if these heretics wished to demolish the forces of nineteenth-century orthodoxy, he wrote, they must attack them in their citadel. No successful attack had yet been made. Then he boldly asserted, "Now I range myself with the heretics. I believe their flair and their instinct move them toward the right conclusion. But I was brought up in the citadel, and I recognize its power and its might. . . . For me, therefore, it is impossible to rest satisfied until I can put my finger on the flaw in that part of the orthodox reasoning that leads to the conclusions which seem to me unacceptable. I believe that I am on my way to doing so."

In this talk he indicated that he disagreed with the heretics that the only remedy for the existing malaise was to change the distribution of wealth or to modify habits so as to increase consumption expenditure. This, he conceded, was a remedy, but there was an alternative, namely, to increase the output of capital goods by reductions in interest rates and other ways. In a brief, popular talk he could not go into details, but his speech is interesting in that it revealed his psychology and the degree of his ego involvement in attacking "the citadel."

In the October 27, 1935 issue of the *New Statesman and Nation,* an article reproduced a conversation that H. G. Wells had with Stalin in Moscow the year before. Kingsley Martin, the new editor of the journal, proud of his scoop, asked George Bernard Shaw to comment on the Wells interview; Shaw had visited Stalin himself and came away convinced, like Sidney and Beatrice Webb, that Soviet Russia was very much like an idealized version of a Fabian state. Wells had been more critical of Stalin's regime, so an old-fashioned row ensued between the two writers. Martin, seeing what wonderful copy it made, asked Ernest Toller and Keynes to comment on the exchange and published the whole correspondence as a pamphlet. In his remarks, Keynes brilliantly analyzed the limitations of Wells's vision of the future and suggested what was lacking, which he was then in the process of rectifying:

"Wells's peculiar gift of the imagination lies in his creative grasp of the possibilities and ultimate implication of the data with which contemporary scientists furnish him. At the same time he is a social and political dreamer—or has grown so as he becomes older—much more than a technical and mathematical dreamer, of the school of Plato, not of Pythagoras or Archimedes. *Wells's misfortune had been to belong to a generation to whom their economists have offered nothing new.* They have given him no platform from which his imagination can leap. But he is fully conscious all the same, and justly so, that his own mind dwells with the future, and Shaw's and Stalin's with the past."

In his contribution to this symposium, Keynes had also been critical of Marx's thought, and this led to a lively exchange with G. B. S. With a good deal of wit and intellectual cogency, he argued in the pamphlet that all three—Stalin, Wells, and Shaw—were wrong and out of date. "Time and the Joint Stock Company and the Civil Service have silently brought the salaried class into power. Not yet a Proletariat. But a Salariat surely." The redoubtable Shaw was not easily convinced; indeed, in a letter dated November 30, 1934, he sought to instruct the Cambridge economist on a few matters. He noted that Marx was now "a best seller" among the serious books in the Everyman Library and that the world was gasping at the Russian Revolution, which had been carried out by men who were inspired by him more directly and exclusively than the Reformation by Luther and Calvin or the French Revolution by Rousseau and Voltaire. He asserted: "In such a situation, it is impossible for a sociologist of any standing to write about Marx as forgotten and negligible. I have picked Marx's mistakes to pieces as meticulously as anybody; but I am always careful to reserve the fact that he was an Epoch Maker."

The class war, he went on to insist, "was perfectly sound as a proposition in political physics. . . . The ruthlessness of capital in pursuit of surplus value (in other words, of cheap labor), as Marx taught, was producing dangerous conflict between our obvious balance-of-power interest in an alliance of England and France with Russia and the USA and the class war pressure to join with Japan in the exploitation of Manchuoko.

"Your article reads as if you had never heard of all this, and therefore, if it is to be reprinted, I think that you ought to revise it sufficiently to avoid this impression."

Keynes replied that it was too late to revise and besides, "as for my view of Marx, I said nothing in that article except to accuse you and Stalin of being still satisfied with his view of the capitalist world which had much verisimilitude in his day but is unrecognizable three quarters of a century later! Surely it is certain that this picture has changed out of recognition.

"My feelings about *Das Kapital* are the same as my feelings about the Koran. I know that it is historically important, and I know that many people, not all of whom are idiots, find in it a sort of Rock of Ages and containing inspiration. When I look into it, it is inexplicable how it can have this effect. His dreary, out-of-date controversializing seems so extraordinarily unintelligible as material for this purpose. Could either of these books carry fire and sword around half the world? It beats me. Clearly there is some defect. Do you, better equipped, believe both *Das Kapital* and the Koran? Or only *Das Kapital*? But whatever the sociological value of the latter, I am sure that its contemporary economic value (apart from occasional and inconsecutive flights of insight) is nil. Will you promise to read it again if I do? Wishing you good health, yours ever."

The redoubtable G. B. S. answered Keynes about two weeks later in a four-page, double-spaced, typewritten letter in which he claimed that Keynes was oblivious of the 1880s and that his Cambridge education was so out of date that it had given him a time lag of about forty years. "I could pile up all sorts of facts from the eighties to show you that your notion of it is postdated by forty years. The real eighties were far more agitated over economics than the present dole-softened money crisis which isn't a crisis at all. It had back of it hunger riots and breaking of windows by the unemployed in Saint James Street and Piccadilly. When trade revived at the end of the eighties, the steam went out of it and the war finished it. And Cambridge forgot all about it and left you under the impression that I am a curate discouraged by reading Goldsmith's *Deserted Village*! Lord help you, you know nothing about it; and Cambridge has convinced you that you know everything, which is the typical university result. You must shake it off, or Cambridge will nullify you as completely as Parliament has nullified McDonald.

"(. . . For all his mistakes, Mahomet was a very wise man for all that, and Marx was also among the prophets!) And you, Maynard, are not merely Marshall's successor. You are a bright and promising youth, frightfully handicapped by the Cambridge nullification process, with some inextinguishable sparks of culture which make you interesting. Hence, my writing all this to save you from one or two blunders as to things which happened before your time."

In his turn, Keynes got around to replying to his combative correspondent on the first day of the new year. "Thank you for your letter. I will try to take your words to heart. There must be *something* in what you say, because there generally is. But I've made another shot at old K. M. last week, reading the Marx-Engels correspondence just published, without making much progress. I prefer Engels of the two. I can see that they invented a certain method of carrying on and a vile manner of writing, both of which their successors have maintained with fidelity. But if you tell me that they discovered a clue to the economic riddle, still I am beaten—I can discover nothing but out-of-date controversializing.

"To understand my state of mind, however, you have to know that I believe myself to be writing a book on economic theory which will largely revolutionize—not, I suppose, at once but in the course of the next ten years—the way the world thinks about economic problems. When my new theory has been duly assimilated and mixed with politics

and feelings and passions, I can't predict what the final upshot will be in
its effect on action and affairs. But there will be a great change, and in
particular the Ricardian foundations of Marxism will be knocked away.

"I can't expect you, or any one else, to believe that at the present
stage. But for myself I don't merely hope what I say, in my own mind
I'm quite sure."

This certainly is an extraordinary statement, both for the general
accuracy of its prediction of the revolutionary impact of the "new
economics" and for its expression of the supreme confidence of a truly
creative mind.

As the new year unfolded, Keynes was going to need all the self-
confidence and tenacity in argument that he could muster, for when he
circulated the proofs of his book, he received very severe criticism. He
sent his first proofs to Dennis Robertson because he still had a very high
opinion of him as an economist and as a friend. Despite a heavy load of
lectures, the latter went about the task with extreme conscientiousness,
making a wad of notes on the first eighteen chapters which were so
voluminous that they approached the dimensions of a book. At first he
found it very hard to make up his mind about the new propositions. He
told Keynes that some of his points expressed "in your old philosopho-
economic manner" were "obviously superb," but finally complained
that he couldn't determine what the linchpin of the new mechanism
was; he found much of it confusing and captious and admitted that a
large part of the theoretical structure was to him "almost complete
mumbo jumbo!" He concluded his letter, "Yours ever—in spite of these
bites at the hand that fed me."

Keynes answered in elaborate detail, his comments and explanations
running to eight printed pages, explaining that the object of the first
part of the book was to show what governs effective demand. But he
had to admit that they were hopelessly at cross purposes. He couldn't
understand how Robertson could contend that most of what he maintained was incompatible with what he already believed. Disappointed
and somewhat put out at Robertson's reference to "mumbo jumbo," he
countered sharply, "For this book is a purely theoretical work, not a
collection of wisecracks. Everything turns on the mumbo jumbo, and
so long as that is still obscure to you, our minds have not really met."

Agreeing to disagree, they broke off their discussion at that point but
resumed it in the fall just before *The General Theory* was published.
Keynes informed his younger colleague that "the great majority of the
passages you specially commented upon have been modified, but

whether you will be satisfied by the modifications is another matter." In answer to Robertson's criticism, he pointed out that he had attacked Pigou and Marshall on the basis of their writings on value theory rather than on business fluctuations and that he had prepared a lengthy appendix on the former's *Theory of Employment* to make good the omission.

During the winter and spring of 1934–35 he continued to plug ahead with his proofs and revision, showing finished work to Kahn and telling him, for example, that his appendix on Pigou "will need your very close eye to make sure that I have not anywhere misunderstood or misrepresented him." In June 1935, he sent his old student Roy Harrod galley proofs of almost the whole book, saying that he was "extremely anxious" to know how it struck him. Fortunately, Harrod was impressed with what he read, writing of its "power and convincingness," but sought to restrain Keynes in his criticism of others. He believed, too, that the book was so difficult to comprehend that another work, a manual of elements, would be necessary to explain it!

Throughout the summer, Harrod continued to send him detailed criticisms from different parts of England and Ireland, probing, arguing for his point of view. Keynes answered at equal length, adopting some of his friend's suggestions and rejecting others. At one point he accused Harrod of misunderstanding his theory, only to have the latter write a precis in his own language, including a valuable graph which became part of the final book. Keynes withdrew his charge. The Oxford professor had tried to get Keynes to mitigate his criticism of the classical school, but he replied that he wanted to "raise a dust" or, shifting metaphors (he had many in his mind), he said he expected that a great deal of what he would write would be "water off a duck's back," unless he was sufficiently strong in his criticism to force the classicals to make rejoinders. One suspects, too, that in his resort to polemics, he was tearing a leaf from the tactics of his old ideal, Jevons, who had taught him the importance of being *épatant*. Harrod differed also on the traditional theory of the rate of interest, insisting that it made sense from one perspective, only to have Keynes inform him, "My own firm conviction is that your mind is still half in the classical world, and that you ought to be accusing me, not of bad manners, but of faulty theory." So it went back and forth, Keynes taking Harrod's "hard knocks" and asking for more, redrafting and using whatever he thought was valid criticism.

It was the same with his voluminous correspondence with Ralph G. Hawtrey, the brilliant Treasury hand whom he had known for so long.

The latter was untiring and meticulous in his criticism; Keynes adopted some of his points, cutting out all reference to "quasi-rents" as being confusing, but could not wholly convince him on interest theory and other matters. He finally turned the correspondence over to Joan Robinson for her comments to see whether there were any other concessions he ought to make. She told him that "an archangel would not have taken more trouble to be fair and clear."

In the summer or autumn of 1935, Keynes was still exchanging notes with Joan Robinson and Kahn (now nicknamed "Alexander" by Lydia to distinguish him from Richard Braithwaite, another fellow at King's). He remarked in a letter to Kahn that he was in "the stage of not liking my book very much. It all seems very angry and much ado about a matter much simpler than I make it appear." Both these friends, while critical, were generally approving. Kahn would write, "I find that it all reads most beautifully. It carries with it an air of finality and inevitability which I find most convincing." And Robinson likewise, though suggesting changes, was very much delighted with the volume and thought it "the most readable book of its weight ever" and that "the eloquent passages come in just at the right points to keep one going." These must have been welcome words for Keynes at this time because, perhaps in reaction to his efforts, he was running a slight temperature and was unable to be as busy as usual. But now, at least, he was in the home stretch, and by late December 1935, after numerous interruptions and five years of hard labor, it was finished. He wrote his mother that he felt like a man of leisure.

Unfortunately, the composition of this revolutionary book had its human costs in that it caused some serious personal wounds that took a long time to heal. In singling out Pigou for his polemical attack on the classical position on unemployment, Keynes stirred up a lot of bad feeling. Pigou believed that his views and those of Marshall had been misrepresented, and when *The General Theory* appeared, he wrote a very critical review of it which reflected his resentment. Later, Keynes in a letter to Robertson said that he was distressed by Pigou's article and "even more so that you should think it worthy of him. . . . I had often wondered how he would take my book, but I never hit on the right answer . . . that his predominant emotion would be that of a sixth-form boy who had been cheeked." Thirteen years later, when *The General Theory* had been thoroughly discussed by the economics profession, Pigou nobly recognized the importance of Keynes's fundamental conception, stating that it was "an extremely fruitful germinal idea. In my original review . . . I failed to grasp its significance and did not assign to Keynes the credit due for it. Nobody before him, so far as I know, had brought all the relevant factors, real and monetary at once, into a single formal scheme, through which their interplay could be coherently investigated."

Reconciliation of the differences between Keynes and Robertson was not so readily achieved. The former was evidently deeply hurt by his colleague's criticisms, so much so that he omitted any acknowledgment to him in *The General Theory*'s preface, despite his laborious efforts in reviewing the manuscript. In a letter to Robertson dated September 20, 1936, Keynes tried to heal the rift between them, saying, "We must try to come to closer touch again." But it was no use, perhaps because Robertson was more of right-wing liberal than Keynes, and he felt that the "new economics" wasn't that original, that, in fact, as he used to say, "it's all in Marshall." In 1944, when Pigou retired, the Cambridge electors offered the chair of political economy to Keynes, but he declined the offer and urged Robertson for the post. The latter took the professorship but, according to some accounts, was never too happy in the position, feeling harried by Keynes's followers at the university. In short, the division between Keynes and Robertson over *The General Theory* was deep and was never closed even at the former's death.

The General Theory of Employment Interest and Money, to give it its full title, is a technical, theoretical book addressed to the economics profession, but its main ideas can be summarized and an indication given of how it bears the mark of Keynes's personality. Essentially, it is an analysis of what the economist calls the short period, meaning that the factors of production, the habits and tastes of consumers, the degree of competition, and the underlying economic structure are taken as given; in other words, it is assumed that they are not capable of being changed in the period under consideration. Keynes presents a theory of output as a whole and demonstrates by his static, aggregative analysis that rather than being self-adjusting, the economy may well reach equilibrium at a level short of full employment. In order to do this, he attacks the classical economic postulates or assumptions, contending that the classical theorists were like Euclidean geometers in a non-Euclidean world. On their assumptions, he argues, money makes no real difference in the functioning of the economy, yet their real-exchange analysis is only applicable to the case of full employment. He regards his theory as being a general one because it embraces the analysis of equilibria at less than full employment instead of being limited to this one case. The classical theory, he says, "represents the way in which we should like our economy to behave," not as it functions in reality.

In developing his own theory of effective demand to explain what determines the level of the national income and employment, he focuses on three independent variables of a psychological nature—the propensity to consume, the schedule of the marginal efficiency of capital (in popular terms, the prospects for profit), and the rate of interest. The dependent variables in this theoretical model are the volume of employment and the national income, both measured in terms of wage units. The propensity to consume (in Professor Alvin Hansen's view, Keynes's major conceptual innovation) states that when income increases, consumption rises but not by as much, the difference being saving. Given the existing unequal distribution of income, there is a tendency under the existing system for savings to rise disproportionately as the national income increases. There is, therefore, a distinct possibility that the volume of savings will become greater than the current rate of investment, with the consequence that the national income and employment will fall until savings and investment are equal. In other words, in a capitalistic economy there is a paradox of savings in that, however beneficial it may be for the individual to save, the aggregate of savings, if it outruns the rate of current investment, is not advantageous to society as a whole because it leads to unemployment.

Now in classical theory this adverse outcome is impossible because of the operation of Say's Law of Markets. In accordance with this theoretical perspective, the economy is thought to tend to full employment automatically because the supply and demand for savings is equated by the fluctuations in the interest rate. But Keynes insists, as he did in *A Treatise on Money,* that the latter price is incapable of performing this function effectively. Economic investment, which constitutes the demand for savings, is dependent on the future yield from capital assets and will be undertaken only when interest rates are at a level which makes a profit possible. Rather than fluctuations of the interest rate determining the quantity of savings, he holds that in the short period the causal chain is reversed—the volume of investment generally determines the level of the national income, and the size of the latter affects the volume of savings. In other words, in terms of what has come to be called the income-expenditure theory, national income and employment reach equilibrium at the point where intended investment equals the current rate of saving.

In the course of his analysis, Keynes develops a new theory of liquidity preference in which money is seen as a link between the present and the future. The motives for holding wealth in a liquid form—for business transactions, as a precaution for unforeseen contingencies, and for speculation—are analyzed subtly to show that uncertainty may cause interest rates to rise to prohibitive levels, thus choking off the inducement to invest. The difficulties in maintaining effective demand at a level high enough to provide full employment, considering the possible association of stable long-term interest rates with a highly unstable marginal efficiency of capital, are stressed. The high liquidity premiums demanded for money seem to Keynes the cause of the world's poverty in capital assets, despite several millennia of steady individual saving.

On the basis of this diagnosis of capitalism's functioning, Keynes is led to advocate a measure of government intervention to achieve greater economic stability and full employment. He says that he expects the state, which can take the long view of marginal efficiency and the general social advantage, to take ever greater responsibility for directly organizing or managing the level of investment; "ordering the current volume of investment cannot safely be left in private hands." Repudiating his views in the *Treatise,* he says that "the right remedy for the trade cycle is not to be found in abolishing booms and thus keeping us permanently in a semislump, but in abolishing slumps and thus keeping us permanently in a quasi-boom." A policy of high interest rates in a boom, he asserts, is a remedy which cures the disease by killing the patient. Such an approach, which assumes that full employment is an unpractical ideal, is unnecessarily defeatist.

In the last section of his book he presents some "short notes suggested by The General Theory in which the style is livelier and more contentious than in the early part. Some of the old arrogance is evident in his characterizing some views as "nonsense" (he changed it to "erroneous"), and there are more metaphorical expressions. In this part, mercantilism, usury laws, stamped money, and other theories of underconsumption, à la Hobson, are defended as being practical measures to overcome high interest rates and stimulate investment and employment. In the last chapter he asserts that the outstanding faults of the existing capitalistic society are its failure to provide for full employment and its arbitrary and inequitable distribution of income. Banking policy alone will be insufficient to determine the optimum rate of investment; "a somewhat comprehensive socialization of investment will prove the only means of securing an approximation to full employment, though this need not exclude all manner of compromises and of devices by which public authority will cooperate with private initiative." State socialism is not called for; the state need not assume the ownership of the instruments of production, so long as it can determine the aggregate amount of resources devoted to their augmentation.

In this division of the book there are many evidences of Keynes the man as we have come to know him: his willingness to admit error in the *Treatise* regarding the natural rate of interest, his constant approval of intuition, his endorsement of the moral quality of Silvio Gesell; and his optimistic faith in reason and ideas. In perhaps his most quoted passage, he concludes that "the ideas of economists and political philosophers, both when they are right and when they are wrong, are more powerful than is commonly understood. Indeed, the world is ruled by little else. Practical men, who believe themselves to be quite exempt from any intellectual influences, are usually the slaves of some defunct economist." Ideas, he added significantly, are not immediately influential because in the area of economics and political philosophy "there are not many who are influenced by new theories after they are twenty-five or thirty years of age," but "soon or late, it is ideas, not vested interests, which are dangerous for good or evil."

When Keynes achieved his scientific breakthrough by developing the theory of effective demand in *The General Theory*, it was generally thought that he was the pioneer, the originator of this revolutionary point of view. It is now recognized that his theoretical innovation was an instance of multiple discovery in science because two other economists were independently arriving at similar insights and conceptualizations. In fact, one of them, Michael Kalecki, an unknown Polish economist, definitely seems to have anticipated Keynes in developing a general theory of output as a whole. In 1933–35, he published three papers in Polish which contain the essential ideas of *The General Theory*. His Polish readers, however, were too uninformed or too orthodox to recognize their originality. He presented his theory to a more sophisticated audience of the International Econometric Association in October 1933 and in articles in *Econometrica* and the *Revue d'Economique Politique* in 1935. But his exposition of his ideas in these media "did not even ripple the placid waters of existing theory. In a word, Kalecki lacked status, authority, and influence." He and his wife went to Stockholm on a Rockefeller Foundation Fellowship the next year, and there he read *The General Theory* upon its publication. He said that it was "an eerie feeling, reading his own thoughts almost word for word expressed by someone else. Even the jokes were the same. As Professor Joan Robinson later attested, the fact that two men, miles apart in space, political outlook, and social circumstances, had come to the same conclusions "was a great comfort."

Kalecki had come to his formulations from a Marxian background, the work of Rosa Luxemburg being especially influential in shaping his views. His system, as a matter of fact, is superior in several respects to Keynes's: It is more dynamic, treats an open economy, and integrates the theory of imperfect competition and oligopoly into its analysis rather than depending on the untenable assumption of perfect competition. Keynes ignored what Professor Shackle has called "the Sraffian Manifesto of 1926, demanding the revision of value theory." He encouraged Joan Robinson to publish her book on imperfect competition, but took little interest in the subject; I was surprised to find that he did not even have a copy of her work in his library.

The other anticipator of *The General Theory* was Professor Gunnar Myrdal, the well-known Swedish economist. In his *Monetary Equilibrium,* published in Swedish in 1931, he formulated an explanation of the variations in output as remarkable as Keynes's. "In all but its assignments of emphasis, *Monetary Equilibrium* anticipated Keynes's *General Theory,*" writes Professor Shackle, "though not conveying Keynes's sense of revolutionary achievement and sense of power." In this connection it is significant that Kalecki agrees that the Keynesian Revolution in Western economics was rightly so called. "For without Keynes's wide sweep, his brilliant polemic, and above all his position within the orthodox citadel, in which he was brought up, the walls of obscurantism would have taken much longer to breach."

During World War II, Kalecki wrote a perceptive article in which he predicted that now that the causes of the commercial trade cycle were known, we should have a political cycle instead. In the boom phase of the cycle, with prices rising and trade unions in a strong position, business and rentier interests would call for "sound finance." But when that type of policy caused unemployment to grow and the next election approached, there would be a return to the vote-catching policy of full employment. And so "the regime of the political business cycle" would go its weary way—a far cry from Keynes's vision of a society of abundance and leisure.

Kalecki died in Poland in 1970, a broken and despondent man, disillusioned with both socialism and capitalism, and emotionally shaken by the Polish repression two years earlier which had been directed at "revisionists" and "Zionists," the latter a thin veil for Jews.

In 1946, when Keynes's book was just ten years old, Paul Samuelson wrote an essay about it in which he contended that nothing in the author's previous life or work quite prepares us for *The General Theory*; the latter, he claimed, was a mutant and comes as a surprise, notwithstanding Keynes's own expressed belief that it represented "a natural evolution" in his own line of thought. Samuelson's view that *The General Theory* has no continuity with Keynes's previous life seems very questionable because certain familiar traits of his personality manifested themselves in its composition. Among them are his supreme self-confidence, as illustrated in his letter to Shaw; his capacity for aggressive polemics; his use of both logic and intuition, a reflection of his double nature; and his receptivity to criticism and ability to change his mind. All these characteristics had a part in the making of this classic.

Keynes knew that he had to attack the views of others with vehemence, with passion or feeling, and that it was unlikely that he would escape reprisal, but he was convinced that he was right and that the times demanded a fresh approach; he was prepared to accept the consequences.

Prominent also in the composition of *The General Theory* was Keynes's employment of both intuition and logic. In his biography of Keynes, Harrod stressed that it was Keynes's "highly developed logical capacity that enabled him to construct a new classification" or model of economic reality. On the contrary, it was Keynes's imagination, not his logical ability, that enabled him to conceive or conceptualize the key variables of his system, as he stated. "To me, the most extraordinary thing regarded historically is the complete disappearance of the theory of the demand and supply for output as a whole, i.e., the theory of employment, after it had been for a quarter of a century the most discussed thing in economics. One of the most important transitions for me, after my *Treatise on Money* had been published, was suddenly realizing this. It came only after I had enunciated to myself the psychological law that when income increases, the gap between income and consumption will increase—a conclusion of vast importance in my own thinking but not apparently, expressed just like this, to anyone else's. Then appreciably later came the notion of interest as being the meaning of liquidity preference, which became quite clear to my mind the moment I thought of it. And last fall, after an immense amount of muddling and many drafts, the proper definition of the marginal efficiency of capital linked up one thing with another."

Keynes's manner of expression may make his accomplishment in writing *The General Theory* seem easy, but, as has been seen, it was only done with considerable strain. As Shackle states, "To start again at the age of nearly fifty and rewrite one's *magnum opus* in a new, more complex, refined, exact, and powerful form was heroic and exhausting. It was, indeed, literally nearly fatal."

Another aspect of Keynes's double nature, namely his receptivity to criticism and others' ideas, is also clearly manifested in the creation of *The General Theory*. This capacity to be passive as well as active as being essential to genius was emphasized by Coleridge in his *Biographia Literaria*. Keynes certainly possessed this ability, as shown by his reliance on the criticism of the Circus, of Kahn, Robinson, and the others. At times it seems that the breakthrough to *The General Theory* was so much a collective effort that it is difficult to assign credit for the accomplishment; Samuelson in a symposium on the subject has even asked the question whether Keynes was "God's midwife for Richard Kahn." However, those who were "present at the creation" are inclined rather to regard the latter as "the perfect foil" for Keynes, but not capable himself of the creative imagination, let alone the persuasiveness, to write such a revolutionary work. One who was very close to the creative process in Cambridge at the time has written, "What seems to me clear is that a group made up of individuals with very different gifts of critical faculties, of energy and persistence, of intuitive perception, is immensely stronger than any one individual in it."

An economist who had a front seat at the creative process when *The General Theory* was being written emphasizes the role of the abnormal in it. Austin Robinson has said that "the Cambridge of 1930–31 ... must seem a madhouse, with the extraordinary personalities of Keynes himself, of Pigou, of Robertson, of Sraffa, and others whom I need not list. But to my mind what is fascinating is how much economics has owed to people who in some sense were very unusual, very abnormal. ... It does not at all surprise me that the really creative work in economics has come from such people." In the remarks from which this quotation is drawn, Robinson did not describe Keynes's extraordinary personality, but one recalls his previous allusion to the androgynous nature of the man, though he did not term it such—"the almost feminine perception of the essential and inevitable pattern of things" and "the curious conjunction of contrasting qualities which made Maynard Keynes so essentially unlike the common run of mankind." This element of the abnormal, on the basis of the testimony of a man who was very close to Keynes for many years, was another essential factor in the creation of *The General Theory*.

The General Theory was the product of Keynes's close involvement in the economic problems of the Western world in the twenties and the thirties. As has been seen, his interest was primarily in economic policy rather than pure theory, especially the problem of unemployment. To understand his work from a methodological standpoint, one must comprehend how he used his historical imagination to construct a "realitic" theory; in contrast to analytic or pure theory, realitic theory seeks a synthetic description of regularities for a particular time and place. While it endeavors to be consistent with analytic theory, it is willing to give up logical rigor or elegance for relevance and practical applicability. Alfred Marshall in his economics sought to combine a static analytical form with a dynamic realitic approach. Many post-Marshallians complained of the obscurities in his thought, but as the obscurities were removed, "the realitic flavor which formed the basis of the Marshallian method was lost." With his firm grounding in the master's method and his own intuitive ability, Keynes in *The General Theory* developed a useful realitic theory which was very relevant to the pressing problem of unemployment. Instead of modifying one assumption at a time, he held several strategic factors constant so that he could focus on the relation of fluctuations in investment to changes in income and employment, thus sacrificing analytical elegance to usefulness. His theory was designed only for an economy in a particular time and place—in that sense it had a historical dimension. It was relevant mainly to capitalistic economies with stable (or declining) prices, high unemployment, and a particular set of financial markets. "When necessary, he [Keynes] included intuitive judgments about the beliefs of actors in the economic system, casual observation of institutional facts, and incorporated these into immediately useful policy prescriptions."

Schumpeter later accused him of committing the "Ricardian vice," which consisted of basing theory on temporary historical conditions; it is true that in making investment dependent on expectations as perceived in historical time, he was in fact departing from the restrictive and unrealistic concept of long-run equilibrium. In Ricardian economics, as Professor Joan Robinson insists, the stationary state was not an equilibrium but "an awful warning" that if Britain did not abolish the Corn Laws and thus reduce the real cost of wages, it would sooner or later bring capital accumulation to an end. Keynes likewise was in effect arguing that unless total investment was maintained at a high level, the resulting unemployment would result in the ultimate destruction of free enterprise and democracy.

Basing his analysis upon his intimate knowledge of Marshallian economics and the functioning of the financial institutions of the City, he formulated a realitic solution to the macroeconomic problem of unemployment without the aid of an independent theory of microeconomics. "He wove together static value theory and a dynamic investment theory into a whole, through the dynamic feedback included in the multiplier, and captured some of the essential dynamic disequilibrium properties of the system." Thus, as is often the case with genius, his creativity in this instance consisted of a recombination of elements rather than a wholly new discovery.

The coincidence in scientific discovery of the basic idea of *The General Theory* has been discussed above, but there was another coincidence in Cambridge at this time, in this case between innovation in economics and in the world of art. In January 1936, Keynes had written his mother, "My book is out of my hands and will be published on February 4. The theatre will open February 3." He was referring to the Arts Theatre of Cambridge which had been his invention and experiment in the very years that he was working on *The General Theory*. Some aspects of his interest in the arts have been touched upon already, but it is worthwhile to examine how his interest and devotion to art originated and developed, considering the enormous amount of time he had to give to his other activities. George Rylands, who was his associate in many artistic ventures, offered three clues to this "mystery": First, he pointed out that Keynes was a Wordsworthian and a follower of Ruskin, Pater, and Arnold.

He shared Arnold's approval of Schiller's dictum that all art is dedicated to joy; he believed in sweetness and light, in spreading the best that has been thought and written in the world, as he believed that money was for spending. He believed in that now-tarnished watchword 'culture.' Second, there was his friendship for artists, Duncan in his younger years, Roger Fry, Vanessa Bell, and now Lydia, who through the ballet brought him closer to the world of drama and the related arts of music and stage design. Third, Keynes would have liked to be a creative artist. It seemed he could do everything to which he turned his trained intelligence; but here was a mystery; here was something— the highest of all things—a world which contained only a few inhabitants, the men of creative genius. As a writer he could open the door into that world.

Today, two tangible memorials of Keynes's interest in the arts remain, his picture collection and the Cambridge Theatre; the history of the latter deserves some consideration. In 1933, when the Camargo Society's affairs were on the decline, Lydia, George Rylands, and he began discussing a theatre project for Cambridge, and the following summer they drew into their discussions Norman Higgins who had opened a cinema in the city the year before. At that time, Cambridge had many cinemas but not a single legitimate theatre. Keynes proposed to Higgins that he close his theatre and accept the post of general manager of this new enterprise. Then, acting as bursar of King's

College, he assembled a site in the very center of the city, hired architects and a local builder, and registered the Arts Theatre as a private company. He also provided most of the share capital, and when the building costs exceeded the original estimate, he made an interest-free loan to the company as well.

As the project proceeded, his interest in the construction work was "all-embracing," no detail being too small to receive his personal attention. He insisted that the dressing rooms in the theatre be as comfortable as the facilities provided up front for the patrons; he went on a shopping tour with Lydia to choose French linen for the restaurant. The latter was another of his ideas, for he thought that a civilized theatregoer should be able to dine within the building. This restaurant, too, would offer opportunity to provide education in the Art of Living and to persuade undergraduates to drink wine instead of spirits. Later, when he noticed that not enough champagne was drunk by the patrons, he proposed that only a small amount be added to the cost of this item rather than the usual markup of fifty percent. A year passed during which he discovered that while more champagne had been purchased at a profit, the total profit on white wine sales had declined, so he discreetly discontinued his little experiment in price discrimination.

After long delays, the Art Theatre opened early in 1936 with a gala performance by the Vic-Wells Ballet, followed the next evening by a film program. Keynes had written of the theatre's purpose in the program: "The object of the Arts Theatre of Cambridge is the entertainment of the university and town. Its name describes, and the form of the pentagon given its auditorium by the architect symbolizes, its purpose of providing a home in Cambridge for the five arts of drama, opera, ballet, music, and cinema. No permanent company will be maintained, but the theatre and its organization will provide opportunities for at least four classes of production."

Actually, the public response during the early years of the venture was quite spasmodic. The ballet, Sadler's Wells Opera, and a few West End productions drew capacity audiences; the other stage productions and films utilized only part of the theatre's seats. However, during the years of World War II the military and government workers who had been evacuated from London flocked to its performances, and Cambridge enjoyed theatrical fare never before possible. The theatre's success was assured.

Once it was in operation, Keynes's interest in every aspect of its functioning was insatiable; he was fascinated by the statistics of bar profits, program money, matinee ices, and even cups of coffee. The first stage presentation after the gala opening were four Ibsen plays—*A Doll's House, Hedda Gabler, Rosmerholm,* and *The Master Builder*—in two of which Lydia had leading roles. Keynes wrote a very interesting introduction for these plays, almost a philosophical disquisition, in which his old fascination with the work of the Norwegian dramatist is evident. He saw these four plays as a commentary on "the profoundest social phenomenon of the period, the emergence of the modern woman." He discussed Ibsen's symbols in the plays and said that they suggest "the supernatural and magic of the north, the Vikings and trolls and little 'helpers and servers' who run among the roots of the trees which are part of the imagination of all of us in our childhood through the folklore and fairy tales of Northern Europe." Here again one sees the hold which these fairy tales of his childhood had on him and how vivid they still were in his mind.

Another evidence of his growing interest in the promotion and provision of the arts for the public was the important broadcast that he gave for the BBC in the summer of 1936 on the relationship between art and the state. In this talk he pointed out that the ancient world of Greece and Rome had recognized that the people needed circuses as well as bread. In later times, after the fall of Rome, the church and the state sponsored and financially supported the creation of works of art and the erection of magnificent buildings. In the eighteenth and early nineteenth centuries, the rich nobility continued to perform this function in a private and attenuated manner. But in the eighteenth century and reaching a climax in the next century, a new view of the functions of the state developed which still prevails, he said, and governs us today. "This view was the utilitarian and economic—one might almost say financial—ideal, as the sole, respectable purpose of the community as a whole; the most dreadful heresy, perhaps, which has ever gained the ear of a civilized people. Bread and nothing but bread, and not even bread, and bread accumulating at compound interest until it has turned into a stone." While poets and artists have protested occasionally against this heresy, only Victoria's Prince Albert was the last protester among the high placed. The Treasury's tightfisted view has prevailed in theory and practice. "We have persuaded ourselves that it is positively wicked for the state to spend a half-penny on noneconomic purposes." Even education and the public health only creep in under an economic alias on the ground that they "pay. . . . One form alone of uncalculated expenditure survives from the heroic age—war. And even that must sometimes pretend to be economic."

Claiming that the United Kingdom was "hag-ridden by a perverted theory of the state," Keynes went on to deplore the neglect of the natural environment, the neglect of irreplaceable national monuments, and the failure to provide those public ceremonies, shows, and entertainments which give the common man some sense of community. "The exploitation and incidental destruction of the divine gift of the public entertainer by prostituting it to the purposes of financial gain," he further declared, "is one of the worser crimes of present-day capitalism." Yet, how the state could best play its part, he admitted, was hard to say. It would probably be necessary to learn by trial and error. But anything would be better than the present system. Citing the BBC as one of the nation's greatest and most successful forms of public entertainment, though even it had to be "furtive" in its progress, he said that it was only the extreme example of the general principle that the Treasury was penalizing music, opera, and all arts of the theatre with crushing taxes.

Arguing that the authoritarian states of Russia, Germany, and Italy were using public entertainment in a manner that was a source of strength to them, he felt that the lack of it was a source of weakness to the democratic societies because it could prove "in some measure an alternative means of satisfying the human craving for solidarity." He concluded with a recommendation that a commission of public places be established to prevent environmental destruction and to preserve precious national monuments and, secondly, that some plans should be made ready to ward off the next slump for the rebuilding of the nation's principal cities. As illustration, he urged that the majority of the existing buildings in London, on the south bank of the Thames from County Hall to Greenwich, be demolished and replaced by "the most magnificent, the most commodious and healthy working-class quarter in the world." "Why should not all London be the equal of Saint James Park and its surroundings?" he asked and forcefully affirmed that there could be no legitimate financial obstacles to such achievements, provided that the labor and material resources were available. That his emotional involvement in the idea of the need for a new relationship of art to the state was profound and passionate was to be amply demonstrated by his work in this field in the postwar years.

Now, in the mid-thirties, he was too busy for wider, more imaginative ventures along those lines because, as he liked to say, Time's winged chariot was moving inexorably on. In August 1937, he fell gravely ill with a cardiac infarction and had to be moved to Ruthin Castle in Wales for specialist treatment. Even while he was there, he and his associates in the Cambridge Theatre completed plans to transfer its ownership to a charitable trust. Under this plan he deeded all his own ordinary shares to that body and agreed to purchase for the trustees an additional £5,000 of unallotted preference shares. In his letters to the mayor of Cambridge and the vice-chancellor of the university, he explained that he regarded his gift "as in some sense a memorial to my parents who have served the university and the town for upwards of half a century." Thus, he assured that others after him would enjoy the beauty, inspiration, and imaginative pleasure that he had experienced for so long in the theatre.

CHAPTER 13

Economic Innovation in
Peace and War

Geniuses *are* very peculiar.
J. M. Keynes

I N THE SPRING of 1936, after the publication of *The General Theory,*
Keynes was occupied, aside from his usual routine as bursar and editor
of the *Economic Journal,* with reviews and expositions of his new book.
At first he felt inclined to turn his mind in other directions, but by early
March he was corresponding with the persistent Hawtrey, the Treasury economist, answering his long letter which had predated the
publication of the book. He was receiving support from his economist
friends, such as G. F. Shove, and discussing moot points with some of
his former pupils. After a drawn-out exchange with Hawtrey, he finally
told him that he was "convinced that nothing I can say will open your
eyes—I do not say to the truth of my argument, but to what the essence
of my argument, true or false, actually is. I doubt if we ought, either of
us, to continue this correspondence any longer." Frustrated, he turned
again to Joan Robinson for advice on how to deal with the Treasury
man. Later, he told Hawtrey that he was thinking of producing what
might be called footnotes to *The General Theory,* dealing with criticism
and obscure points of which, he admitted, there were several. "Of
course, in fact, the whole book needs rewriting and recasting. But I am
still not in a sufficiently changed state of mind as yet to be in a position to
do that."

The impact of *The General Theory* on the economics profession was substantial, to say the least, but it took a while for many to digest it all. While the majority view was favorable, there were others who took a very dim view of it. As an example of the latter, consider the following: "However much we may admire Mr. Keynes's crusading zeal, his latest work is likely to remain for the academician but an interesting exhibit in the museum of depression curiosities. To the inflationist, who will be able to bolster his specious arguments by appeal to authority, it will serve as *vade mecum*."

Even as Professor Alvin Hansen, who was to become a leading American Keynesian in the future, at first took a very critical view of it. All in all, in the ten years after the book's publication there were no fewer than three hundred articles in major professional journals commenting on or expounding it, without taking account of books and monographs. In this early postpublication period, Keynes was engaged in discussing some of these early expositions of his work. Sir William Beveridge had criticized the volume, and Professor John R. Hicks had written two well-known articles, "Mr. Keynes's Theory of Employment" and "Mr. Keynes and the Classics." Professor Harrod wrote a sympathetic sketch of it, which led Keynes to remark concerning the critical reactions that "experience seems to show that people are divided between the old ones whom nothing will shift . . . and the young ones who have not been properly brought up and believe nothing in particular."

In retrospect, Keynes's remark about the young economists seems to have been unduly cynical, especially so far as the American ones were concerned. In fact, his ideas had an unusual impact on them, as has been recounted in years past by Professors Galbraith, Herbert Stein, and Robert Lekachman. Paul Samuelson later described most vividly the reaction to *The General Theory* of some of his contemporaries among graduate students in 1936. "Bliss was it in that dawn to be alive, but to be young was very heaven!" Samuelson at the time did not share that rapture, but others did. Professor Kenneth Boulding has recalled his enthusiasm to an earlier Keynesian work: "I shall never forget the excitement, as an undergraduate, of reading Keynes's *Treatise on Money* in 1931. It is a clumsy, hastily written book, and much of its theoretical apparatus has now been discarded. But to its youthful readers it was a peak in Darien, opening up vistas of uncharted seas— Great [*sic*] was it in that dawn to be alive, and [*sic*] to be young was very heaven."

While one wonders how many economists were so poetical, it is indisputable, as Erik Erikson has shown us, that the young have a deep need for an ideology to bolster their shaky identities, and these young economists were presumably no different. In a time of profound collective economic crisis, Keynes's ideas and vision had a deep resonance in their minds, and his nonconformist life and personality probably had somewhat of a charismatic appeal to them. His book, while proclaiming its revolutionary character, embodied a middle-of-the-road ideology that met a need in their personalities. Rejecting the pessimistic hypothesis of scarcity, it based itself upon the optimistic vision of abundance—that through full employment, achieved through the instruments of a mixed economy, the paradox of poverty in the midst of potential plenty could be overcome. While leaving open a flexible view of the future, it seemed to constitute a step toward "a higher stage of rationalization of economic life," a move toward conscious planned achievement of high-level consumption which was consistent with the contemporary requirements of mass production and the growth of mass democracy. Schumpeter criticized Keynes for reverting to the Ricardian vice of "offering, in the garb of general scientific truth, advice which carries meaning only with reference to the practical exigencies of the unique historical situation of a given time and country." But Keynes's vision of abundance through full employment was not only based on a shrewd, imaginative appraisal of the historical situation, it was compatible with a powerful set of economic interests. It was to give new life to the old ideology of progress and national economic growth.

In the United States, as Professor John Kenneth Galbraith has demonstrated, Harvard was the principal academic institution through which the Keynesian ideas passed to the underlying population. Professors Alvin Hansen and Seymour Harris of that university were indefatigable disciples of the master in disseminating his ideas, while others, such as Robert B. Bryce were doing the same, for example, in Canada. The first manifesto of the young Keynesian school, *An Economic Program for American Democracy,* appeared in October 1938, and shortly thereafter the Temporary National Economic Committee, which was holding hearings on economic concentration, gave further publicity to the new ideas. In December of that year, Professor Hansen in his presidential address to the American Economic Association emphasized the thesis that the United States was probably suffering from "secular stagnation" or economic maturity and that consequently there might be a need for permanent deficit spending.

It is evident from this and other contemporary developments that there were probably different degrees of Keynesianism in the United States at that time. Some were mere "fundamental-theoretical Keynesians"; others were cyclical Keynesians; and still another group went all the way with the stagnationist theory. In general, there was a "widespread conversion to Keynesianism in these years after the publication of *The General Theory* and a good deal of controversy and criticism from the more conservative business community. Many businessmen and others had been very critical of the Roosevelt administration's spending earlier and in the 1936 campaign, so much so that, as one economist aptly expresses it, Keynes and the New Deal were practically "synonomous profanities" to some people. Though it is pretty well established that FDR was a "reluctant Keynesian," by 1940 Keynes's ideas "had very largely swept the field of the younger economists," many of whom were later to be high in decision-making councils in Washington.

In the spring of 1936, Keynes spent more time than usual at Tilton; his house was being rebuilt to provide more rooms and he had acquired additional acreage, but as yet he didn't know what he would do with it. In the meanwhile, the foreign situation was taking on a more ominous nature, but he was inclined to be optimistic about the objectives of the fascist nations. He thought that the "brigand powers" were not likely to attack Britain's immediate interests directly, but he did see a threat to other minor peoples in various parts of the world.

In the summer he prepared a lecture which he later gave in Stockholm entitled "Further Reflections on Liquidity Preference," in which he sought to differentiate his theory from the orthodox one. He and Lydia went on a visit to Sweden and Russia in the early autumn. Though they were traveling eight nights out of the twelve that they were away, they had a very restful holiday. Keynes liked slow transportation and thought that there should be special trains on which one would pay a special fare for their going slowly. While on this trip he was able to read proof on some of the new books being published by his younger followers, such as Joan Robinson's *Essays in the Theory of Employment* and her *Introduction to the Theory of Employment,* which she referred to as her "told-to-the-children book."

Before leaving on this holiday, Keynes had given an important speech on the BBC on "Art and the State," a subject which was of growing interest to him. Then in July and August in the *New Statesman and Nation* he took a strong stand in favor of rearmament and against those who thought that Great Britain was so pro-fascist at heart that it couldn't be trusted with arms; he even offered a defense of the Baldwin government.

In the fall, four articles by Professors Wassily Leontief, Dennis

Robertson, Frank W. Taussig, and Jacob Viner appeared which contained some important criticism of *The General Theory,* much of which Keynes said that he accepted and from which he hoped to benefit. These conciliatory remarks were made in a piece which he wrote by way of reply and in which he took the opportunity of reexpressing some of his basic ideas. In this essay, which Professor Shackle has hailed as "the apotheosis of his thought," he spelled out the philosophical implications of his new theory. He stated modestly enough that he was more attached to the simple fundamental ideas which underlie the theory than to the particular forms in which he embodied them. "If the simple basic ideas can become familiar and acceptable, time and experience and the collaboration of a number of minds will discover the best way of expressing them." In other words, he was seeking in this essay to express the ultimate ground for the existence of involuntary unemployment in a capitalistic society.

In its essential character, Keynes's theory of unemployment is related to those philosophical challenges to rationalism which were mentioned at the beginning of chapter six. He believed that the nineteenth century in its complacency had used the rationalism of the Benthamite school to "reduce the future to the same calculable status as the present" and that even contemporary thought was still influenced by "some such pseudo-rationalistic notions." In this manner an untenable conception of man's rational behavior had been incorporated in classical economic theory. Deriving from the Age of Reason and Newtonian celestial mechanics, equilibrium economics evolved from the Smithian "obvious and simple system of natural liberty" into a system of thought which assumed rationality of behavior and perfect knowledge and foresight in its theoretical analysis. But he insisted that in the real world our knowledge of the future is "fluctuating, vague, and uncertain; the occurrence of certain events are so unknowable in advance that we cannot even form any calculable probability of their happening. "We simply do not know." Yet action and the necessity for action forces man to assume either that the present is a serviceable guide to the future, that the future is already discounted in current prices, or to fall back in a conformist way upon conventional judgment. The decisions of the boardroom that are based upon such flimsy foundations are always subject to vague panic fears or equally unreasoned hopes. Writing somewhat like Thorstein Veblen, Keynes says the classical economic theory is "one of these pretty, polite techniques which tries to deal with the present by abstracting from the fact that we know very little about the future." In effect, it ignores those ways in which we conceal from our conscious selves our ignorance of the future. In the actual economic world, he went on to state, "our desire to hold money as a store of wealth is a barometer of the degree of our distrust of our own calculations and conventions concerning the future. ... The possession of actual money lulls our disquietude; and the premium which we require to make us part with money is the measure of our disquietude." In the face of this inescapable uncertainty, investment is of necessity an irrational activity, or at least a nonrational one. Enterprise, which depends on hopes stretching into an unknown future, depends as much on "animal spirits" as it does on mathematical expectation, as he put it in *The General Theory*. The existentialist perspective of Keynes's thought in this essay is summed up well by Professor Shackle when he says, "The possibility of massive general unemployment thus springs from the bearing of a human institution, that of money, upon the ultimate nature of human existence, the human being's endless journey into the void of time." Keynes restated his other basic concepts in this article, but this is its major message, the ineluctable facts of uncertainty and ignorance in economic life and the consequent central role of money and of expectations and conventional judgments in economic behavior.

During this year, when he could get away from his desk, Keynes spent many hours at the auction rooms at Sotheby's. Lord Lymington was disposing of the papers of Sir Isaac Newton, and finding that they were being sold "extraordinarily reasonable," he bought almost everything which he thought ought to remain in Cambridge. In the summer he must have been perusing these new acquisitions with great interest; he wrote his mother, "Newton absorbs more time than he should, but that is a hobby."

While he was pursuing his scholarly avocation, Lydia was giving another notable performance as Celimene in Molière's *The Misanthrope* at the Ambassador Theatre in London. Raymond Mortimer in his review noted that "Mme Lopokova's voice has improved enormously, both in power and variety, but the particular power of her acting must always be in the flash of her eyes, the poise of her elbows, the carriage of her head. Her whole body talks, and how happy we are to listen."

Early in 1937, Keynes broke into print again with three articles in *The Times* under the title, "How to Avoid a Slump." These have since become a subject of controversy because, though Britain had not attained full employment at the time, he stated in one of them that the country was "more in need today of a rightly distributed demand than of a greater aggregate demand" and that the local authorities should retard or hold back investment. Professor Terence W. Hutchison has argued that this shows he was concerned with the possible dangers of inflation when unemployment was still around eleven to twelve percent, but this interpretation has been strongly disputed. In his articles, Keynes advocated the establishment of a public investment board to prepare schemes of public outlay for when they should be needed. In the following years the rearmament program, which he was anxious to see accelerated, began to mop up unemployment.

In February, he delivered the Galton Lecture before the Eugenics Society, returning to another of his old interests and talking on the subject, "Some Economic Consequences of a Declining Population." He was concerned in this talk with the possible effect on investment of a stationary or declining level of population, an important question because on the basis of his calculations a little less than half of the demand for new capital in the nineteenth century was attributable to the demands of a growing population, the other half to technological innovations. If population stability or decline was in the offing and prosperity and civil peace were to be maintained, he held that it would be necessary to increase consumption by achieving a more equal distribution of income and by establishing low interest rates to stimulate investment. This article undoubtedly influenced Professor Hansen and others who shortly after became concerned about the prospect of secular stagnation.

Keynes was unusually busy in the spring of 1937, lecturing on Harrod's new book, *The Trade Cycle,* on the *ex ante* and *ex post* approaches to interest theory, and corresponding at length with Bertil Ohlin on the Stockholm theory of savings and investment. Early in March, not feeling well, he went off with Lydia to Cannes for eight days. He felt better after that stay but still complained of breathlessness and chest discomfort after walking. Upon his return he consulted Sir Walter Langdon-Brown, his uncle, who was a chest specialist, but before the diagnosis was complete he suffered a thrombosis of a coronary artery while he was in Cambridge. The doctor, in a letter to his mother, later explained that his condition was that of pseudo-angina. "The treatment is that of the underlying neurosis, and the prognosis is a good one, sudden death not occurring." Still later he wrote that Keynes must not drive himself in the way that he has been accustomed to. "Keep the brakes on him as much as you can, for we must realize that he has had a narrow squeak." This is the first and only reference that one finds in the Keynes papers to a neurotic condition.

In June he was moved to Ruthin Castle in Wales to convalesce under the care of a Dr. Janos Plesch, a Mayfair heart specialist, who was formerly the most eminent man in his field in Germany. Keynes was his patient for practically the rest of his life, and the two grew quite fond of each other. Joking about "the ogre," Keynes would say that his doctor was something between a genius and a quack, but recommend him to his friends, and Plesch got to like Maynard so well that he would write, "I look forward to seeing you to my great pleasure from more than one point of view."

While convalescing in Wales, Keynes managed to arrange with W. H. Auden and Christopher Isherwood for the production of their play, *On the Frontier,* in which Lydia later played a part. Her role in life was now drastically changed—whereas formerly she was ever his cheerful companion, now she had to supervise his life closely as to diet and rest so that he would not be overtaxed. She did it all without complaint, and gradually he was nursed back to better health, but he was never after without the threat of another heart attack.

With her loving help and with assistance from Richard Kahn, Keynes resumed his writing and correspondence, publishing an article on "Alternative Theories of Interest" in June and engaging in further controversy with Robertson and Pigou in the *Economic Journal.* The former questioned Keynes's definition of liquidity preference and sharply stated, "Of course, J. M. K., like Humpty Dumpty, can use words to mean what he chooses them to mean." Pigou had written an article on "Money Wage Rates in Relation to Unemployment" for the *Economic Journal,* but Keynes in his capacity as editor thought the piece was so muddled that he should have a chance to reconsider. At the time Pigou was also suffering from a heart condition, though not as serious as Keynes's. He was also nursing a young man who, while on a climbing holiday at his cottage in the Lake district, had a near fatal fall from a cliff. Taking account of his colleague's troubles, Keynes was seeking to protect him from publishing what he regarded as "outrageous rubbish." In the fall Pigou wrote him, "You're a marvel. How the devil do you continue to be so intelligent when you're unfit?" Kahn had sent Keynes a copy of Pigou's latest book, *Socialism versus Capitalism,* and Keynes was led to comment, "As in the case of Dennis Robertson when it comes to practice, there is really extremely little between us. Why do they insist on maintaining theories from which their own practical conclusions cannot possibly follow? It is a sort of Society for the Preservation of Ancient Monuments."

In the latter part of the year Keynes was asked to review a League of Nations publication, J. Tinbergen's *A Method and Its Application to*

Investment Activity, as well as a volume of the latter on business cycles in the United States. He was rather loath to undertake this particular task because, as he said, he had the utmost difficulty "making heads or tails" of the books. In fact, he felt almost persecuted by the request because he disagreed strongly with the underlying econometric logic, writing to Kahn that he thought it was "all hocus." Nevertheless, he wrote a lengthy critique of the method for the *Economic Journal,* even though he was not persuaded that "this brand of statistical alchemy is ripe to become a branch of science." Experts in econometrics, such as Professor Samuelson, believe that "Keynes did not really have the necessary technical knowledge to understand what he was criticizing," but there was a basic methodological difference between the two. In any case, perhaps out of considerations of honor, he was elected president of the Econometrics Association for two years (1944 and 1945).

Another offshoot or development which stemmed from *The General Theory* was economic growth theory. In August 1938, Roy Harrod submitted to the *Economic Journal* the draft of "An Essay in Dynamic Theory" which was to be the forerunner of the Harrod-Domar type of growth economics which became so important in the postwar years. Keynes did not fundamentally agree with Harrod's piece, but he told him that it was "exceptionally interesting" and thought that he was "on a fruitful line of analysis." He had a long exchange with the Oxford economist, trying to clear up obscure points and improve the exposition. Typically, in one letter he told him that he had "seen in a flash what it was all about. My intuition told me that your conclusion could be true *in general,* but only subject to specified conditions." The basic assumption, which he stated he was allowing Harrod to get away with, was the existence of a warranted rate! He urged him to express his analysis in a way that would permit his readers' intuition to work on the right lines, and then they would see what it was all about. In closing he said, "I have found it rather comforting in these days to muddle one's head with this sort of stuff." Given his own more psychological and historical approach, with its emphasis on uncertainty and ignorance, it is no wonder that he differed with the more mechanistic analysis of Harrod. The causes and consequences of these methodological differences between Keynes and his followers will be further explained in the Afterword.

In August 1937, the American economy, which had been recovering up to that time, underwent a severe recession which added three million to the rolls of the unemployed within a year. Secretary of the Treasury Henry Morgenthau was so intent on balancing the federal budget that there had been a sharp turn from deficit to surplus financing and this, coupled with other destabilizing developments in the economy, seems to have contributed to the economic contraction. Keynes had been watching these events closely—he had taken severe personal losses on securities in the March 1937 decline on the New York Stock Exchange—and now on February 1, 1938, he addressed an unsolicited letter to President Roosevelt on the recession. The key to recovery, he maintained, was spending. Easy money and an improved system of relief would not in themselves turn the economy around. Recovery would only be achieved by a large-scale recourse to public works and other investments in capital goods guaranteed by the government. The administration, he contended, had handled the housing problem very badly, and yet that sector was essential to economic recovery. He advised putting "most of the eggs in the housing basket" and making sure that they were hatched, if necessary through the use of direct subsidies. He also criticized the deadlock on the public utilities; too much was being made of the "wickedness" of the utility holding companies because the "real criminals" in that industry had cleared out long ago. Personally, he asserted, he thought that there was a good deal to be said for government ownership of all the utilities, but if public opinion was not yet ripe for this, there was no point in "chasing the utilities around the lot every other week." He discussed the railroads as potential sources of new investment expenditure, urging either that they, too, should be nationalized or, if not, pity should be taken on the problems of their management and "let the dead bury the dead." Affronting two nationality groups at once, he said, "To the Englishmen, you Americans, like the Irish, are so terribly historically-minded!"

The recession, he maintained, was partly psychological in origin, and the President's attitude to businessmen had contributed to a loss of confidence on their part. He wrote: "Businessmen have a different set of delusions from politicians and need, therefore, different handling. They are, however, much milder than politicians, at the same time allured and terrified by the glare of publicity, easily persuaded to be 'patriots,' perplexed, bemused, indeed terrified, yet only too anxious to take a cheerful view, vain perhaps but very unsure of themselves, pathetically responsive to a kind word. You could do anything you like with them, if you would treat them (even the big ones), not as wolves and tigers, but as domestic animals by nature, even though they have been badly brought up and not trained as you would wish. It is a mistake to think that they are more *immoral* than politicians. If you work them into the surly, obstinate, terrified mood, of which domestic animals, wrongly handled, are so capable, the nation's burden's will not get carried to market; and in the end public opinion will veer their way." It is not recorded how American businessmen reacted to this metaphor which pictured them as domestic animals, but so many of them were already so anti-Keynesian that it didn't make any difference.

President Roosevelt's response to this letter was to turn it over to Secretary of the Treasury Morgenthau for him to reply. The latter, whose opposition to more government spending had been long known, was deliberately noncommittal in his letter. "It was very pleasant and encouraging to know," he wrote, "that you are in agreement with so much of the Administration's economic program. This confirmation, coming from so eminent an economist, is indeed welcome. Your analysis . . . is very interesting. The emphasis you place upon . . . housing . . . is well placed." Morgenthau simply ignored Keynes's emphasis upon public spending and, in accepting this reply for his own signature, President Roosevelt could not have had any doubt about what it implied. The Treasury secretary felt that he could still conquer the recession without giving in to the spenders; in February and March, he recommended a number of remedies which it was thought would force or induce a degree of private spending that would make the Keynesian policy unnecessary and undesirable. He insisted that "Keynes and his disciples had a set of delusions all of their own."

As it was, Keynes had other preoccupations during the summer of 1937. As the fascist menace to Europe's peace mounted while he was convalescing in Wales, he was doing considerable thinking about foreign policy. In the previous year he had written no fewer than eight columns of letters to *The New Statesman and Nation,* replying to Marxist or pacifist points of view. His most distinguished opponent in this debate was Bertrand Russell, who persisted in his pacificism in the thirties despite the aggressive actions of the Nazis and Mussolini in those years. Keynes also found himself at odds with Kingsley Martin, the editor of the aforementioned journal, who opposed appeasement and urged a collective alliance with the Soviet Union. According to the latter, Keynes supported appeasment "even after Munich" with the objective of ending the injustices of the treaty of Versailles.

Others who had opposed that treaty, such as Walter Lippmann, had already come to regret their opposition. The American journalist, writing in July 1930, stated that "if I had it to do all over again, I would take the other side; we supplied the Battalion of Death with too much ammunition." Considering that Lippmann's previous opinion had been heavily influenced by Keynes's tract, this was quite a significant repudiation. Keynes himself, it would appear, might have been entertaining second thoughts about his role in that matter. Sometime in 1936, after the March 29 "election" in Germany which consolidated Hitler's power, Elizabeth Wiskemann, a German-born, Cambridge-educated historian, met him at a social gathering in London. Suddenly, she reported later, she found herself saying, "I do wish you had not written that book [meaning *The Economic Consequences,* which the Germans never ceased to quote], and then longed for the ground to swallow me up. But he said simply and gently, 'So do I.'"

Later, in March 1938 when Anthony Eden resigned in protest over Chamberlain's supine policy, Keynes's views changed, and he came out strongly against the insufferable attitude of the prime minister. Still, even in September of that year, he was in favor of revision of Czechoslovakia's frontier as a means to peace. His stand at that perilous time was one of "living from hand to mouth in international affairs" because, as he put it, "the successive links in the causal chain are so completely unpredictable."

In February 1938, Keynes made his first public appearance after his heart attack, at the annual meeting of the National Mutual Life Insurance Society. Again, his speech on that occasion made headline news, but he was growing tired of his feud and rows with the stiff-necked Establishment types of the boardroom. He really despised the conventional bankers, and it must be admitted that he was never popular himself in the City. He resigned in October 1938 from the National Mutual but retained his chairmanship of the Provincial Insurance Company because he was friendly with the Scott family who held the controlling interest in the firm.

One person whose admiration he finally and definitely won about this time was Virginia Woolf, who wrote the following encomium about their versatile, mutual friend to her sister:

Maynard is a great man, I rather think. They [the Keyneses] had caught three mice on one trap; this excited him to the verge of hysteria. Now that's true greatness; combined as it is with buying a whole flock of sheep; ditto of cows; he had been also dictating a letter to *The Times;* is overcoming the innumerable actors and actresses who won't act Phèdre; had also a complete knowledge of tuberculosis in cows; meanwhile gave permission for Auntie to drive with Edgar [chauffeur] to Lewes to buy stockings; all details are referred to him; yet he remains dominant, calm; intent as a terrier to every word of L[ydia]'s play; spotted at sight things I'd never seen from sheer vacancy; and left me crushed but soaring with hope for a race that breeds men like Maynard. And I kissed him and praised to the skies his Memoir Club paper, by which, most oddly to my thinking, he was really pleased.

In this period of reduced activity he continued to write letters to *The Economist* and *The Times* on Treasury financial policy and foreign affairs, but his main occupation seems to have been his old love, book collecting. Now he concentrated on the first editions of the great English thinkers—Newton, Hume, Bentham, and others, as well as certain of the continental writers. His brother Geoffrey, also an avid collector, gave him an *Abstract of Hume's Treatise of Human Nature,* originally published in 1740. It had been thought that this was the work of the young Adam Smith who had made this abstract of his friend's *Treatise.* With the assistance of Piero Sraffa, Keynes discovered that the *Abstract* had been written by Hume himself to promote his own original work which had sold badly. This must have been a source of deep intellectual satisfaction to him because of the high esteem in which he held the skeptical Scottish philosopher.

After 1939, his interest as a bibliophile turned to English literature of the Elizabethan and Stuart periods; he energetically bought the works of sixteenth- and seventeenth-century authors, particularly those of the dramatists and poets. His letters to George Rylands show the solace which he found in this pursuit. In one, written as he was leaving for America on September 3, 1943, he wrote, "I have been comforting my declining days by buying lots of quarto plays from Shakespeare to Congreve, and can now boast that I have more than forty."

One byproduct of his book collecting was his fascinating biographical essay on "Cambridge's greatest son," entitled "Newton, the Man," written apparently toward the end of the thirties. (This piece was later read by Sir Geoffrey Keynes at the Newton Tercentenary Celebration at Trinity College on July 17, 1946, and was published in the 1951 edition of *Essays in Biography*.) In some respects this remarkable sketch of the great physicist has been somewhat neglected among Keynes's writings, despite the fact that it may contain some clues to an interpretation of his own life. At the very outset of the essay, Keynes stated very emphatically, "Geniuses *are* very peculiar." He went on to explain that since the eighteenth century, Newton had been thought of as the first and greatest of the scientists, a rationalist, the embodiment of the Age of Reason. But, wrote Keynes rather forcefully, "I do not see him in this light." He was rather "the last of the magicians and indeed, in vulgar modern terms ... profoundly neurotic of a not unfamiliar type, but—I should say from the records—a most extreme example. His deepest instincts were occult, esoteric, semantic—with a profound shrinking from the world, a paralyzing fear of exposing his thoughts, his beliefs, his discoveries in all nakedness to the inspection or criticism of the world." This "wrapt, consecrated solitary," who had been born a posthumous child with no father on Christmas Day 1642, grew up devoted only to his mother. "Like all his type," added Keynes, indirectly advancing a theory of homosexuality, "he was wholly aloof from women." "This strange spirit" lived like a monk of science in his Trinity rooms and garden, largely alone, for twenty-five years, intensely pursuing his studies with an introspection and a mental endurance never equalled, until his *magnum opus,* the *Principia,* was published. Keynes insisted that behind all of Newton's secrecy there was "extreme method in his madness." All his unpublished works on esoteric and theological matters were just as sane as the *Principia,* but they embodied a major heresy for his time. From his study of the ancient authorities, Newton had concluded that the prevailing religious orthodoxy, the doctrine of the Trinity, was fallacious, and in the light of his own investigations he had become instead "a Judaic monotheist of the school of Maimonides." This was the "dreadful secret" that he took pains to conceal all his life. Being, in effect, a Unitarian, he refused to take holy orders and had to receive a special dispensation to hold his chair and fellowship at Trinity College; nor could he become master of that college because of his beliefs. All the incriminating evidence, stated Keynes, went into a big box which some of his later biographers were reluctant to open, or when they did, they covered up their tracks with "carefully selected extracts and some straight fibbing."

In 1689, Newton's mother to whom he was so attached died, and three years later he suffered a severe nervous breakdown, marked by melancholia, sleeplessness, and fears of persecution. After two years he recovered, but he had lost "the former consistency of his mind." He could not concentrate in his former fashion or do any fresh work. His friends, concerned for his health and future, were finally successful in persuading him to move to London where he lived with his niece Catherine Barton, "one of the most brilliant and charming women in the London of Congreve, Swift, and Pope." His old and loyal friend, the Earl of Halifax, who was chancellor of the exchequer and was reputed to have had Catherine Barton as his mistress, arranged to have Newton made master of the mint in 1699. Newton held this post very successfully through the remaining twenty-eight years of his life, during which he also reigned as president of the Royal Society. At this point Keynes added, "He liked to have clever young men about him to edit new editions of the *Principia*—and sometimes merely plausible ones, as in the case of Fatio de Duillier."

Keynes felt that Newton's preeminence as a scientist was due to "his muscles of intuition being the strongest and most enduring with which a man has ever been gifted." He could "hold a problem in his mind for hours and days and weeks until it surrendered to him its secret." Mathematical proofs were not the instrument of his discoveries; it was his intuition that was "preeminently extraordinary." Keynes also noted Newton's versatility, stating that "he possessed in exceptional degree almost every kind of intellectual aptitude—lawyer, historian, theologian, not less than mathematician, physicist, astronomer." In addition, like himself, he was a very successful investor of funds and, as a consequence, survived the terrible financial crisis of the South Sea Bubble, dying a rich man.

A summary does not do justice to this charming, perceptive essay, but it cannot be left without asking why its subject had the unusual fascination that he obviously had for Keynes. Great men aroused his interest, and with his flair for biographical analysis he was naturally drawn to sketch Newton's portrait, but was there something more? Did he unconsciously realize that he, too, had his "dreadful secret" and was a heretic in a most crucial way—a practicing homosexual in the years before World War I at a time when that inclination could be as disastrous to a public figure as Newton's religious heterodoxy was in his? He undoubtedly sensed the other parallels in their lives—the attachment of both to their mothers, their common employment of intuition in a powerful way, and the contrast between their private and public lives. And finally, in his reference to the clever young men who surrounded Newton in his declining years, was he not suggesting that the famous Cantabrigian was homosexually inclined? It is some slight confirmation of this thesis of parallelism between the two men to recall that in the years before World War II in conversation with Michael Kalecki, Keynes, disheartened by the reception given his *General Theory,* "drew a parallel between his theory and that of Newton, which no one under the age of forty understood at the time."

From his voluminous correspondence it is apparent that Keynes was not only a devoted son to his parents, but was very fond of his sister and her family, as well as being very generous with his old friends. His sister Margaret had two sons and daughters, and Maynard became a good uncle to them all. He stood as godfather for Geoffrey's son, Stephen, gave them all fine Christmas presents, and when they were grown made presents of one hundred pounds a year for seven years to Polly and David. When the boys were old enough, he liked very much to have them come down to Tilton for the pheasant shoots.

There is much evidence, too, that he went out of his way to help his other relatives. He gave financial advice to his old playmate Kenneth Brown, and when Neville Brown, another cousin, needed work he interceded with Walter Layton at *The Economist* to get him a job. Later, when Neville decided to go into the camera business, he lent him three thousand pounds, with interest to be paid only when the ordinary shares of the company paid a dividend. Three years later he told Brown that he shouldn't worry about the loan.

These instances of his generosity to his relatives are quite apart from the assistance that he gave over the years to friends in need. Perhaps the most significant instance of the latter was in 1937 when he provided a settled income for Duncan Grant, who was then fifty-two. The painter wrote at the time, "Dearest Maynard, I do not know how to thank you for what you are doing for me. . . . But honestly it is the greatest blessing that I need no longer worry about old age and decrepitude making me a burden on the rates, quite apart from all the pleasure it will give me to have a little extra money now. . . . I am only telling my mother and Vanessa about it at the moment because if it gets about that I am a moneyed man, no one will buy any more pictures. Much love, Duncan."

As his health improved in 1938 and 1939, Keynes took a more active but cautious part in social and political activities. In May he was awarded honorary degrees at Oxford and Glasgow, and about this time he prepared a paper entitled "The Policy of Government Storage of Food Stuffs and Raw Materials," which was read by his old pupil Gerald Shove to the British Association at its meeting in Cambridge. In this essay he urged the government to acquire surplus stocks of such materials in order to stabilize prices and contribute to moderation of the trade cycle. He elaborated further on this idea of "stock piling" during the war and looked forward to the use of this strategy in postwar reconstruction.

In August there was the Munich crisis, and he took as usual an optimistic (and erroneous) view of its outcome in a letter to his mother: "It is a tremendous relief to get last night's news—though my reasoning self has never wavered from the conclusion that it was ten to one against the war. Hitler has never had much to gain from calling off the bluff until the last possible moment; he needed the fleet maneuvers and the air raid precautions to convince him that we would really act. Given the latter, I have always believed the former would follow. The prime minister has shown extraordinary charity and courage and good motives. But his sympathies are distasteful. And if he gets us out of the hole, it was he (and *The Times)* who got us into it by leading the Nazis into the belief that at the bottom the sympathies of the English ruling class were with them. I should have thought that Mrs. Chamberlain could have told him that kindness and consideration are the wrong way to handle a hysteric."

Later, as he digested the significance of Munich, he concluded that "the whole nation had been swindled as never before in its history. . . . We have suffered one of the worst pieces of trickery in history. Honorable international policy has suffered a terrific reverse by the inscrupulous intrigues, quite unsupported by public opinion, of our own pro-Nazis."

When early in 1939 Sir Stafford Cripps sought to organize a united front of progressives against the detestable policy of Munich, Keynes made a contribution to his fund. But now, as the war became more imminent, his mind turned to questions of war finance. He wrote two articles on the subject for *The Times,* advocating a policy of low interest rates, control of capital exports, and establishment of a department of coordination with an economic general staff. Broadcasting on the BBC, he discussed the conditions of full employment which would follow rearmament and analyzed possible financial policies in two more articles in *The Times.* Then, in August he went off with Lydia on a holiday to Royat, France, to take the steam baths and massage, but he could take only half the cure because the hotel had to close down as a result of the French mobilization. The war was now very close.

At the outbreak of hostilities with the Nazi invasion of Poland on September 3, 1939, Keynes was back in England. Apparently, at first he didn't dream of reassembling his old "A" Division and, furthermore, most of the old-timers, Falk, Ward, and others, were either in the Treasury or otherwise engaged. Instead, as he wrote Roy Harrod, "my plan is to come up here [to King's] to run a good part of the bursary of the college, the *Economic Journal,* and teaching in the economics faculty, which . . . would in due course release more active people. . . . Committee work, which would involve quiet drafting in my own room and occasional visits to London, would be the sort of thing I might be fit for." In the following months he did spend most of his time in Cambridge, only going down to London for a few days in the middle of the week.

Almost inevitably his mind turned to the economic problems of the conflict, and by September 14 he had sent his first contribution—a memorandum on price control—to Lord Stamp and a day later to the Treasury. In this he argued against a policy of preventing any price rise as impracticable and urged instead a moderate increase in British prices. Ten days later he sent a paper on exchange control to Sir Richard Hopkins and Sir Frederick Phillips in the Treasury in which he reminisced a good deal about World War I practices and advised these officials to be cautious and cagey in its control system. At this time he was hosting at 46 Gordon Square the "Old Dogs," ex-officials such as H. D. Henderson, Sir Arthur Salter, Sir William Beveridge, and Sir Walter Layton, and out of these discussions came several more memoranda—one on blockade policy he sent to Sir Frederick Leith-Ross, but it didn't affect official policy. In a second memorandum on the food blockade which he sent to Beveridge, the foreign office, and the ministry of economic warfare, he suggested that wheat should be removed from the list of contraband as a step toward humanizing the war; he also tried to persuade Winston Churchill of the soundness of this idea, but got nowhere. Finally, at the suggestion of others he prepared "Notes on the War for the President" [Roosevelt] in which he advised the United States to break off diplomatic relations with Germany and declare a state of nonintercourse. The credits granted by the United States to Britain (there should be no private credit transactions) should carry no interest and should be repayable over a short period of years into a reconstruction fund, all this with a view to preventing the spread of communism in postwar Germany. In this paper he had referred to the United States's gold stock as "lunatic," but in redrafting changed it to "useless." Publicly he was writing to *The Times* on Sir John Simon's first war budget, urging a low interest policy on government borrowing.

In October the Swedish Academy of Science awarded him a medal for his "valuable contributions to the evolution of economic theories and their application to international problems of the greatest importance." Shortly thereafter, G. B. S. got him involved in a foreign policy matter, Shaw having written a letter to *The New Statesman* urging Britain to give up the pretense of war and to allow Russia and Germany to come to terms by themselves. Keynes advised Kingsley Martin not to publish such foolishness, but when it appeared, he wrote in as well: "The intelligentsia of the Left were loudest in demanding that the Nazi aggression should be resisted at all costs. When it comes to a showdown, scarce four weeks have passed before they remember that they are pacificists and write defeatist letters to your columns, leaving the defense of freedom and civilization to Colonel Blimp and the Old School Tie, for whom Three Cheers." This was all in the period after the Stalin-Hitler pact when the Stalinists made a sharp reversal of the party line.

In the early months of the war a parliamentary by-election for

Cambridge University became necessary as a result of the illness of its representative. The master of Magdalene College, A. B. Ramsey, now approached Keynes with the offer of the nomination. All three parties were ready to support him for the post, and he found the offer very attractive. It was a "tormenting decision," but after consulting Dr. Plesch, who approved, he finally decided not to accept because he felt that he was more useful as a publicist than he would be as a regular member at Westminister.

Since the beginning of hostilities, Keynes had been giving much thought about how to obtain the real resources for the war without inflation, which led him gradually to devise his plan for "compulsory savings." He had tried out the idea in a lecture to the Marshall Society, the undergraduate economics society at the university, and then reworked it for publication in *The Times* where it eventually appeared. Copies had been circulated to the chancellor of the exchequer and other officials, and the initial reactions were encouraging. He had come to regard the increase in aggregate demand brought about by armament expenditure and the resulting threat of inflation as "the central problem of the home economic front" and one which required for its solution the coordination of price policy, budget, and wages policy. Up to that point all this had not been honestly and squarely faced by the nation; now he was determined to make it do so. By siphoning off the excess purchasing power through compulsory savings, or what he later called "deferred pay," he not only hoped to check the ravages of inflation, but also achieve a greater degree of social justice by spreading the increased national debt among every class in the community. He proposed to credit workers with deposits in the Post Office Savings Bank for part of their pay and thus prevent the excess demand from causing prices to skyrocket.

The day after *The Times* articles appeared he sent Sir Richard Hopkins and Lord Stamp "the statistical background out of which the particular magnitude of my proposals emerges" and later published in the *Economic Journal* a detailed analysis of "The Income and Fiscal Potential of Great Britain," utilizing the expertise of Colin Clark, the statistician, and of Erwin Rothbarth, a refugee student who was an assistant in statistical research at Cambridge.

The Times article gave rise to a considerable amount of comment and criticism to which Keynes responded with amazing vitality and force. He wrote letters, took part in discussions, spoke over the air in a dialogue with Donald Tyerman, addressed the Labor Front Bench, the leaders of the Trade Union Congress, members of the Fabian Society, and a large gathering of MPs. He secured support for his plan from eminent bankers and financiers, including Montagu Norman, with whom he was personally reconciled after a long estrangement. Perhaps most gratifying of all, most of the academic economists agreed with his novel proposal, at least in principle, including Professors Hayek, Robertson, and Robbins.

Encouraged by this wide interest, he prepared a pamphlet entitled *How to Pay for the War,* and upon its publication in February 1940, he managed to get Lord Balfour to initiate a debate in the House of Lords on its contents. As he had done so often in the past, he circulated almost one hundred copies of his little book before publication among friends, colleagues, and those whom he was anxious to persuade. It is interesting to note that he had modified his plan in the light of suggestions and criticisms so that he could emphasize that it represented a positive social improvement and promoted social justice. His complete scheme now included universal family allowances in cash, the accumulation of working-class wealth under working-class control, a linking of wages and pensions to the cost of a limited range of rationed articles of consumption, and a general capital levy after the war to provide for the deferred consumption without increasing the national debt. His book set out very lucidly and cogently his case for this innovation in wartime finance. Somewhat later he prepared a *Budget of National Resources* which sought to relate the ideas of *How to Pay for the War* to the figures of the forthcoming budget.

After the book's appearance he maintained a campaign of persuasion and propaganda by further correspondence, meetings, and visits. He was seemingly indefatigable in his efforts in behalf of what he regarded as the only specific new proposal to deal with the threat of wartime inflation in a fundamental way. In the past and even later, many would think of his economics as being concerned primarily with the problems of depression and unemployment; now in *How to Pay for the War* he showed how his technique of analysis could be applied to the economics of excessive demand as well. In a preface to a French edition of this book, he said that he thought of his plan as "a first installment of a comprehensive social policy to regulate the general rate of spending so as to avoid the disastrous alternations of boom and slump which otherwise will continue to undermine the foundations of society."

In a long, rather neglected article in the *New Republic* in which he sought to relate his plan to the changing economic conditions in the United States, he made the previous point quite explicit, namely, that in the circumstances of war the facts are the reverse of those of depression, and as a consequence "the practical advice of the economist must suffer a sea change. More war investment and *less* private spending become the new order of the day." In this piece he made some remarks about the difficulties of attaining full employment in peacetime that deserve more attention than they have received. He wrote: "Even if a complete harmony between the Roosevelt administration and private enterprise had achieved, momentarily, a satisfactory economic recovery, it would not have endured more than a few months, with institutions and the distribution of purchasing power what they are today. That full employment would have been reached even so, I do not believe—any more than it was in 1928–29.

"It is, it seems, politically impossible for a capitalistic democracy to organize expenditure on a scale necessary to make the grand experiments which would prove my case—except in war conditions." He continued to hope, nevertheless, that good might come out of evil and that as a result of its wartime experience the United States would learn "the first principles governing the production of wealth" and would put such ideas to good use in postwar reconstruction. But it is necessary to note that in concluding his essay, he asked, "Is it vain to suppose that a democracy can be wise and sensible? Must the poison of popular politics make impotent every free community? So much hangs on the issue that it is our duty to believe that we can do what we should, until the opposite is proved."

Casting his lot with the reformers, he eloquently argued the case for a more conservative approach to the problems of transition. "In a world of destroyers" such people must "zealously protect the variously woven fabric of society, even when this means that some abuses must be spared." Reverting to that emphasis on tradition and Burkean ideas which was so noticeable in the philosophizing of his later years, he said, "Civilization is a tradition from the past, a miraculous construction made by our fathers of which they know the vulnerability better than we do, hard to come by and easily lost." Rejecting the invalidism of the Left and the sclerotic thinking of the old guard of the Right, he warned the latter, "Let them learn from the experiences of Great Britain and of Europe that there has been a rottenness at the heart of our society, and do not let them suppose that America is healthy."

In retrospect it can be seen that despite his heroic and strenuous efforts for "compulsory savings," this plan which he came to consider "the centerpiece of war finance" was only partially implemented in British governmental policy. True, Keynesian aggregate economics led to calculations of the "inflationary gap," and this approach contributed to the restraint on wartime inflation; further, his influence manifested itself in the low interest rate policy which was followed through the war years. As to "deferred pay," he proposed to raise £550 million a year by that means, though an annual average of £121 million was, in fact, achieved by this method. Still, his idea was adopted in the form of "postwar credits," and his scheme for family allowances was also utilized toward the end of the conflict.

Another aspect of wartime economic policy that commanded his attention early in 1940 was exchange control. He had discussed this question with Sir Frederick Phillips on February 22 and the next day with the governor of the Bank of England, but it was under the prodding of Richard Kahn who was now on the Board of Trade that he was spurred to more activity. Soon he was pursuing this matter with the same vigor and imagination that he had invested in his compulsory savings plan. He believed that the war on its economic side had to be waged with the nation's might and determination, and he felt very strongly that the management of foreign exchange restrictions had been handled very badly since its outbreak. If Britain was to marshal all its resources for an all-out effort, she needed to conserve and mobilize all the foreign exchange possible to pay for the sinews of war, and in this matter he had all the experience of his work on world war financing to draw upon. He spoke on the subject to the Parliamentary Monetary Committee and then in May, after receiving criticisms of his draft from Henry Clay and other Bank of England officials, he submitted a detailed memorandum on "Exchange Control and Exchange Policy" to Phillips at the Treasury. In this paper he opposed blocking sterling exchange completely, but argued for more stringent controls on security transactions by foreigners, limitation of imports, and tighter administration of exchange and import regulations generally. He wanted concerted action on these matters throughout the British, French, Dutch, and Belgian empires and comprehensive exchange agreements to be effected, supported by the common financial resources of the group. He advised finally that a special joint department of the Treasury and the Bank of England should be established to run this system.

In June, he sent an aide-mémoire to the chancellor of the exchequer embodying his ideas on "The Mobilization of our Foreign Resources as a Weapon of War," which stressed the need for a spectacular, imaginative policy. He outlined a "grand scheme" involving a complete pooling in gold, securities, and current trade balances of the British, French, Dutch, and Belgian empires and rapid establishment of uniform exchange control between this area and the rest of the world. Almost in mercantilist fashion, he advised bilateral exchange control of the Allied area with each country outside it, and provisions for clearing and uncleared balances. With such a scheme in operation, he felt that it would be possible to assure the war departments of finance for three years or longer of all the imports that it was physically possible for them to acquire. It is very clear that he, at least, was ready for total economic war.

In another forceful memorandum to the chancellor of the exchequer a week later, he warned against establishing financial relations among the allies on "a pseudocommercial basis, which apes the conventions of foreign investment." Instead, assistance and cooperation should be determined by what was physically possible and should be tied up "to the least possible extent with formal financial arrangements." In this paper he sought to assure the French government, which was reeling under the blows of the Wehrmacht, of a real pooling of resources (material as well as military) in this war to save civilization. There should be no question, as there was after World War I, of one ally owing large sums to the other. As for the United States, whatever credits it extended to such allies should bear no interest and should be repayable to a fund for the postwar reconstruction of Europe. The United States, it was to be hoped, would in addition contribute £5,000 million in gold out of its redundant and useless stock to provide bank reserves for the nations in need of reconstruction. He warned that unless Britain freed herself from "the taint of pseudocommercial transactions" with France, it would spoil the prospect of right arrangements with the United States.

About this time Keynes also involved himself with problems of manpower allocation, writing to *The Times* on the subject early in June. With the fall of France in that month, he became even more concerned about the fate of some of his refugee friends among the economists. With the intensification of the war and the threat of invasion, the British government decided on a roundup of enemy aliens who had previously been exempt from all restrictions. Such people were shipped to the Isle of Man with the idea that they would later be sent to the Dominions when shipping was available. It was indicated, however, that "valuable" aliens would be permitted to remain in the country with some freedom of movement. With that in mind, Keynes immediately intervened with the authorities for the release of such economists as Piero Sraffa, Erwin Rothbarth, H. W. Singer, and Edward Rosenbaum. Sraffa, with whom he was most friendly, wrote him expressing how grateful he was for all the trouble that he had taken about him and asking if Keynes's mother would keep in touch with his mother because she was without friends in Cambridge. Maynard asked his mother to do this. His efforts, by the way, for Sraffa and the other emigré scholars were successful; they were eventually released for teaching and research activities.

The defeat of the British in Norway early in May brought an end to the "phoney war" and led to the downfall of the Chamberlain administration and the formation of the coalition government under Winston Churchill. The new chancellor of the exchequer was Sir Kingsley Wood, and one of his first steps in office was to appoint a consultative council composed of representatives of industry, commerce, banking, and the trade unions; Hubert Henderson and Keynes were appointed to serve as economists on this body. The latter, as usual, kept his mother informed of the developments: "I have got a small job of work, which seems to be well suited to try out my present capacities without involving any strain. The chancellor of the exchequer is setting up an advisory council in the Treasury, and I am to be a member of it. It will require no regular attendance. I should say that most of the other members are people who will do no work at all and that I can make my own work just what I choose. I have, as you know, a strong prejudice against advisory as compared with executive jobs. But I think that it is probably wise to start with something minor like this, and it will have the great advantage of giving me direct access to the chancellor of the exchequer with any bright ideas I may have. I don't know much about it yet."

At first Keynes thought that the work of the council would be "exiguous," but by the end of July he wrote that he was "extremely busy giving the Treasury unsolicited advice." In August he was given a more extensive function in that department, being put on the Exchange Control Conference and assigned a room which was adjacent to that of Lord Thomas Catto, a financier who was also an advisor to the chancellor. He and Keynes got along very well and were affectionately referred to as "Catto" and "Doggo." In effect, Keynes was now advising from within the Treasury, though he was not a civil servant and received no salary. In late August, writing to his mother again, he said, "They could not be kinder to me at the Treasury than they are. This week I have been putting in about five hours a day there, and such work as there is is interesting and important. But like Polly Hill [his niece], I am only just able to occupy my time and have not *really* enough work to do. You know how Keyneses hate that."

London at that time was being "blitzed" by the Germans; on one occasion Keynes reported that he and Lydia were forced to spend an hour in a deep cellar in Piccadilly. Naturally enough, his initial work in the Treasury had to do with a war damage compensation scheme which he presented to the consultative committee at its first meeting and eventually pushed through to adoption as law. He submitted at least three memoranda on the subject, urging a definite policy of full compensation for damage in order to bolster general confidence. Typically Keynesian, in one he quoted from Gibbons's *Autobiography* and concluded another, "We lose on every score if we fail to exercise imaginative foresight and act accordingly beforehand." By September of that year he could tell his mother of his long conversation with the prime minister at the Other Club and of his placing "my new war damage scheme" in his speech that afternoon and of his hope that it would really be adopted. It was.

In the period after the outbreak of the war, British budget policy was at first slow to face up to the difficult problems of the nation. Sir John Simon's budgets of April and September 1940 were the subject of much criticism, especially in the columns of *The Economist*. The reliance on voluntary saving and the level of taxation reflected the ambiguous feelings of the public and the politicians in this period of the "phoney war." But the summer of 1940, which saw the German invasion of Belgium and the Netherlands, the collapse of France, and Dunkirk, brought about a national change of heart and a commitment on the part of the British people to total war and victory, no matter how long it might take. Keynes was drawn into the long, difficult deliberations at the Treasury which finally resulted in a drastic revision of fiscal policy. Again, he reported to his mother, "I am now occupied in trying to put across to the big guns a comprehensive budget of financial policy. But it is too soon to say whether I shall have the least success."

In several long notes on the budget submitted in July and September–October, he blocked out the main lines of the new policy. Using the basic concepts of the aggregate national income approach, he hammered at the idea that the main objective of a war budget was not simply to finance the military effort, but to prevent the social evils of inflation, and to do this in a way that satisfied the popular sense of social justice. He calculated the inflationary gap and argued for the stabilization of the cost of living through increased direct taxation and forced saving. In the budget strategy sessions with the chancellor, he explained how he arrived at his estimate of a budget gap of £400–450 million and how he proposed to close it. His argument was strengthened at this time by the social surveys carried out by Charles Madge for the National Institute of Economic and Social Research; these showed that workers had improved their real economic position and that they would be agreeable to the idea of deferred pay. Throughout the rest of that year, Keynes produced a stream of memoranda for the chancellor and his advisors, changing his proposals, adding new information, pressing the case that the task was beyond the powers of voluntary methods. Again one notes a characteristic emphasis: "What the public requires is a sense that imagination has been used, that a novel fiscal instrument has been forged, that social justice has been preserved, and that a basis for further social improvement has been laid."

Sir Kingsley Wood's budget of 1941, which became the cornerstone of Britain's internal financial policy for the rest of the war, adopted many of Keynes's ideas, several in modified form. It was the first budget to use a national income analytical framework; after the chancellor's budget speech, a White Paper was published which furnished an analysis of the sources of war finance and estimates of the national income for 1938 and 1940. This was another significant innovation in which Keynes had a major part. It came about in this fashion: Sir Austin Robinson, who had been much impressed by Keynes's idea of compulsory saving, persuaded two key officials that authoritative national income estimates were necessary for the economic planning of the war and the shaping of fiscal policy. Professor James Meade, who had been working for the League of Nations in Geneva, and later Richard Stone of the Central Economic Information Service, soon began work on a framework for the proposed national accounts. Keynes took an enthusiastic interest in their efforts when he joined the Treasury in July and circulated their paper, "National Income, Saving, and Consumption," to the Treasury budget committee. The data in this monograph were essential to the formulation of the chancellor's innovative 1941 budget. The theory of inflationary finance which underlay that budget was more readily accepted by the Treasury officials than the basic arithmetic. Hubert Henderson and Dennis Robertson were skeptical of the estimates, but the chancellor in the end accepted them. Keynes had insisted all along that the budget must be regarded as a part, and only a part, of a comprehensive economic policy. In his *Notes for the Budget Statement, 1941,* which he prepared for the chancellor's use, he sounded a note of satisfied accomplishment: "I fancy that a first-class revolution in our fiscal system has happened almost silently in the last year. The country has finally converted to the great superiority of direct taxation at all levels of income. With that conversion we have reached, so to speak, a higher standard of fiscal civilization. We have made up our minds that for all of us, the wage earners not least, direct taxes are better than higher prices."

The most novel feature of the 1941 budget was its treatment of part of the increased income tax as a "withholding tax"—a tax that was to be paid after the war. In the end, Kingsley Wood's stabilization budget did not involve a complete implementation of the Keynes deferred pay plan, nor did the amount collected in the succeeding years come anywhere near what his scheme would have required, but it was a significant contribution to a rational financial policy. Keynes himself was very satisfied with the outcome, as the following letter to his mother clearly indicates: "I am as well satisfied with the budget as I could reasonably expect; and indeed got my way on a number of points as much as is good for me. The limited acceptance of deferred pay is most associated with me publicly. But the two points I attached most importance to and where I played a part were the stabilization of prices, for which I have been fighting very hard, and the logical structure and method of a wartime budget which, together with the new White Paper, is really a revolution in public finance. The chief officials, Sir Richard Hopkins and Sir Horace Wilson, as well as the chancellor, have been extraordinarily good to me and open-minded and ready to be persuaded; and Lord Catto has been a great help all through. Indeed, we were a wonderfully united team. The opposition, which has given me trouble and worn out my nerves, was mainly from Hubert Henderson."

In November 1941, in his notes on the budget, Keynes suggested that it should be described as a social policy budget and should aim at correcting some of the anomalies which had developed out of the war situation. For example, among other matters he urged that married women who were employed should be given an allowance to reduce the level of taxation on their earned income. Broadly speaking, he contended that "the strengthening of the economic position of the family unit should be the main purpose of social policy now and after the war." He was also influential in enabling Britain to fight the so-called three percent war. He wrote several sophisticated notes on loan policy, drawing upon his long experience in the City—he was especially keen on shortsighted issues, but he was not always successful in his efforts at persuasion. Early on he drafted a forceful memorandum on the excess profits tax, urging modifications which were eventually adopted, and toward the end of the war he was interested in control of new capital issues. Reform-minded, he wrote, "Instead of complaisant stonewalling on a position which will surely have to be abandoned very soon, we should be tackling this imminent task with life and vigor and invention of mind."

During all of his strenuous work in the Treasury in the fall of 1941, London was being heavily bombed by the Germans. In September he was bombed out of Gordon Square; Bloomsbury had been badly hit— Duncan and Vanessa had their studios demolished, and the Woolfs' house nearby had been wrecked. During this period Keynes returned to Tilton each night. He described his new routine to Dr. Plesch: "I have breakfast every morning at 7:00A.M., leave the house before 8:00 A.M., and do not get back until about 8:30 P.M.; whilst my day at the Treasury, which is now my headquarters for all purposes, gets fuller and fuller every week. Nevertheless, all this and the suppressed strain of the blitzkrieg seems to do my health nothing but good. I get reasonably tired, but no distressing symptoms."

Despite the strain of these months, there were some consoling and gratifying developments which probably bolstered his morale. Even before he joined the Treasury he had been elected a fellow of Eton to represent the masters on the governing body. Though he had to cross swords in that council with the very eloquent and sarcastic provost, Lord Quickswood (formerly Lord Hugh Cecil), he held his own and undoubtedly enjoyed the contribution he was able to make to the improved administration of the college's bursary. He also persuaded the governing body to adopt a more active investment policy such as he had introduced at King's.

Meanwhile, prospects brightened a bit for the British in the winter of 1940 after the terrible ordeal of the Battle of Britain. President Roosevelt had been reelected in November, and in the following January lend-lease was announced. Britain had been spending on a scale that endangered her whole financial solvency, but now there was some hope of economic salvation. It was in this latter connection that Keynes made the first of his six visits to the United States. He had been in consultation with Benjamin Cohen of the White House staff on these questions, and the American now suggested to Ambassador John Winant that it would be desirable for him to make a personal visit to the United States to explain the British situation in detail. Accordingly, he flew first to Lisbon, where he participated in negotiating a monetary agreement with Portugal, and then with Lydia to New York and Washington. He was accompanied by Lucius Thompson who served as his assistant. He had been given a roving mission which embraced as matters of discussion the scope of lend-lease, problems of British

exports and investments, the American program of mobilizing resources for war production, inflation, and postwar aims. It was a big
order, but the way had been cleared in part by Sir Frederick Phillips
who had established good relations with Secretary Morgenthau of the
Treasury Department. Keynes, too, had old friends in the States, such
as Walter Stewart, Professor Frankfurter, and Walter Lippmann, and
after an uncertain start he was soon on good terms with the Secretary
and many other important officials in the Treasury. Secretary Morgenthau later appraised him in this fashion: "He was a gentle soul. . . . He
was a very fine and pertinacious negotiator; every visit he paid advanced
the British cause. He was the best emissary they could have chosen;
they were not always so happy in their choice. . . . He had a very fine
intellect but, unlike many intellectuals, was never cold, so that one
always had a feeling of intimacy with him."

Meanwhile, Maynard and Lydia were enduring the trials of the
Washington social circuit and its steamy climate. "In the first five weeks
here I lunched and dined out forty-seven times, which really is service at
the front and certainly not more dangerous than the blitz. However,
health stands up to it, and indeed I haven't felt so well for years. It is
the cessation of liverishness [an old complaint] which makes the
difference.

"Yet, I shouldn't have survived without Lydia, who provides constant rest, discipline, and comfort.

"It is difficult to pick one's way through the tortuous and suspicious,
yet kindly, Washington world; and they are the slowest people to do
business with I've ever experienced. But I get on well enough and have
made some good friends. Arthus Purvis, the head of the Supply
Council, is a grand chap to whom England will owe much, if all goes
well, than to most people in this war." Sadly, Purvis died in Washington less than two months later; Keynes, in writing home, spoke of his
death as a "terrible loss."

In one of the numerous dinners that he referred to, given to enable
him to meet Leon Henderson and other officials of the Office of Price
Administration, he advocated a more repressive fiscal policy to check
incipient inflation in the American economy. In correspondence with
Walter S. Salant, he learned to his satisfaction that American economists were already employing the multiplier as well as the acceleration
principle in their analyses of the impact of defense expenditures on the
economy. He noted in one of his letters to Salant the difference in
perspective between the younger and older economists: "There is too
wide a gap between the intellectual outlook of the older people and that

of the younger. I have been greatly struck during my visit by the quality of the younger economists and civil servants in the Administration. I am sure that the best hope for good government in America is to be found there. The war will be a great sifter and will bring the right people to the top. We have a few good people in London, but nothing like the *numbers* you can produce here." There was probably in these words an intimation or sensing on Keynes's part of the rapidity with which the younger American economists would accept the ideas of the "new economics."

On the whole, Keynes's first mission to Washington had been a success. The scope of lend-lease had been broadly blocked out; the principle of a loan against the deposit of British securities had been established; an agreement had been reached on American acceptance, at least in part, of pre-lend-lease commitments and on Britain's need for some basic good reserve. Most important of all, he learned, Britain could rely upon the friendship and support of Secretary Morgenthau. In this account of these negotiations no mention has been made of the difficult question of "consideration" in the form of the elimination of discrimination in international trade which the State Department insisted on and which eventually became the famous Article VII of the Mutual Aid Agreement of February 1942. That delicate issue will be discussed in the next chapter.

On the fiscal front during the rest of the war he made a number of broadcasts over the BBC in which he expounded and explained Treasury policy, and he continued, too, to submit memoranda on the subsequent budgets, but these did not offer opportunity for the type of innovation that had gone into his earlier effort. In fact, budgetary policy for the remainder of the war operated pretty much within the principles that had been established in that pathbreaking policy action. This was hard on him, as he liked the new and challenging; he explained to his mother: "The last two days I have been writing a big wad of the budget speech—a heartbreaking job—for I know well by experience that the better I make it the less likely it is to be used!" In another letter two weeks later he spelled out what he meant: "Every phrase, every fact in what one provides which could conceivably attract attention is erased. For anything which is capable of attracting attention might also attract criticism! It is indeed the dregs of human dignity and morale. Or as Hoppy [Sir Richard Hopkins] more politely expresses it, 'the chancellor proceeds from the pedestrian.'"

If life at the Treasury did not offer as much excitement and challenge as it had in earlier years, there now developed an opportunity which

Keynes had not anticipated. In September 1941 he was elected a director of the Bank of England to fill the vacancy caused by the death of Lord Stamp who had been killed in an air raid. This created quite a stir, for, as Harrod remarks, had he not been "the foremost assailant of the policy of the Bank for twenty years?" Gerald Shove wrote him, "Well, well, well. . . . Another of the forts of folly taken. What a triumph. One almost begins to believe that there is some hope for the world after all. But nobody but you could have brought it off. Take care of yourself."

Two months later he was involved in correspondence with the Archbishop of York in which he gave advice on a publication which the latter had written entitled *Christianity and the Social Order*. The archbishop was evidently insecure about his knowledge of economics and had written Keynes asking for his assistance. His reply shows not only his sensitivity and willingness to help one with whom he had little in common theologically, but it is very illuminating concerning his view of the relationship of economics to ethics. In returning the proofs of the archbishop's book, he wrote that he had found it extremely interesting and expressed the opinion that it would attract much favorable attention. He reassured him, in fact, that in his first chapter he had understated his case on the relationship between religion and the "dismal science." He continued: "Along one line of origin, at least, economics more properly politico-economy is a side of ethics. Marshall used always to insist that it was through ethics he arrived at political economy, and I would claim myself in this, as in other respects, to be a pupil of his. I should have thought that nearly all English economists in the tradition, apart from Ricardo, reached economics that way. There are practically no issues of policy as distinct from technique which do not involve ethical considerations. If this is emphasized, the right of the church to interfere in what is essentially a branch of ethics becomes more obvious.

"It was a very recent heresy indeed to cut these matters out of its province." He went on to cite the contributions of Dean Swift, Bishop Fleetwood (the author of the first scientific treatise on prices and the theory of index numbers, according to Keynes), Bishop Berkeley, Bishop Butler, Archdeacon Paley, Archbishop Sumner, and the Reverend Thomas R. Malthus who, he wrote, was "the greatest economist writing in the eighteenth century after Adam Smith."

In his painstaking reply, Keynes pointed out an error regarding the national debt in one of the chapters and disagreed with the archbishop on the public schools which, he argued, "should not be injured by stealing from them a limited number of their most promising pupils." A loyal Etonian, he was very anxious that the tradition of the public school not be destroyed.

About a month later the Archbishop of York answered him, thanking him most sincerely for his aid and stating that he was "very much encouraged that you should take so much trouble about my extremely amateur production." Keynes's letter has been quoted at length because it reveals so well the man and his conception of economics as a moral science.

CHAPTER 14

Bretton Woods and the
Anglo-American Loan Agreement

Originality must be passionate.
Michael Polanyi, *Personal Knowledge*

INTERNATIONAL RELATIONS occupied much of Keynes's attention in the last years of his life. In his role, as he put it, of "a demi-semi-official" in the Treasury, he had firsthand knowledge of the United Kingdom's increasingly desperate financial situation in the period before the adoption of lend-lease and, of course, he also realized the extremely difficult economic problems that would have to be faced at the end of the struggle. It is testimonial to the shrewdness of the British that they cast him in the role of a statesman in this, their time of troubles. In this chapter it will not be possible to examine in much detail all the technical questions he confronted so splendidly; that has been done by others with superior skills in such matters. Instead, the focus will be on the influence of his creative personality on the events and policies with which he had to deal.

As has been seen, Keynes was in Washington in the summer of 1941 negotiating and laying Britain's "cards on the table" with the American officials. To understand his mission, it is helpful to recall that at the outbreak of the war the United States Neutrality Act forbade lending to a belligerent, and the Johnson Act of 1934 prohibited loans to any country that had defaulted—as Britain had—on the debts of World War I. In November 1940, however, Congress had amended the

[328]

former law to allow Britain and her allies to purchase war supplies, provided that they paid cash and did not use American shipping. This "cash and carry" legislation permitted the British to step up their orders considerably, but as fast as they ordered their dollar balances dwindled. To finance the struggle, Britain was divesting herself of gold and dollar balances. In December 1940, Prime Minister Churchill wrote President Roosevelt and told him, among other things, "The moment approaches when we shall no longer be able to pay cash for shipping and other supplies." Brooding over this letter as he cruised the Caribbean, the President later announced the principle of lend-lease under which, as he said, he sought to "eliminate the dollar sign." Under his plan the government would purchase all the munitions and would lease to Britain, subject to mortgage, those that would be more useful in her hands. In a fireside chat to the American people, he explained that his policy was simply to provide the implements of war for others to do the fighting in order "to keep war away from our country." The materiel and equipment "necessary for the defense of the United States," as the lend-lease phrased it, could be handed over to Britain if the president thought this the most efficient way of using them; the goods so transferred were not to be paid for in money but would be acknowledged in the form of some "consideration" which was to be negotiated. Thus, under this, "the most unsordid act in history," as Winston Churchill called it, the main principle that governed the flow of supplies to Britain was settled for the remainder of the war.

The Lend-Lease Act was signed by the President on March 11, 1941. In accordance with the terms of this act relating to "consideration," the President had instructed the State Department rather than the Treasury to prepare a draft, with the collaboration of Keynes, for his review. Dean Acheson drew up a nondiscrimination clause which stated that the United Kingdom received defense aid from the United States, and in return therefore agreed "to promote mutually advantageous economic relations between them and the betterment of worldwide economic relations; they shall provide against discrimination in either the United States of America or the United Kingdom against the importation of any produce originating in another country; and they shall provide for the formulation of measures for the achievement of these ends." This was to become Article VII of the Mutual Aid Agreement.

The impasse between the two countries over this provision was ended by language which had been worked out in the State Department. It stated merely that "at an early convenient date conversations shall be undertaken between the two governments with a view to determining ... the best means of attaining the above-stated objectives." Until that time there was no commitment.

Keynes returned to London with this draft of Article VII and explained its nuances to the authorities. He pointed out that it meant there would be no war debts after the close of hostilities, in short, no deliveries of cash or goods having merely economic significance. As for the " 'discrimination' clause, whatever that may mean," he said that it was of an awkward character and, in his mind, ambiguous. Dean Acheson, however, in conversation with him had indicated that it would preclude a system of imperial preferences as well as of import and exchange controls. Secretary Cordell Hull had been campaigning for nine years against such restrictions on international trade, and Keynes referred to it as his "pet idea." In speaking of the first draft of this article, in fact, he had called it "the lunatic proposals of Mr. Hull."

In the Atlantic Charter of August 1941, the British won a minor victory over this matter of phraseology—the discrimination clause was not used. The fourth point of the British draft merely spoke about striving to bring about fair and equitable distribution of essential produce. President Roosevelt wanted to add "without discrimination and on equal terms," but Prime Minister Churchill insisted that he couldn't accept such wording without consulting the Dominions. The President did not press the matter; the offensive words were omitted.

In his earlier discussion with the Americans on this issue of discrimination in international trade, Keynes had taken the position that the mere elimination of discrimination in trade practices was insufficient. He argued that "unless there was a large joint Anglo-American effort to restore equilibrium of trade," Britain would have to adopt restrictionist measures. "What he had in mind was the application with American assistance of Keynesian remedies for unemployment and trade depression on a world scale" and also "the appalling problem that Britain would face after the war in the matter of her own trade balance."

To understand Keynes's thought on these matters it must be remembered that in his pamphlet, *The Means to Prosperity,* he had taken the view that the tariffs, quotas, and exchange restrictions which had proliferated in the depression years were largely defensive measures, stating that "insofar as these things are not the expression of deliberate national or imperial policies, they have been adopted reluctantly as a means of self-protection and are symptoms, not causes, of the tension on the foreign exchanges." He went on to criticize the tendency of international conferences, such as that assembling in London at that time, to pass pious resolutions deploring symptoms, but to leave the basic disease untouched.

It was with such ideas in mind that he prepared in September 1941 the first draft of his proposals for an international currency (or clearing) union, which was circulated in the Treasury. In it he stated that the world needed an instrument of international currency having general acceptability between nations so that the blocked balances and bilateral clearings would be unnecessary. This currency union would manage an international clearing bank which would act basically as a central bank for the central banks of the member countries. Their accounts would be denominated in an international currency which, in his fourth draft of the plan, Keynes called "bancor." This bancor would be defined in terms of gold, but its value was not to be unalterable; the union would have the power to change its value if it deemed this desirable. Like a British bank, the clearing union would create debit balances through the form of overdrafts rather than make specific loans. It would charge interest, however, on both credit and debit balances. This feature was deliberate because it was part of Keynes's scheme to place part of the burden of balance of payment adjustments on the creditor countries. In other words, he wished to discourage credit balances to avoid the contradictory effect on international trade of large balance of payments surpluses, but he also stressed the need for debit balances to be controlled.

In a memorandum entitled *Postwar Currency Policy,* which he distributed in the Treasury at the same time as this clearing union proposal was making the rounds, he called attention to Dr. Hjalmar Schacht's barter schemes without which Germany would not have embarked on a course of war. He indicated his agreement with Hubert Henderson that while this method was used in the service of evil it should not blind us to its possible technical advantages in the service of a good cause. And he suggested that the alternative to his international currency union plan was "not a return to the currency disorders of the epoch between the wars . . . but a refinement and improvement of the Schachtian device." Then, in even stronger language, he asserted, "It would be madness on our part to deprive ourselves of the possibility of action along the above lines until we have a firm assurance of an equally satisfactory solution of a different kind. Anyone who at this stage would agree to sign away our future liberty of action would be as great a traitor to his country as if he were to sign away the British navy before he had a firm assurance of an alternative means of protection." It is evident that in his mind, as Harrod states, his clearing union embodied the minimum terms on which Britain could participate in a movement for greater freedom of international trade. It was his answer, in effect, to the proposals that the United States Department of State had stressed in the discussion the previous summer.

Keynes's document on the clearing union circulated within the Treasury and went through many drafts. Some officials thought it too grandiose or even Utopian. But Sir Richard Hopkins, the second secretary who was in charge of external finance, gave it his qualified support, and even Hubert Henderson, who had parted with much of Keynesian economics, made some constructive suggestions. Dennis Robertson, who was working in the Treasury in his dedicated way, was enthusiastic because he regarded it as a departure from Keynes's more nationalistic views of the prewar years. "I sat up late last night reading your revised proposals with great excitement—and growing hope that the spirit of Burke and Adam Smith is on earth again. . . . And then also a growing hope that we shall choose the right things and not the wrong ones to have such rows with the Americans as we must have."

Robertson was certainly right about the prospect of rows with the Americans because the United States Treasury had also prepared a proposal for exchange stabilization entitled "Suggested Program for Inter-Allied Monetary and Bank Action." This became known ultimately as the White Plan because its author was Harry Dexter White, Secretary Morgenthau's leading economic advisor during the war years.

In White's earlier years as an academic, he had admired Keynes as a theorist. But now his relation to him was different; he was often cast in the role of a protagonist, opposite a man with a very different social class and cultural background. Actually, he was not wholly at a disadvantage in their various encounters; he was very bright, witty, and capable of forceful and blunt speech, and he was not afraid to stand up to the older, more distinguished economist from the other Cambridge. In truth, as has been said, the relationship between the two was a curious combination of respect and exasperation.

While Keynes's monetary plan emphasized the reconstruction and revitalization of world trade, White's scheme focused more narrowly on the stabilization of exchange rates and the abolition of restrictive practices such as multiple currency rates and bilateral clearing arrangements. Unlike the clearing union, it was a contributory plan with subscriptions originally intended to total at least $5 billion. Keynes envisaged a fund with credits of a much larger amount, $25 billion, enough to induce governments to terminate their discriminatory restrictions on trade. White's plan, too, underwent an evolution as a result of intradepartmental conferences. As circulated in April 1942, it was entitled *Preliminary Draft Proposal for a United Nations Stabilization Fund and a Bank for Reconstruction and Development of the United and Associated Nations*. It covered, therefore, what ultimately became both the International Monetary Fund and the International Bank for Reconstruction and Development.

Meanwhile, Keynes was drafting and redrafting his clearing union proposal, taking advantage of every suggestion that had merit, showing his characteristic receptivity to new ideas. Harrod writes of him being "extraordinary open-minded" and adds that "he was entirely lacking in the kind of obstinacy which so often results from pride of authorship." When his attention was called to a paper that he had presented in 1938 to the British Association at Cambridge on buffer stocks, he took up the idea "with zest" and wrote a full memorandum on the subject. He showed, too, a "passion for detail" that would send him at times to attend low-level committees or lead him to talk with the "backroom boys" with whom he was on good terms because he was ready to learn from them.

When the White Stabilization Fund proposals became available in London in July 1942, Keynes was very favorably impressed with them. He found it encouraging that the objects sought by the Americans were the same as those that he had been pursuing. On the other hand, he felt that the White Plan would be helpful only to countries which already had a gold reserve and would provide assistance to them in proportion to that reserve. Other differences between the two plans were as follows: (1) under the White Plan the fund would operate with what was later called "a mixed bag of currencies"; the clearing union, with bancor; (2) the stabilization fund was designed to correct the maldistribution of gold; the clearing union would relegate gold to a secondary position; and (3) the stabilization fund would abolish exchange control; the clearing union offered no objection to exchange controls and indeed permitted control of capital movements by member countries. There were other structural and procedural differences, but these cannot be examined here.

As a result of his study of the two plans Keynes now made another draft—his fifth—of the clearing union proposal. He set out in a preamble what he regarded as the deficiencies of the American proposals and suggested also that the fund should have executive offices in London as well as New York, with its board of managers to meet alternately in London and Washington. By this time his plan had become the official Treasury proposal, and he was able to write his mother with evident pride, "The final text of my masterpiece on the future currency system of the world has just been printed, ready for communication to the Americans."

Just at this time Keynes had much more to be proud of than his proposal for the future currency system of the world. In May 1942, he had received another honorary degree, a Doctor of Laws, from Manchester University. Then later in the month he heard that his name was to be submitted to the King for a barony of the United Kingdom—he was to be Baron Keynes of Tilton; the phrasing of the title was his own idea. Not only did he have pride of ancestry, as Harrod described his probable reaction, but this honor may have fulfilled a long and deep fantasy which, as has been seen, manifested itself occasionally in his youth. His mother, who was absorbed in the family genealogy, was of course delighted. She wrote him that she liked the coat of arms he had selected and exclaimed, "And now you have put the crown on the family fortunes!"

Many congratulatory letters were written to him on his receipt of this honor, including one even from Lloyd George, leading Keynes to comment in a note, "So I suppose we must regard the latest quarrel as made up." Ex-Prime Minister Baldwin sent "a very nice letter," and the incumbent, Winston Churchill, proposed his health at dinner. He took his seat in the House of Lords in July—he had decided to sit with the Liberals—with his mother and Lydia in attendance. His father received a wonderful letter from Master R. A. Butler of Pembroke, his old college, signed by all the fellows present. The next day his mother wrote him again, saying that it was a proud and happy day for her and ending, "Do tell me how I ought to address you!"

He did not make his maiden speech in the chamber until the following May; it was a short one, but he received plenty of compliments on it, as he put it, "for what they were worth." In the meantime, he had a long weekend with the prime minister at Chequers, reporting after that it was "all very interesting. He [the prime minister] is in present condition a truly supernatural being." Keynes himself was working very hard that spring, but his health was surprisingly good. At this time he liked to dine with an old friend, the Spanish ambassador, the Duke of Alba. He also gave a dinner party at his club for his Treasury associates which was a great success.

To his friends he had become "the squire of Tilton" and, in fact, he played the role of the country gentleman with a certain gusto. Still, according to Vanessa's son, Professor Quentin Bell, who worked as a young man on the Keynes estate, there was something incongruous about Maynard being a country gentleman. His farm workers admired him, but somehow he never established a happy relationship with them. His efforts to please them were sometimes too deliberate, and most of them, accustomed to the familiar, calculable stupidity of their former employer, did not know how to react to such a brilliant master. "In matters of business, he came amongst them like a man armed with a rapier who meets rustics armed only with clubs."

There was a certain awkwardness even when the Keyneses invited friends or local farmers to come to Tilton to shoot partridges. Usually, recounts Bell, such a party was conducted with a good deal of English style—Maynard had a professional keeper and usually an army of beaters—but then when the sportsmen assembled in the hall at Tilton beneath Matisses and Seurats, Lydia might greet them by pointing to the lavatory and saying, "Now you boys will want to do your little waters in here." Alas, it was inevitable because, though her husband had strenuously sought to educate her in the niceties of English deportment, Lady Keynes's natural impishness and love of fun would lead to remarks like that.

On his sixtieth birthday, Keynes was made High Steward of Cambridge, an honorary post that entailed no duties but was associated with many great names in England's past. Again his love of tradition and his sense of being of the elect must have made this occasion a source of great satisfaction. Still, he was more concerned that the swiftly passing years had brought him to the sixty mark. Almost in anguish he wrote his mother, "Well, it's a shocking thing to be sixty. . . . It is a warning, though, that if I were really a civil servant (as I pretend to be), I should be compulsorily pensioned today as no longer capable of carrying on. Old friends are giving me a birthday dinner in King's this evening."

There was no question of his carrying on. All that spring he had worked very hard on the budget and international monetary matters, and in the fall he assumed even more onerous tasks in the formulation of the postwar financial plans in Washington. Happily, he was able to relax at Tilton during part of the summer; he had received a favorable report on his health from Dr. Plesch.

About this time he had to give some avuncular advice to Milo Keynes, Geoffrey's son, who had been exempted from military duty because he was studying medicine. Uneasy about his status and thinking about enlisting, Milo had written Maynard for his view; this in itself showed the affection he had for him. Keynes replied: "My advice is that you should stay where you are—and with a good conscience.

"... It seems to me unlikely that the war will last long enough, at any rate in a fashion which requires great numbers of foot soldiers, to make an interruption of your work really useful to the country.

"In time of war, fortune is not evenly distributed to the children of men; some are lucky, some are unlucky. You, compared with many, are lucky—both in the date of your birth, which settled a good deal, and in the accident of your chosen profession. So enjoy your luck and do not repine. Perhaps some version of abstract justice requires equal suffering. That, perhaps fortunately, is not what happens.

"I am not sorry that you have worried a bit about it. But, if the thing is once settled, do not tease yourself about it any more. Ever your affectionate." The empathy that this letter demonstrates is another illustration of the sensitivity and understanding that Keynes displayed in his relations with those he loved.

In his informal, noncompensated role in the Treasury, Keynes was not part of the chain of executive responsibility, and consequently he was free to offer advice on a wide range of economic and financial problems. He interacted closely with many of the officials, high and low; some seem to have regarded him as something of a prima donna, but that characterization did not seem justified. P. D. Proctor, who knew him well in his advisory capacity, recalled that while he had his faults, "some of them he deployed so engagingly that it is hard to call them so. He was a most unscrupulous advocate; he handled statistics like india rubber and used his sharp, but not bitter tongue, to overwhelm his opponents; he was wildly inconsistent and would maintain opposite theses with equal virulence in two simultaneous correspondences; he would rend a colleague for carrying out a policy which he himself had forced on him a month or two back. What did it matter? It was all part of the delightful process of being turned upside down and, above all, being made to think for oneself where before one had taken things on trust, with a wonderful raree-show of wit and mental acrobatics thrown in."

In the preceding chapter, the way in which Keynes's macroeconomic approach was employed in framing the domestic budget was described; in view of that fact, it was natural for him to take a keen interest in the prospects and problems of maintaining full employment after the end of the war. As it happened, the principal documents submitted by the Treasury to the Committee on Postwar Internal Problems had been prepared by Sir Hubert Henderson, an ex-colleague of Keynes's on the

New Statesman who, nevertheless, was very critical of the new Keynesian theory and pessimistic about unemployment in postwar Britain. Keynes's comments on Henderson's "Note on the Problem of Maintaining Employment" as well as on a similar memorandum submitted by J. E. Meade of the economic section of the War Cabinet provide a most interesting insight on his view of the postwar prospects and of the appropriate economic policy. He contended in his own memorandum that after the war there were likely to be three phases:

"(i) when the inducement to invest is likely to lead, if unchecked, to a volume of investment greater than the indicated level of savings in the absence of rationing and other controls;

"(ii) when the urgently necessary investment is no longer greater than the indicated level of savings in conditions of freedom, but it [*sic*] still capable of being adjusted to the indicated level by deliberately encouraging or expediting less urgent, but nevertheless useful, investment;

"(iii) when the investment is so far saturated that it cannot be brought up to the indicated level of saving without embarking upon wasteful and unnecessary enterprises."

He declared that the first phase might last five years after the close of hostilities, during which controls would be maintained on investment and consumption; in the second phase, these government controls (except on foreign lending) could be suspended, and he then envisioned that "if two-thirds or three-quarters of the total investment is carried out or can be influenced by public or semi-public," then the potential range of fluctuation in investment (and therefore in employment) could be narrowed. Incidentally, he stated his opinion that "the proportion of investment represented by the balance of trade, which is not easily brought under short-term control, may be smaller than before." The length of this second phase was difficult to predict, but he thought that it might last another five or ten years, when the nation would pass insensibly into the third phase. With the onset of this latter "golden age," as he termed it, "the object will be to slowly change social practices and habits so as to reduce the indicated level of saving. Eventually, depreciation funds should be almost sufficient to provide all the gross investment that is required." These statements are exceedingly fascinating because they reveal that his vision of long-term capital saturation, which he had first mentioned in his essay on "Economic Possibilities," still dominated his imagination. In view of the development of compensatory fiscal policy in the United States in the war and postwar periods, it is equally relevant to note that he expressed skepticism about the value of stimulating short-period changes in consumption in order to offset short-period fluctuations in investment, except for a proposal by Meade to vary social security contributions according to the state of employment, which he endorsed. He repeated this opinion in a subsequent letter to Meade and in one to Josiah Wedgewood, a fellow director of the Bank of England. In the latter he stated, "What I attach primary importance to is the scale of investment in the postwar period and am interested in the low interest rate as one of the elements furthering this. But I should regard state intervention as probably a more important factor than the low rates of interest in isolation." He added that he held this view because "at the present stage of things, it is very much easier socially and politically to influence the rate of investment than to influence the rate of consumption." Presently, these passages are important because they are seen by some economists as demonstrating that Keynes was not a believer in fiscal "fine-tuning." It will also be noticed that Keynes endorsed two quotations of Henderson's in the aforementioned note, stating that they "seem to me to embody much wisdom." In the second, Henderson had written: "We are more likely to succeed in maintaining employment if we do not make this our sole, or even our first, aim. Perhaps employment, like happiness, will come most readily when it is not sought for its own sake." In the light of subsequent developments, that might seem to be a very embarrassing endorsement.

From memoranda that Keynes wrote at this time, it is clear he thought that as a result of the technological stimulus provided by the war such British industries as textiles, coal, building, and the whole of the engineering industry, both heavy and light, were learning their lesson and had gone a long way toward overtaking American practice. With characteristic optimism, he remarked that "with modern methods of application behind them, they should again be able to lead the world." However, his involvement in such questions was at the time relatively light because his energies were directed toward the formation of what became the International Monetary Fund.

Early in September 1943, in fact, he and Lady Keynes sailed for the United States. This was their second visit to Washington, and gradually they were becoming more at home in the capital. They were acquiring a circle of close American friends; the Lippmanns, the Frankfurters, the Achesons, the Chatfield-Taylors, and the poet Archibald MacLeish were among their acquaintances. Walter Lippmann later recollected, "My friendship with Keynes was one of the happiest of my life."

At this time Quentin Keynes, one of Geoffrey's sons, was stationed in Washington, and he would sometimes serve as the couple's aide-de-camp and drive them on weekends through the surrounding country-side. It was a relaxing routine between the very arduous negotiations in which Keynes and his colleagues were now engaged.

To illustrate, between September 15 and October 9 the British delegation, headed by Keynes, had no fewer than nine meetings with a United States group led by Harry White, covering a wide range of highly technical matters. The outcome of these sessions was the first draft of what eventually became the International Monetary Fund. The discussions focused on some fourteen points on which there were differences between the two countries. At their close, agreement had been reached on only a half dozen of these topics, though most of the disagreements were resolved before the Bretton Woods conference assembled. These differences reflected the divergent objectives of the two countries in their international economic policies as well as their respective economic and political structures. The United States was interested primarily in achieving multilateralism in international trade (in other words, no discrimination among trading countries), whereas Britain was more concerned with domestic full employment and economic reconstruction in the postwar period. The disparities in the degree of dependence on foreign trade and investment and the differences in the constitutions and political processes of the two countries also seriously complicated the negotiations.

The biggest and most important disagreement financially centered on the differences between the Keynes and White plans which have already been described. The most conspicuous contrast between the two schemes was in the amount of liquid resources they made available. The overdraft facilities of the clearing union would amount to $25 billion, whereas White's stabilization fund was limited to $5 billion. Keynes wanted to resolve the dilemma between internal and external financial stability, to obtain, as he put it, the advantages without the disadvantages of an international gold currency. White was more concerned with ending economic warfare by banning restrictive practices and achieving stability in exchange rates. The plans differed also in their mechanisms of adjustment of international payments. White's proposal contained sanctions against both debtor and creditor countries to induce them to achieve equilibrium in their balance of payments, without recourse to exchange controls or currency depreciation. Keynes's clearing union dealt more leniently with debtors; they could draw upon the liberal overdraft facilities of the union before being called to account. Neither plan made adequate provision for the difficult transitional problems at the end of the war before permanent equilibrium was attained. It is notable that in the public discussion of the two plans the Americans tended to support the White Plan and the British, Keynes's proposals. However, Dennis Robertson, in a letter to Keynes during the negotiations, referred to "the Whines Plan," combining syllables from the names of the two principal negotiators. Keynes himself, in the debate on financial collaboration in the House of Lords, stressed the essential similarity of the two plans.

After much wrangling and more new drafts, the experts achieved a compromise on the establishment of an international monetary fund, and this was published in April 1944. Keynes had yielded to the Americans on many points, but the British were mollified in part by the inclusion in the agreement of a "scarce currency clause" that made it possible for debtor countries to discriminate against, say, American goods if dollars were in short supply. Some Britishers were enthusiastic about this provision, but Keynes apparently thought at first it was "a half-baked suggestion" that would ultimately be withdrawn. Actually, later in his statement to the ministers, he spoke of it as a revolutionary step and took it as a sign of American fairmindedness and sense of responsibility to the other nations of the world. Meetings were held during these months on other topics, such as Keynes's buffer stock proposal, commercial policy, and international investment. Some of these matters were deferred and others were thought to be too contingent on future developments, though progress was made on commercial policy which eventually led to the formation of the International Trade Organization.

Back in England, Keynes was soon immersed in Treasury business. While he made a relatively slight contribution to the drafting of the steering committee's report on postwar employment (the White Paper) that appeared early in 1944, he hailed it as "a revolution in official opinion" and made detailed comments on it. He was disappointed at the failure of the report to emphasize the idea of capital budgeting of investment, but was pleased at the prospect of increased statistics on economic activity, saying "The new era of 'Joy through Statistics' ... can begin" and exulting that "theoretical economic analysis has now reached a point where it is fit to be applied." He was unable to make any further contributions to the evolving report because of his involvement in the formulation of external economic policy and because of illness. White's proposal for an international bank for reconstruction and development had arrived from America and had to be considered. In March 1944, there were meetings with the Dominions, but Keynes was unable to attend because of Dr. Plesch's orders. His heart symptoms had recurred; the doctor required rest in bed. The next month he was well enough to listen to the debate in the House of Commons, where much opposition was being voiced against the international monetary fund. Those on the political left thought that it would interfere with the attainment of full employment; rightists, on the other hand, saw it dooming imperial preferences (a system of mutual preferences in trade among the nations of the British Commonwealth), and bankers thought that it would mean the decline of London as a financial center. Listening to the argument in Commons, Keynes was bitterly disappointed. "I spent seven hours in the accursed gallery, lacerated in mind and body," he wrote. The next day he made a powerful speech in the House of Lords, defending the compromise proposal and reassuring his listeners that Britain's domestic policies would be immune from criticism by the fund. He denied that the proposal involved a return to the gold standard, insisting instead that it was "the exact opposite of it." At one high point in his speech, he asked: "Was it not I, when many of today's iconoclasts were still worshipers of the Calf, who wrote that 'Gold is a barbarous relic'? Am I so faithless, so forgetful, so senile that, at the very moment of the triumph of these ideas when with gathering momentum, governments, parliaments, banks, the press, the public, and even economists have at last accepted the new doctrines, I go off to help forge new chains to hold us fast in the old dungeon? I trust, my lords, that you will not believe it."

Continuing his defense of the proposed fund, he argued that in its operation the primary responsibility for a scarcity of dollars would be placed on the United States because of the scarce currency clause. Nor would Britain have to discard exchange control or reciprocal trade agreements with other countries. Obviously, he had to make some broad concessions to the skeptical; whether they would all be acceptable to the Americans remained to be seen. It would appear that at the time of his plea there were still ambiguities and differences in the understanding of what the White Plan entailed.

By the spring of 1944, the European war was approaching a climax. D-Day was set for June 6, and on the financial front there was also significant movement. In April, Secretary Morgenthau had dispatched invitations to forty-four governments to attend a formal conference on monetary cooperation at Bretton Woods, New Hampshire, on the following July 1. Accordingly, the Keyneses embarked on the *Queen Mary* in the third week of June so that they could attend a preliminary drafting conference at Atlantic City, New Jersey, during the latter half of the month. En route to New York, Keynes found that there were other delegates who might confer on the subject of the international bank, which had not received much attention until now. A meeting was held, he became enthusiastic about the idea, and a draft was prepared.

In Atlantic City, the British sought to reach agreement on some matters (such as exchange stability and the transitional period) which would give them more liberty of action. The Americans were able to make some concessions, so progress was made. At these meetings the British and Americans played the principal parts, with some assistance from the Canadians present; in addition to high officials from the Treasury and the foreign office, also participating were Professors Robbins and Robertson and Redvers Opie who served as economic advisor to the British Embassy. Keynes addressed a joint session with the Americans on the bank, which Robbins described in his journal:

"Keynes was in his most lucid and persuasive mood; and the effect was irresistible. At such moments, I often find myself thinking that Keynes must be one of the most remarkable men that have ever lived— the quick logic, the wide vision, above all the incomparable sense of the fitness of words, all combine to make something several degrees beyond the limit of ordinary human achievement. Certainly, in our age, only the prime minister is of comparable stature. He, of course, surpasses him. But the greatness of the prime minister is something much easier to understand than the genius of Keynes. For, in the last analysis, the special qualities of the prime minister are the traditional qualities of our race raised to the scale of grandeur. Whereas the special qualities of Keynes are something outside all that. He uses the classical style of our life and language, it is true, but it is shot through with something which is not traditional, a unique unearthly quality of which one can only say that it is pure genius. The Americans sat entranced as the godlike visitor sang and the golden light played all around. When it was all over there was very little discussion."

After this preliminary session, the Bretton Woods conference assembled at the Mount Washington Hotel in its beautiful setting amidst the White Mountains of New Hampshire to draft the articles of the international monetary fund and the international bank. In all, there were 730 delegates and their staffs from 44 member countries of the United Nations, not to mention representatives from Congress and the executive offices of the United States government. The agenda for this three-week confab was huge, and when it was completed it resulted in more than 500 documents and 1,200 printed pages. Three commissions were set up to do the work: White chaired one on the fund, and Keynes another on the bank, with the third, which dealt with other forms of international financial cooperation, led by Eduardo Suarez of Mexico. These commissions seldom met; the main work was done in committees, with Keynes and Harry White staying in their rooms to resolve controversial points as needed. Later, Keynes graphically described what it was like: "It is as though . . . one had to accomplish the preliminary work of many interdepartmental and Cabinet committees, the job of the . . . draftsmen, and the passage . . . of two intricate legislative measures numbering anything up to 200 persons in rooms with bad acoustics, shouting through microphones, many of those present . . . with an imperfect knowledge of English, each wanting to get something on the record which would look well in the press down at home, and . . . the Russians only understanding what was afoot with the utmost difficulty. . . . We have all of us worked every minute of our waking hours . . . all of us . . . are all in."

Keynes wrote his mother that he thought he had never worked so continuously hard in his life. His efforts were actually less gruelling than that of the others because Lydia would not allow him to go to meetings after dinner, whereas the other delegates used to sit at interminable sessions until 3:30 A.M. and then start again at 9:30 A.M. Professor Robertson and Edward Bernstein played especially essential roles because they formulated the final texts out of the drafts of the various committees. Keynes wrote his mother, "Dennis Robertson is perhaps the most useful of all—absolutely first-class brains do help!" He also confided that he wouldn't have survived without Lydia, who took constant care to see that he did not overexert himself—no easy task. Otherwise, she had a very boring time because there was no shopping within two hundred miles. As it was, Keynes did have one incident which showed how careful he had to be. After a heavy day's work and dinner with Secretary Morgenthau, he ran upstairs in the hotel to keep an appointment for which he was late. As a consequence, he suffered a light heart attack which kept him in bed; the resultant publicity in England about this attack annoyed him a good deal.

On the last day of the conference Keynes moved the acceptance of the final act in one of his most felicitous speeches. Characteristically, he had references in it to sprites and Puck and Bottom, and even had a good word to say for the lawyers in attendance. At its conclusion the whole body of the assembly rose to their feet and cheered him for several minutes, and as he moved toward the door, they sang, "For He's a Jolly Good Fellow." Professor Robbins later recorded in his journal: "In a way, this is one of the greatest triumphs of his life. Scrupulously obedient to his instructions, battling against fatigue and weakness, he had throughout dominated the conference."

The Keyneses left Bretton Woods for Canada in the limousine of the high commissioner of that country—he had official Treasury business to do in Ottawa, and Lydia wanted to make up for lost time on her shopping; Keynes wrote that she bought a seersucker suit and a pair of shoes every day! Now they were able to relax almost as if they were on holiday. Keynes penned home, "Tell Fay [his old Eton friend] that we confirm his opinion that Canada is a place of infinite promise. We like the people, and if one ever had to emigrate, this should be the destination, not the U. S. A. The hills, lakes, and forests make it a perfect holiday place—and they have the effect of making it a place of peace and repose of mind, such as one never finds in the U. S. A."

As they steamed home he did so with a great sense of elation and accomplishment. In the course of the war his theoretical ideas were making a remarkable impact on two continents, and now in the field of practical politics, through his creativeness and ability to persuade, he had helped to devise proposals for financial cooperation to implement the theory. At the same time he realized much more than most officials the magnitude of the financial and economic burdens that Britain would face at the end of the fighting.

Keynes was not to stay long in England. In the fall he and Lydia were again bound for America on what he termed "the most important and most difficult of all my missions." In fact, he was to substitute for the chancellor of the exchequer in conversations with the Americans on the subject of lend-lease during the period known as "Stage II," as the interval between the defeat of Germany and that of Japan came to be called. The matters to be discussed were extremely intricate and vitally important for the United Kingdom's economic present and future. In the prosecution of the war, certain members of the Commonwealth were piling up huge sterling balances in London; Britain's financial reserves of gold and dollars were running low, and it was estimated that Britain would need to quintuple her exports after the defeat of Germany to stay financially solvent. The Stage II negotiations had been preceded by a meeting between President Roosevelt, Prime Minister Churchill, and the chiefs of staff at Quebec (the Octagon Conference) which was primarily concerned with military strategy, but the British did manage to raise some central economic issues. Secretary Morgenthau was most interested in pushing his plan for the pastoralization of Germany, apparently with the idea that the suppression of German industry would contribute to solving Britain's long-range economic problems. Harry White had been instrumental in drafting the comprehensive plan to permanently reduce Germany to a fifth-rate power and persistently pressed for the adoption of such a policy. But his efforts were forestalled by the opposition of Secretary Henry L. Stimson, Anthony Eden, and the British Treasury. President Roosevelt and Prime Minister Churchill managed a strategic political retreat from that ill-conceived plan.

Agreement was reached on some lend-lease matters at Quebec and on the need to liberate the United Kingdom's export trade; further, the United States was to allow supplies to continue to flow to Britain to enable her to move toward reconversion. The details of these questions were to be worked on by an Anglo-American team of which Keynes was a member. Incidentally, a story is told of this conference that illustrates amusingly the difficulties that statesmen had in keeping up with his very flexible mental processes. It seems that Churchill sent Keynes a note that read: "Am coming around to your point of view," only to get back an answer: "Sorry to hear it; have started to change my mind."

Late in September, Keynes entered into discussions in Washington on these Stage II matters; by that time the British reserve position had grown worse. For these negotiations he had to master all the details of lend-lease and of the British and Dominion economic situation, but he was equal to it, thanks to the assistance of many capable aides, including his old friend and coeditor, Austin Robinson, who was a member of the British party. It was two months of hard work, but in the end the British delegation left satisfied, even though they had obtained few American signatures on the complex agreements. Under the American political order, as some Britishers did not appreciate, executive officials could not commit Congress as readily as is done under a parliamentary system. Through it all, Keynes's health survived the pressures, and so he and Lydia were able to return home for Christmas, bringing back her vast reserve of presents. At Tilton for four days during the holiday season, they had a grand old-fashioned Christmas party for their farm families, with a tree and entertainment provided by themselves and their guests.

Early in 1945, Keynes became involved in another aspect of postwar employment policy. Deputy Prime Minister Clement Attlee had requested advice from the Treasury on the possibility of a postwar capital levy, and James Meade had suggested that the inquiry be widened to embrace the whole question of the postwar burden of the national debt. As a consequence, in January the government established a national debt inquiry, chaired by Sir Edward Bridges and including Professors Meade, Robbins, and Keynes. At the second meeting the latter gave a very thorough exposition of his new theory of the relation between savings and investment, discussing the nature and effects of changes in interest rates and debt management policy generally.

The events of the last year of World War II came with a suddenness that shocked the British and many others, seriously complicating economic adjustment to the postwar era. First, the tragic death of President Roosevelt on April 12, 1945, brought to the White House a president who had not been in close contact with Britain's problems; the necessary changes and the discontinuity in the personnel of the new administration produced difficulties for the British negotiators. Secondly, the defeat of Germany the following month caused an economy wave to sweep through the administration and Congress, and led to the decision that lend-lease supplies were to be restricted to those required for direct use against Japan, though foodstuffs were exempted from this directive. And, lastly, the capitulation of Japan on August 15 caused the abrupt termination of lend-lease to all Allied nations five days later in strict accordance with statute. The latter was the worst bombshell of all, since it meant that Britain had to pay for all future supplies; they had expected some tapering off of aid rather than unilateral cessation without any prior negotiation. Prime Minister Churchill, who was still in office, indicated to Parliament that he was sending Lord Halifax and Lord Keynes back to Washington to enter into immediate conversations with the Americans on a wide range of issues.

Keynes had been studying Britain's desperate economic position through the spring and summer, and had prepared a brilliant memorandum which was eventually endorsed by the Attlee Cabinet at the start of the mission. As he saw it, Britain had three courses open to it: "Starvation Corner" would result from doing nothing about her external debt; it would mean a completely directed economy "somewhat on the Russian model," but it would probably provoke retaliation. The second option, termed "Temptation," would be to accept an American loan of from $5 to 8 billion on their terms; this he also rejected because it would mean that Britain would be faced with a greater external debt than the Germans. The third course, labelled

"Justice," would be to ask (i) for $3 billion "as sort of retrospective lend-lease to replace the equal sum spent in the United States before lend-lease came into full operation, for what afterwards became a common war; and (ii) up to a further $5 billion at call over a period 'at a token rate of interest and on easy terms of repayment.'" If the Americans were agreeable to these ideas, Britain in turn would be able to commit itself to progress toward a multilateral trading system. Keynes knew that he had to convince the United States and Canada that Britain's future strength should be a major concern to them, but he also knew that "our chief trouble will be to prevent the attachment of inconvenient strings."

Early in September he and Lydia were again on the high seas, bound first for Quebec. Keynes would need all the fortitude and good health he could achieve because the negotiations were starting under rather different conditions than had prevailed during the war. After the trials of that struggle, the American people were in a mood to end controls, reduce taxes, and return to normalcy. One symptom of the change was that the Secretary of the Treasury was now Fred M. Vinson, a border-state Democrat who had succeeded the sympathetic Morgenthau shortly after President Truman assumed office. He was one of the conservative Democrats whose influence had grown within the Administration during the later years of the war. He was not disposed to be innovative but rather saw his duty as translating the will of the electorate into governmental policy. Keynes, on the other hand, had become persuaded that he should base his case for further American help on the principle of "equality of sacrifice," and that such assistance might take the form of a $6 billion grant-in-aid or, at the very least, an interest-free loan.

The discussions that were held in the august chambers of the Federal Reserve building opened with an exposition of the British position by Keynes which lasted three days. Completely in command of the complex questions, he spoke with a lucidity and integrity that impressed his listeners. After his opening presentation, the negotiators formed themselves into commissions on financial problems, commercial policy, lend-lease, and surplus property disposal. In these proceedings the discussions extended over three months. It finally became evident that a grant-in-aid or an interest-free loan was not acceptable to the Americans, and they were insistent not only on Britain's commitment to multilateral trade but to sterling convertibility at an early specified date. The British had agreed to the former by signing Article VII of the Mutual Aid Agreement of February 1942. But the latter, and particularly convertibility at a premature date, posed grave dangers for Britain. When this idea was mentioned, according to one American witness, Keynes "hit the ceiling." In the end, the Americans were so insistent that it was agreed sterling should be convertible one year after the effective date of the agreement, on December 31, 1946. This provision had great dangers for the British because it applied to the large sterling balances that the Commonwealth nations had piled up in London during the war. Keynes, however, secured some possible relief in the form of a clause for postponement of convertibility after consultation. As it turned out, when the British made the unsuccessful step to convertibility in 1947, they did not invoke this particular clause.

When he was in England, Keynes had perhaps unduly raised the expectations of his fellow countrymen that he could secure a favorable settlement from the Americans. Now, in the final settlement, they learned that the assistance was to be in the form of a loan, with interest at two percent, extending over a period of fifty years. A five-year period of grace was granted on the payment of interest, and no interest was to be paid in any year in which British visible and invisible exports did not suffice to buy imports at the prewar volume. Keynes had originally asked for $6 billion as a gift, but this was scaled down when it became clear that such an arrangement was unacceptable to the Americans. One American negotiator suggested $4 billion, but Secretary Vinson was of the opinion that Congress would not grant more than $3.5 billion. President Truman relied on the principle of "splitting the difference" and made the amount $3.75 billion. The purpose of this line of credit, as the financial agreement phrased it, was "to facilitate purchases by the United Kingdom of goods and services in the United States, to assist the United Kingdom to meet transitional postwar deficits in its current balance of payments, to help the United Kingdom to maintain adequate reserves of gold and dollars, and to assist the Government of the United Kingdom to assume the obligations of multilateral trade, as defined in this and other agreements." One notes the last clause among these purposes because it was one of the major "strings"; other language in the agreement committed the British to end discrimination in trade and exchange controls. Finally, it should be recalled that the British lend-lease obligations were remitted entirely.

Though he wasn't happy with all of these provisions by any means, Keynes felt that they were the best terms that could be obtained under the circumstances. However, the authorities at home were reluctant to accept the realities; public opinion in both countries, England and the United States, was diverging and making agreement doubly hard. One respected news commentator suggested that the main difficulty facing the negotiators was not "what would be the right and wise thing to do. ... What they are trying to decide, and all of them are seriously troubled by it, is how far Congress and Parliament, the American public and the British, will permit them to solve the problem." It was the old story of the "inside opinion" and the "outside opinion" which Keynes had analyzed in the *Tract* years before, but now it was being illustrated on an international stage.

His difficulties were magnified by the fact that he didn't have much rapport with Secretary Vinson. He was accustomed to rag or tease his fellow negotiators in a most intimate way. His colleagues sought to warn him that in dealing with Vinson he was "dealing with Kentucky." Well, replied Keynes defiantly, "Kentucky will have to like it." One incident illustrates the gulf between the two men. Vinson, in trying to make a point, had asked Keynes a hypothetical question whether Britain's capacity to service a loan would not be enhanced "'if suddenly, tomorrow, you found currency in a cave.' 'Why, of course,' Keynes exclaimed. 'Any currency found in caves—we'll have that in the agreement!' There was a roar of laughter at this riposte. Vinson turned black with rage. He did not quickly forget the incident."

Keynes's role in this delicate diplomacy between the two nations was not an enviable one. Between London and Washington, he was being ground between the upper and the nether millstones. At first he was his optimistic self, as in this early letter to his mother: "The strain of work and responsibility has been severe. ... But I have stood up to it under Lydia's discipline, which has been strict on diet, rest, icebags, and sleep.

"This has been the toughest assignment I have ever had; it doesn't look too good, yet I expect to reach an acceptable conclusion. So I remain ... optimistic, and with the onset of senility, don't worry anything like as much as I use to."

Two weeks later, the strain and the anguish were more noticeable: "But my difficulties in bringing London along to a reasonable compromise are not less than those in moving Washington. Last week was very worrying, and I could not see how I was to extricate myself from all the nets of obstinacy and misunderstanding which were closing in on me from all sides. Obstinate and tiresome though the Americans are, they are full of goodwill and good intentions and kindness. What a country of opposites!" Happily, his spirits were buoyed up at this time by the prospect of going for a picnic with the Walter Lippmanns in Virginia in glorious autumn weather. Two weeks later, when he said he was feeling more fatigue, though still well, he pathetically wrote, "May it never fall to my lot to have to persuade anyone to do what I want with so few cards in my hand!"

Exasperated with the lack of understanding that was being shown in London, on one occasion when he was instructed to avoid any specific commitment on the sterling balances to be included in the financial agreement, he lost his patience. Upon receipt of a particularly obnoxious cable from his superiors, he wired back: "We are negotiating in Washington repeat Washington. Fig leaves that pass muster with old ladies in Threadneedle Street wither in a harsher climate."

Meanwhile, the deadline for the conclusion of the negotiations was nearing; the Americans wanted to "wrap up everything" by the end of the year, and this included approval by Parliament. But now the Cabinet began to waver on the prospect of an interest-bearing loan tied to rigid multilateral commitments. It considered recalling Keynes for further consultation. Instead, since his health would not permit a return by air, it sent over Sir Edward Bridges, a leading Treasury official, but upon his arrival he found that he couldn't budge the Americans either; they were united against further concessions. Faced with the alternative of acceptance of the existing terms or complete failure of the mission, the Cabinet decided on the former course, and so the financial agreement was finally signed on December 6.

The day before, Chancellor of the Exchequer Hugh Dalton, who had studied under Keynes years before, wrote him:

My dear Maynard,
Thank you from the bottom of my heart for all you have accomplished in this long, hard fight—against great odds.
You have, I know, strained yourself, mentally and physically, to the very limit. And you have got us the dollars, without which—though I have more than once thought that a break might have to come—the near future would have been as black as the pit!
I am deeply grateful to you, and so are my colleagues. Even those who least like some details of the agreement are loud in praise of your skill, resource, and patience.
And now come home and rest.
I look forward very much to seeing you again and shaking your hand. Yours ever. . . .

A few days later the Attlee government presented Parliament with an omnibus resolution embracing the financial agreement, the lend-lease settlement, Bretton Woods, and the proposals on commercial policy. The government had a majority in the Commons, but the House of Lords was in control of the Conservatives and many of its members were strongly opposed to the agreement. There was little enthusiasm for it on either side of the House. The tone of the often hostile debate was shown by Robert Boothby's remark that it constituted "an economic Munich," and he warned the Labor government that it had no mandate to "sell the British Empire for a pack of cigarettes."

To those who were critical of multilateralism, the whole agreement seemed like blackmail. Lord Woolton, the Conservative leader, spoke of "dollar dictation" and exclaimed, "I do not like this tacking of a loan to Bretton Woods. It is not a respectable way to treat a great country." While the conservatives saw the American objective as the destruction of imperial preference, a Socialist such as G. D. H. Cole contended that the American government was using "our own economic difficulties arising out of the war as an opportunity to prevent our government from applying its socialist principles to international trade."

On the whole, up to that point the financial agreement had received a very weak defense in Parliament. Then Keynes made a very powerful speech in the House of Lords in which he attacked the opponents of multilateralism with merciless sarcasm. He dismissed their program as an attempt to build up a separate economic bloc that excluded Canada and consisted of countries to which, he said, "we already owe more than we can pay, on the basis of their agreeing to lend us money they have not got and buy only from us and one another goods which we are unable to supply." The government's resolution had passed the House of Commons by a vote of 343–100, but 169 members had abstained; the revolt in the House of Lords subsided after Keynes's masterly statement. In the final decision, a majority of the press and of the public came out for approval; the nation seemed to have reluctantly reconciled itself to the financial agreement.

The following spring the British loan was debated in Congress, and the argument over it became even more acrimonious than that in England. The climate of opinion was equally unfavorable for its passage; polls showed that a majority of the public opposed it. The isolationists in Congress had a field day, and the defenders of the agreement stirred up British antagonism by their indiscreet remarks about breaking up the sterling dollar pool. One congressman, Emanuel Celler of Brooklyn, argued that the loan would "promote too much socialism at home and too much damned imperialism abroad." Such Americans apparently thought that approval of the loan involved an endorsement of the Labor Party's socialism, while another chauvinist congressman announced that he would not vote one dollar for Britain

"as long as they have got the crown jewels in London." Others feared
that the loan would give an impetus to Anglo-American imperialist
elements, antagonize the Russians, or force us into an alliance with
Britain such as Churchill proposed in his Fulton, Missouri, "iron
curtain" speech. In retrospect, the debate did little to improve Anglo-
American relations or understanding. What ultimately turned the tide
in the loan's favor was not the arguments for multilateralism, but the
growing deterioration of relations with the Soviet Union and the
feeling that solidarity and support of Britain was a vital investment in
the unstable world of the "cold war." President Truman signed the law
authorizing the British loan on July 15, 1946.

Upon his return home, Keynes had many activities to resume after
his long stay in the United States. There was his involvement in the
promotion of art and, in particular, the new Covent Garden scheme.
Then there were honorary degrees which came to him in considerable
number at this time. He had been nominated for a honorary doctor of
laws at Edinburgh in April 1945, and now in the new year he received
an honorary doctorate from the Sorbonne. Even more satisfying, in the
same month he was awarded an honorary doctor of science by his own
university. His family was elated, too, by this last distinction and
planned a gathering after the award of the degree; even his father, now
very advanced in age, wanted to walk in the procession, but Maynard
thought that it would not be advisable.

The inaugural meeting of the board of governors of the International
Monetary Fund and of the International Bank was to be held in
Savannah, Georgia, early in March. The agenda for the Savannah
meeting was simple enough—the choice of a site for the fund and the
bank, and the delineations of the functions and salaries of their executive directors. Behind all these matters, however, was a more important
issue relating to the fundamental nature of the new institutions. Were
they purely financial institutions to be managed by a group of civil
servants or would their functioning involve such critical economic and
political questions as to require close control by their member governments? Keynes had argued at Bretton Woods for the former view; he
wanted these organizations to be relatively passive, allowing an almost
automatic access to credit. The Americans, always sensitive to what
Congress would approve and fearful of unlimited financial liability for
the United States as the largest contributor to the fund and the bank,
favored the latter conception. Keynes wanted the new institutions to be
clear of "the politics of Congress and the nationalistic whispering

gallery of the embassies and legations." But the Americans had come to the conclusion that there was no separating the political and economic angles of a loan. Furthermore, Secretary Morgenthau and Harry White as New Dealers had wished to see a transfer of the control of international finance from Wall Street to Washington; the British, having reserved their decision to locate the fund and the bank in the United States at Bretton Woods, had favored New York as the site for the institutions. Earlier, Keynes had discussed this latter matter with officials of the Federal Reserve Bank in New York and found them in complete sympathy. Now, just before the Savannah meeting opened, he learned from Secretary Vinson that the American delegation was under an absolute instruction from the President to place both institutions in Washington, and they were not free to depart from this position under any circumstances. The Truman Administration, it would appear, felt that it was entitled to decide for itself what the locations should be, without consultation with the British or anyone else.

At the opening session of the board of governors, which convened at the General Oglethorpe Hotel on Wilmington Island off Savannah, thirty-eight member countries of the fund were represented. Secretary Vinson was in the chair. The business of the meeting went smoothly until Keynes, in his capacity as governor of the United Kingdom, rose at the rostrum as the final speaker. He spoke of the privilege of being present at the hour of birth of the two institutions, a privilege which he "would not have readily forgone." He was at his most eloquent and imaginative; he chose to speak of a christening attended by the usual fairies, veiled in beards of Spanish moss, and carrying appropriate gifts. The first fairy would bear a multicolored Joseph's coat to signify that these children belonged to the whole world. The second would carry a box of mixed vitamins to nourish the delicate infants. A third, being older, would represent the spirit of wisdom and discretion because if "these institutions are to win the full confidence of the suspicious world, it must not only be, but appear, that their approach to every problem is absolutely objective and ecumenical, without prejudice or favor." But then a darker note emerged in his address; he hoped that there was no "malicious fairy, no Carabosse [he had seen Robert Helpmann in that role in *The Sleeping Beauty* a month before] had been forgotten and coming uninvited should curse the children, 'You two brats shall grow up politicians; your every thought and act shall have an *arrière-pensée;* everything you determine shall not be for its own sake or on its own merits but because of something else.'

"If this should happen, then the best that could befall—and that is how it might turn out—would be for the children to fall into an eternal slumber, never to be heard again in the courts and markets of mankind." It was a remarkable example of how readily he could invoke the fairies from his imaginative mind, as he had done at Versailles years before. The speech reflected, of course, his unspoken thoughts about the way things were turning out, and the reference to Carabosse had not been lost on Secretary Vinson. He assumed that it was he who had been pictured as Carabosse and was greatly displeased. One delegate recalled that he grumbled, "I don't mind being called malicious, but I do mind being called a fairy."

Keynes fought a rearguard action on this matter of the location of the two institutions, but to no avail. The second controversial issue had to do with the functions and compensation of the executive directors of the fund and the bank. The Americans wanted twelve full-time directors for each institution, with alternates, the compensation to reflect their full-time status. On the other hand, the British, wanting to minimize the influence of national governments on the fund's daily operations, thought the directors might hold other posts and be paid accordingly. Under the American proposal, Keynes believed the directors would be drawing high salaries for light duties; the Americans were slipping back into their old notion of the fund as a "schoolmistress" which he had previously denounced. On this question of management he succeeded in securing a compromise on the provision to the effect that both directors and their alternates need not be on full-time duty.

On the third and final issue, that of the renumeration of the directors, the Americans proposed that they should be paid $25,000 (net of taxes) and finally obtained approval for $17,500. Keynes fought against this action vigorously, but again in vain. He termed the salaries to be paid "scandalous" and refused to the very end to give his government's approval to them. To him the problem was that many of the nations voting were prospective beneficiaries from the United States and therefore did not approach these questions objectively. Holding the balance of political and economic power, the Americans were able to "railroad" their decisions through the conference. "It seemed that all his fine protestations on behalf of American goodwill and cooperativeness were belied. They no longer discussed; they decided matters in advance. His castles were falling around him."

His pessimism about the whole situation is evident in the last letter he wrote to Richard Kahn from Savannah on March 13: "The Americans have no idea how to make these institutions into operating international concerns, and in almost every direction their ideas are bad. Yet they plainly intend to force their conception through regardless of the rest of us." The Americans "think they have the right to call the tune on practically every point. If they knew the music, that would not matter so much, but unfortunately they don't."

Five days later he and Lydia took the night train for Washington. Savannah, which he had come to love, now seemed hateful to him. His sleeper was in the front of the train. Next morning, feeling hungry, he walked through the swaying cars to the dining car over the moving platforms. It seemed an endless journey; he was tired and exhausted, but finally he made it. After breakfast, feeling revived, he started back, but before he had gotten far, he collapsed. He was carried to the dining car, where he lay for two hours. It was the worst heart attack that he had ever had.

From New York the Keyneses embarked on the *Queen Mary* for the voyage home. Unfortunately, the liner had a rough passage and in addition was in a filthy state, having been used on the previous voyage to transport brides of American soldiers returning from Europe, many of them with babies. As a consequence, some form of dysentery affected many of the passengers. Keynes had not been well when the ship sailed, but on the second day out he became very weak. To make matters worse, he had to prepare a memorandum for the Cabinet on the deliberations at Savannah. It appears that he at first wrote one that condemned American policy with "extraordinary ferocity" and recommended that the government refuse to ratify the fund and the bank agreement. At this time the American government had not as yet ratified the loan proposal, but such a memorandum would have badly affected the approval of both the American and Canadian loans. Two British officials who had been at Savannah were on board, Sir George Bolton, a Bank of England director, and Ernest Rowe-Dutton, a Treasury civil servant, and they spent much of the voyage trying to persuade Keynes to abandon his draft. Finally, he agreed to destroy it, and Rowe-Dutton reviewed and approved the final memorandum which he submitted to the chancellor of the exchequer two days after his arrival. The result was a sober and well-written document that bore few signs of his previous sense of disappointment and disgust. It read in part:

"Nevertheless, the outcome at Savannah, though discouraging to our previous efforts and a doubtful augury for the efficient working of the new institutions, must be viewed in the right perspective. No specifically British interest has been injured. In the judgment of the members of the British delegation, the strength of the new institutions has been impaired, both for effective action and for unwise interference alike. The outfit of experienced whole-time directors and alternates was imposed by the Americans because they wanted their own representatives to be of the highest caliber and to be free to play a significant and, perhaps, decisive part in the management.

"By the time the conference was coming to an end, the Americans were becoming increasingly conscious of the force and justice of our criticisms. . . . They nearly confessed, in private, to cold feet about the effect of what they had been doing on the daily efficiency of the young twins."

In his memorandum, Keynes took note of the fact that under the Bretton Woods Act, Congress had set up a National Advisory Council to act as "an organ for international collaboration on economic and financial affairs which is relatively independent of Congress." This was a development of which he approved, and he stated that its importance could not be underestimated. Then he added rather significantly, "It may have been rather stupid of us not to tumble to all this sooner. Some of our criticism and opposition may have seemed childish and a little way off the point. But we were not handled in a way which made apprehension easy."

In submitting his memorandum to the chancellor, Keynes suggested that its opening section was "too long and has the effect of giving a greater emphasis of discontent than I really intend. . . . The truth is that my own reactions to the conference changed with further reflections." He had offered to revise the document, but the chancellor did not press him to do so. In its published version as a Cabinet paper, there were no real changes of substance. One paragraph alluding to the bad motives of certain delegates in voting for high salaries for the executive directors was modified slightly, and the following paragraph was deleted:

"In spite of the bad atmosphere of the early days, which I have mentioned above, the conference mellowed, as generally happens, toward the end. My last memory is of Dr. Harry White, with vine leaves (or were they cocktails?) in his hair, leading into the dining room a Bacchic rout of Satyrs and Sileniuses from Latin America, loudly chanting the strains of 'Onward Christian Soldiers.' So we must hope for the best."

This characteristic note of optimism was evident also in Keynes's last published work, his article on "The Balance of Payments of the United States," which did not appear until after his death. In this short essay he examined the statistics on America's external account, saying it was not his object to make definite predictions. Nevertheless, after reviewing the relevant data he remarked that, after pondering these figures, "may not the reader feel himself justified in concluding that the chances of the dollar becoming dangerously scarce in the course of the next five to ten years are not very high?" In the long run, he went on to say, "more fundamental forces may be at work, if all goes well, tending toward equilibrium, the significance of which may ultimately transcend ephemeral statistics. I find myself moved, not for the first time, to remind contemporary economists that the classical teaching embodied some permanent truths of great significance, which we are liable today to overlook because we associate them with other doctrines which we cannot accept without much qualification. There are in these matters deep undercurrents at work, natural forces, one can call them, or even the invisible hand, which are operating toward equilibrium. . . . The United States is becoming a high-living, high-cost country beyond any previous experience," and as a consequence, he argued, it was likely to develop "ways of life which, compared with the ways of the less fortunate regions of the world, must tend toward, and not far away from, external equilibrium." Continuing, he found hope and "provisional comfort" in the contemporary American proposals for an international conference on trade and employment as indicating that the United States was directing its efforts toward creating "a system which allows the classical medicine to do its work." He was quick to say, however, that reliance on the classical medicine was insufficient; quicker and less painful aids such as exchange variation and overall import controls were the most important expedients. "The great virtue of the Bretton Woods and Washington proposals, taken in conjunction, is that they marry the use of the necessary expedients to the wholesome long-run doctrine." In an age of uncertainty, of flux and change, no plans will work for certain. Therefore, in the meanwhile, "for us the best policy is to act on the optimistic hypothesis until it has been proved wrong. We shall do well not to fear the future too much."

Keynes had sent the proofs of this article to White in Washington. Upon returning them, the latter stated that he agreed on the whole with his assessment of the prospective balance of payments of the United States and concluded, "Altogether the possibility of scarcity of dollars during the next five years seems to me, as it does to you, to be remote— barring, of course, untoward international political developments." At the end of the war, White as well as others in Washington looked forward hopefully, believing that mankind would move rapidly toward what Wendell Willkie in a famous phrase called "one world." No influential person in Washington, he later wrote, expressed the expectation that international relations would worsen.

In the postwar era, Keynes's last essay has become a subject of considerable controversy, with some contending, as does Harrod, that Keynes was not professing to be diagnosing the immediate future, but only the long-term trend, whereas Lord Balogh argues that Keynes was predicting that the balance of world trade would be restored "within the next two years," and he says contemptuously, "I wouldn't have even posthumously written that." And even Richard Kahn asserts that "Keynes's vision of the postwar world has turned out to be seriously defective."

The hopes of the architects of the Bretton Woods institutions were suddenly dashed by the stern and unanticipated realities of the postwar years. They had hoped, as has been seen, that after a short period of adjustment the world would move toward political as well as economic adjustment. But in Britain's case, after a short period of illusionary prosperity in 1946, her balance of payments went into catastrophic deficit, and the "dollar shortage" became a monstrous fact. Under the Anglo-American agreement, the British were required to make sterling convertible by July 15, 1947, and when they did so the dollar drain became so huge that they were forced to suspend convertibility the following August. Next, the principle of nondiscrimination in trade had to be summarily scrapped because of the perilous state of her finances. Thus, the abortive attempt to implement multilateralism came to an abrupt end, and a large part of the American loan was dissipated in an effort to stave off financial collapse.

In 1948, with the eventual realization of the seriousness of Britain's financial situation and the general deterioration of economic conditions in Europe, the Marshall Plan and the Truman Doctrine took precedence over all previous arrangements. With the beginning of the European Recovery Program, the International Monetary Fund practically ceased operation and the bank discontinued loans for reconstruction. The world entered the period of the Cold War, and the United States shifted from the goal of global multilateralism to the more limited objective of recovery and integration of Western Europe. Harry White, who had been appointed by President Truman as the United States's executive director of the fund in those early years, concluded: "A candid appraisal of the contributions which both institutions have so far made toward the stated objectives would force us to the conclusion that achievement has been much less than anticipated." Tragically, the world after 1945 was becoming more uncertain and unpredictable than either he or Keynes had ever expected.

In previous chapters Keynes's activities in behalf of such artistic endeavors as the London Artists Association, the Camargo Ballet, and the Arts Theatre of Cambridge have been described. During the early years of World War II, the scope of his involvement in the arts widened further. In February 1942, to be exact, R. A. Butler, then president of the Board of Education, invited him to be chairman of the C. E. M. A. —the Committee for the Encouragement of Music and the Arts. This organization had come into existence in 1939 to administer a sum of twenty-five thousand pounds provided by the Pilgrim Trust, one of the philanthropies of the American, Edward S. Harkness. At first, Keynes hesitated to take on this new responsibility because he was heavily involved in important work at the Treasury and, of course, his health was still uncertain. Nevertheless, he accepted partly because he probably thought that the activity would offset his rather different duties at Whitehall, but more important was the fact, as Harrod pointed out, that he saw in the C. E. M. A. "the germ of a great idea." In the future, as he had prophesied in his essay "Economic Possibilities for Our Grandchildren," there would be a greater amount of leisure for the mass of the population. They should be able to enjoy the fine arts as the rich and the privileged had in the past. Now was the time to prepare the ground.

In the years to follow, right down to his death, he put much of his waning energy and strength into the problems and management of the C. E. M. A., maintaining a close control over its affairs through correspondence with its secretary, Miss Mary Glasgow, from his office in the Treasury or from wherever he was when abroad. He supervised the operation of the C. E. M. A. with remarkable thoroughness, but the various quarrels and controversies which occurred made his position as chairman very wearing. Still, there was a bright side to all the difficulties of his position: the system of guarantee against loss which he had backed was coming into its own; the C. E. M. A. was gradually evolving toward the vision and the principles of the Arts Council under which the government assumed the permanent patronage of the arts. Before World War II ended, it had been decided to put the C. E. M. A. on a permanent basis. Keynes arranged to have the public grant transferred from the Ministry of Education to the Treasury, and in that way ensure that it would be subject to less government interference. On the occasion of the council's formation, he gave a radio talk in which he spoke of the history of the organization and its underlying philosophy, saying:

> I do not believe it is yet realized what an important thing has happened. State patronage of the arts has crept in. It has happened in a very English, informed, unostentatious way—half-baked, if you like. . . .
>
> At last the public exchequer has recognized the support and encouragement of the civilizing arts of life as part of their duty. But we do not intend to socialize this side of social endeavor. [He was referring here to the recent discussions in broadcasts of the Labor Party's program of nationalizing certain industries, and then went on to say,] Everyone, I fancy, recognizes the work of the artist in all its aspects is, of its nature, individual and free, undisciplined, unregimented, uncontrolled. The artist walks where the breath of spirit blows him. He cannot be told his direction; he does not know it himself. But he leads the rest of us into fresh pastures and teaches us to love and enjoy what we often begin by rejecting, enlarging our sensibility and purifying our instincts.

Finally, he spoke in this broadcast of the future of London as an artistic center, though for this purpose, as he said, it was presently "half a ruin." During the war the Queen's Hall had been destroyed; the Royal Opera House at Covent Garden had been converted to a dance hall; and the Crystal Palace had been burned to the ground. But now plans were afoot for the London County Council to allot a site for a National Theatre; the Arts Council had joined with the trustees of the Crystal Palace to make it once again a great People's Palace; and most opportunely, the Covent Garden was to be reopened early the following year as the home of the opera and the ballet.

As chairman of the Covent Garden trustees, Keynes had involved himself in almost every aspect of the preparations for this historic event. He might well have regarded it as the climax of his work for the arts and a symbol of what he hoped would be realized in the future. He closely followed the negotiation of a special Treasury grant to make it financially possible and even extend his attention to the details of the redecoration of the auditorium. At last, on February 20, 1946, the opera house opened under the new auspices. The program had been carefully chosen; it was to be *The Sleeping Beauty,* with Margot Fonteyn dancing as the princess and Robert Helpmann doubling in the parts of Carabosse and the prince.

The evening turned out to be a virtual national triumph. Keynes subsequently received letters from various guests who told how much they had been moved by the gala event. A few days later he wrote his mother about his own reactions: "The first night went off in great glory. . . . The occasion seems to have struck them, that is, the audience, emotionally with a greater strength than one had anticipated. The explanation is, I think, that many people had come to fear in their hearts more than they were admitting to themselves that all the grace and elegant things from the old world had passed permanently away, and it caused an extraordinary feeling of uplift when it was suddenly appreciated that perhaps they had not entirely vanished."

Occasions such as this reopening of Covent Garden gave him deep satisfaction because they were so much in accordance with his social philosophy of promoting the art of living. Just the year before he had made a speech which has become a famous illustration of his viewpoint. It was at a dinner given him by the Council of the Royal Economic Society upon his retirement from the editorship of the *Economic Journal* after thirty-three years in the post. According to those who heard it, it was one of his best—light, smoothly flowing, and full of amusing anecdotes about eminent figures and those with whom he had contact as secretary of the society. Finally, he came to the toast. He said, "I give you the toast of the Royal Economic Society, of economics and economists, who are the trustees"—and here he paused—"not of civilization, but of the possibilities of civilization." His phrasing of that toast was not a mere rhetorical flourish; it embodied a distinction which he felt was very significant. Economics was important—he had devoted his life to it—but he believed that it should be regarded as but the means to the higher achievements of art and culture.

CHAPTER 15

The End of a Passionate Pilgrimage

Men must endure
their going hence, even as their coming hither,
Ripeness is all.

Shakespeare

IN THIS STUDY of Keynes's life, much attention has been given to the nature of his sexuality and its relationship to his creativity, but his social background, or what Harrod termed "the presuppositions of Harvey Road," has not been neglected in interpreting his complex personality. From his secure middle-class family and his elite education at Eton and Cambridge, his close friendship with the sophisticates of Bloomsbury and intimate acquaintance with the rich and powerful, he had evolved into the Liberal aristocrat, supremely and often arrogantly confident of his intellectual superiority. With this heritage and class position there went, fortunately, a strong sense of social responsibility, of *noblesse oblige,* if you will, which explains his patriotism and dedication in matters of statecraft and social welfare. In his middle years and beyond, he became less the rational individualist and more impressed with "the extraordinary accomplishments of our predecessors" and with the social "rules and conventions skillfully put across and guilefully preserved," to quote his essay, "My Early Beliefs." In short, in his own mind he became more conservative and interested in preserving those traditions of social life which he thought sustained freedom of belief, of action, and of individuality.

One recalls these familiar facts about his life because they illuminate a document which his mother disclosed after his death and which, strangely enough, has not been mentioned or commented upon by his previous biographers. She said that it was from an introduction to a book which he never had time to write, possibly an autobiography. It is reproduced in full:

The pride of ancestry has in great measure passed away, for the fast-rising wave of democracy day by day obliterates the old landmarks and traditions that were once held dear.

Some, however, I trust there are, to whom the great names of the past remain in living memory, who shape their course in the world under a deep sense of responsibility of bearing them; and fill their appointed position and do their appointed work

commanded
by the dead gaze of all their ancestors.

One does not need to elaborate on these solemn lines which remind us so much of the sentiments and even of the phraseology of deTocqueville or of Edmund Burke. Obviously, their reference is to the Keynes Connection, of which his early study of the family's genealogy had made him so conscious; this surely was one figure that was woven indelibly into the Keynesian carpet. Still, if one lived with so severe an idealized image—always conscious of "the dead gaze of all their ancestors"—one could conceive it contributing to emotional conflict, but perhaps Keynes wrote in this vein more for literary purposes than for any other. In any case, he never published these lines. But enough of such speculation; it is more worthwhile to turn back to an account of his last days.

Upon his return from the monetary conference at Savannah, Keynes had quickly resumed his routine of work and leisure; he would spend the middle of the week in London and repair to Tilton on the weekends for rest and relaxation. He still had responsibilities at the Treasury and the Bank of England, and there were meetings of the Provincial Insurance Company and of the National Gallery trustees that he had to attend. There was time, of course, for dining, visiting art exhibits, and enjoying the ballet and the theatre. Even when he was at Tilton he could not relax completely, for there would be a daily pouch from the Treasury containing papers which he had to review. Still, it was an agreeable life, and he was well enough to enjoy it. Honors continued to come to him—in April he was recommended for election as a fellow of the Royal Society and asked to accept appointment to the Order of

Merit. In his letters he was still capable of the old banter and gaiety; for example, in writing to his brother-in-law A.V. Hill to accept the former honor, he closed thus: "Something clearly gone wrong with the weather. This is definitely not old England. Is it sunspots? My mother is quite extraordinary well; my father writes long letters. Must be sunspots."

In these last years he liked to have the family with him, especially when he was at Tilton. At Christmas 1945, he and Lydia had their nephews down for the shoot, and on Boxing Day they had a large party for their neighbors with songs, sketches, and refreshments in which some of the Charlestonians joined. Lydia distributed her "Washington booty" on a lavish scale, and all had a jolly time. The following spring she and he planned to spend the whole week before Easter at Tilton; his parents met him in Bloomsbury, and they drove down together to the Sussex estate.

The weather remained beautiful so that the whole family was able to enjoy the English countryside at its best. Keynes loved to stroll about the grounds of his farm, discussing plans for the workers with his loyal helper, Logan Thomson. One morning, clad in his favorite country garb, a Cambridge blue jacket and a shady straw hat, he showed his mother the supply of meat that was being prepared for the Easter feast. A calf had been killed, and joints of meat were laid out on a table in the barn, allocated to the families according to the number of its members. It was a time of serenity and peace after the long ordeal and trials of the war.

In his leisure, Keynes liked to sit in his garden reading—he was still buying rare books, especially of Elizabethan authors, and he would peruse what he had bought. Another of his great delights was to go to the top of Firle Beacon on the Downs where he used to walk with his friends in the old days, enjoying the fabulous view of the countryside and the sea.

Twice before during the week he had driven with his mother to the top of the Downs. It was a lovely Saturday afternoon, and he decided that they should drive to the area; Lydia was to join them, and he declared his intention to return with her by the footpath. He had not done this for years since his long illness, and he felt quite fit to do it now. His mother lovingly recalled the scene:

"I stood watching the two of them as they disappeared gradually below the brow of the hill—he, bending down to her in animated talk, she looking up in eager response. She told me afterwards that he had been describing a poem by Thomas Parnell, a friend of Pope and Swift, the first edition of which had just reached him. He had ended with the words: 'And the meaning of it all is: "Don't worry, there is always divine Justice." '"

"On Easter Sunday after breakfast," as Lydia later informed the Lippmanns, "there came a sudden fatal heart attack—I lost my everything." Maynard had been taken from her in his sixty-second year. She would survive another thirty-five years.

In her *Memorial,* Keynes's mother expressed her deep sorrow at her son's passing with a few lines from Shelley:

> Thou were the morning Star
> among the living,
> Ere the pure light had fled;
> Now, having died, thou are as
> Hesperus, giving
> New luster to the dead.

At the memorial service in Westminster Abbey a few days later, Lydia and she walked up the aisle with John Neville Keynes, aged ninety-three, and heard the grateful tributes of the nation and the condolences of Keynes's many friends. Earlier, under the graceful fan vaults of King's College Chapel, they had listened as Maynard's old colleague, Provost John Sheppard, recited a passage from *The Pilgrim's Progress:* "I do not repent me of all the trouble I have been at to arrive where I am. My sword I give to him that shall succeed me in my pilgrimage, and my courage and skill to him that can get it."

The Transformation of Keynes's Vision

The children of the mind are like the children of the body. Once born, they grow by a law of their own being and if their parents could forsee their future development, it would sometimes break their hearts.

R. H. Tawney, *Religion and the Rise of Capitalism*

WHILE THE QUARTER CENTURY following World War II has been dubbed "the age of Keynes," it would in fact be preferable and more accurate to speak of it as the "age of the Keynesians," thus distinguishing the ideas of the followers from those of their creator. In the closing pages of *The General Theory,* Keynes had speculated about what reception capitalistic society would give his new theory, asking, "Is the fulfillment of these ideas a visionary hope? Have they sufficient roots in the motives which govern the evolution of political society? Are the interests they will thwart stronger and more obvious than those which they will serve?" He did not attempt to answer those questions in his book, but concluded instead with his famous tribute to the power of ideas in history. He thus neglected the possibility, already demonstrated by the intellectual history of the theories of Adam Smith, Karl Marx, and others, that rather than being ignored his new theory might undergo a strange and drastic metamorphosis in the course of its exegesis.

While Keynes was still alive, a Keynesian school of thought had developed in the United States, Great Britain, and some other countries, and during World War II this intellectual development was strengthened and resulted, for example, in the British White Paper on

Employment and the adoption in the United States of the Employment Act of 1946. Both these nations thereby made strong commitments to full employment as a goal of public policy. Governments in Canada, New Zealand, Australia, Sweden, and the Union of South Africa likewise accepted national responsibility for high levels of employment at the war's end.

In attacking the postulates of the classical economics, Keynes was in effect challenging Bentham's pleasure/pain calculus on which the "real" relations of the theory were based. He sought to overthrow this basic concept of a balancing mechanism by an appeal to what he repeatedly called "the facts of observation." In criticizing this century-old tradition of inventing axioms and making logical derivations from them, he allied himself instead with those thinkers who relied on intuition and who "preferred to see the truth obscurely and imperfectly rather than to maintain error, reached indeed with clearness and consistency and by easy logic, but on hypotheses inappropriate to the facts." In doing so, he brought economics methodologically closer to twentieth-century modes of thought in other fields of science, but his challenges to the conventional rationalism in economics was so profound that it is a wonder not that it was distorted, but that it survived at all.

Keynes saw the economic world differently from his more orthodox colleagues; his cognitive style or epistemological assumptions derived from his experience in a world war, the social and economic upheavals of the twenties and thirties, the rise of totalitarian governments in Europe, his personal involvement in finance, and not least his homosexuality, which made him skeptical of the conventional way of looking at reality. The misprision or misconstruction of *The General Theory*, which it is now increasingly recognized as having occurred, can be significantly explained by the differences between his cognitive style (with its heavy emphasis on the facts of observation and intuition, and the shifting historical, uncertain context of economic problems) and that of the relatively nonhistorical and highly mathematical approach of the so-called neo-Keynesians. In other words, a significant shift in the methodological frame of reference occurred as Keynes's ideas in *The General Theory* passed from him to his followers. Professor Alex Leijonhufvud, who has closely studied this aspect of macroeconomics, goes so far as to generalize, "It is in the nature of all major innovations that the visions of the innovator and his audience are at variance. A flawed model is therefore likely to be 'corrected' so as to correspond to the interpreter's view of the world rather than the originator's. This, it appears, is what happened to Keynes."

The process of interpretation of *The General Theory* had started promptly with a crucial article by Professor J. R. Hicks of Oxford entitled "Mr. Keynes and the Classics" that was based on a paper he had read at that university in September 1936, six months or so after the book's publication. In this celebrated essay, which was written before Keynes's *Quarterly Journal of Economics* article on "The General Theory of Employment," Hicks took the latter to task for attacking the classical economics and sought to show that, with revisions and qualifications, *The General Theory* was not new. In this "potted version" of the book, as Hicks himself later termed it, he argued that its economics was not much different from Marshall's doctrine. He presented a diagram in his article, based on the general equilibrium approach historically associated with the name of Léon Walras, a nineteenth-century French economist, and showing both the real and monetary sectors of the economy, in which both the rate of interest and the level of output were simultaneously determined. This so-called IS–LM framework seemed to be pedagogically useful in demonstrating certain aspects of Keynes's theory; it was taken up and popularized by Professor Hansen and became a fixture in textbook expositions of Keynesian economics for the next forty years, even though it is a rather dubious representation of the latter. Keynes had written Hicks about his article, expressing relatively little disagreement with it to the latter's surprise, though he did object to making the inducement to invest dependent on current income rather than on the relevant variable, expected income for the period of the investment. The fact is that Hicks's analysis is hardly compatible with "the dark forces of uncertainty and ignorance" which Keynes had emphasized in his article on "The General Theory of Employment" published about this time, because it conceals the pervasive existence of uncertainty in economic life. In brief, the attainment of equilibrium in the economic system, even in so-called special cases, is not guaranteed.

Later, in the forties, other economists, such as Alvin Hansen, Lawrence Klein, Franco Modigliani, and Paul Samuelson, expounding the "simple mathematics of income determination," moved closer to what is called "the neoclassical synthesis," at the same time cutting Keynes's analysis loose from real historical time. Samuelson's forty-five-degree diagram in his famed text, which was useful in popularizing the essentials of demand management via fiscal policy and other such treatments, tended to ignore the aggregate supply analysis of Keynes's original work and its related economic implications. By the fifties, Professor Sidney Weintraub began criticizing this orthodox macroeconomics as a perversion of Keynes's views, and then in 1968, Professor Leijonhufvud even more forcefully and brilliantly showed the disparity between the economics of Keynes and that of the dominant school of Keynesianism.

Finally, in 1976, to conclude this brief account of a bizarre episode in intellectual history, Professor John Hicks, by now a Nobel laureate, practically recanted on his famous diagram, stating that the failure of the neoclassical Keynesians to recognize the concept of calendar time in Keynes's theory meant that the Keynesian revolution had gone off "at half cock. The [general] equilibrists did not know that they were beaten. . . . They thought that what Keynes had said could be absorbed into their equilibrium system; . . . I must say that that diagram [the IS–LM] is now much less popular with me than I think it still is with many people. It reduces *The General Theory* to equilibrium economics; it is not really *in* time."

Does that statement signify the end of the neoclassical thermidor or counterrevolution in macroeconomic theory? Professor Shackle, a respected British theorist, summed up his view of the state of affairs somewhat earlier when he wrote, "He [Keynes] did escape from the made-up world of classicism; his critics did not."

Considering this tale of misinterpretation and distortion in the exposition of Keynes's economics in the years after World War II, there is a certain fascination in an earlier correspondence between him and an American economist, John M. Clark, about the development of the Keynesian school in the United States. The latter had written the Cambridge economist to say that his "income flow" analysis was a coherent, logical, theoretical system or formula which had the quality of a mechanism and possessed tremendous analytical power, adding that it also had "the danger of too undiscriminating application." Keynes replied to Clark, stating that he agreed about "the danger of a school, even when it is one's own." Nevertheless, despite his evident misgivings about possible misinterpretations of his original conceptions, in succeeding years the Keynesian revolution was formalized, culminating finally in "the neoclassical synthesis."

This version of Keynesianism in the form of the income-expenditure model was expounded in innumerable texts and became the basis of much academic discussion in the postwar period. In the realm of public policy, despite allegations of the "truimph" of Keynes's ideas, fiscal legislation in these years was actually rather timid and unimaginative, with the possible exception of the 1964 tax cut in the United States. In Great Britain likewise, even though both the Conservative and Labor governments were committed to full employment, obsession with the foreign balance of payments and the "stop-go" character of financial management conspired to produce an economic performance which Keynes would hardly have approved. In the United States, as *The Economist* acutely observed in 1967, "the mortal defect in the application of Keynesian economics . . . is that it will always be a one-way street, used when the economy needs stimulation, not when it requires restraint." Thus, while the academic expositors of Keynes's ideas were casting them in the mold of "a static and nonhistorical system" which deviated markedly from his own conception, the implementation of his theory in the form of fiscal policy was being reduced to one of expansionary demand management rather than the economics of control. Keynes himself had contributed somewhat to this distortion of his theory. As Leijohhufvud has pointed out, he "had tried to bend the tools of traditional statics to the analysis of a conception of a basically 'dynamic and historical nature.' In a way, the degree to which he succeeded is remarkable. Had this method indeed been entirely sound, however, it is hard to imagine that Keynesianism would have succumbed so meekly to the neoclassical synthesis. This, I think, is true, although his concentration on the involuntary unemployment state, in which the income constrained-process ensues, also contributed to mislead later economists into giving his system a purely static and ahistorical interpretation."

However one distributes the blame for this tragic misinterpretation, the result was a fundamental revision of Keynes's own vision and goal of the economic process, causing his old colleague Joan Robinson to declare, "The twenty-five years after the war that passed without a major recession has been called the Age of Keynes, but it was not much like his vision. It turned out closer to Kalecki's sardonic description of the regime of the political trade cycle."

Keynes's classic had been formulated basically as an answer to the problem of the Great Depression. It was, as Hicks contended, an "economics of depression" in that it was a short-run analysis that abstracted from the elements of reality not pertinent to the solution of the problem of mass unemployment. Richard Kahn, who was in an excellent position to know, has written also that "Keynes's concepts were designed for an economy in a state of depression." In particular, by working with a constant wage unit, Keynes's model of the economy excluded the price level from consideration, though he did have a chapter on that subject in which he explained that there could be "semi-inflation" before full employment was reached. He wrote that these critical points of semi-inflation have "a good deal of historical importance. But they do not lend themselves to theoretical generalization."

Keynes himself had a considerable respect for monetary policy in coping with the problem of economic instability, but the Keynesians in policy making in the postwar years showed a distinct preference for fiscal remedies. Then, in the mid-1950s as inflation began to be a more important problem, the "new economics" was challenged by a monetarist counterrevolution led principally by Professor Milton Friedman who resurrected the quantity theory in a new conceptual form.

In the midst of this battle of economic theories during and after World War II, the institutional structure of the Western industrial economies continued to undergo rapid change and transformation. In general, governments came to play a larger part in their economies' functioning, and other elements of the welfare state, such as social security and unemployment insurance in the United States, grew more important. Corporations expanded in size, and trade unions became more powerful in some sectors of the economy. In time, with Western industrial cultures committed to mass consumption and economic growth as a source of jobs, these collective organizations readily adapted themselves to the new Keynesian regime of demand management, utilizing their market power to assure themselves of a stable or increasing share of the national income. In the United States, for example, as President Eisenhower candidly observed in his last message to the nation, there was the emergence of what he called "the military-industrial complex" as the large corporations and their associated unions became ardent supporters of what has been termed "military Keynesianism"; in short, both groups were willing to accept deficit financing of the federal budget, so long as the government did not compete with them, but provided jobs and profitable new business. Increasingly, too, the large unions bargaining with such oligopolistic corporations were able to secure higher money wages or more liberal fringe benefits because the resulting higher unit costs could be passed on to the ultimate consumer. In the light of such institutional developments, Professor Galbraith could persuasively argue in 1973 that "the Keynesian revolution was, in effect, absorbed by the planning system of the large corporations."

In the world of economic theory as contrasted with this real world of incessant institutional change, developments have proceeded along two broad lines. One path, as has been seen, involved an effort to reconcile Keynesian macroeconomic theory with neoclassical microeconomics, resulting in the neoclassical synthesis. The members of this school refer to themselves as neo-Keynesians; Professor Joan Robinson has baptized them more irreverently as the "bastard Keynesians."

The other path of theoretical development evolving out of Keynes's thought has taken the form of an extension of his analysis along Ricardian lines, though not on the basis of perfect competition or the marginal productivity theory of distribution, both of which were abandoned by the members of this school of thought. This group has been referred to in the professional literature as "post-Keynesian." Basically, it sees itself as developing a new paradigm in economic theory since, in its view, the Keynesian revolution was aborted. It seeks to extend Keynes's analysis in his *Treatise on Money* and *The General Theory* to an economic system expanding over time in the context of actual history rather than of theoretical equilibrium. (In this connection, Professor Shackle, a keen British student of contemporary economic theory, reports that Keynes once remarked, "Equilibrium is blither.") The dynamic element in this theory is an outgrowth of Harrod's early work on the trade cycle which he discussed with Keynes while he was still alive. Another contribution stems from Joan Robinson's *The Accumulation of Capital* and Lord Kaldor's important article, "Alternative Theories of Distribution," both published in 1956.

Another distinguishing characteristic of post-Keynesian theory is that it treats distribution as a variable linked to the rate of economic expansion. Further, it retains the fundamental approach to a monetized economy outlined by Keynes in his last two major works and emphasizes the role of discretionary expenditures in determining the level of economic activity. Finally, this approach operates with a very different conception of the pricing decision than that employed in neoclassical economics, giving more attention to the price policies of the oligopolistic corporations and contends that the markups of such companies take account of their investment needs as well as covering their current costs.

This bare sketch of theoretical developments since Keynes's passing (no account has been taken of radical political economy) must suffice at this point because it is desired to make some closing remarks about public policy as influenced by his thought. It has been demonstrated above that the objective of Keynesian "demand management" policies in the post-1945 years was full employment without inflation, but controversy persists over the extent to which action based on the "new economics" has been beneficial. Those who support Keynesianlike measures assert that in the quarter century after World War II the world economy grew faster than in any similar span of years largely because of the stabilizing effects of the policies he advocated. On the other hand, there are those who with an equal sense of conviction argue that "the age of Keynes" inevitably led to "the age of inflation" because of the inflationary bias in the politicians' fondness for public spending and deficits rather than for taxation and budgetary surpluses.

With the emergence of "stagflation" in the sixties—defined as deep recession in terms of unemployment coupled with continued rapid inflation—there has been stronger criticism to the effect that we are witnessing "the crisis in Keynesian economics" or, more definitely, "the end of the Keynesian era." Defenders of the economics of Keynes as distinguished from the formulations of his followers, such as the neo-Keynesian school, attribute the declining relevance of the latter's doctrine to its lack of historical perspective. In the former's view "hydraulic Keynesianism"—so called because it conceives of the economy in terms of disembodied and homogeneous flows of expenditure, income, or output—does not properly take account of the changing institutional structure of capitalism. The neo-Keynesians are said to lack the vision or historical imagination to redefine their models to conform with current economic reality.

In retrospect, it is not likely that Keynes himself would have been prone to such a shortcoming if he had lived longer to confront the complex economic problems of the postwar era. While he was by no means infallible, he showed his reluctance on various occasions in his life to accept what was being urged in his name. No genius, it has been said, is ever a true disciple of the "ism" which is named after him; that epigram is probably especially apropos in his case. His contemporaries have cited several instances in which he expressed misgivings about the policies which were being espoused or supported in his name. Indeed, one critic goes so far as to say, "It may well be that, had he lived, he would have become the leading anti-Keynesian."

In all this rather futile debate over what Keynes would have done or said if he was still alive, one needs to recall that in *The General Theory* he himself emphasized that "the object of our analysis is not to provide a machine or method of blind manipulation which will furnish an infallible answer, but to provide ourselves with an organized and orderly method of thinking out particular problems; . . . this is the nature of economic thinking."

If the economic and cultural dilemma of our time is to be surmounted or at least alleviated, it must be in the spirit that animated his "long struggle to escape from the habitual modes of expression and thought" of his day, not by conformance to the Keynesian letter. The free spirit with which he worked never stopped him from seeking better solutions. Once he jotted down on a piece of paper a few words which succinctly expressed his philosophy: "I do not hope to be right. I hope to make progress."

Like most politico-economic systems, Keynes's thought as set forth in *The General Theory* and some of his earlier writings may be said to have related analytical and normative elements. In the preceding section it has been explained how his personal analytical vision was misinterpreted or distorted in the course of the development of "Keynesian economics." Similarly, it can be suggested that his normative vision, his conception of the good life or the good society, has been somewhat obscured by its ideological absorption in the policy goal of full employment. It is true, in fact, that he himself contributed to this tendency, but it also is clear that he regarded economics and economic means as but instruments for the attainment of the larger ends of civilized life. His position on these social ends or values does not seem to have undergone any significant change in the years after the publication of *The Economic Consequences of the Peace.* His stance on means, however, underwent a basic shift in the twenties and thirties toward acceptance of "a positive policy of collective action through government." With his vision of the diminishing marginal propensity to consume in the long run and the parallel tendency of investment opportunities to decline in the advanced capitalistic economies, he was disposed to accept the prospect of slower economic growth and the possibility of satiation with respect to the consumption of material goods. This Millsian attitude toward the idea of the stationary state was quite in line with his philosophic conservatism. As has been noted above, he was quite explicit about his anti-Benthamism, indicating *laissez-faire* capitalism as being "absolutely irreligious, without internal union, without much public spirit, often, though not always, a mere congeries of possessors and pursuers." With this outlook, and assuming another hundred years of economic growth led by the purposive men, he could hope and believe, as he put it in the preface to his *Essays in Persuasion,* that "the day is not far off when the Economic Problem will take the back seat where it belongs, and that the arena of the heart and head will be occupied, or reoccupied, by our real problems—the problems of life and human relations, of creation and behavior and religion."

The latter is a rather broad statement, and some will find it a strange concern for an economist, but it must be kept in mind that Keynes was more than an economic technician or mere specialist. He regarded himself as a Marshallian in his general approach to economic life, and that meant he was concerned about man's ultimate ends. With his Apostolic background, his knowledge of Burke's and Coleridge's thought, and his probable familiarity with Edward Carpenter's views, one is inclined to conclude that he was prepared to substitute a humanist ethic of human fulfillment in community for what he regarded as the obsolescent ethic of work and saving.

Recently, in a highly critical portrait of Keynes, the late Harry G. Johnson and his wife pictured his approach to art and leisure as being essentially that of the patrician who sought to do good with a strong Victorian philosophy of social betterment. He thought of these subjects, they contended, "in terms which reflected his own social background" and "looked forward to more automation, less work, and the enrichment of leisure time by cultural activities provided by the state." While Keynes was undoubtedly influenced by the esthetic movement of the late nineteenth century in Great Britain, the Johnsonian interpretation overlooks altogether the liberating effect of Bloomsbury with its interest in the visual arts on his developing value system. Is it not plausible to believe that he was enthusiastic about art because he felt that Victorian industrial society strongly repressed important dimensions of human existence? In his own life he had known the stimulus that the arts give to the imagination, and he probably agreed with Matthew Arnold in his *Culture and Anarchy* that without an informing vision all the technique or "machinery" of civilization has no meaning. Further, it is a misconception to think that he favored "cultural activities provided by the state"; in this area of life he was a strong advocate of individual enterprise with some degree of state subsidy.

Having said that, it is necessary to admit that Keynes's vision of abundance in another generation or two (as set out in his "Economic Possibilities for Our Grandchildren"), with men freed to cultivate the art of life itself, does reflect the values and even wishful thinking of an Edwardian esthete. One should note, however, that he qualified his prophecy with the observation that his "Utopia" would not be within sight even in that period unless mankind acquired the will to control population, the determination to avoid wars, and the willingness to entrust to science matters which are properly the concern of science. His vision of the future assumed that factory work could not be made psychologically satisfying and fulfilling, and therefore the goal should be to mechanize it completely and seek to establish the conditions of fulfillment in leisure time. This conception is no longer acceptable to many modern social scientists; in the latter's view a postindustrial society will aim to make work as well as leisure self-fulfilling. Keynes's image of the future had the limitations of its time; it was vintage 1930 and resembles the progressive thought that emerged in Great Britain and the United States at the turn of the century. *In toto* it still remains as remote from realization as when it was conceived, though certain important aspects of it are still coming to the fore, as will be noted below. World War II, with its enormous destruction of natural and manmade wealth, and its profound dislocation and impoverishment of Great Britain, obviously necessitated a revision of his forecast of the economic and cultural future, but he was generally too ill and preoccupied with other duties during that period to undertake it.

In appraising this phase of Keynes's thought, one should recognize that he was usually able and willing to admit his errors and to sense his own limitations. Four years before his death he said as much in a very poignant letter to his old friend and co-worker Oswald Falk: "The basic trouble is, I expect, that I am getting too elderly to have any ideas well in advance of the times. I have run as fast as I could and am now out of breath. If practical forces catch one up, what can I do about it? Certainly no help to transfer into monkish rumination."

In a practical assessment of the man, what were the values which were foremost in his moral outlook? Or, more broadly, what were the values implicit in his life-style which he predicted would eventually prevail when "we shall once more value ends above means and prefer the good to the useful"? Aside from his interest in the arts and his championing of that individualism which safeguarded "the variety of life" even for "immoralists," it is probable that he would emphasize love and reason, which he said were so central in the life of his friend Dillwyn Knox. Like E. M. Forster, he was critical of the Englishman with an "undeveloped heart," and in his own case this attitude extended to a genuine concern for others, the ideal of public service which his mother's life so nobly exemplified. In his essay "Economic Possibilities for Our Grandchildren," he stated that in the future economy of growing abundance, "it will remain reasonable to be economically purposive for others after it has ceased to be reasonable for oneself." This was the motive he exhibited so magnificently in working for the common good during World War II and after, even though his personal means made it wholly unnecessary.

Another value that stands out in his life was the admiration and appreciation of women—for his mother and wife, for Mary Marshall, Vanessa Bell, Ottoline Morrell, and others. This kind of sympathy and understanding undoubtedly derived from the duality of his own personality that enabled him to perceive (as Jean Baker Miller has perceptively stated quite recently) that male-led society, in projecting into women's domain some of its most troublesome and problematic necessities, may have "simultaneously and unwittingly delegated to women not humanity's 'lowest needs but its highest necessities'—that is, the intense, emotionally connected cooperation and creativity necessary for human life and growth."

It has often been remarked that the reputation of the great figures of history fluctuates with the passing of time because each successive generation tends to view them from a different perspective. As an instance of this, at present Keynes is being appraised mainly from the standpoint of the validity and usefulness of his economic theories—his critics write books about him with somber titles such as *The Shadow of Keynes* or *The Consequences of Keynes*—but the time may come, given the fleeting relevance of many economic theories, when he will be damned or praised more for the cultural or noneconomic values and ethos which he and Bloomsbury stood for than for the "deficit finance" or unbalanced budgets. In general and in philosophic perspective, his life points to a humanist world view, a transformation of the human outlook that would fuse the unifying powers of the poetic imagination with the powers of reason.

In terms of economics as it relates to these ultimate ends, it is clear that to Keynes, if not to the Keynesians, full employment was decidedly a short-run macrogoal, since it grew out of a short-run analysis of the Western economies at a particular juncture of their history. To make it a superior, overriding end of social policy would be tantamount to accepting what to him was the detested Benthamite principle of making the increase of the happiness of the greatest number the sole or dominant criterion of government action. In the long run of actual historical time, Keynes did not see us as "all dead," as his quip so often quoted out of context has it; he envisioned economics rather as the handmaiden of civilization, the servant of all the arts of living rather than of the single standard of GNP growth. In other words, on the basis of this reading of his work, he was not a growth fetishist.

Economic growth in the past has been fostered by the heavy emphasis placed on so-called instrumental values, many of which derive from a patriarchal heritage that neglected the expressive values of life. It is the belief of several commentators on the contemporary American scene that our culture is currently in the process of making an epochal shift in the balance between instrumental values and the expressive ones.

Daniel Yankelovich, a pollster and philosophical analyst of changing values in the United States, finds that "by the seventies a majority of the American people had reached a conclusion comparable to that reached by cultural critics of industrial civilization in earlier years, namely, that our civilization is unbalanced, with excessive emphasis on the instrumental, and insufficient concern with the values of community, expressiveness, caring, and with the domain of the sacred." Judging by his own efforts at reform, as one who valued ends above means, Keynes would probably approve of such efforts at a cultural awakening, believing as he did that the challenges of life and of civilization could only be met by flexible persistence.

The present time, both nationally and internationally, is one of such deep, radical, and convulsive change that there is a widespread personal and social disorganization. In such a disordered world, people seek direction and a sense of vision from their leaders. The ancient Chinese, it is said, considered this problem in terms of what they called "the dilemma of the Reformation and the Sage. But so long as the world is disordered, no Sage can appear. The resolution of the dilemma lies in the fact, often proved in history, that genius can arise in spite of disorder, pointing to a way out." Maynard Keynes patently displayed elements of genius in his life, and while alive pointed to a way out of the desperate conditions of the Great Depression. Whether his values as described in the preceding pages point in a direction leading out of the present cultural crisis, each individual must decide for himself.

Source Notes

The sources of quotations and other matter in the following notes are indicated in the consecutive order in which they appear in each chapter. The abbreviation CW refers to *The Collected Writings of John Maynard Keynes,* published for the Royal Economic Society by Macmillan and Cambridge University Press in thirty volumes.

INTRODUCTION

The issue of *Time* magazine referred to is that of December 31, 1965; see also *Business Week,* February 5, 1966; M. Keynes, ed., *Essays on John Maynard Keynes;* K. Martin, review of Harrod's life of Keynes, *New Statesman and Nation,* February 3, 1951, p. 133; the Oxford memoir on Harrod is in W. A. Eltis et al., eds., *Induction, Growth and Trade* (Oxford: Clarendon Press, 1970), p. 14; R. F. Harrod, *The Life of John Maynard Keynes;* A. Robinson, "John Maynard Keynes, 1883–1946," *Economic Journal,* March 1947, pp. 1–68; the quote from Henry James will be found in the front of L. Edel, *Henry James, 1843–1870, The Untried Years* (Philadelphia: J. B. Lippincott, 1953).

CHAPTER 1

The Dictionary of National Biography (Oxford: Oxford University Press); F. A. Keynes, *Gathering Up the Threads,* appendix I; M. Keynes, ed., *Essays; N. G.* Annan in *J. H. Plumb, Studies in Social History; Keynes Papers,* King's College Library; Harrod, *The Life; Diary of John Neville Keynes,* Cambridge University Library; J. C. Gowan, *Development of the Psychedelic Individual* (Buffalo, N.Y.: Creative Education Foundation, 1974), pp. 54, 71; J. T. Spence and R. L. Helmreich, *Masculinity and Femininity, Their Psychological Dimensions, Correlates and Antecedents* (Austin: University of Texas Press, 1978), *passim.*

CHAPTER 2

D. Garnett in *The New Republic,* May 7, 1951; J. Gathorne-Hardy, *The Old School Tie;* Letters of J. M. Keynes, King's College Library; *Diary of J. N. Keynes;* J. Boswell, *Christianity, Social Tolerance and Homosexuality;* A. J. Ayer, *Part of My Life;* V. L. Bullough, *Sexual Variance in Society and History;* A. L. Rowse, *Homosexuals in History;* P. Fitzgerald, *The Knox Brothers;* J. Jaynes, *The Origins of Consciousness and the Breakdown of the Bicameral Mind.*

CHAPTER 3

B. Russell, *Autobiography of Bertrand Russell, 1872–1914;* M. Holroyd, *Lytton Strachey;* E. M. Forster, *Goldsworthy Lowes Dickinson; Diary of J. N. Keynes;* D. Proctor, ed., *The Autobiography of G. Lowes Dickinson;* B. Askwith, *Two Victorian Families;* H. M. Hyde, *The Love That Dared Not Speak Its Name;* P. Levy, *Lytton Strachey, The Really Interesting Question and Other Papers;* F. M. Brookfield, *The Cambridge Apostles;* CW, vol. X; B. Russell, *Autobiography;* P. Levy in M. Keynes, ed., *Essays;* R. F. Harrod, *The Life;* N. Annan, "The Rise of the Cult of Homosexuality" (mimeographed); J. Ronsley, *Yeats' Autobiography.*

CHAPTER 4

Erich Fromm quote is from A. Maslow, ed., *New Knowledge in Human Values,* p. 157; the second Fromm quote is from his *Escape from Freedom,* p. 184; Harrod, *The Life,* M. Holroyd, *Lytton Strachey;* J. M. Keynes, *Letters;* Strachey, *Letters;* R. Wohl, *The Generation of 1914;* M. Secrest, *Being Bernard Berenson;* R. Shone with D. Grant in M. Keynes, *Essays;* R. Shone in D. Crabtree and A. P. Thirlwall, eds., *Keynes and the Bloomsbury Group,* Letters of L. Strachey to L. S. Woolf (The Berg Collection), New York Public Library; Letters of J. M. Keynes to D. Grant, The British Library; CW, vol. XV.

CHAPTER 5

J. M. Keynes, *Letters;* CW, vols. XI and XV; G. Keynes, *Henry James at Cambridge;* G. Keynes, *The Gates of Memory,* pp. 196–198; correspondence of J. M. Keynes and G. L. Strachey, The British Library; K. Pearson and E. M. Elderton, *A First Study of the Influence of Parental Alcoholism on the Physique and Ability of the Offspring,* London, 1910; Keynes's article was in the *Economic Journal,* September 1911; W. M. Bartley III, *Wittgenstein;* R. S. Sayers, "The Young Keynes," *Economic Journal,* June 1972, p. 592.

CHAPTER 6

The quotation of B. A. Corry is from D. Crabtree and A. P. Thirlwall, *Keynes and the Bloomsbury Group;* "Old Bloomsbury" in V. Woolf, *Moments of Being;* M. Holroyd, *Lytton Strachey and the Bloomsbury Group: His Work, Their Influence;* Gordon Square as a lion's house is from N. Nicolson and J. Trautman, *The Letters of Virginia Woolf,* vol. 2; Q. Bell, *Bloomsbury* and the same author's *Virginia Woolf, A Biography;* P. Rose, *Woman of Letters, A Life of Virginia Woolf;* V. Woolf, *Roger Fry;* R. F. Harrod, *The Life;* R. Williams in Crabtree and Thirlwall, *Keynes;* L. Woolf, *Sowing;* on the Mill-Colridgean school, W. Stone, *The Cave and the Mountain, A Study of E. M. Forster;* H. S. Hughes, *Consciousness and History;* CW, vol. X; on the Homintern, see N. Annan, "The Rise of the Cult of Homosexuality," (mimeographed); on androgyny in Bloomsbury, see C. Heilbrun, *Toward the Recognition of Androgyny;* V. Woolf, *A Room of One's Own;* Bullough, *Sexual Variance;* B. Fassler in *Signs,* Winter 1979; on bisexuality and creativity, see S. Freud, "Dostoevsky and Parricide," *Collected Papers,* vol. V. New York: Basic Books, 1960, pp. 222–242; H. Lowenfeld, "Psychic Trauma and Productive Experience in the Artist," *Psychoanalytic Quarterly,* 1941, 10; E. Bergler, *The Writer and Psychoanalysis,* New York: Doubleday, 1950; M. Besdine, "The Jocasta Complex, Mothering and Genius," *Psychoanalytic Review,* 1968, 55, 2; C. Martindale, "Femininity, Alienation in the Creative Personality,"

Psychology, 1972 issue; for discussion of the relationship between genius, psychopathology and creativity, see *American Imago,* vol. 24, nos. 1–2, 1967; E. Carpenter, *The Intermediate Sex;* C. Tsuzuki, *Edward Carpenter,,* p. 154; S. Freud, "Civilized Sexual Morality and Modern Nervousness" in his *Collected Papers;* S. Arieti, *Creativity, the Magic Synthesis;* A. Koestler, *The Act of Creation;* S. T. Coleridge, *Specimens from the Table Talk of Samuel Taylor Coleridge;* Keynes's essay on W. Stanley Jevons in the CW, vol. X; B. Wiley, *Samuel Taylor Coleridge;* on the androgyny of homosexuals, see L. C. Bernard and D. J. Epstein, "Androgyny Scores of Matched Homosexual and Heterosexual Males," *Journal of Homosexuality,* Winter 1978; L. Woolf's remark about Keynes being "a mental hermaphrodite" is quoted in L. Edel, *Bloomsbury, A House of Lions,* p. 49; L. Edel, *Henry James: The Conquest of London, 1870–1881;* M. Keynes, *Essays;* on the three B's, see J. Jaynes, *The Origin of Consciousness in the Breakdown of the Bicameral Mind,* p. 44.

CHAPTER 7

The Henry James quote is from P. Lubbock, ed., *Letters of Henry James,* vol. 2, p. 384, as quoted in S. Hynes, *The Edwardian Turn of Mind; CW, vol. XVI; Economic Journal,* September, November, and December 1914; Letters of J. M. Keynes; Diary of J. N. Keynes; Keynes-Strachey correspondence; C. Hassal, *Rupert Brooke, A Biography;* Letter of F. Bekassy to N. Olivier, dated May 1915, enclosed in a letter from the latter to J. M. Keynes, October 22, 1915; Harrod, *The Life;* Nicolson and Trautman, *The Letters of Virginia Woolf,* vol. 5; Letter of J. M. Keynes to Mrs. B. Bagenal, July 8, 1945; M. Holroyd, *Lytton Strachey,* vol. 2; P. Levy in M. Keynes, *Essays;* A. O. Bell, *The Diary of Virginia Woolf,* vol. 1; CW, vol. XXVI; Nicolson and Trautman, *Letters of V. W.,* vol. 2; letter of A. Marshall to J. M. Keynes, June 13, 1917; D. Garnett, *The Flowers of the Forest.*

CHAPTER 8

H. Elcock, *Portrait of a Decision;* CW, vols. X and XVI; H. C. Hoover, *The Ordeal of Woodrow Wilson;* D. Garnett in M. Keynes, *Essays;* A. O. Bell, *The Diary of Virginia Woolf,* vol. 2; S. A. Schuker in *The Journal of Economic Literature,* March 1980; P. F. Drucker, *Adventures of a Bystander;* J. M. Keynes *Letters;* Harrod, *The Life;* S. G. Millin, *General Smuts;* E. Mantoux, *The Carthaginian Peace, or The Economic Consequences of Mr. Keynes;* CW, vols. II and XVII; A. S. Link, *The Higher Realism of Woodrow Wilson and Other Essays;* J. Campbell, *Lloyd George, The Goat in the Wilderness, 1922–1931;* Letter of J. M. Keynes to D. Grant, July 17, 1919; Veblen's essay is in M. Lerner, *The Portable Veblen;* A. Rothenberg, *The Emerging Goddess;* C. Barnett, *The Collapse of British Power;* W. Churchill, *The Aftermath;* Harrod, *The Life;* letter of J. M. Keynes to F. Frankfurter, September 20, 1919; CW, vol. XVII; B. Baruch, *The Making of the Reparation and Economic Sections of the Treaty;* CW, vols. X and XVII; *The Collected Poems of W. B. Yeats;* Harrod, *The Life;* on paleological thinking, see Arieti, *Creativity;* J. A. Schumpeter, "Science and Ideology," *American Economic Review,* March 1949, p. 350; Harrod, *The Life;* H. E. Jensen, "J. M. Keynes as a Marshallian," *Journal of Economic Issues,* Spring 1983; H. E. Phillips, *Felix Frankfurter Reminisces.*

CHAPTER 9

CW, vol. XVII; H. Minsky in oral remarks at the American Economic Association; Harrod, *The Life;* P. N. Furbank, *E. M. Forster, A Life;* letters of "Sebastian" Sprott to J. M. Keynes, August 27, 1922; also letter of G. L. Strachey to S. Sprott, June 6, 1922; R. B. Braithwaite in M. Keynes, *Essays;* CW, vols. VIII and X; P. Samuelson's remark in R. Lekachman, *Keynes's General Theory: Reports of Three Decades;* S. Hynes, *The Edwardian Turn of Mind;* R. Buckle in M. Keynes, *Essays;* C. W. Beaumont, "The Return of Lopokova" in *Dancing Life,* November 1921; D. Kramer, *Heywood Broun, A Biographical Portrait;* R. Buckle, *Diaghilev;* M. Keynes, *Essays;* L. Woolf, ed., *A Writer's Diary;* Nicolson and Trautman, *The Letters of Virginia Woolf,* vol. 2; CW, vols. III and XVII; on "trustees of the possibility of civilization," see "Economic Possibilities for Our Grandchildren" in CW, vol. IX, p. 332; Nicolson and Trautman, *The Letters of Virginia Woolf*, vol. 3; Rowse on Chicherin in A. L. Rowse, *Homosexuals in History;* CW, vol. XVIII.

CHAPTER 10

CW, vol. IX; D. Dillard, "Revolutions in Economic Theory," *Southern Economic Journal,* April 1978; R. Skidelsky, "The Reception of the Keynesian Revolution," in M. Keynes, *Essays;* J. R. Commons, *The Legal Foundations of Capitalism;* CW, vol. IX; on W. Whitman's phrase, see J. Kaplan, *Walt Whitman, A Life;* CW, vols. IV and XVIII; the Moggridge quote is from D. E. Moggridge, *Keynes*, p. 70; Harrod, *The Life;* W. W. Bartley III, *Wittgenstein;* CW, vol. X; CW, vol. IX; D. E. Moggridge, *British Monetary Policy, 1924–1931;* on Keynes as conflicting with class consciousness, see H. J. Sherman, *Elementary Aggregate Economics;* the quote on "the creative possibilities of freedom" is from S. E. Harris, *John Maynard Keynes, Economist and Policy Maker;* C. W. Beaumont, *The Diaghilev Ballet in London;* the description of Lopokova by the American reporter was quoted in the obituary of the *New York Times,* June 30, 1981. For anecdote about the barristers, Harrod, *The Life;* Nicolson and Trautman, *The Letters of Virginia Woolf,* vol. 3; CW, vol. X; on Lytton Strachey's apparent anti-Jewish bias, see letter of G. L. Strachey to D. Grant, August 15, 1905, in which he asks, "Are you really able to paint with all the juives and Americaines and schoolboys and spook-secretaries creeping and crawling around?"

CHAPTER 11

Nicolson and Trautman, *The Letters of Virginia Woolf,* vol. 3; A. O. Bell, *The Diary of Virginia Woolf,* vol. 3; CW, vol. VI; "The British Balance of Trade, 1925–1927," in *Economic Journal,* December 1927; CW, vol. IX; J. M. Buchanan and R. E. Wagner, *Democracy in Deficit;* J. K. Whitaker, *The Early Economic Writings of Alfred Marshall, 1867–1890;* A. C. Pigou, *The Theory of Unemployment,* p. 252; J. Robinson, *Contributions to Modern Economics;* CW, vol. IV; G. Mehta, *The Structure of the Keynesian Revolution* quotes the remark about the "invasion by barbarians" which was made by A. W. Marget in his *Theory of Prices,* chapter 1; J. B. Conant, *On Understanding Science;* J. A. Schumpeter, *History of Economic Analysis;* A. W. Coats, "Sociological Aspects of British Economic Thought (ca. 1880–1930); *Journal of Political Economy,* 1967; J. A. Hobson, *Confessions of an Economic Heretic;* CW, vols. V, VI, and VII; Lord Annan, "The Victorian Counter-Culture" (mimeographed); D. H. Robertson, "The Monetary Doctrines of Foster and Catchings," *Quarterly Journal of Economics,* May 1929; CW, vols. XII and XIII; B. Ohlin, "The Reparation Problem," *Economic Journal,* June and September 1929; S. E. Harris, *John Maynard Keynes;* J. Robinson, "Kalecki and Keynes" in *Contributions to Modern Economics;* CW, vol. IX for Keynes's essay on "Economic Possibilities for Our Grandchildren"; D. Dillard, "The Influence of Keynesian Economics on Contemporary Economic Thought," *American Economic Review,* May 1957; R. Skidelsky, *The End of the Keynesian Era; The* (London) *Times,* January 14, 1937; M. J. Weiner, *English Culture and the Decline of the Industrial Spirit, 1850– 1980;* D. Patinkin, *Keynes's Monetary Thought, A Study of Its Development;* CW, vol. V; G. L. S. Shackle, *The Years of High Theory;* CW, vol. VII; K. Wicksell, *Geldzins and Guterpreise;* H. Parker Willis in the *New York Times,* March 22, 1931.

CHAPTER 12

Samuelson quote is from J. E. Stiglitz, ed., *The Collected Scientific Papers of Paul A. Samuelson;* D. Patinkin and J. Clark Leith, *Keynes, Cambridge, and the General Theory;* Harrod, *The Life;* R. F. Kahn, "The Relation of Home Investment to Unemployment," *Economic Journal,* June 1931; *The New Statesman and Nation,* March 7, 1931; Lord Robbins, *Autobiography of an Economist;* CW, vol. IX; Patinkin and Leith, *Keynes, Cambridge, passim;* CW, vols. V and XIII; F. von Hayek in *Economica,* August 1921 and February 1932; CW, vol. XXIX; CW, vol. XIII; J.

Robinson, "Parable on Savings and Investment," *Economica,* February 1933; *The New Statesman and Nation,* A. Boyle, *The Fourth Man;* J. M. Keynes in "Democracy and Efficiency," *New Statesman and Nation,* January 28, 1939; Nicolson and Trautman, *The Letters of Virginia Woolf,* vol. 5; D. E. Moggridge, "From the *Treatise* to *The General Theory:* An Exercise in Chronology," *History of Political Economy;* Nicolson and Trautman, *Letters,* vol. 5; A. Bell, *The Diary of Virginia Woolf,* vol. 5; Q. Wright, ed., *Unemployment as a World Problem;* D. Patinkin, *Keynes's Monetary Thought;* CW, vol. XIII; CW, vol. XXIX; *The Collected Poems of W. B. Yeats;* G. Holton, "On Trying to Understand Scientific Genius," in Y. Elkana, ed., *The Interaction between Science and Philosophy;* T. S. Kuhn, *The Structure of Scientific Revolutions;* D. Dillard, "A Monetary Theory of Production: Keynes and the Institutionalists," *Journal of Economic Issues,* June 1980; CW, vol. VII; A. Rothenberg, *The Emerging Goddess;* CW, vols. IX, X, and XIII; J. Robinson in *Contributions to Modern Economics;* Harrod, *The Life;* F. Perkins, *The Roosevelt I Knew;* letter of W. Lippmann to J. M. Keynes, Yale University Library; CW, vol. XXIV; Keynes-Shaw correspondence in CW, vol. XXVIII; J. C. Gilbert, *Keynes's Impact on Monetary Economics* for Keynes's relations with D. H. Robertson and A. C. Pigou from which much in the text is drawn; G. R. Feiwell, *The Intellectual Capital of Michael Kalecki;* G. L. S. Shackle, *The Years of High Theory;* CW, vol. XIV; Samuelson in Patinkin and Leith, *Keynes, Cambridge;* A. Robinson in Patinkin and Leith, *Keynes, Cambridge;* D. C. Colander and K. J. Koford, "Realitic and Analytic Syntheses of Macroeconomics and Microeconomics," *Journal of Economic Issues,* September 1979; J. Robinson, *What Are the Questions and Other Essays;* G. L. S. Shackle, *The Nature of Economic Thought;* CW, vol. XIII; Council of King's College, *John Maynard Keynes, A Memoir;* M. Keynes, *Essays;* on "Art and the State," see CW, vol. XXVIII.

CHAPTER 13

The epigraph on geniuses is taken from Keynes's essay on Isaac Newton, for which see CW, vol. X; B. Beckhardt in *Political Science Quarterly,* December 1936; on the Keynesian literature, see Moggridge, *Keynes;* J. R. Hicks in the *Economic Journal,* June 1936 and in *Econometrica,* April 1937; R. F. Harrod in *Econometrica,* January 1937; J. K. Galbraith, "How Keynes Came to America," in M. Keynes, *Essays;* R. Lekachman, *The Age of Keynes;* H. Stein, *The Fiscal Revolution in America;* D. Dillard, "The Influence of Keynesian Economics on Contemporary Economic Thought," *American Economic Review,* May 1957; R. V. Gilbert et al., *An Economic Program for American Democracy;* U. S. Printing Office, *Hearings* of the Temporary National Economic Committee; A. H. Hansen, "Economic Progress and Declining Population Growth," *American Economic Review,* 29 (1930); J. M. Keynes's letter to J. N. Keynes, July 15, 1936; *The New Statesman and Nation,* July 18, August 8, 15, 29, and September 12, 1936; the remark about Keynes and the New Deal being "synonomous profanities" is in H. Stein, *The Fiscal Revolution;* the four articles by Professors Leontief, Robertson, Taussig, and Viner are in *The Quarterly Journal of Economics,* November 1936; J. M. Keynes, "The General Theory of Employment," CW, vol. XIV; G. L. S. Shackle in *The Years;* R. Mortimer's review was in *The New Statesman and Nation;* J. M. Keynes, "How to Avoid a Slump," *The Times,* January 12–14, 1937; T. W. Hutchison, *Keynes versus the Keynesians;* J. M. Keynes, "Some Economic Consequences of a Declining Population," CW, vol. XIV; letter of Sir Walter Langdon-Brown to Mrs. F. A. Keynes, June 11, 1937, King's College Library; Keynes on Tinbergen in CW, vol. XIV; P. Samuelson in R. Lekachman, *Keynes's General Theory, Reports of Three Decades;* Keynes's quote from J. M. Blum, *From the Morgenthau Diaries, Years of Crisis, 1928–1938;* K. Martin, *Editor;* on W. Lippmann's quote on the "battalion of death," see R. Steel, *Walter Lippmann and the American Century;* E. Wiskemann, *The Europe I Saw;* Nicolson and Trautman, *The Letters of Virginia Woolf,* vol. 6; A. N. L. Munby in M. Keynes, *Essays;* on Newton, see CW, vol. X; on Isaac Newton see F. E. Manuel, *A Portrait of Isaac Newton,* which has much influenced the author; G. R. Feiwell, *The Intellectual Capital,* and private correspondence with the author, dated July 17, 1979; letter of D. Grant to J. M. Keynes, April 21, 1937; J. M. Keynes to Mrs. F. A. Keynes, August 29, 1938; J. M. Keynes to K. Martin, October 1, 1938, is quoted in K. Martin, *Editor;*

The Times, September 28, 1939; CW, vol. XXIII; *The Times,* November 14 and 15, 1939; CW, vols. IX and XXII; J. M. Keynes, "The United States and the Keynes Plan," *New Republic,* July 29, 1940; J. M. Keynes to Mrs. F. A. Keynes in CW, vol. XXII; J. M. Keynes to Dr. Plesch quoted in Harrod, *The Life;* letter of J. M. Keynes to Mrs. F. A. Keynes, June 28, 1940; J. M. Keynes to W. Salant, July 28, 1941, quoted in Harrod, *The Life;* letter of J. M. Keynes to the Archbishop of York, November 19, 1941.

CHAPTER 14

R. S. Sayers, *Financial Policy, 1939–1945* (Official History of the Second World War); R. N. Gardner, *Sterling-Dollar Diplomacy;* see also J. M. Blum, *From the Morgenthau Diaries;* Harrod, *The Life;* CW, vol. IX; J. K. Horsefield, *The International Monetary Fund, 1945–1965,* vol. I, *Chronicle;* Lord Kahn, "Historical Origins of the International Monetary Fund," in D. Crabtree and A. P. Thirlwall, eds., *Keynes and International Monetary Relations;* on H. D. White see *Harry Dexter White, A Study in Paradox;* Harrod, *The Life;* J. M. Keynes to Mrs. F. A. Keynes, August 23, 1942; July 2 and 9, 1942; Q. Bell, "Recollections and Reflections on Maynard Keynes," in Crabtree and Thirlwall, eds., *Keynes and the Bloomsbury Group;* letters of J. M. Keynes to Mrs. F. A. Keynes, June 5, 1943 and July 21, 1943; P. D. Proctor in *John Maynard Keynes, A Memoir;* CW, vol. XXVII (our brackets); A. H. Meltzer, "Keynes's *General Theory:* A Different Perspective," *The Journal of Economic Literature,* March 1981 and comments on same in *ibid.,* March 1983; the Lippmann quote is from R. Steel, *Walter Lippmann;* Letter of D. H. Robertson to J. M. Keynes, July 13, 1943, in the Franklin Roosevelt Library; J. M. Keynes to Mrs. F. A. Keynes, October 18, 1943; CW, vol. XXVII; Keynes's House of Lords speech is taken from S. E. Harris, *The New Economics;* Harrod, *The Life;* J. M. Keynes to Mrs. F. A. Keynes, August 7, 1944, and September 7, 1945; the Keynes-Vinson dispute is discussed in Gardner, *Sterling-Dollar;* J. M. Keynes to Mrs. F. A. Keynes, October 21, 1945, and November 4, 1945, and November 21, 1945; H. Dalton letter to Keynes from CW, vol. XXVII; debate on the British loan in the United States is from Gardner, *Sterling-Dollar;* J. M. Keynes to Mrs. F. A. Keynes, February 15, 1946; Keynes's speech at Savannah is in Harrod, *The Life;* J. M. Keynes letter to R. F. Kahn is in Thirlwall, *Keynes and International Monetary Relations;* on Keynes abandoning his draft, see G. Bolton, "Where Critics Are as Wrong as Keynes Was," *The Banker,* November 1972; J. M. Keynes, "The Balance of Payments of the United States," *Economic Journal,* June 1946, reproduced in CW, vol. XXVII; H. D. White quotes from Rees, *Harry Dexter White;* Lord Balogh quoted in Thirlwall, *Keynes and International;* R. F. Kahn quote is from R. F. Kahn, "On Re-reading Keynes," *Proceedings* of the British Academy, vol. LX; the last H. D. White quote is from Gardner, *Sterling-Dollar;* on Keynes's activities at the C.E.M.A., see M. Glasgow, "The Concept of the Arts Council," in M. Keynes, *Essays;* Harrod, *The Life; The Listener,* July 12, 1945; letter of J. M. Keynes to Mrs. F. A. Keynes, February 23, 1946.

CHAPTER 15

Mrs. F. A. Keynes in *In Memoriam, Papers of John Maynard Keynes,* King's College Library; J. M. Keynes to A. V. Hill, April 15, 1946; *In Memoriam;* Lady Keynes to Helen and Walter Lippmann, The Lippmann Collection, Yale University Library.

AFTERWORD

CW, vol. VII; on Keynes's challenge to rationalism, see P. V. Mini, *Philosophy and Economics, The Origins and Development of Economic Theory,* esp. pp. 228–230; J. R. Hicks, "Mr. Keynes and the Classics, A Suggested Interpretation," *Econometrica,* April 1937; Keynes-Hicks exchange of letters in CW, vol. XIV; S. Weintraub, "Micro-Foundations of Aggregate Demand and Supply," *Economic Journal,* 1957; also Leijonhufvud, *On Keynesian Economics;* Hicks's recantation in A. M. Tang et al., *Evolution, Welfare and Time in Economics;* G. L. S. Shackle, "Keynes and Today's Establishment in Economic Theory: A View," *Journal of Economic*

Literature, June 1973; J. M. Clark's letter to J. M. Keynes, July 24, 1941, and the latter's reply, July 26, 1941, from the Roosevelt Library, Hyde Park, N. Y.; *The Economist,* September 23, 1967; J. Robinson quote from M. Keynes, *Essays;* R. F. Kahn, "Some Aspects of the Development of Keynes's Thought," *Journal of Economic Literature,* June 1978; on the monetarist counterrevolution, see H. G. Johnson, "The Keynesian Revolution and the Monetarist Counter-Revolution," in *Further Essays in Monetary Economics* by the same author; on this subject, see also J. C. Gilbert, Keynes's *Impact on Monetary Economics,* esp. chapter 6; Galbraith quote is from J. K. Galbraith, *Economics and the Public Purpose;* on post-Keynesianism, see A. S. Eichner, *A Guide to Post-Keynesian Economics;* Keynes's remark about equilibrium being blither is from G. L. S. Shackle, *Keynesian Kaleidics;* J. Robinson, *The Accumulation of Capital and The Review of Economic Studies,* 1957, as (2); the phrase, "the end of the Keynesian era" is from J. R. Hicks, *The Crisis in Keynesian Economics;* on the lack of historical perspective in neo-Keynesian economics, see R. X. Chase, "Keynes and U. S. Keynesianism: A Lack of Historical Perspective and the Decline of the New Economics," *Journal of Economic Issues,* September 1975; also A. Coddington, "Keynesian Economics: The Search for First Principles," *Journal of Economic Literature,* December 1976; on the possibility of Keynes becoming the leading anti-Keynesian, see H. W. Hutt, *The Keynesian Episode, A Reassessment;* Keynes's quote from Johnson and Johnson, *The Shadow of Keynes;* on Keynes's shift in the twenties, see W. S. Gramm, "Natural Selection in Economic Thought: Ideology, Power and the Keynesian Counter-Revolution," *Journal of Economic Issues,* March 1973; on *laissez-faire* capitalism, see "A Short Review of Russia," in CW, vol. IX; H. G. and E. Johnson, *The Shadow of Keynes;* letter of J. M. Keynes to O. S. Falk, June 2, 1942; the Miller quote is from J. B. Miller, *Toward a New Psychology of Women;* D. Yankelovich, *New Rules, Searching for Self-Fulfillment in a World Turned Upside-Down;* on genius pointing to a way out, see L. W. White, *The Universe of Experience.*

Bibliography

I. Primary Sources

By far the most important primary sources of this biography have been the letters of Lord and Lady Keynes in the King's College Library, the diaries of John Neville Keynes in the Cambridge University Library, the magnificent collection of the letters of Lytton Strachey in the British Library, the correspondence of the latter with Leonard Woolf and others in the Berg Collection of the New York Public Library, as well as the Keynes-Lippmann holdings of the Sterling Memorial Library, Yale University, and Keynes's correspondence in the Princeton University Library and in the Franklin D. Roosevelt Library at Hyde Park, New York.

II. Secondary Sources

The most valuable source of Keynes's own writings, public papers, and of letters other than mentioned above is *The Collected Writings of John Maynard Keynes,* edited by A. Robinson and D. Moggridge and published for the Royal Economic Society by Macmillan and Cambridge University Press, vols. I–XXX.

Keynes's Life and Times

A. Alpers, *The Life of Katherine Mansfield.* New York: Viking Press, 1980.
B. Askwith, *Two Victorian Families.* London: Chatto and Windus, 1971.
A. J. Ayer, *Part of My Life.* New York: Harcourt Brace Jovanovich, 1977.

W. M. Bartley III, *Wittgenstein*. Philadelphia: J. B. Lippincott, 1973.

N. T. Bazin, *Virginia Woolf and the Androgynous Vision*. New Brunswick: Rutgers University Press, 1973.

C. W. Beaumont, *The Diaghilev Ballet in London*. London: Putnam, 1940.

A. O. Bell, ed., *The Diary of Virginia Woolf*, 5 vols. New York: Harcourt Brace Jovanovich, 1977.

C. Bell, *Old Friends*. London: Chatto and Windus, 1956.

Q. Bell, *Bloomsbury*. London: Futura Publications, 1974.

————, *Virginia Woolf, A Biography*, 2 vols. New York: Harcourt Brace Jovanovich, 1972.

A. Boyle, *The Fourth Man*. New York: Dial Press/James Wade, 1979.

F. M. Brookfield, *The Cambridge Apostles*. London: Pitman, 1906.

R. Buckle, *Diaghilev*. New York: Atheneum, 1979.

S. T. Coleridge, *Specimens of the Table Talk of Samuel Taylor Coleridge*, 2nd ed. London: John Murray, 1836.

Council of King's College, *John Maynard Keynes, A Memoir*. Cambridge: Cambridge University Press, 1949.

D. Crabtree and A. P. Thirlwall, eds. *Keynes and the Bloomsbury Group*. London: Macmillan, 1980.

S. J. Darroch, *Ottoline, The Life of Lady Ottoline Morrell*. New York: Coward, McCann and Geoghegan, 1975.

P. Delaney, *D. H. Lawrence's Nightmare*. New York: Basic Books, 1978.

P. F. Drucker, *Adventures of a Bystander*. New York: Harper and Row, 1980.

L. Edel, *Bloomsbury, A House of Lions*. Philadelphia: J. B. Lippincott, 1979.

P. Fitzgerald, *The Knox Brothers*. New York: Coward, McCann and Geoghegan, 1977.

E. M. Forster, *G. Lowes Dickinson*. London: Edward Arnold, 1934.

P. N. Furbank, *E. M. Forster, A Life*, 2 vols. New York: Harcourt Brace Jovanovich, 1977.

D. Garnett, *The Golden Echo*. London: Chatto and Windus, 1953.

————, *The Flowers of the Forest*. London: Chatto and Windus, 1955.

————, *The Old Familiar Faces*. London: Chatto and Windus, 1962.

J. C. Gilbert, *Keynes's Impact on Monetary Economics*. London: Butterworth, 1982.

M. Green, *Children of the Sun, A Narrative of "Decadence" in England after 1918*. New York: Basic Books, 1976.

P. Grosskurth, *John Addington Symonds*. London: Longmans, 1964.

R. F. Harrod, *The Life of John Maynard Keynes*. London: Macmillan, 1951.

C. Hassal, *Rupert Brooke*. New York: Harcourt Brace World, 1964.

M. Holroyd, *Lytton Strachey, A Critical Biography*, 2 vols. New York: Holt, Rinehart and Winston, 1968.

W. Houghton, *The Victorian Frame of Mind, 1830–1870*. New Haven: Yale University Press, 1957.

H. M. Hyde, *The Love That Dared Not Speak Its Name*. Boston: Little, Brown, 1970.

S. Hynes, *The Edwardian Turn of Mind*. Princeton: Princeton University Press, 1968.

H. G. and E. Johnson, *The Shadow of Keynes: Understanding Keynes, Cambridge, and Keynesian Economics*. Chicago: University of Chicago Press, 1979.

J. K. Johnstone, *The Bloomsbury Group*. London: Secker and Warburg, 1954.

F. A. Keynes, *Gathering Up the Threads*. Cambridge: W. Heffer and Sons, 1950.

G. Keynes Kt., *Henry James at Cambridge*. Cambridge: Heffer, 1967.

———, *The Gates of Memory*. Oxford: Clarendon Press, 1981.

M. Keynes, ed., *Essays on John Maynard Keynes*. Cambridge: Cambridge University Press, 1975.

D. Kramer, *Heywood Broun, A Biographical Portrait*. New York: Current Books, 1949.

R. Lekachman, *The Age of Keynes*. New York: Random House, 1966.

P. Levy, *Lytton Strachey, The Really Interesting Question and Other Papers*. London: Weidenfeld and Nicolson, 1972.

———, *Moore, G. E. Moore and the Cambridge Apostles*. London: Weidenfeld and Nicolson, 1979.

J. D. R. McConnell, *Eton—How It Works*. London: Faber and Faber, 1967.

H. Marder, *Feminism and Art: A Study of Virginia Woolf*. Chicago: University of Chicago Press, 1968.

K. Martin, *Father Figures, The Evolution of an Editor, 1897–1931*. Chicago: H. Regnery, 1966.

———, *A Second Volume of Autobiography, 1931–1945*. London: Hutchinson, 1968.

B. Mazlish, *James and John Stuart Mill, Father and Son in the Nineteenth Century*. New York: Basic Books, 1975.

D. E. Moggridge, *Keynes*. London: Fontana/Collins, 1976.

H. G. Nicolson, *Diaries and Letters*, edited by N. Nicolson. New York: Atheneum, 1966–68.

N. Nicolson and J. Trautman, *The Letters of Virginia Woolf*, 6 vols. New York: Harcourt Brace Jovanovich, 1975–1980.

J. H. Plumb, *Studies in Social History, A Tribute to G. M. Trevelyan*. London: Longmans, Green, 1955.

J. B. Priestley, *The Edwardians*. New York: Harper and Row, 1970.

D. Proctor, ed., *The Autobiography of G. Lowes Dickinson and Other Unpublished Writings*. London: Duckworth, 1973.

G. Raverat, *Period Piece*. New York: Norton, 1976.

P. Rose, *Woman of Letters, A Life of Virginia Woolf*. New York: Oxford University Press, 1978.

B. Russell, *The Autobiography of Bertrand Russell, Vol. 1, 1872–1914*. London: Allen Unwin, 1967.

M. Secrest, *Being Bernard Berenson*. New York: Holt, Rinehart and Winston, 1979.

R. Shone, *Bloomsbury Portraits, Vanessa Bell, Duncan Grant, and Their Circle*. Oxford: Phaidon Press, 1976.

G. Spater and I. Parsons, *A Marriage of True Minds*. London: Jonathan Cape and Hogarth Press, 1977.

R. Steel, *Walter Lippmann and the American Century*. Boston: Little, Brown, 1980.

W. Stone, *The Cave and the Mountain, A Study of E. M. Forster*. Stanford: Stanford University Press, 1966.

D. Sutton, ed., *The Letters of Roger Fry*. London: Chatto and Windus, 1972.

L. Trilling, *E. M. Forster*, rev. ed. New York: New Directions, 1964.

C. Tsuzuki, *Edward Carpenter, 1844–1929, Prophet of Fellowship*. Cambridge: Cambridge University Press, 1980.

G. H. von Wright, *L. Wittgenstein: Letters of Russell, Keynes and Moore*. Oxford: Basil Blackwell, 1974.

M. J. Weiner, *English Culture and the Decline of the Industrial Spirit, 1850–1980*. Cambridge: Cambridge University Press, 1981.

B. Willey, *Cambridge and Other Memories, 1920–1953*. London: Chatto and Windus, 1968.

————, *Samuel Taylor Coleridge*. New York: Norton, 1972.

E. Wiskeman, *The Europe I Saw*. New York: St. Martin's Press, 1968.

R. Wohl, *The Generation of 1914*. Cambridge: Harvard University Press, 1979.

L. Woolf, *Sowing*. New York: Harcourt, Brace & World, 1960.

————, *Growing*. New York: Harcourt, Brace & World, 1961.

————, *Beginning Again*. New York: Harcourt, Brace & World, 1964.

————, *Downhill All the Way*. New York: Harcourt, Brace & World, 1967.

————, *The Journey Not the Arrival Matters*. New York: Harcourt, Brace & World, 1969.

————, *A Writer's Diary*. New York: Harcourt, Brace & World, 1954.

V. Woolf, *Roger Fry: A Biography*. New York: Harcourt Brace Jovanovich, 1940.

————, *A Room of One's Own*. Frogmore, St. Albans, Eng: Triad/Panther Books, 1977.

G. M. Young, *Victorian England, Portrait of an Age*, 2nd ed., London: Oxford University Press, 1953.

Keynes's Economics and Economic Policies

C. Barnett, *The Collapse of British Power*. New York: William Morrow, 1972.

B. Baruch, *The Making of the Reparation and Economic Sections of the Treaty*. New York: Harper, 1920.

J. M. Blum, *From the Morgenthau Diaries, Years of Crisis, 1928–1938*. Boston: Houghton Mifflin, 1959.

K. E. Boulding, *Ecodynamics, A New Theory of Societal Evolution*. Beverly Hills: Sage Publications, 1978.

W. A. Brown, Jr., *The International Gold Standard Reinterpreted, 1914–1934*, 2 vols. New York: National Bureau of Economic Research, 1940.

J. Buchanan et al., *The Consequences of Mr. Keynes*. London: The Institute of Economic Affairs (Hobart Paperback No. 78), 1978.

J. Campbell, *Lloyd George, The Goat in the Wilderness, 1922–1931*. London: Rowman, 1977.

P. Davidson, *Money and the Real World*. London: Macmillan, 1972.

A. S. Eichner, ed., *A Guide to Post-Keynesian Economics*. White Plains, N. Y.: M. E. Sharpe, Inc., 1979.

H. Elcock, *Portrait of a Decision, The Council of Four and the Treaty of Versailles*. London: Eyre Methuen, 1972.

G. R. Feiwell, *The Intellectual Capital of Michal Kalecki*. Knoxville: University of Tennessee Press, 1975.

J. K. Galbraith, *Economics and the Public Purpose*. Boston: Houghton Mifflin, 1973.

R. N. Gardner, *Sterling-Dollar Diplomacy*, rev. ed. New York: McGraw-Hill, 1969.

S. E. Harris, *The New Economics*. London: Dennis Dobson, 1948.

————, *John Maynard Keynes, Economist and Policy Maker*. New York: Charles Scribners, 1955.

F. von Hayek, *The Road to Serfdom*. Chicago: University of Chicago Press, 1944.

———, *A Tiger by the Tail*. London: Institute of Economic Affairs, 1972.

J. Hicks, *The Crisis in Keynesian Economics*. Oxford: Basil Blackwell, 1974.

H. C. Hoover, *The Ordeal of Woodrow Wilson*. New York: McGraw-Hill, 1958.

J. K. Horsefield, *The International Monetary Fund, 1945–1965*, 2 vols. Washington, D.C.: International Monetary Fund, 1969.

T. W. Hutchinson, *A Review of Economic Doctrines, 1870–1929*. Oxford: Clarendon Press, 1953.

———, *Economics and Economic Policy in Britain, 1946–1966, Some Aspects of their Inter-relations*. London: Allen and Unwin, 1968.

———, *Keynes v. the Keynesians*. London: Institute of Economic Affairs (Hobart Paperback No. 11), 1977.

———, *On Revolutions and Progress in Economic Knowledge*. Cambridge: Cambridge University Press, 1978.

R. Kahn, *Selected Essays on Employment and Growth*. Cambridge: Cambridge University Press, 1972.

L. Klein, *The Keynesian Revolution*. New York: Macmillan, 1947.

A. Leijonhufvud, *On Keynesian Economics and the Economics of Keynes, A Study in Monetary Theory*. New York: Oxford University Press, 1968.

R. Lekachman, ed., *Keynes's General Theory: Reports of Three Decades*. New York: St. Martin's Press, 1964.

A. S. Link, *The Higher Realism of Woodrow Wilson and Other Essays*. Nashville: Vanderbilt University Press, 1971.

E. Mantoux, *The Carthaginian Peace, or The Economic Consequences of Mr. Keynes*. New York: Charles Scribners, 1952.

P. Mattick, *Marx and Keynes: The Limits of the Mixed Economy*. London: Merlin, 1971.

G. Mehta, *The Structure of the Keynesian Revolution*. London: Martin Robertson, 1977.

S. G. Millin, *General Smuts*. London:

H. P. Minsky, *John Maynard Keynes*. New York: Columbia University Press, 1975.

D. E. Moggridge, *The Return to Gold, 1925: The Formation of Economic Policy and Its Critics*. London: Cambridge University Press, 1969.

———, *British Monetary Policy, 1924–1931*. Cambridge: Cambridge University Press, 1972.

D. Patinkin, *Keynes's Monetary Thought, A Study of Its Development*. Durham: Duke University Press, 1976.

D. Patinkin and J. C. Leith, *Keynes, Cambridge and The General Theory*. Toronto: University of Toronto Press, 1978.

A. C. Pigou, *The Theory of Unemployment*. London: Macmillan, 1933.

J. R. Presley, *Robertsonian Economics, An Examination of the Work of D. H. Robertson on Industrial Fluctuations*. New York: Holmes and Meier, 1979.

L. C. Robbins, *The Autobiography of an Economist*. London: Macmillan and St. Martin's Press, 1971.

D. H. Robertson, *Banking Policy and the Price Level*, reprint of 1926 ed. New York: Kelley, 1969.

J. Robinson, *Problems of Economic Dynamics and Planning: Essays in Honor of Michal Kalecki*. Warsaw: 1964.

————, *Collected Economic Papers,* 4 vols. Oxford: Basil Blackwell, 1951–1979.

————, *Contributions to Modern Economics.* Oxford: Basil Blackwell, 1978.

E. Roll, *The World After Keynes.* New York: Frederick A. Praeger, 1968.

R. S. Sayers, *Financial Policy, 1939–1945* (Official History of the Second World War). London: H. M. S. O., 1956.

S. A. Schuker, *The End of French Predominance in Europe.* Chapel Hill: University of North Carolina Press, 1976.

J. A. Schumpeter, *History of Economic Analysis.* New York: Oxford University Press, 1954.

G. L. S. Shackle, *The Years of High Theory, Invention and Tradition in Economic Thought, 1926–1939.* Cambridge: Cambridge University Press, 1967.

————, *Epistemics and Economics: A Critique of Economic Doctrines.* Cambridge: Cambridge University Press, 1972.

R. Skidelsky, ed., *The End of the Keynesian Era, Essays on the Disintegration of the Keynesian Political Economy.* New York: Holmes and Meier, 1977.

H. Stein, *The Fiscal Revolution in America.* Chicago: University of Chicago Press, 1969.

J. E. Stiglitz, *The Collected Scientific Papers of Paul A. Samuelson,* 2 vols. Cambridge: M. I. T. Press, 1966.

A. M. Tang et al., *Evolution, Welfare and Time in Economics, Essays in Honor of Nicholas Georgescu-Roegen.* Lexington, MA: Lexington Books, 1976.

S. Weintraub, *Keynes, Keynes and the Monetarists.* Philadelphia: University of Pennsylvania Press, 1978.

————, *Capitalism's Inflation and Unemployment Crisis; Beyond Monetarism and Keynesianism.* Reading: Addison-Wesley, 1978.

J. K. Whitaker, *The Early Economic Writings of Alfred Marshall, 1867–1890.* New York: Free Press, 1975.

D. Winch, *Economics and Policy: A Historical Study,* rev. ed. London: Fontana, 1972.

Homosexuality, Androgyny, and Creativity

S. Arieti, *Creativity, the Magic Synthesis.* New York: Basic Books, 1976.

F. Barron, *Creativity and Psychological Health.* New York: Van Nostrand, 1965.

C. Berg, *Homosexuality.* London: George Allen and Unwin, 1958.

A. A. Brill, ed., *The Basic Writings of Sigmund Freud.* New York: Modern Library, 1938.

J. Bronowski, *The Visionary Eye: Essays in the Arts, Literature and Science.* M. I. T. Press, 1978.

V. L. Bullough, *Sexual Variance in Society and History.* New York: John Wiley, 1976.

E. Carpenter, *The Art of Creation, Essays on the Self and Its Powers.* New York: Macmillan, 1917.

————, *The Intermediate Sex.* London: George Allen and Unwin, 1918.

J. Gathorne-Hardy, *The Old School Tie, The Phenomenon of the English Public School.* New York: Viking Press, 1978.

W. J. Gordon, *Synectics: The Development of Creative Capacity.* New York: Harper and Row, 1961.

J. C. Gowan, *Development of the Psychodelic Individual.* Buffalo, N. Y.: Creative Education Foundation, 1974.

C. Heilbrun, *Toward the Recognition of Androgyny*. New York: Knopf, 1973.

H. S. Hughes, *Consciousness and History*. New York: Knopf, 1958.

J. J. Jaynes, *The Origin of Consciousness in the Breakdown of the Bicameral Mind*. Boston: Houghton Mifflin, 1976.

A. C. Kinsey et al., *Sexual Behavior in the Human Male*. Philadelphia: W. B. Saunders, 1948.

A. Koestler, *The Act of Creation*. New York: Macmillan, 1964.

E. Kris, *Psychoanalytic Explorations in Art*. New York: International Universities Press, 1969.

L. S. Kubie, *Neurotic Distortion of the Creative Process*. Lawrence: University of Kansas Press, 1958.

J. Marmor, ed., *Homosexual Behavior, A Modern Reappraisal*. New York: Basic Books, 1980.

J. B. Miller, *Toward a New Psychology of Women*. Boston: Beacon Press, 1976.

R. E. Ornstein, *The Psychology of Consciousness*. Harmondsworth, Eng: Penguin Books, 1975.

A. Rothenberg, *The Emerging Goddess, The Creative Process in Art, Science and Other Fields*. Chicago: University of Chicago Press, 1979.

A. L. Rowse, *Homosexuals in History, A Study of Ambivalence in Society, Literature and the Arts*. London: Weidenfeld and Nicolson, 1977.

C. W. Soccarides, *The Overt Homosexual*. New York: Grune and Stratton, 1968.

J. T. Spence and R. L. Helmreich, *Masculinity and Femininity, Their Psychological Dimensions, Correlates and Antecedents*. Austin: University of Texas Press, 1978.

E. Wilson, *The Wound and the Bow, Seven Studies in Literature*. New York: Oxford University Press, 1965.

General

E. Carpenter, *Towards Democracy*. New York: Mitchell Kennerly, 1922.

———, *Civilization, Its Cause and Cure and Other Essays*. Arden Library, 1978.

K. Clark, *Civilization, A Personal View*. New York: Harper and Row, 1969.

E. H. Erickson, *Identity: Youth and Crisis*. New York: W. W. Norton, 1968.

———, *Life History and the Historical Moment*. New York: W. W. Norton, 1975.

C. E. Kerman, *Creative Tension, The Life and Thought of Kenneth Boulding*. Ann Arbor: University of Michigan Press, 1974.

F. Manuel, *A Portrait of Isaac Newton*. Cambridge: Belknap Press, 1968.

T. Parsons, *The Structure of Social Action*, 2 vols. New York: Free Press, 1968.

D. Rees, *Harry Dexter White, A Study in Paradox*. New York: Coward, McCann and Geoghegan, 1973.

F. J. Sulloway, *Freud, Biologist of the Mind: Beyond the Psychoanalytical Legend*. New York: Basic Books, 1979.

L. Trilling, *The Opposing Self*. New York: Viking Press, 1955.

L. W. White, *The Universe of Experience*. New York: Harper and Row, 1974.

N. I. White, *Harry Dexter White—Loyal American*. Waban, Mass.: Bessie (White) Bloom, no date.

Index

Abatti, A. H., 236
Abelard, Peter, 47
Abrahams, Lionel, 81, 88, 89
Abstract of Hume's Treaties of Human Nature, 308
Acheson, Dean, 329, 330, 338
Acton, Harold, 36
Adams, Franklin P. (F.P.A.), 181
Adams, Jane, 172
Adler, Alfred, 35
"Age of Keynes," the, 366, 370, 373
Agricultural Adjustment Administration, 276
Alba, Duke of, 334
Albert, Prince, 293
Alston, L., 70
"Alternative Theories of Interest," 303
American Economic Association, 298
American Economic Review, 254
American Political Economy Club, 274
Androgyny, 15, 18, 103, 107, 111, 112, 123
Annan, Lord, 2, 3, 38, 237
Apostles, The, xv, 43, 49, 53, 74, 85, 95, 96 100, 226, 241, 242, 264, 375
Arieti, Silvano, 105–106, 107, 113
Arnold, Matthew, 26, 245, 291, 375
Arnold, Thomas, 160
Arts Council, 359, 360
Arts Theatre of Cambridge, 291, 292, 294, 359
Arts Theatre, London, 266
Asgard, 16
Ashley, W. J., 131
Asquith, Herbert H., 119, 127, 148, 155, 177
Asquith, Margot, 172, 176
Atlantic charter, the, 330
Attlee, Clement, 345, 346, 350
Auden, W. H., 303
Ayer, A. J., 30

Bagehot, Walter, 8
Bagenal, Faith, 125
Bagenal, Nicholas, 125
Baines, Keith, 228
Balance of Payments, 370
Balfour, Sir Arthur, 153, 315
Baldwin, Stanley, 197, 198, 199, 204, 231, 334
Balogh, Lord, 112, 358
"Bancor," 331, 333
Bank for International Settlements, 253

Bank of England, 116–17, 136, 207–9, 215, 216, 217, 218, 230, 256, 317, 326, 338, 355, 363
Barnett, Corelli, 162
Barocchi, Randolpho, 181, 222
Bartley, William W. III, 211
Barton, Catherine, 309
Baruch, Bernard, 167, 168, 189
Bayeaux, Bishop of, 2
Beaumont, Cyril, 179, 222, 223
Beazley, J. D., 46
Bedford, Eng., 3, 15
Bekassy, Ferenc, 85
Bell, Angelica, 126
Bell, Clive, 41, 62, 94, 95, 126, 160, 264
Bell, Julian, 264
Bell, Quentin, 97, 113, 335
Bell, Vanessa, 41, 94–98, 125, 127, 128, 131, 133, 148, 175, 176, 181, 227, 228, 264, 291, 323, 376
Benson, Robert H., 27
Bentham, Jeremy, 7, 100–1, 192, 308, 367
Benthamism, 7, 45, 100, 300, 377
Berenson, Bernard, 56, 175
Berenson, Mary, 56, 57, 78
Bergson, Henri, 101, 113
Berkeley, Bishop, 326
Berlin, Isaiah, 102
Bernard of Cluny, Saint, 25
Bernstein, Edward, 343
Besdine, Matthew, 106
Beveridge, William, 204, 297, 313
Bevin, Ernest, 256
Birrell, Francis, 72, 98
Birth control, Keynes on, 221–2
Bisexuality, 106, 161, 203
Bismarck, Prince Otto, 152
Blackett, Basil, 116, 117, 130
Blake, William, 6
Bloomsbury, xv, 94–114, 125, 126, 149, 160, 179, 180, 203, 204, 221, 223, 228, 323, 362, 375, 377
Blunt, Anthony, 264
Boer War, 27–28
Bolsheviks, 130, 137, 138, 140, 142, 158, 194, 221, 229, 265
Bolton, Sir George, 355
Boothby, Robert, 351

[393]